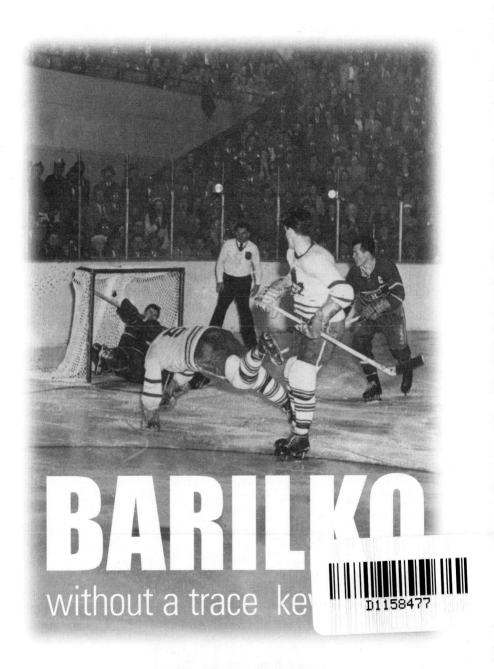

BARILKO

without a trace ke

Fenn Publishing Company Ltd.
Bolton Canada

BARILKO
WITHOUT A TRACE
A Fenn Publishing Book / First Published in 2004

Fenn Publishing Company Ltd.
Bolton, Ontario, Canada

Distributed in Canada by H. B. Fenn and Company Ltd.
Bolton, Ontario, Canada, L7E 1W2
www.hbfenn.com

Library and Archives Canada Cataloguing in Publication

Shea, Kevin, 1956-
    Barilko: without a trace / Kevin Shea.

ISBN 1-55168-256-6

Barilko, Bill, 1927-1951. 2. Toronto Maple Leafs (Hockey team)
Hockey players – Canada – Biography. I. Title.

GV848.5.B37S432004   796.962'092   C2004-903140-6

Printed and Bound in Canada

To Anne Klisanich,
who relived the laughter and sadness of a life
shared with her brother, Bill Barilko.

Also, to Gerry McNeil and Sid Smith,
who passed away during the writing of this book,
shortly after contributing their memories.

CONTENTS

FOREWORD

Our parents, who went through the Great Depression, shared an appreciation of hard work, thrift, self-reliance and self-esteem. Those same values were taught to the three of us — my brothers Alex and Bill, and me. Because we were raised in humble surroundings, we continued to live life that way.

It makes my heart rejoice that God gave me caring parents, my Mama and my Papa, two wonderful brothers, a loving husband, Emil Klisanich, and two wonderful sons, Frank and Barry.

Frank met Chris at the University of Western Ontario, where both graduated. They got married and blessed us with three lovely grandchildren — John, Michael and Caroline. Frank and his family moved to Minnetonka, Minnesota in 1996, and still reside there.

Barry enjoys his life as a bachelor and is still waiting for the right girl.

Emil, Barry and I volunteer at the Hockey Hall of Fame. It is a privilege and an honour to be affiliated with such a prestigious organization.

Although our time with Bill was too short, I'll treasure the memories for a lifetime. I've been so incredibly proud to be Bill's sister and to be able to share my scrapbooks and memories with people who are still so interested in Billy's life. I just can't get over the fact that, more than 50 years after we lost Billy, people are still so interested in him. I look back at all the tributes made to Bill. He's unforgettable. I just can't believe it!

My mother always said that her Billy would be famous again, and she was so right — between The Tragically Hip, BB 16, newspaper stories and television specials, I'm still heartened by all the attention my brother gets.

I was so proud of what my brother achieved in his hockey career in such a short period of time. Four Stanley Cups in five years. It was a glorious moment when Billy scored the goal that won the Cup in 1951. It was a magic moment, and then four months later, there was tragedy.

Sharing my scrapbooks and photo albums of Bill makes life a richer experience for me. Although his time with us was too short, having him in our lives is something we'll treasure for a lifetime.

I am a very fortunate person indeed!

Anne (Barilko) Klisanich
August 1, 2004

PREFACE

Overtime Overture

It is an annual rite of spring; an enduring love affair between a city and its hockey team. Simultaneous with the emerging of blossoms on what were dormant twigs mere weeks before, so too is a city's intense passion for its Maple Leafs rekindled with the first signs of the Stanley Cup playoffs.

Every spring, Torontonians convince themselves that this is "our year." It is an annual occurrence, as ingrained as daylight saving time. Since the Toronto Maple Leafs last hoisted the Stanley Cup in that miraculous spring of 1967, a city has clung to the fervent hope that this would again be "our year." They allow themselves to dream that hockey's Holy Grail will at last return to Toronto, the home of 13 Stanley Cup championships since the formation of the National Hockey League in 1917 — one for the Toronto Arenas in 1918, one in 1922 for the Toronto St. Patricks and 11 for the Toronto Maple Leafs — 1932, '42, '45, '47, '48, '49, '51, '62, '63, '64 and '67.

On April 21, 1951, the charismatic yet combative Bill Barilko scored an overtime goal that clinched the Stanley Cup for the Toronto Maple Leafs. The goal has been immortalized in song ("Fifty Mission Cap" by the Tragically Hip) and in photography, but most enthusiastically in spirit. More than 50 years after Barilko's shot rifled over the shoulder of Montreal Canadiens' netminder Gerry McNeil at 2:53 of the first overtime, fans still recount the legend of Bill Barilko every spring.

Statistically, there is little reason to commit Bill Barilko's career to memory. Twenty-six goals scored in five NHL seasons does not a Hall of Fame career make. But remarkably, through his five seasons as a Maple Leaf, Barilko played an integral role in four Stanley Cup championships (and surviving teammates swear that Toronto should have won in the fifth year as well). And although Bill scored just five goals in 47 playoff contests, there is reason to remember only one.

As buoyant away from the rink as he was belligerent on the ice, the Leafs' hard-hitting Number 5 might very well be forgotten today, like so many of his contemporaries, had it not been for four months in 1951.

Bill Barilko's Stanley Cup–winning goal on April 21 turned out not only to be the last goal he ever scored, but his final act on a National Hockey League rink. That summer, on August 24, Bill Barilko and Dr. Henry Hudson embarked on a fishing trip to a remote river on the east side of James Bay. The plane never returned — it was lost without a trace.

The fortunes of the Toronto Maple Leafs spiralled downwards after Barilko's daring goal. Both the Detroit Red Wings and Montreal Canadiens enjoyed dynastic eras throughout the '50s, while Toronto, the predominant team of the 1940s, not only struggled but suffered the ultimate indignity, finishing last in the NHL in 1957–58. Then, in an eerie coincidence, Toronto broke an 11-year drought by winning the Stanley Cup on April 22, 1962, and just over a month later, on June 6, the remains of Bill Barilko and Dr. Hudson were discovered in the dense, unforgiving bush approximately 100 miles north of Cochrane, Ontario. Their skeletal remains were still strapped into the cockpit of their plane at the crash site.

The Barilko legacy is built as much on the tragedy of his untimely death as it is on the majesty of his Stanley Cup goal. In fact, the two are so intertwined that they have forged an indelible mark on the hearts of Leafs fans. What might have been an asterisk or a series of anecdotes instead has brought Bill Barilko enduring fame. Andy Warhol, the noted artist and social chameleon, stated, "In the future, everyone will be famous for 15 minutes." But then, Warhol never knew the incomparable Bill Barilko.

CHAPTER 1

Gold and Cold

When an outsider thinks of Timmins, two words invariably come to mind: "gold" and "cold." Mention of the place conjures up images of men descending thousands of feet into the earth to carve the rock beneath their boots, and of a climate made up of 10 months of snow and two months of lousy hockey conditions.

The area known as "The Porcupine" is comprised of the communities of Timmins, Schumacher, South Porcupine and Porcupine. Timmins is at the hub, with Schumacher a mile away, South Porcupine seven and Porcupine not quite eight. Since the communities were amalgamated in 1973, the City of Timmins occupies 1,240 square miles of land, making it Canada's largest city in terms of area. There are close to 500 lakes in the Porcupine, too.

The region can be a paradox — vast expanses of granite intersecting with tracts of lush green foliage as far as the eye can see. Lakes such a deep blue in colour that they're almost violet are interspersed between the rocks and the trees. But that's on the surface. Most of the region's history took place below ground.

In the first few years of the 1900s, gold was discovered in various locations along the Precambrian Shield in northern Ontario that included the Porcupine region. A few relatively insignificant discoveries were made, but it wasn't until a railway line was established between North Bay and Cochrane in 1908 that the district attracted substantial attention and surrendered its precious minerals.

The Porcupine Gold Rush began in June of 1909 when a party led by Jack Wilson stumbled upon a vein of gold in Tisdale Township that was so extensive, it was known as the Golden Stairway. Wilson's cache became the Dome Mine, and a flood of prospectors dreaming of great wealth descended upon the region. Within months, Benny Hollinger and Alex Gillies had started the Hollinger Mine after discovering rich veins of gold in the Pearl Lake area. After arriving in the region from his native Scotland, Sandy McIntyre, who had changed his name from Alexander Olifant, founded a third mine, the McIntyre Mine.

Those involved in the Hollinger Mine settled in the area known today as Timmins, named for Noah Timmins, a developer who purchased the claims of the Hollinger camp. Nearby, the employees of the McIntyre Mine huddled in an area now known as Schumacher, named after druggist Frederick Schumacher. Word spread like a spark in the tinder-dry brush, and the area's population exploded, becoming a prosperous and important centre of mining in Ontario.

Prospectors staking gold claims throughout the mineral-rich area founded Timmins in 1912. The town prospered as hordes of adventure-seeking men and women moved into the region in search of their fortunes. The three gold-producing mines were all located in Tisdale Township. Deposits in the area proved to be so plentiful that, during the first half of the twentieth century, the Porcupine produced more of the precious metal than any other region in North America. Since the Porcupine Gold Rush, more than 56 million ounces of gold have been extracted from the Porcupine.

Mining towns are not pretty: open pits and slag heaps dot the landscape, as do grizzled men who despise their occupations, any gentleness removed by years of hard labour and fear — fear of collapse; fear of silicosis, the disease of the lungs, caused by years of inhaling mineral dusts, that leaves those afflicted perpetually short of breath; and fear of the mine closing and stealing both their identities and their livelihoods.

It's a confusing paradox that the Porcupine's natural beauty should be fused with the man-created ugliness inherent to mining to form a region that provided careers for generations of men. Hard-working men. Men who played as hard as they worked. Men who needed to forget the week they had just completed on Friday night in one of the many bars that dotted the vicinity.

*　*　*

Steve Barilko was one of those men who worked the mines in the Porcupine. "My father was born in Dobuchin, in the Polish district of Pruzana," begins Anne Klisanich, the youngest of the three Barilko children. "On his naturalization certificate, his birth date was listed as April 15, 1893, but we have since discovered letters that state Papa was born in 1892. My father and his brother John left Antwerp and arrived at the port in Quebec on May 2, 1910." The Barilko boys made their way to the north, looking for a steady income and a better way of life than they would have known back home in Poland. They landed in Timmins and were luckier than most. "Both my father Steve and my uncle John found work as cooks in various mining camps in the Porcupine area," states Anne.

Steve was a pleasant-looking man — five foot eight with brown hair, grey eyes and a head that tilted to the right at a jaunty angle. "We never wanted to hurt Papa's feelings, so we never asked him why his head tilted," Anne admits. "I did ask my mother why our father's head leaned to the right and she told us that when Papa was a baby, his mother didn't change his sleeping position and it caused his head to slant that way.

"My mother was born Feodosia Karpinchuk in the town of Malech in the Polish district of Pruzana on September 3, 1899," smiles Anne. Feodosia's birthplace is now part of Belarus. "Mama was a wonderful woman; a real loving person. She was five foot four with brown eyes and black hair. She was a very gentle lady," says Anne. "Everybody spoke very fondly of her. She did not ask for much in life. She laboured hard for those she loved."

Russia and Poland had skirmished over religious and political differences for several centuries. Although Poland was perched on the western edge of Russia, these neighbours had a long, bitter history of mistrust. After the end of the First World War, Poland renewed hostilities with Russia — in 1920 — and subsequently pushed the border more than 70 miles to the east, placing 80,000 Russians under Polish rule. Fleeing the Russian Revolution, Feodosia travelled third class on the steamship *Zeeland* and landed in Halifax on December 27, 1924. "My mother was a refugee when there was a problem between Poland and Russia," Anne explains.

The Karpinchuk family led a meager existence and the family often went hungry. Life was often cruel, and families were forced to be enterprising. Poverty also fuelled new habits rooted in deep-seated fears. Anne relates a story about her mother's twilight years: "I used to drive her to the grocery store. I'd laugh and say, 'Mother, you have more groceries in your pantry than I do.' She said, 'Anne, you never mind. When I was a child growing up in Russia, you never saw animals on the street. We'd use them as food. All through your life, you've never known hunger. I'll never be hungry again. I'll always make sure that I have food in my cupboards.'"

A cousin, Tom Kozloff, had sponsored Feodosia, who went by the more common "Faye" when she arrived in Canada. Tom arranged for Faye to live in Timmins. It's more than 1,200 miles from Halifax to Timmins, and 25-year-old Faye climbed aboard the train with her few earthly possessions and stared out the window in amazement throughout the entire trip. It was a brave new world for the young Polish woman who spoke no English and knew nothing of local customs.

On the trip, Faye was mesmerized by a man sitting across the aisle from her whose mouth and lips moved constantly. She felt sorry for the man and his affliction. After arriving in Timmins, Faye told others about the odd man with the peculiar behaviour. "He doesn't have any problem," they laughed. "The man is chewing gum!" Faye had never seen such a thing before. "Very odd, very odd," she frowned, shaking her head.

"Everybody in the old country thought the streets in Timmins were lined with gold," laughs Anne. "They had heard there was a lot of gold there and were very disappointed when they discovered the climate was comprised of long, cold winters and short summers."

"This must have been an arranged marriage," guesses Anne about her mother's union with Steve Barilko. "Mama never told me that, but it's all I can assume because they were married January 18, 1925. Mother had only arrived in Canada three weeks earlier."

The young immigrant couple started a new life together, but from the very beginning it wasn't easy. "Transportation during the winter in Timmins in those days was by horse and sleigh," relates Anne. "Because my Dad worked as a cook in the mining camps, he'd only get home on weekends."

And because Steve Barilko worked alongside the men in the mine, he had a good grasp of the English language and refined it through the years. Conversely, Faye Barilko had arrived in the midst of a culture and language that were completely unfamiliar to her. "My Dad really helped Mother with her English. She didn't have any education. Through her entire life, she could never read or write. My father gave her tips on cooking, as well."

As more and more immigrants landed in Canada, they gravitated to places like Timmins because they could be guaranteed work, in spite of linguistic or cultural differences. "Timmins was multicultural before the rest of Canada knew what the word meant," boasts Victor M. Power, the mayor of Timmins. "In the early days, the shafts of the mine were sunk by men of different nationalities — Ukrainian, Finnish, Italian, French. In fact, the second Sunday in June we have Multicultural Day at the McIntyre [Arena] where all the ethnic groups come together. It's quite impressive!"

As the region exploded in population and interest, an inferno fuelled by dry timber and intense winds cut a swath 40 miles wide by 160 miles long through the region during July 1911. To avoid the blaze, 2000 residents prayed for salvation by wading into a nearby lake, but the water temperature escalated so rapidly that many were scalded to death by the seething waters, and many of those who weren't perished in the ensuing panic. The Dome Mine was destroyed in the fire. The devastating blaze took an enormous toll on the area, yet survivors refused to abandon their dreams of fortune, and, astonishingly, the camps were rebuilt within two months.

The area grew exponentially over the next few decades. Whereas the Great Depression plundered much of North America, the Timmins area dodged the financial losses of other areas and maintained its pattern of growth. Mining provided steady employment and, for a time, the place seemed immune to the ravages of the Depression. As the area grew through the 1920s and '30s, more and more people gravitated toward it, hoping to find at least one place where they could still prosper. Mines offered jobs, of course, while lumbering and farming offered above-ground alternatives to those arriving in Timmins.

"In 1934, President Roosevelt raised the price of gold from $22 U.S. per ounce to $35 per ounce," Mayor Power explains. "Thirty-five dollars was a lot of money in those days. As a result, Timmins and other mining towns were places in Canada where people could find work. There wasn't much work during the Depression. That was the big thing that brought Timmins along through the Depression."

And in 1938, while the Porcupine flourished, local businessman constructed a building that would play an integral role in the community.

J.P. Bickell, the chairman of McIntyre-Porcupine Mines in Schumacher, conceived the idea for the McIntyre Arena. Back in 1931, Bickell had been instrumental in getting Toronto's Maple Leaf Gardens built, and was named the first president of the Gardens holding company. "It was his idea that an arena should be built [in Timmins] along the scale of Maple Leaf Gardens," said Mayor Power. "In 1938, he built the arena for the employees of the mine, which was flourishing in those days, but really, it was for the entire community. It was placed in Schumacher because the McIntyre-Porcupine Mine operated there.

"There were very few places in Ontario with artificial ice at that time," Power continues. "Schumacher and St. Catharines were the only two places in Ontario outside of Maple Leaf Gardens. There were a lot of well-organized leagues at the McIntyre Arena at that time, and outdoor rinks supplemented them. In those days, winters were colder, and there were outdoor rinks everywhere — every school, playground, church had an outdoor rink and they lasted from well before Christmas until well into March. They would install lights on some of them and the kids would skate and play hockey for a long time after school."

Winter activities were important to all communities, but few enjoyed these sports as much as Timmins. "Hockey and figure skating were big things in those days," continues Mayor Power with pride. "A lot of young ladies from the Timmins area went into professional figure skating, including my wife, Clarice Dillon. In those days, Barbara Ann Scott trained at the McIntyre Arena in the summer. Every spring, there'd be a skating carnival the likes of which you wouldn't see other than in big cities, and that was because this was one of the few arenas that had artificial ice."

Above all, it was hockey that put the Porcupine on the map. A list of talent from the area includes Frank and Peter Mahovlich, Dean and Eric Prentice, plus the three Hannigan brothers, Gord, Pat and Ray, all from Schumacher; another pair of siblings, (Father) Les and Murray Costello, hailed from South Porcupine, as did Bob Nevin and Pete Babando, and from Timmins proper, there were Allan Stanley, Bep Guidolin, Real Chevrefils — and, of course, Bill Barilko.

CHAPTER 2

Cedar and Sixth

Soon after celebrating their first wedding anniversary, Steve and Faye Barilko were blessed with the birth of their first child. Alex was born February 4, 1926, in the township of Tisdale, where Steve was working at the mine. Just over a year after Alex's arrival, the Barilkos welcomed a second baby boy. William arrived on March 25, 1927 — again at the site of the mining camp in Tisdale Township. The family's third child, Annie, was born September 5, 1930.

Annie, who has gone by Anne for the better part of her life, sits in her beautifully decorated home and speaks lovingly of the brother she lost so many years ago. Life has been good to Anne, who retains every ounce of the charm and all of the playfulness she would have had as a younger lady. And she has lost none of the looks that won her the title of the Purim Ball's Queen Esther at the Riverside Pavilion in Timmins all those years ago. The home she shares with her husband, Emil, and son, Barry, is tidy and organized — which will come as no surprise if you speak to Anne for any length of time.

On a table spread out like a sumptuous feast sit the scrapbooks that chronicle, in meticulous detail, the career of Bill Barilko. Through more than 50 years, Anne has cut out every written word and picture related to her beloved brother. And there have been a lot — an awful lot. Each scrapbook vividly recalls a certain period of time. Each article and picture has been carefully affixed to a page with the date written in the upper-right-hand corner. Since she was 16, Anne has been the principal archivist of all news Barilko-oriented, from Bill's exceptional life, to his equally extraordinary death, to his lasting legacy. Anne spent five years bursting with pride as her brother Bill played with the Toronto Maple Leafs, 11 years wondering how he had disappeared without a trace and the past four decades animatedly narrating the remarkable story of Bill Barilko.

"He was a blond, blue-eyed baby, and Mama used to brag about her little Billy's weight," smiles Anne, recalling a baby picture of Billy lying naked on a bearskin rug. At six months, he weighed 24 pounds. "When he started to play hockey, my mother said, 'See, he was born with that bum to give bodychecks.'"

As children, Bill and Anne were inseparable. "Growing up, I was closer to Billy because he was closest to me in age. Alex was just over 13 months older than Bill, and Billy was three years older than me. Billy and I had a real admiration for our older brother," states Anne.

The Barilko family didn't have much as the children grew. "We saw our parents go through a lot of hardship," Anne admits. "Seeing that as you grow up teaches you a willingness to make sacrifices. We just did the best we could." A strong work ethic and resilience were handed down from one generation to the next. But so was an insistence that, no matter the circumstances, it was important to retain one's dignity and, above all, treat others with great respect. "All our lives, my mother insisted we remain friendly with people we met through the day," reflects Anne. "Mother used to always tell us that it doesn't cost anything to say hello."

The family had a close-knit group of friends and relatives. The three Barilko children shared several godparents — the Denisavitches, the Hriskeviches and the Hways, all from Timmins, and the Konopelkys from Cochrane. "We called our godfathers 'Papa Krasni' and godmothers 'Mama Krasna' — carry-overs from our Russian-Ukrainian heritage."

John Denisavitch had been a sailor in the Royal Russian Navy and went by the nickname "Matros," the Russian word for *sailor*. Matros married Olga Barilko, Steve's cousin, and moved to Timmins from their native Russia. They had four children: Johnny Jr., Mary, Anne and Steve. Matros and Olga bought property in Kapuskasing and Timmins, including the Welcome Hotel.

Mary Panchuk, who is Anne's godmother and was born a Denisavitch, recalls seeing the Barilko family socially. "Steve Barilko was a great dancer. He loved to waltz and we loved to watch him dance when we went to weddings," she recalls. At that time, parents took their children to social events.

Steve and Faye Barilko were also very close to Steve's brother John and John's wife Katy. "Uncle John was a cook in the mines just like my father," Anne states. John and Katy Barilko had three daughters, Ann, Leda and Nina. "When Uncle John and Aunt Katy moved to South Porcupine, they bought a property known as 'the old hospital.' They converted it into a rambling home. It was spotlessly clean and after they purchased it, it didn't resemble a hospital in the slightest."

Ann married Bernie Dillon but died at the age of 20 giving birth to their first child. Leda married Walter Soknacki and had two sons. Peter is a successful businessman. The eldest, David, is a Toronto city councillor as well as the city's budget chief.

Nina, the last of the first cousins, married Conn Weseluck and has two children, Mark and Cathy. "I was the youngest of the cousins," starts Nina. "I looked up to my cousin Bill and thought, 'Wow, what a sweet guy.' I used to like to get that hug from him. We lived in South Porcupine and used to take the train to visit my cousins in Timmins. You'd think we were going across the country, but it was only seven miles away! We had a lovely stay for a few days. My aunt was always so kind and we had such great meals, but whenever I used to see Bill, he was always outside playing with a hockey stick in his hand. He'd wave to me and off he'd go with his friends."

With three children to raise, in April 1931, Steve and Faye Barilko purchased the modest house they had been renting from Sam Gurevitch. Bought at an auction sale for a thousand dollars earned through intense sweat and saving, the Barilko home was a tri-plex in the north end of Timmins. "We lived on the main floor, which consisted of three bedrooms, a living room and a kitchen," remembers Anne. The other two floors were rented out as income properties.

The Barilko home was located at 63 Sixth Avenue in Timmins, right on the corner of Cedar Street. In the early 1940s, the address was changed to 121 Cedar Street North. Such an apparently minor change threatened to have serious consequences for the Barilko children. "When we lived on Sixth Avenue, we went to Central School, which was two blocks from our house," Anne explains, "but when the same house was renumbered to 121 Cedar Street North, we were transferred to Birch Street Public School [later Queen Elizabeth Public School], which was a mile from home. Mama was furious because that meant a longer distance for us to go, so the neighbours got together and spoke up and we ended up going to Central School again."

The house featured a glassed-in veranda with big red geraniums sitting on the windowsills. The Barilko children played for hours on that porch. "On rainy days, we worked on jigsaw puzzles or played games like Monopoly," recalls Anne. "I remember one time, Bill said, 'Let's play Cowboys and Indians.' Billy found some rope and put me on a wooden chair and tied my arms behind my back. Then he went outside and forgot about me. I was there for quite some time and I was screaming. My mama was out in the garden. I rocked myself back and forth until I tipped the chair forward and landed on my chin — I still have the scar. Mother came in and found me there on the floor, bleeding, with my arms tied behind me. You can imagine the punishment Bill got for that!"

Bill was always full of mischief from the time he was young, reports his sister. "'Come on. Let's play restaurant,' he said to me," laughs Anne. "I said, 'Oh, okay.' He said, 'Make up a menu and I'll be the customer.' So I made a menu and gave Billy a choice between a tomato sandwich or a cheese sandwich — something very simple. Then, I had to prepare it, serve it to him and then I had to clean up."

"After that, I smartened up," Anne admits. "'That's enough of that, Bill. I have to do all the work. We're not playing restaurant anymore!'"

Eating in a restaurant was as foreign a concept to the Barilko family as eating on the moon. "We never thought about going to eat in a restaurant when we were growing up. We always ate at home. Sometimes my brothers would go and get chips with gravy, but we never went to a restaurant as a family," states Anne. Yet the home at 63 Sixth Avenue had neither a refrigerator nor a telephone until Bill joined the Toronto Maple Leafs and was able to acquire them for his mother. One Sunday a month, the Barilkos would buy a brick of Neapolitan ice cream, a three-coloured treat made of chocolate, vanilla and strawberry. "Because we didn't have a fridge, we took turns each month running to the corner store, buying the brick of ice cream, then running back home. Alex, Billy and I would argue over who got the biggest slice," giggles Anne.

Faye Barilko was enterprising, and after being coached by her husband who prepared meals in the mines for a living, she became a wonderful cook. "Mama made the best soups, cabbage rolls and perogies," Anne says. She also made borscht (beet soup), kapusta (cabbage soup) and the more traditional vegetable soup and chicken rice soup.

"Mama prepared food for the long, cold winter," the youngest of the Barilko children continues. "She made homemade dill pickles that were stored in a wooden barrel in our basement. I can still picture the barrel with a board placed on top and a large rock placed on top of that to keep the pickles intact. She also made sauerkraut using a special wooden cutter with blades to slice the cabbage. It took her hours and hours."

Mrs. Barilko also put up jars of fruit preserves. "I remember blueberries, strawberries and peaches, mainly. The jars were placed neatly in rows in a special cupboard we had in our basement. She also baked the most delicious sweet buns, two dozen at a time. Mmmm," reminisces Anne, closing her eyes as she relives the memory.

The cold cellar also housed sacks of flour and sugar as well as baskets of carrots, beets and onions picked from the family's garden during the summer months. The home was renowned for both its vegetable and flower gardens, which boasted well-kept flower beds and lush lilac trees.

Anne smiles and admits she was Daddy's little girl. "My papa spoiled me. Whenever my mother made a big pot of chicken soup, vegetable soup, borscht or kapusta, I didn't want to eat it. My father would say, 'I'll give you a nickel if you eat your soup.' Well, then I ate my soup!" Faye was upset that her husband resorted to bribing Annie to eat her meals. "She'd say, 'Oh sure, she gets everything because she's the '*panya*.' Billy said, 'Mama, what's a *panya*?' My mother said, 'Annie is Papa's princess — a *panya*.'" The boys laughed and, in time, gave their sister the nickname of "Pun," a label she carried into high school. "I was never Anne or Annie; I was always Pun."

Steve Barilko played the penny stocks quite heavily, dreaming of making his fortune so that life would be easier for his wife. The dream never came true. "He was a good father, but it was difficult for my mother because if she didn't have a grasp of the purse strings, that money would go to buying stocks on margin."

On some Saturday nights in the 1930s, Faye and Steve Barilko went to the Timmins Steambath on nearby Algonquin Boulevard. Occasionally, the kids would get to tag along for a special treat. "They charged 25 cents per person, which included a towel," laughs Anne heartily. "We would giggle when Mama and Papa were in the steambath together."

"We didn't have a bathtub in those days," Anne adds. "My mother would fill a large round laundry tub she'd place on the floor near the wood stove in the kitchen. Mama would stand there and hold a sheet so I could have my bath first, and then Billy would have his, and finally Alex would have his. Eventually, we got a bathtub. I can still remember it — it had clawed feet. Now, I laugh when I see they're back in style."

Faye and Steve would often go for a draught beer on a Saturday night. "Mama and Papa would go to the Welcome Hotel, owned by the Denisavitches," recalls Anne. "We would be taken along, although we'd have to sit in the lobby and wait for our mother and father. They'd buy us a treat to tide us over until we got home — usually a bag of peanuts and a soda pop."

But Saturday night was also *Hockey Night in Canada.* "Our Stromberg-Carlson floor model radio was our link to the outside world," Anne admits. "Billy and I would both have a ruler, and we'd use a marble to play hockey while we listened to Foster Hewitt on the radio on Saturday nights. I don't know where we got the nickel, but we always had a bottle of Pepsi-Cola, too." A game of marbles could be a lot of fun, too, Anne remembers. "Bill always ended up being the winner, and he sure had quite a collection. He treasured them and kept the marbles in old coffee cans my father would bring home from the kitchen at the mining camps."

One winter, Bill made a snow fort in the backyard. "He really spent a lot of time on it. I can still picture it," recalls Anne. "Billy went into the house and asked my mother for a candle. She said, 'Why you want candle?' He said, 'I want to put it in my igloo.' He said, 'Don't worry. There can't be a fire because it's snow.' Well, I was curious. I said, 'Billy, can I go in your igloo?' He snapped, 'No, you can't! Stay out! It's just for boys!' I was mad. I was a tomboy and thought I should be able to go into this igloo that Billy had made. We kept our hockey sticks outside the back door; I grabbed a stick and hit Billy over the head with it. When I saw the blood dripping down his face, I ran for my life. 'My God, what have I done? Am I ever going to get it!' I ran over to my friend Mary Stefanich's house and said, 'Let me in! I've got to move in with you! I clobbered my brother over the head with a hockey stick and my mother's going to kill me!' I stayed away from home until after dinner. When I finally went home, boy oh boy, did I have to pay for it! I had to face the music and got my punishment."

Although they were good children most of the time, Alex, Bill and Anne were punished when the occasion required. "Sometimes we would have to go in the corner or some part of the house where Mama could watch us. We'd have to get down on our knees and sit there. It was terrible! We'd say, 'Mama, our knees are sore!' 'That okay,' she'd say. 'You learn something?' But she was never cruel."

On Saturday mornings, Bill and Anne picked the big, plump blueberries found at the Sand Claims, also known as "The Buckets," as well as in the bush across the road from the cemetery where Bill is now buried. "We talked and sang and just enjoyed being together," smiles Anne, remembering a wonderful time. "We picked our blueberries in old three-pound shortening pails Papa brought home from the mine when he was cooking there. Mama would wash them out and we'd fill them to the top with blueberries. Then we'd sell the blueberries to our neighbours for 25 cents. The neighbours were practically waiting in line for them! We gave Mother 10 cents and we'd keep 15. I remember once Billy bought a pack of cigarettes with a nickel, but most of the time, the money was enough to get us into the movies."

Going to the movies was a rare but special luxury for the Barilko kids. Anne remembers some of the Timmins' theatres she and Bill visited as youngsters. "Bill loved cowboys and Indians, so we went to Goldfield's Theatre to see Roy Rogers, Dale Evans and Trigger, Gene Autry and Champion and Buck Jones. The Palace was an absolutely gorgeous theatre — probably the nicest in northern Ontario. We used to go to Shirley Temple movies there. The Palace is where I got to see *Gone with the Wind*. We got to go at night — what a treat that was!"

The Broadway and Victory theatres were well appointed, and occasionally the Barilkos would go to the Empire, but Anne remembers that visits to the Cartier Theatre were extra special. "Oh, we used to laugh so hard at the Laurel and Hardy movies and the Three Stooges, but the Cartier also gave out dishes every two weeks." With the aid of friends and neighbours, Faye ended up getting six complete settings, which were used only on special occasions. "Our everyday dishes were the plain, white, heavy glass dishes that were going to be thrown out at the mine camps where Papa was the cook."

The Barilko family did not have a family car, although neither did most of the families in the neighbourhood — except one. "Mr. and Mrs. Alex Peters had a car, but they only took it out on Sundays," Anne remembers. "They just kept it to themselves. We used to envy them because they had this lovely car. She was a seamstress and did a lot of sewing for my mother and me. They had one child, a son named Andrew who I used to invite to my birthday parties." Anne starts to laugh as she remembers Andrew Peters. "He was terrified of the police. His parents must have threatened him — 'Andrew, if you're bad, the police are going to come and get you.' Well, my brothers and the other kids on the block used to tease him, saying, 'Andrew, a policeman is coming,' and we'd watch Andrew run for his life and hide any place he could find a spot. Of course, there was no policeman coming.

"But you know the funniest thing? Andrew eventually became a policeman!"

The Barilko boys received hand-me-down clothing and skates from their father's boss, Mr. MacPhail. "The first hockey equipment Billy and Alex ever got was from Mr. MacPhail," Anne says. "He was the mine manager where my father was the head cook."

The MacPhails had four children: Roddy, Ross, Margaret and Ann. The MacPhails lived in an affluent area of Timmins commonly known as Snob Hill. "Once a year, Mrs. MacPhail would invite us to her home for afternoon tea. I was used to seeing my mother in a housedress with her hair pushed back. She always looked old to me," grimaces Anne. But Faye Barilko would get all dressed up and have her hair done beautifully for her visits to the MacPhails'. "She'd put my hair in ringlets. The MacPhail home was so lovely. Mrs. MacPhail used her best china and served tea and cookies and chatted with Mama. She taught my mother a few English words.

"I remember asking to use the bathroom just so I could see the beautiful black and white tiles," Anne says. "The MacPhails were very, very good to the Barilko family," she emphasizes.

Faye wore simple dresses, some homemade and others bought at Bucovetsky's department store, Friedman's, Fishman's or Economy Dry Goods. "Mama always wore a homemade apron to protect her clothes when she was preparing food," says Anne. "She made the aprons from flour and sugar sacks, then embroidered them with flowers."

Monday was laundry day in the Barilko home. Anne remembers, "Mama did the laundry and I would help with the ironing. But Mama always seemed to choose Monday morning to make a rice or bread pudding, too. We always came home for lunch and got to know that we'd have pudding on Monday before we went back to school."

Passions learned young are usually burned indelibly into adulthood, and Bill Barilko's life was no different. But his childhood interests take on an eerie sense of premonition. "Even as a boy, Bill was fascinated by airplanes," Anne remembers. "Bill liked to buy model airplane kits for 10 cents at Kresge's, Woolworth's or Metropolitan's. He liked to put those together."

Alex and Bill would occasionally be sent by train to visit family friends in Kirkland Lake. "We called them Uncle Nick and Aunt Anne, but the Kozloffs were really third cousins," recalls Anne (Klisenich). "They wouldn't take all three of us kids at once, so the boys would be invited to their camp to fish and hunt. That's where Billy got his first BB gun.

The young man's fascination with the outdoors was also legendary in the neighbourhood. Bill loved to venture into the surrounding wooded areas, where he explored, hunted and fished. "Billy liked to hunt. He had a hunting rifle and he and his friends would go into the woods to shoot rabbits," his sister recalls. "But most of all, he loved fishing on the local lakes with his friends and our neighbours — George Floria, Peter Stefanich and Joe Chopp. There was a small workshop in our basement and Bill would putter down there for hours, sorting out his fishing tackle so he'd always have it handy for his next expedition. He really didn't have very good equipment. The boys used to catch suckers. Mother used to get so angry. She'd say, 'Billy, suckers all you bring home. They full bones.' Mind you, she cooked them and we ate them. But Bill didn't care much for fish."

Gillies Lake was across Lakeshore Road, about a mile from the Barilko home. Anne remembers going there often as youngsters. "It was the only beach in Timmins, and my brother liked to swim," she acknowledges. "In the winter, we'd skate or borrow a sleigh from our neighbours. There was a nice hill there." But the lake afforded a different adventure for Bill Barilko during the winter of 1938. "Bill saw a boy riding his bicycle on Gillies Lake and the bike broke through the ice. Bill thought it was our brother Alex, so he jumped in and rescued the boy," recounts Anne. The 14-year old boy, Donald Beauseigle, had been warned repeatedly by his father to keep his bicycle off the ice on Gillies Lake. Bill, who was only 11, rushed out onto the ice to save the boy and fell through the ice himself. Someone near enough to hear the commotion ran out with a ladder to save the boys. Meanwhile, the Timmins Fire Department responded to a panicked phone call and pulled Beauseigle and Bill out of the icy lake.

"When Billy got home, he was soaking wet and shivering. Mama was furious. She couldn't understand what Billy was doing at Gillies Lake," continues Anne. Bill stood there, dripping wet, being reprimanded by his mother. Annoyed, he yelled, "Mom, I thought it was Alex and I tried to save him!" Faye didn't believe him until the following day, when the

Timmins *Daily Press* confirmed Bill's story. "My mother was most apologetic," Anne admits. It was the first time Bill Barilko's name would appear in print. Bill had learned what it was like to be a hero, a feeling he would rediscover 13 years later.

The resourceful Bill found a way to get to ride a bicycle, like the other boys did, without owning a bike of his own. "I had a bicycle and whenever I had a flat tire, Bill would repair it for me," laughs his cousin, Mary Panchuk. "He would keep in touch with me to make sure the bike was okay. That way, he got to ride my bike."

Leo Curik, Bill's best friend, lived half a block away on Balsam Street. "Bill was a bully; a tough bugger," Leo states. "He was always a big boy. He'd hold the young kids down and not let them up. He'd block the doorway and he wouldn't let anybody in. A big guy would come along and Bill would say, 'Sorry, you can't come in here,' and he'd take them on."

While Bill was more interested in the outdoors, his brother Alex was more sports-minded. "Alex was the one who got Billy playing hockey," Anne readily admits. "Billy really looked up to Alex. So did I. Alex always did well in school. My mother used to call him 'Smart Alex.' Billy didn't do well in school, but I wanted to be like my brother Alex and get good marks."

School was difficult for Bill Barilko. "For one thing, he was a very poor speller," admits Anne. "We had a nurse named Diane Vienneau renting a room at our house. She worked at St. Mary's Hospital, which was only a block from us. She used to help Billy with his spelling." But Barilko was good with his hands and became skilled at making things. "He'd take a clock apart or whatever he could get his hands on," his sister remembers. "In Grade 8, he made a small wooden bench which my mother used for years and years. On the end of this bench, Bill carved what looked like a wolf." In an interesting coincidence, three years later, Bill Barilko would begin his pro hockey career in earnest with the Hollywood Wolves.

The academic challenges Bill struggled with forced him to spend three years in the eighth grade before he packed it in at the age of 15. "We could see that he wasn't going anywhere in school, so my mother said, 'There's no use going back to school because you're just not interested. You better get a job,'" Anne explains. "She warned him that he was going to end up being a truck driver."

"He had no education and little talent," admits Leo. "It appeared that Bill would follow the path of so many of his peers — he would work in the mines."

Faye Barilko was right: Bill did end up driving a truck for the Delnite Mines. "That lasted one year," Anne continues. "Bill was such a charismatic boy that he fit nicely into that environment. He enjoyed making deliveries and chatting with the people along his route. He enjoyed that job."

Leo adds, "Bill did a lot of lifting, which really helped him develop the physique and strength that afforded him so well once he got to the National Hockey League."

Young Bill didn't express an interest in what he wanted to do for a living, although Anne says that playing hockey for a living was a dream of his, as it was for nearly every other youngster. Neither Steve nor Faye Barilko was athletic at all. "They didn't know what sports were until we got involved in athletics," shrugs Anne. It seems ironic in light of the children's later exploits. "Mother wasn't interested in hockey. She didn't understand anything like that," laughs Anne. "I listened to the hockey on the radio with my brothers, but I didn't know any of the players. I didn't even know what 'NHL' stood for. I just knew Foster Hewitt's voice."

One of those who became friendly with the Barilko boys was Hall of Fame defenceman Allan Stanley. "I was Alex's age. I didn't know Bill too well until later on. Bill ran with the Curik boys. They were closer to his age." Through the years, Allan came to be a frequent visitor to the Barilko house. "Mrs. Barilko was a wonderful lady; a loving mother," he recalls. "She was so friendly — we had great chats for a number of years."

Leo Curik recounts how his friendship with Bill Barilko began. "One day, I saw Bill at a restaurant. He was standing outside. I said, 'How ya doin', Bill?' I thought maybe he was waiting for somebody. This went on a couple of times. I said, 'Bill, you waitin' for anybody?' He said, 'No.' I said, 'Come on with us.'" From that day on, Leo Curik and Bill Barilko were the best of friends.

The Curiks owned the Victory Hotel on Cedar Street, one of 22 beverage hotels in the area at that time. "Timmins was known as the beer capital of Canada for decades," boasts Emil Klisanich, who would later marry Bill's sister, Anne. The Klisanich family owned the Pearl Lake Hotel in Schumacher at that time. Emil played baseball with eldest brother Alex, and at the time didn't know either Bill or Anne.

Bill and his friends the Curiks, Allan Stanley and Gaston Garant went to the Victory Hotel nearly every night they were all home. "If Billy wasn't home, Mother knew he'd be at the Victory Hotel," smiles Anne.

"I grew up with the Barilkos and the Curiks," says Garant. "Allan Stanley was one of the boys, too. They were hockey players, but I never played hockey. I was never interested in hockey, but all my friends are hockey players — Bep Guidolin and Real Chevrefils are both good friends of mine, too."

Although born in Thorold, Ontario on the Niagara Escarpment, Bep Guidolin grew up in Timmins. Born in 1925, he was about a year and a half older than Bill. "I was baptized in Rouyn, Quebec. My dad was working in the mines there. After that, he went up to Timmins and I went to school there." While the Barilkos, who lived in the north end, went to Central School, Guidolin called the south end home and attended Moneta Public School. "Our side was mostly Italians and their side was a mix of English, French, Romanian and Ukrainians," says Guidolin, "but we all got along well and everybody worked in the mines together. There was no animosity — we used to go to their dances and they used to go to ours."

As the boys got a little older, they started to earn their own money. Bill was driving the truck for the mine and Alex worked for McIntyre Mines. "He played baseball for McIntyre Mines," explains his sister. "If you played ball for the mines, you were assured of having a summer job. A lot of athletes came up to northern Ontario for jobs — they'd play baseball and hockey, then get a job in the mines." Alex worked on the garden crew at the beautiful McIntyre Park in Timmins. "My husband worked there, too," mentions Anne. "One summer, Alex also went down to Niagara Falls and picked fruit. He enjoyed that."

Anne earned her spending money by babysitting for the neighbours; then, when she turned 16, she took a job as a waitress. "At the time, there were some very good restaurants in Timmins — the Paradise Grill and the Golden Arrow both had great Chinese food, and the McIntyre Coffee Shop at the McIntyre Arena was a good place for breakfasts and snacks. I guess one of the most popular spots was the Fern Cottage, where I got my first real job," Anne recollects. "Alex and Bill didn't like the idea that their sister was a waitress. Anne Kozloff, a relative from Kirkland Lake, was visiting us and said, 'Let her go. When she finds out how hard it is to be a waitress, she'll be so glad to go back to school.'

"My brothers were concerned about me getting home at night. The owner of the restaurant, Albert Zincone, assured all the students that he would make sure they got home all right. It was only four blocks away from our home."

The experience was invaluable to the young Anne Barilko. "I tried to please everyone. A lot of the figure skaters from the United States came up to Timmins and Schumacher during the summer to attend a summer figure skating school at the McIntyre Arena. Barbara Ann Scott used to come up in the summer. The skaters used to come to the Fern Cottage and we were quite honoured when we'd see them."

Before long, Anne got the idea that she was making enough money that she could donate all her old clothes to the Salvation Army and outfit herself with a new wardrobe. "My mother thought, 'Aha. *This* will teach her the value of a dollar.'"

"I went shopping at Bucovetsky's and Freidman's, two local department stores that carried very fashionable clothes," Anne continues. "I had $150 and spent every penny, but I came home and thought, 'This is all I got with all that money?' I didn't realize that it wouldn't buy very much. I asked my mother, 'Where are the clothes I was giving away to the Salvation Army? I hope you didn't give them away yet!' I learned my lesson there."

"Bill and I enjoyed each other's company immensely," concludes his proud sister. "Billy always had a big smile on his face. You couldn't help but like him. As we got older, he had his friends and I had mine. When we were teenagers, they didn't want their little sister around, of course. Both Alex and Billy were terrific brothers. They really watched over me. They were always very good to me."

Although there was barely enough money for food, clothing and the roof over their heads, the Barilko family had no shortage of affection. And the lessons of strength, resiliency and humility remained with Alex, Bill and Anne their entire lives. "I guess because we were raised with humble beginnings, we continued to live our lives that way," nods Anne. "Especially Bill."

CHAPTER 3

Lost in the Woods

The headline in the Porcupine *Advance* screamed, "Searchers Believe Barilko Alive."

Frantic with anxiety and exhaustion, those involved in the search had valiantly spent a frustrating night trudging through the woods and wading through muskeg trying to locate Bill Barilko, lost in the woods north of Timmins. "If he is not alive, we would have found his body for we have combed every inch of that territory. We have scoured it," announced Constable Strickland of the Ontario Provincial Police.

Curiously, this newspaper account isn't about Bill Barilko, the second-born child of Steve and Faye Barilko, and the futile search for the Toronto Maple Leaf hockey player. *This* search actually took place through the night on September 20, 1937 — fourteen years before the big defenceman vanished without a trace.

"There were three Barilko families in Timmins," recalls Anne Klisanich, the kid sister of the hockey playing Bill Barilko. "There was our family, my Dad's brother John's family, which was John and Katy Barilko and their girls Ann, Leda and Nina. And my father Steve had a cousin, Steve Barilko. My Dad's cousin owned a hotel on Cedar Street called the International Hotel, and had five children — Mary, Bill, Nick, Eddie and Alex. Mary married Carlo Cattarello, the hockey coach from the Holman Pluggers. They have a daughter Sandra and a son named Carlo Jr., who was the mascot for the Holman Pluggers."

So, at one time in Timmins, there were two Steve Barilkos, two Bill Barilkos, two Alex Barilkos and two Anne Barilkos, although the other Ann didn't have an *e* at the end of her given name. "You can imagine this got a lot of people confused," laughs Anne.

In a community the size of Timmins, it seems so unlikely that there could be two Bill Barilkos, but that, in fact, was the case. "The other Bill

Barilko would have been our third cousin," explains Anne, attempting to untangle the mystery.

The search for the other Bill Barilko carries eerie parallels to the 1951 search for his namesake, the Toronto Maple Leafs' Stanley Cup hero. Both were Timmins boys in their early twenties when they were lost in densely forested areas outside of town. Both were with friends in search of wildlife. Both were the subject of aerial searches.

"The going is bad for searchers. They are working in muskeg and there is mud and water to their knees. After searching all day yesterday and last night, their eyes red from lack of sleep, they took to the air today to further the hunt," read the 1937 newspaper account.

Charlie Angus, leader of a fine band called the Grievous Angels, New Democrat member of Parliament for the massive Timmins–James Bay riding and an outstanding writer who chronicles life in northern Ontario, devoted a chapter to the Barilko story in his book, *Mirrors of Stone: Fragments from the Porcupine Frontier.* "I know that it's nothing more than coincidence — a fluke of fate, time and names. But the story that unfolds in the 1937 account carries a similar sense of urgency and concern that was shared during the 1951 search. In the first search, the residents of the Porcupine clung to the fading hope that the boreal forest would free young Bill Barilko and return him to his family. In the end, their prayers were answered and the forest relented. Fourteen years later, however, the forest changed its mind."

CHAPTER 4

Miner Hockey

Life below the earth's surface is unpredictable. Draining. Daunting. Tough. Exciting. And the toll it exacts affects all those in the community above, just as the economy relies on the earth surrendering its riches.

For many, escape was found through either sports or drinking (or, for some, both). In the 1940s, the Porcupine boasted more taverns per capita than any other community in Ontario. And the climate of the area was ideally suited to winter sports.

During the winters of Bill Barilko's youth, skating rinks would have dotted the town at every school, church and vacant lot in the area. Every neighbourhood had a rink, and every kid on it had a dream — a dream of playing in the National Hockey League. For a kid in the Timmins area, the way to avoid a life in the mines was to play sports. The better you played, the better your chance of leaving behind a life spent underground.

Bill Barilko's dreams were no different than those of any other boy growing up in the region. He sat and listened to Foster Hewitt describe the games and imagined himself swirling effortlessly around Maple Leaf Gardens, carving a seamless arc out of the chalky white ice as he glided over its surface. At times, he imagined he was Charlie Conacher — the Big Bomber — firing a shot so hard it would catch the back of the net before the goaltender had a chance to react. Other times, he pretended he was Leafs defenceman Red Horner, the league's "bad boy," body-checking the opponents into submission.

But although Barilko's dreams were no different than those of other boys, they were no more realistic, either.

The fact was, Bill couldn't skate. Other boys in the neighbourhood had been skating for several years before Alex and Bill got their first pair of hand-me-down skates. Alex took to skating with relative ease, but Bill struggled — so much so, in fact, that he was posted in the goal crease. Bill Barilko began his hockey career as a bespectacled goalie who was short on skill but long on desire.

"He was a well-built boy who was very physical while playing, but he did not have the speed to skate as a centre or the ability to skate backwards as a defenceman, so he played as a goalie," Leo Curik remembers.

Working diligently to perfect his craft, Barilko became quite proficient as a goaltender. He played for the Central School team, which won the Halperin Cup as Interscholastic Intermediate elementary school champions of the region in 1940–41. With Bill in goal and his friend Leo Curik playing forward, Central also took the Interscholastic Intermediate hockey championship of the Porcupine District in 1941–42, and the following year, Central School captured the Timmins Senior School championship.

Curik recalls that while Bill played goal for Central School, he paid special attention to one Maple Leaf as he listened to *Hockey Night in Canada*. "Bill idolized Turk Broda," laughs Leo. Broda and Barilko were to become good friends as teammates with the Toronto Maple Leafs. During an intermission interview on *Hockey Night in Canada* in 1967, Turk Broda was asked to name the best defenceman ever to play in front of him. Broda's answer? Bill Barilko.

"Billy and Alex would get up at six o'clock in the morning to go off to Central School to help prepare the ice for the coming winter along with other young hockey enthusiasts," remembers their sister. "They would put the boards up and shovel the ice. They didn't think anything of getting up so early. I remember the teacher, Don Finlayson. He was in charge of the boys' hockey team."

The public school teams in the area played on outdoor rinks, but Timmins winters can be bone-chillingly cold. Anne Klisanich remembers her youngest brother complaining about the frigid air. "Bill said, 'Gee, I'm so cold when I play goal,' and my brother Alex replied, 'Well, if you learned to skate, you could become a defenceman.' So Billy took his advice and learned to skate." In a 1947 interview with the *Toronto Daily Star*, Bill confirmed the reason for his move from the crease to the blue line. "I couldn't skate and they made me play goal," Barilko admitted. "A couple years in the nets was enough. I about froze to death."

But there was another driving factor behind Bill's transformation to a position player. Photographs of the young Barilko show the defenceman wearing glasses. "Billy wore thick glasses, and he had to wear them when he played back then," notes Anne. "Our parents were of modest means and money was hard to come by." Replacing Bill's glasses would strain the family's finances, and there was a greater chance of them being damaged if he continued in goal. His fate was therefore sealed: Bill Barilko was going to learn to play defence.

"I was on the ice morning, noon and night learning to skate," Bill told the Toronto radio station CFRB in 1947. Barilko learned that Toronto Maple Leafs star Charlie Conacher had also been pushed into the net as a boy because it was the path of least resistance for poor skaters. Conacher had worked hard to address his deficiency and become an NHL star, and Bill was determined that he would follow in the Big Bomber's skate tracks. "I was determined to stay on defence if I had to skate 18 hours a day," he said.

❋ ❋ ❋

Timmins boasted several juvenile hockey teams in the late 1930s, and Allan Stanley, an Honoured Member of the Hockey Hall of Fame, remembers the simple process by which one of them was organized. "There was a businessman in Timmins who wrote his company and said, 'I have a bunch of kids around here who want to play hockey. Will you buy sweaters and stockings?' And the company wrote back and said, 'That's a good idea.' That was the Holman Pluggers. We were together five years."

Bill Carroll was the man who initiated the Holman Pluggers and acted as the team's manager. Carlo Cattarello was the first coach.

"My Dad goes way back," explains Carlo Cattarello Jr., who as a boy was a mascot for the teams his father coached. "At 16, my Dad was playing Senior A hockey in the Porcupine, which was quite an accomplishment. He got out of playing hockey in his early thirties and turned his talents to coaching.

"It used to disappoint my Dad that a lot of the good players would end up going down south," Carlo Jr. states. The scouts would swoop through the area and pluck the better players for teams in southern Ontario. Carroll and Cattarello were determined to give hometown talent the opportunity to develop in their own backyard.

"The calibre of hockey was really good. A lot of the families were in the mines. It was dangerous work and they didn't want their sons to go underground, so they figured hockey was a great outlet," hypothesizes Cattarello Jr., who spent some time underground himself. "They had so many open-air rinks and everybody was on the ice. People just loved hockey." A search through the archives indicates that there were 14 or 15 outdoor rinks when Barilko was learning to skate; one at each of the schools, one at the Timmins Armouries and one at Gillies Lake. Although nearby Schumacher boasted the McIntyre Arena, the only covered rink in Timmins proper was the Timmins Arena at the corner of Second and Balsam, which burned down in 1947. "They went years without an arena in Timmins," says Cattarello Jr.

In 1937, Ontario Premier Mitchell Hepburn donated a trophy that was to be awarded to the juvenile hockey champions of the province. That first year, the Mitchell Hepburn Championship Trophy was won by a team from Iroquois Falls.

Sudbury perennially iced a strong team, finishing behind Oshawa in 1938 but capturing the championship the next year. In both 1940 and '41, Sudbury again found itself in the role of runner-up, to St. Catharines and Hamilton. Kirkland Lake won the championship in 1942.

In 1943, Timmins finally got its chance.

The Holman Pluggers had enjoyed a sensational season, with a lineup studded with players who would go on to grace professional hockey lineups. Pete Babando played in the National Hockey League with Boston, Detroit, Chicago and New York. Eric Prentice, better known as "Doc," would debut later that year as the youngest player ever to pull a Toronto Maple Leafs sweater over his head, playing five NHL games and later becoming a teammate of Bill Barilko's in Hollywood. And then there was Allan Stanley, a future four-time Stanley Cup champion and veteran of more than 1,000 NHL games with the New York Rangers, Boston, Chicago, Toronto and Philadelphia. "Allan Stanley started as a centreman, but my Dad moved him back to defence because he was too slow at centre," chuckles Carlo. Alex Barilko went on to the Pacific Coast Hockey League, as did Billy Adamo, Bill Curik, George DeFelice and Roy McKay.

"The Holman Machine Shop was selling drills to the mines back then," says McKay. "They decided to sponsor hockey for some local boys and came up with the Holman Pluggers. There were seven or eight juvenile teams in Timmins at that time, and the Holman Pluggers were one of them. I started playing with them in the team's first year. I was only 15."

Looking on from the bench was Bill Barilko. Not good enough to play with the Pluggers, Bill was conscripted to be the team's stick boy. "Bill was a little younger than us," explains Allan Stanley. "His brother Alex was with us. Alex was closer to my age." Anne adds, "Our brother Alex would say, 'Come to the rink with me and you can be the stick boy.' That's how Billy got to be the stick boy for the Holman Pluggers."

"Bill just lived on the open-air rinks," relates Carlo Cattarello Jr. "My Dad would tell me that when Bill was stick boy, he wanted to get into games, but he was still young and wasn't quite ready. These guys [the Pluggers] were very talented, but Bill was always out there scrimmaging. He wasn't the greatest skater, but he had so much drive. He really worked at his skating."

Pluggers' coach Carlo Cattarello Sr. recalls that Bill would gamely do anything he could to help the team. "When we'd have practices, he always wanted to play. If given a chance to play, he'd put on the pads when we were short a goaltender and he'd join the practice."

"He just wanted to be part of the team so badly," says Carlo Jr.

The Holman Pluggers defeated an excellent team from Kirkland Lake — one that featured future NHL stars Gus Mortson and Ted Lindsay — to capture the Northern Ontario Hockey Association's juvenile championship. With that, they earned the right to play St. Catharines in a one-game sudden-death playoff at Maple Leaf Gardens. "That had to be the biggest thrill for a kid," Stanley remembers. "Even to be in Maple Leaf Gardens at that time would be tremendous." Carlo Cattarello Jr. adds, "It was the first time any of the players had been to Maple Leaf Gardens."

The day before the championship contest, William A. Hewitt, the longtime secretary of the Ontario Hockey Association and Foster's father, arranged for a 30-minute practice for the Pluggers. During the workout, Bill — in his first time on the Gardens ice on which he would later earn his living — played goal. The Ottawa St. Pats, coached by Hall of Fame netminder Alex Connell, were scheduled to take the ice after the Pluggers. The St. Pats were in Toronto for the All-Ontario junior final against the Oshawa Generals. "As we were leaving the ice, Alex Connell, who had been watching us, suggested our team stay on the ice and play a one period game against his squad," recalls Pluggers' coach Carlo Cattarello. The Holman Pluggers won the abbreviated contest 5–2. Astonished, Connell asked Cattarello, "Where did you get those guys?"

The next afternoon, April 3, 1943, the Pluggers faced a formidable challenge from a fine St. Catharines team that didn't have a star-studded lineup but played a fierce team game.

* * *

The Holman Pluggers edged the St. Catharines Lions 6–5 that Saturday afternoon to win the Mitchell Hepburn Trophy as provincial juvenile champions. "That started my career, and those of a lot of other guys," states Allan Stanley. "I was scouted by Boston and went to the Bruins' training camp the next fall. I think nine players off that team went to professional camps. Two of us went to Boston, [Eric] Prentice went to Toronto and there were about six who went to Detroit's training camp. I don't think any of those guys played in the National Hockey League, but some of them played in the American Hockey League and other leagues around. We [Timmins] were well represented."

Bill Barilko watched his colleagues compete for the All-Ontario championship. It was an eye-opening glimpse inside the storied Maple Leaf Gardens, a venue he had envisioned while listening faithfully to Foster Hewitt's *Hockey Night in Canada* radio broadcasts each Saturday night.

By witnessing a strong, competitive level of hockey and being exposed to a talented group of young hockey players, Bill realized how much he wanted to play for the Holman Pluggers. "That's where he really got interested in hockey," states his sister.

Allan Stanley assigns much of the credit for the team's success to the coach. "We were all 16 or 17 years old, but that's the way it was. It was during the war and all the senior guys were in the service. We had a talented team and an excellent coach. He coached for two or three years and he did a really great job working with kids."

Carlo Jr. was the Pluggers' mascot while his dad coached. "I idolized all the players," he smiles. "Whenever we went on trips, the players all went out of their way to treat me well. Dad never carried extra players — he never liked to cut anybody. Some of the players would buy me lunches. They figured maybe that way, they could crack the lineup."

"They were a great group," he continues. "The players all got along. You never saw a selfish player." But not only were they good sportsmen, the Pluggers were excellent hockey players. "My father could really spot a good hockey player. If he thought there was any hope, my Dad felt he could make a hockey player out of him."

Bummer Doran was one. "At 17, he was at the Leafs' camp. Conn Smythe found out that Doran had been having a few beers after practice, and that just didn't go in those days. Smythe called Tommy Naylor, the trainer, and said, 'If you don't get that guy on the next train to South Porcupine, you're going to be looking for a job yourself.' That was it for Bummer."

"Another guy was Eddie Brown," says Carlo. "He lied about his age to get into the army. My Dad said he was probably the best to come out of the Porcupine. He played in an all-star game against the famous Kraut Line [Milt Schmidt, Bobby Bauer and Woody Dumart of the Boston Bruins] in Europe during the war, and this guy was the first star of the game. And he was just 16. After the war in 1945–46, he was playing for the St. Louis Flyers of the AHL. He was heading to Detroit to join the Red Wings and in the very last game he played in St. Louis, he lost an eye." Hockey can be a cruel game, and circumstances like these punctuate the fragility of a professional career.

Carlo Cattarello Sr. devoted his life to hockey, spending more than 25 years on the executive of the Northern Ontario Hockey Association. In October 2001, the 88-year-old native of South Porcupine was honoured with the highest civilian award available to Canadians, the Order of Canada.

🍁 🍁 🍁

With so many players signing to play elsewhere, the Holman Pluggers made wholesale changes after their triumphant 1942–43 championship season. "Carlo Cattarello went off to war and the Pluggers changed considerably," says Cec Romain. Roy McKay and Stewart Pirie were the sole holdovers from the previous year's club. The Pluggers of 1943–44 would boast Bill Arundel coaching, while Ray Hannigan and Les Costello, both of whom played with Barilko on the Toronto Maple Leafs in 1948–49, joined the lineup.

The Holman Pluggers went on to repeat as northern Ontario juvenile champs in 1943–44, and defended their All-Ontario title against the St. Catharines Lions. This time, the finals consisted of a best-of-three series to be played at the McIntyre Arena, marking the first time the juvenile championship was to be contested in the north. The Pluggers prevailed and were crowned provincial champions for the second year in a row.

While Bill Barilko had been the stick boy and occasional practice goaltender with the Holman Pluggers in 1942–43, he wasn't yet ready to crack the drastically revamped squad in 1943–44. But he was nothing if not determined; that year, he made his transition from netminder to defence and played on two teams. Of his play with the Kiwanis Air Cadets, the Timmins *Daily Press* remarked, "The bespectacled rearguard is a real ice general and adds some size to a line-up that has a lot of midgets." Bill also skated with the Central School Seniors, who won the 1943–44 Porcupine District Schools' championship in a sudden-death victory over South Porcupine.

※ ※ ※

With many of the Porcupine's older boys joining the war effort, some of the more capable younger players were able to accelerate their hockey development. "In 1944–45, I was the goalie with the Timmins Canadians," recalls Cec Romain. "I played with them for four years from the time I was 15. Bill Arundel was the coach." Romain also remembers the rambunctious Barilko. "Bill tried out and joined the Timmins Canadians that year. Bill could really skate, especially backwards. He was a big, solid boy even then."

There seemed little doubt that a player like Allan Stanley was destined for the National Hockey League. But with the NHL consisting of only six teams at that time, no matter how deep the local talent pool appeared to be, it seemed unlikely that any other Timmins-trained player would debut in the big league. And certainly a player of Bill Barilko's calibre wasn't about to measure up to a talent like Allan Stanley's. Bill seemed ticketed for a life working in the mines.

But his drive was extraordinary, and he skated at every opportunity. By the fall of 1944, only two years after he became a defenceman, Barilko had improved enough not only to earn a spot with the Timmins Canadians, but to play senior hockey with the Hollinger Mines Greenshirts. "The mines were all very rich and were very competitive. They had lots of money to spend on hockey and baseball," explains Gus Mortson, the tough Leafs defenceman who was born in New Liskeard. By this time, Bill's game had developed hints of the bashing, daring style for which he would later become renowned. "It was fun bouncing guys and being bounced," Bill attested in an interview several years later.

After performing admirably with both teams during the 1944–45 campaign, Barilko was recruited to join the Porcupine Combines Junior A club for their contest against St. Michael's College in the All-Ontario junior finals to be played at the revered Maple Leaf Gardens. To be invited to join the Combines, even if only for two games and in a losing cause, was a major indicator that Bill had made extraordinary — and extraordinarily rapid — progress over the course of the season.

Johnny Mitchell, the coach and manager of the Pittsburgh Hornets of the American Hockey League, had watched Bill play at the McIntyre Arena in the fall of 1944, and again in the spring against St. Mike's. Having witnessed his dramatic improvement firsthand, Mitchell invited Barilko — as well as Leo Curik and, from Kapuskasing, Doug Davidson — to try out for the Hornets in the autumn of 1945.

CHAPTER
5
Hooray for Hollywood
(1945–47)

Northern Ontario was bursting with hockey talent, and it made Toronto Maple Leafs scout Bob Wilson question why NHL teams didn't put more value on the region as a source of prospects. "If clubs could give a little assistance to juvenile and junior teams in the North, they could tie up talent from North Bay to Timmins and west to Sault Ste. Marie," Wilson suggested. "There's some very fine talent in the North."

Harold "Baldy" Cotton, a star with the Leafs' first Stanley Cup championship team in 1932, had turned to scouting after retiring from playing in the NHL. In 1946, while employed by the Boston Bruins, he proclaimed, "The territory between Sudbury and Timmins is one of the best breeding grounds in Canada, bar none." Cotton did his fair share of prospecting for hockey talent in northern Ontario, and he tapped into a rich vein; Real Chevrefils, Wayne Connelly, Leo Labine, Doug Mohns, Jean-Paul Parise, Larry Regan, Ron Schock and Jerry and Zellio Toppazzini are a few of those who went on to the NHL after the Bruins' signed them on Cotton's advice.

Another key to the Bruins' success in recruiting in the Porcupine region was Bep Guidolin. When he first stepped onto the ice in a Bruins uniform in November 1942, he was only 16 years old; to this day he remains the youngest player ever to play in the NHL. "I brought Pete Babando, Allan Stanley, 'Moose' Lallo and Dutch Delmonte to Boston," states Bep. "Art Ross was our manager and coach, and I phoned him and said, 'I've got four good hockey players up here who want tryouts. He said, 'I'm going to send you some A Forms. Tell them to sign them and we'll bring them down.' The Bruins lost nine players to the war, plus they had the Boston Olympics, the farm team that played at the Boston Garden. Two of my Timmins boys made the NHL and two made the

Boston Olympics. So Mr. Ross said, 'You got any more up there?' I said, 'Oh yeah, there's a few more up there.'"

Johnny Mitchell, who had spent eight years playing with the Duluth Hornets of the AHA in hopes of a chance to crack the NHL, had been named manager of the Pittsburgh Hornets in 1944, the same year the Toronto Maple Leafs chose the team as their AHL affiliate. Mitchell made a pilgrimage to Timmins to scout what was developing into a hockey hotbed. He remembers seeing a young prospect named Bill Barilko. "It was the fall of '44 at the McIntyre Arena in Schumacher. Bill was all alone on defence with two men coming in on him. Instead of trying to outwit them, he walked into the guy on the right and started a battle. I liked his moxie and decided if he ever learned to skate, he'd make the grade. The next spring [1945], I saw him playing for the [Porcupine] Combines against St. Mike's and I couldn't believe my eyes. Instead of struggling up the ice, he was whizzing along as fast as any of the Irish [nickname for St. Mike's players]." Maple Leafs manager Conn Smythe had also seen Barilko play. "Conn liked Barilko's style and his skating so he put him on the Toronto negotiation list," said Mitchell, whom Smythe told to keep a close watch on.

The Toronto Maple Leafs had a deep farm system. In addition to the AHL Hornets, who were stacked with prospects, there were the Tulsa Oilers, who played in the United States Hockey League, one step below the American league.

Coached by former Leaf Gus Marker, the Oilers made an overture to have Barilko join their team in 1945–46. The lineup that season included Bill's future teammates Gus Mortson and Johnny McCormack, as well as prospects Jack Forsey, Hugh Mair and Nick Knott. A letter provided by Toronto Maple Leafs historian Allan Stitt shows that Marker was alerted to the talents of two Timmins-area boys by scout Ernie Orlando. The letter, written July 27, 1945, reads in part:

> I have approached two brothers who played on last year's Porcupine Combines Juniors who were eliminated by St. Mike's in the all-Ontario finals. They are Alex and Bill Barilko, both husky lads. Alex is about 5'11" and weighs 175 pounds and is 19 years old, almost 20. His brother Bill is 18 years old and about the same build. Both play defence but Alex is also a fast skater and has played forward. Alex was down at the Red Wings training camp last fall and won a berth with the Detroit Red Wings sponsored club, the Galt Red Wings of the OHA junior circuit. He played a few games and came home to play for the local juniors due to an argument with Galt coach Al Murray who, as Alex says,

is a little too strict. This I can vouch for since my brother Ralph played for Murray in 41–42 season at Guelph.

The Barilko boys are yet undetermined as to their future plans since they have another offer from Johnny Mitchell of Pittsburgh Hornets. I told them that the International League [prior to 1940, the AHL had been known as the International-American Hockey League] is still a little fast for them and they're sure to be farmed out to the EAHL, which is worse than our senior league here. I told them that if Doc Prentice is only dressed by the Hornets for about 15 games a season, they'll have little chance to tag along. They are gradually seeing things my way and after I relayed your message to them about Tulsa, they seem to like the idea of trying out but they still want to wait until Mitchell comes here next week and see what he has to offer. I'll let you know about them later.

Based on Orlando's recommendation, Marker offered both Barilko brothers a tryout with Tulsa. The offer was politely declined in a letter Alex wrote to Marker:

> My brother and I have come to an agreement that we would not break [up], so since he too signed with Pittsburgh, I am also going there. I'd like to take this opportunity to thank you for giving us this tryout, however, should we not come to an agreement at Pittsburgh, we would be glad to try out with your club.

Only a couple of years before, Bill Barilko had been unable to make his local juvenile team as anything other than a stick boy and practice goaltender. Now, he was a prized prospect who was entertaining competing offers from professional teams. He had also been invited to join the Oshawa Generals, a powerhouse junior club in the Ontario Hockey Association, but the parties were unable to structure a deal. Anne Klisanich recalls that Johnny Mitchell paid a visit to the Barilko home and asked Faye Barilko for permission to sign her 18-year-old son to a contract that would make him the property of the Pittsburgh Hornets. "I think he signed for $125 a week," recalls his friend Leo Curik.

At training camp, Pittsburgh coach Max Kaminsky, a former NHL forward, spent time working with Bill, who was wearing the number 5 he would later immortalize in Toronto. Mitchell recalled arriving at the Duquesne Arena to watch his prospects just in time to see Barilko in the midst of a brawl. A stray fist cold-cocked the defenceman. "He looked to be badly cut over one eye so I went to the first aid room. I could hear him roaring away down the hall. When I arrived, he yells, 'Get that doctor outta here. I want to get back out there and get even with the guy that hit me!' That sold me on him."

Bill was sent to Hollywood for seasoning, with the promise that, if he kept working at his game, he would be strongly considered the first time Pittsburgh needed a replacement on the blue line.

❋ ❋ ❋

The guns of World War II were finally silenced in 1945, to be replaced by the renewed clatter of hockey talent returning to North America, anxious to find a place to play.

Since the collapse of the Patrick brothers' Western Hockey League in 1926, professional hockey had been most firmly rooted in the eastern portion of North America. The National Hockey League's six franchises ventured no further west than Chicago. The American Hockey League's ever-shifting lineup stretched from New England to the Midwest. In the latter territory, it had absorbed markets that had been orphaned when the American Hockey Association collapsed in 1942. And as the name would imply, the Eastern Amateur Hockey League traced an arc from Boston to Baltimore.

Although hockey had been played on the west coast of North America since the Patrick brothers introduced artificial ice, via their Pacific Coast Hockey Association, in 1911, hockey didn't really take root until the debut of the Pacific Coast Hockey League in 1944–45. The 10-team league was divided into three conferences. The Northern Division was made up of teams that had been part of the Northwest International Hockey League the year before: the Seattle Ironmen, Seattle Stars, Portland Eagles and Vancouver (Washington) Vanguards. The Central Division consisted of just two teams, the San Francisco Shamrocks and Oakland Oaks. And the Southern Division, which had evolved out of the short-lived Southern California Hockey League, included the Los Angeles Monarchs, San Diego Skyhawks, Pasadena Panthers and Hollywood Wolves.

The National Hockey League regarded Portland, Seattle and Vancouver as hockey territories belonging to the suspended domain of Lester and Frank Patrick after their WHL (the successor to the PCHA) suspended operations following the 1925–26 season, and the NHL therefore demanded sizable fees from the new PCHL for the territorial rights to these cities. The PCHL balked and decided to incorporate as an amateur league, which it remained until 1948–49.

A pair of enterprising brothers, Cliff and Phil Henderson, played a pivotal role in developing hockey on the west coast. The Hendersons pioneered hockey in the Los Angeles area and were the original organizers of the PCHL. They realized that hockey could very well take several years before it found a substantial audience, but they were willing to take the risk, hoping to hit paydirt by one day emerging with an NHL franchise. To commemorate their efforts in establishing hockey in California, the PCHL's playoff champions were awarded the Henderson Cup.

The Henderson brothers introduced two teams to the Los Angeles area, the Hollywood Wolves and Los Angeles Monarchs, both of which played out of the ultramodern, streamline-styled Pan-Pacific Auditorium. Since its opening in 1935, the 5,862-seat venue had hosted political events, conventions, basketball events and concerts. Elvis Presley would make his Hollywood debut in a concert at the Pan-Pacific on October 27, 1957. But by the early 1970s, the arena had fallen into disuse. It was added to the National Register of Historic Places at the end of the decade, and shortly afterward the condemned building's exterior appeared in the Olivia Newton-John film *Xanadu*. But on May 24, 1989, the landmark was destroyed in a fire.

In their debut season, Hollywood finished third in the Southern Division with nine wins, eight losses and a tie for 19 points in 18 games. San Diego finished first with 22 points.

※ ※ ※

Excited but nervous about leaving home for the first time, the 18-year-old Bill boarded his first airplane in the fall of 1945 to cross the wide-open spaces of the American Midwest on his way to a new life in California. "Imagine," says Anne, "coming from Timmins, where the weather is so cold, down to California to play hockey — it's just unbelievable! Just the thought of going to California with all the Hollywood stars and the warm weather was so exotic to us back home. My mother and I couldn't quite figure out where they were going to find ice surfaces to play on in California!"

It's a long way from Timmins to Hollywood in every conceivable way. Bill stepped off the plane, stretched, grabbed his well-worn suitcase and stood on the tarmac in awe. The sun was bright and beat down on his fair skin, forcing Bill to take off his sports coat and drape it over his arm. Barilko didn't know whether to be excited or scared, but as always, he was up for an adventure. He hailed a cab and made his way to the address written on the sleeve of paper folded in his pocket: PAN-PACIFIC AUDITORIUM. 7600 WEST BEVERLY BLVD.

The taxi pulled up in front of the grand building. Bill was impressed, but not to the point of distraction; after all, Schumacher had a terrific arena of its own. The McIntyre Arena back home had been built in 1938, just three years after the Los Angeles facility, and, having been modelled after Maple Leaf Gardens, was a beautiful multi-purpose auditorium in its own right. Inside the Pan-Pacific, Barilko was met by Bob Gracie, a former NHL star and the playing coach of the Hollywood Wolves.

The two looked over the Wolves lineup to see if there were any names familiar to Bill. Deed Klein had played in the NHL with Boston and the New York Americans, but Bill didn't recall having heard of him. But a handful of games into the season, Bill was pleased to discover that an old friend from home was joining the Wolves. Doc Prentice, whose given name was Eric, was just seven months older than Bill. Doc was a Schumacher boy, and in 1942–43 — the year Bill had been the Holman Pluggers' stick boy — Prentice had played for the championship team. In Timmins, Prentice was a legend. In 1943–44, at only 17 years of age, he had played five games for the Toronto Maple Leafs, making him the youngest player ever to dress in the blue and white. In the fall of 1945, Toronto traded Prentice to Detroit, and he started the season with the Omaha Knights of the USHL, a team that featured a young Gordie Howe. But after only three games, Doc was released from the Knights and he joined the Hollywood Wolves.

Bill rented a room in a home at 265 South St. Andrew's Place in a conservative, well-to-do area just below Hollywood and next to Hancock Park. It was a two-mile cab ride from his door to the Pan-Pacific.

Bill, Doc Prentice and a few of the other Wolves would occasionally spend a free evening at the Pan-Pacific Bowling Lanes, next door to the arena. Sometimes, they walked down to Chester's, where they would stay up half the night talking about the game and about girls. Bill took particular delight in joining some of the boys for drives along the Pacific Coast Highway, twisting and winding along the California coastline, watching the waves crash against the rugged coastal rocks that rise out of the sea.

But as much as he enjoyed the open spaces and wildlife of California, Bill also loved being a tourist in Hollywood. And while there, he developed a keenness for clothes, a passion he'd never been able to afford to indulge. On days off, Bill also liked to head down to Santa Monica Beach. Whenever he played host to a visitor, Bill loved to point out the home of film star Gene Autry. The bustle of activity in Hollywood was new to Barilko. Timmins was a small town, sleepy in comparison to "Tinseltown." Back home, Bill was happy to meet up with his pals at the Victory Hotel and laugh over shared stories. But Hollywood was a different experience altogether — so much to do, so much to see.

Although the Wolves were well down the developmental rungs of hockey's ladder, players loved to ply their trade in Hollywood, and Bill was no different. The press emphasized Barilko's "matinee good looks — tall, blond and handsome with wavy blond hair and beautiful blue eyes. An easy grin, baby face and handsome head of hair give the lie to the fierce competitive nature he owned." Leo Curik adds, "He was built like [Tarzan's] Johnny Weissmuller." And that is the paradox. Off the ice, Barilko was soft-spoken, polite and well-mannered, with movie star looks. But during games, "Bashin' Bill" displayed a mean streak and dished out ferocious hipchecks with abandon to halt opposing forwards.

Hockey was also becoming a hot topic in the Hollywood community. In December 1945, several PCHL players, including Wolves coach Bob Gracie, were recruited for skating parts in a hockey-themed film entitled *Gay Blades*.

Celebrity status helped the shy young man develop a gregarious personality, but it was the strong competition that helped advance Barilko's career. "When he came home that first summer, we all saw that he was well coached because of the improvement in his skating," admits Leo Curik.

The team was well taken care of by its owners. Many of the boys were given jobs at Del Mar Racetrack, a playground for the stars located 100 miles south of Los Angeles. The team travelled to most of its games in a pair of long, black limousines. And one day each season, the owners took the entire team by bus across the border to Tijuana, Mexico.

For the 1945–46 season, the Pacific Coast Hockey League had been realigned into two divisions: North and South. Hollywood was in the South, along with San Diego, Los Angeles, Oakland and the San Francisco Shamrocks. Hollywood would finish second to the Oaks, owned by the Hall of Fame defenceman Eddie Shore. Over their 40-game schedule, the Wolves won 21 and lost 19 for 42 points.

Wearing Number 4 and nicknamed "Billy the Kid" by a local writer who described him as "rough, tough and fearless," Bill led the Wolves in penalty minutes that season with 103, the third-highest total in the league. In 38 games, Barilko collected four goals and five assists. Doc Prentice contributed six goals and six assists in the 21 games he played in Hollywood that season. Coach Bob Gracie dressed for 16 games and picked up 14 points.

The Wolves battled through the playoffs and won the South Division. They challenged the Vancouver Canucks, who had won the Shipstad and Johnson Ice Follies Trophy for finishing first in the North Division in the regular season. The Canucks defeated Barilko and the Wolves four games to one to take the Henderson Trophy as PCHL champions.

Bill spent the summer back at home with his mother, brother Alex and sister Anne. "He came home that summer and brought me the most wonderful clothes," Anne recalls. "My brothers were very good to me." Anne would get the opportunity to show off her new outfits when high school resumed in the fall. "Miss Everard, one of the teachers, said, 'I suppose that's another outfit your brothers sent back from California.' She was a beautiful dresser herself. She's now Mary Last and she's become one of my closest friends."

"I thought it was wonderful that my brothers were playing hockey in California," Anne adds. "They were looked upon as celebrities. I was so proud of both of them."

During the summer of 1946, the Barilko home was the spot where Bill, Alex and their friends would congregate for a quick meal in their mother's kitchen before heading off for an evening at the Victory Hotel, the tavern over on Cedar Street owned by the Curik family. "The boys went there nearly every night," chuckles Anne.

But as much as Bill might have basked in his status as a pro hockey player, there was sadness that summer as well. His father, Steve, died in a Gravenhurst hospital on August 6. "Papa never saw Billy play hockey with the Toronto Maple Leafs," Anne confirms.

Mining had evolved exponentially during the 1930s. Roads leading to and from the mines had been improved and mass transportation had been initiated. But with that progress came a blow that struck at the very core of the Barilko family. The mines no longer needed the bunkhouses used to house their employees during the week, which eliminated the need for a cook on the premises; Steve Barilko's role at the mine had been made redundant. Nor were there other opportunities for him to ply his trade. "There were few hotels or restaurants, so there was no demand for cooks anywhere," Anne states. "Papa took a job in the stock-room at the Broulan Mine. And then, even though my Papa didn't work underground, he developed tuberculosis at the age of 50."

But it wasn't silicosis, the scourge of anyone working in the mines, that caused Steve Barilko's death. "He fell going down a flight of stairs and likely hit his head," says Anne, the youngest of the Barilko children. The Barilkos had not yet been able to afford the luxury of telephone service, so the phone rang at a neighbour's house. "Faye! Anne! Hurry, it's the hospital for you," shouted the neighbour.

Anne ran next door, only to be told, "Your father fell down the stairs. There was brain damage and he's passed away."

🍁 🍁 🍁

There was an interesting development on August 28, when general manager Conn Smythe announced that the Toronto Maple Leafs had officially added the Hollywood Wolves to their growing farm system, which also boasted minor pro affiliates in Pittsburgh and Tulsa and a total of four junior clubs: the Toronto Marlboros, the St. Michael's College Majors, the Winnipeg Monarchs and, on a less formal basis, the Oshawa Generals.

On September 16, the Maple Leafs conducted a rookie camp in St. Catharines, Ontario, and Bill Barilko was one of 22 hopefuls who attended. All harboured dreams of being chosen to stay on for the main camp that followed immediately afterward, rather than being dispatched to one of the farm teams for seasoning or released outright. Bobby Copp, who had played with the Maple Leafs during the 1942–43 season, originally accepted an invitation to attend the camp, but later declined so that he could open his own dental practice in Ottawa. Garth Boesch, Vic Lynn, Howie Meeker, Gus Mortson, Tod Sloan and Bill Barilko were a few of those who later played for the parent club. Barilko was teamed with a young Port Colborne defenceman named Eddie Young.

Smythe and coach Hap Day liked what they saw in several of the prospects and invited three to attend the main Leafs camp: Meeker, Lynn and Mortson. They also noted the big defenceman who was throwing his body in front of everything in sight, but felt he needed seasoning before he would be ready for the National Hockey League.

Bill was assigned to the Pittsburgh Hornets' training camp being conducted down the road in Welland. Although the Hornets sent Barilko back to Hollywood, the Toronto brain trust kept tabs on him through coach Bob Gracie and veteran defenceman Tommy Anderson. He would be playing in Hollywood, but Barilko remained property of the Hornets, the Leafs' American Hockey League affiliate — oddly enough, a team with whom he would never play a single hockey game.

When Barilko returned to the coast in September 1946, he was joined by 11 members of the previous year's team, including Blink Bellinger, the Wolves' top scorer, and Doc Prentice from Timmins. Former NHLer Gus Mancuso, who had played only six games at the end of the 1945–46 season, would be with the Wolves for the full year. There were also some new faces, the most notable of whom was Tommy Anderson.

Anderson was winding down his career with the Hollywood Wolves in 1946–47. Nicknamed "Cowboy," the Scottish-born Anderson had made his NHL debut as a Detroit Red Wing in 1934–35, but was sold to the New York Americans before the start of the next season. In New York, he starred on a team that, to that date, had been consistently awful, missing the playoffs in every season but one since its inception. The Americans would qualify for the postseason in four of the next five seasons.

Just prior to the 1941–42 campaign, Red Dutton, the general manager of the Americans, changed the name of the team to the Brooklyn Americans, hoping to stimulate an enhanced rivalry between his team and the New York Rangers. At the time, Dutton commented, "We had fans mostly from Brooklyn while the Rangers had the hotsy-totsy ones from New York." Although both shared residency in Madison Square Garden, a Brooklyn–New York City rivalry never did materialize.

Anderson led the sad-sack Americans in scoring with 41 points (12 goals and 29 assists) in 1941–42, good for 10th place in the NHL's regular-season scoring parade. Even though he played for the last-place team, the league awarded Anderson the Hart Trophy as its most valuable player.

The outbreak of the Second World War robbed NHL teams of substantial numbers of young players who withdrew to contribute to the war effort. The Americans' lineup was severely depleted, as Anderson, goaltender Chuck Rayner, Kenny Mosdell and Jack Church, among others, enlisted in the Canadian military. Dutton suspended operation of the team before the 1942–43 season, but the franchise was never resuscitated, leaving the NHL to weather the next quarter-century with a complement of six teams that has been incorrectly labelled the "Original Six."

When the Americans ceased operations, the Brooklyn players were allocated to the remaining NHL clubs in a special dispersal draw held on October 9, 1942. The rights to Tommy Anderson were transferred to the Toronto Maple Leafs. When Anderson returned from World War II, he was unable to crack the strong Leafs lineup and was dispatched to the American Hockey League. After a year with the Providence Reds, Anderson joined the Hollywood Wolves.

In 1946–47, at the age of 36, Anderson was slated to play defence with a prospect just one year out of the mining country of northern Ontario. As Bill Barilko's mentor, Anderson helped the 19-year-old work on his positional game and on his skating, specifically his backwards skating. "Tommy Anderson worked with Bill a lot," recalls Babe Gresko, one of the Wolves' rookies that season. "In fact, Tommy wasn't a great skater himself. He was a choppy skater and he had bowlegs, but he was a very good hockey player." One press clipping read, "Like the old bird dog, Tommy Anderson knows the shortest distance between two points, gets there on schedule and usually breaks up some well-oiled play the opposition wants to put through."

Leo Curik, Bill's best friend, asserts that Hollywood developed Barilko into an NHL-calibre player. "When he got to Hollywood, they really taught him hitting and how to skate backwards. He became a great backwards skater."

Toronto-born Babe Gresko was new to Hollywood that year. "My given name is William," chuckles Gresko as he explains his nickname. "We had 16 people living in our house and I was the baby of the family. It was a long time before they gave me a name, so I was called Babe. It stuck with me all my life, and wherever I played sports, I was always Babe."

The athletic Gresko didn't begin a hockey career until he was a teenager, although he quickly caught up to his contemporaries and soon was playing junior hockey in his hometown. "[Former Leaf] George Parsons asked me to play major junior with the [Toronto] Native Sons, which was his team at Maple Leaf Gardens. Howie Meeker was on that team with me, but we didn't have too good a team."

As was the case for so many young men, World War II came along and altered his career plans. "It was in the army that I learned most of my hockey," says Babe. "I was in a place called Shilo, Manitoba. I was the physical training instructor. We would play hockey in all the little towns around. Then I went overseas, and that's where I came in contact with [Leafs players] Turk Broda and Bud Poile."

After starring with a Canadian military hockey team that played in Brighton, England, Babe discovered his skills had not gone unnoticed. "When I came back, I was recommended by Broda and Poile to Bob Davidson, who was later the head scout of the Toronto Maple Leafs. I had played on a line with Bud Poile and a guy named Gordie Bruce, who played for the Boston Bruins at the time. Bob Davidson contacted me and I went to the Leafs' training camp in Pittsburgh. There were about 40 fellows there, and I made the team."

Gresko was assigned to the roster of the Hollywood Wolves. "I only weighed 140 pounds. I wasn't that big, but I was just happy to be playing hockey. I would love to have played in the NHL, but I knew it probably wasn't going to happen."

The Wolves left training in Pittsburgh with a solid roster. "We had some good goalies," remembers Babe. "We had Baz Bastien and Gordie Bell and a fellow named Pat Boehmer. Bastien was the goalie most of the year for us. He was an excellent goalie." The trio of netminders spent much of the season shuttling back and forth between Hollywood and Pittsburgh. Although several years older than Barilko and Doc Prentice, Bastien was also from Timmins, and the three would often swap stories about their hometown.

Babe also remembers the impression a young defenceman made on him. "Bill Barilko went to training camp with the Leafs that year. They trained in St. Catharines, but our training camp was in Pittsburgh. He came right from St. Catharines to us, so he was in good shape. He was 19 years old, weighed about 180 pounds and was a tall, good-looking boy. He looked very powerful. After training camp, we flew out west. Bill was a comical guy. It was physical comedy. I was always telling jokes but

Bill was always doing practical jokes. If you were sitting down, he'd tie your shoelaces together. He was a very funny guy."

As much as Bill loved to joke off the ice, he was every bit as competitive on the ice. Any opponent skating into his end of the ice was fair game. Bill dared opposing forwards to try to get around him, and when they did, he didn't just try to knock them down; given the opportunity, he tried to put them through the boards. The intimidating Barilko had a presence that loomed large.

The quality of hockey played in the PCHL was quite good. The combination of experienced veterans winding down their professional careers and rookies trying to earn their shot at the big time proved to be an irresistible combination for fans who came out to watch the Wolves at the Pan-Pacific Auditorium. The spectators, who tagged themselves "Pan Fans," saw some great hockey. The Pony Line of Joey Peterson, Harry Hilliard and Blink Bellinger created much of the Wolves' offence. *The Goalie*, a newsletter published by the league, reported that Bill Barilko was "a bit wild last year, giving every play that good old college try. The Barilko [whom Bob] Gracie brought home to Hollywood this year has grown up."

The writing in *The Goalie* was often as exciting as the hockey at the Pan-Pacific itself. "The Film City Quintet [the Wolves] rocketed to their fourth straight as Oakland Oaks [who, incidentally, included Alex Barilko] reclined in their usual horizontal posture at the Pan. For two periods, the game was close as A to B. The Oaks, as unattractive as smog when the Wolves tarred them 8–2 Wednesday night, were considerably livelier tonight. Whippet-fast Steve Black played some solo polo to thrust the Oaks to the front. But the third period was as wild as the Western frontier. Harry (Hurry) Currie, Bill Barilko and Babe Gresko performed Mazda massacre during the final session."

The excitement of hockey in Los Angeles attracted the interest of a new medium, too, although the sparks were definitely fanned by the exuberance of Cliff and Phil Henderson. Hollywood Wolves hockey games were regularly being broadcast by KTLA-TV in Los Angeles. To put this in perspective, television was still very much a novelty at that time. The only NHL team having games broadcast on television was the New York Rangers, also commencing in October 1946. The Detroit Red Wings first had their games televised in October 1947, while the Montreal Canadiens started in October 1952 and Toronto Maple Leafs in November 1952.

As enthusiasm for the Wolves gained momentum, so did their exposure to the celebrity element. Babe Gresko remembers being introduced to many Hollywood stars during that season. "There was a great big guy, a sound effects man from NBC studios who came to our hockey games. He took us backstage and I met Bob Hope. We also met Ish Kabibble, who played with Kay Kyser's band." During the 1930s and '40s, Ish Kabibble was a household name thanks to his silly appearances on the immensely popular radio show, *Kay Kyser's Kollege of Musical Knowledge.*

"There were nine or 10 players who were in Hollywood the year before. They all knew each other quite well," Gresko recalls. "When I got there, eight of us lived in a hotel they called the Halifax Apartments. It was one block from Hollywood and Vine. There were four guys in a room. We'd have a party one night, then the next night there'd be another party, then another party. I said, 'Gee, I'm going to get out of here. This is too much for me.' Johnny Morrow and I got a room together in a private home.

"We went to a couple of parties up in the Hollywood Hills," continues Gresko. "There was a songwriter named Johnny Green. He wrote 'Body and Soul' and we went up to his mansion in the Hills, right at the top. You could see the beautiful view of Los Angeles and Hollywood and you could see the spotlights going back and forth. He had some showgirls there, and we're all up there having a party, so we had some good times."

Those attending games at the Pan-Pacific Auditorium wouldn't have been surprised to see Alan Ladd, Carmen Miranda, Gracie Fields, George Raft or William Bendix glued to the hockey action. Babe remembers others who were fans, too. "I met Ruth Warwick [who starred in *Citizen Kane* with Orson Welles]. She used to come into the rink there. We had our pictures taken with a girl named Vera-Ellen. She played with Bing Crosby and Danny Kaye in *White Christmas.*" Vera-Ellen was signed to the Samuel Goldwyn studio. In searching for as much publicity as possible, the studio paired Vera-Ellen with hockey because of its burgeoning popularity, and she became the official mascot of the Hollywood Wolves.

But actors didn't drop by the arena just to enjoy a hockey game. "We used to practise every day except when we played, and Cary Grant used to be around the arena all the time," Babe smiles. "I spoke to him every day for weeks. He was making a movie called *The Bishop's Wife* and there were some skating scenes in it. David Niven was in it, too." The playing coach of the Los Angeles Monarchs, John Polich, was teaching Grant how to skate for his role in the film.

The Bishop's Wife was released in 1947, and Grant played an angel who comes to Earth. It garnered five Academy Award nominations. Karolyn Grimes, a child actress who appeared in the film — her best-known role was as Zuzu Bailey in *It's a Wonderful Life*, in which she immortalized the line, "Every time a bell rings, an angel gets its wings" — recalls the skating scenes well. "Cary could really skate, and every day at lunchtime, he would pull me around on a sled while he practised his skating," she writes. "He practised with a coach [Polich] and a chair on the ice. As a child growing up in California with no ice or snow, I had a blast just watching. I found it all so exciting that I begged my mother to arrange skating lessons for me."

For Bill Barilko, the PCHL in 1946–47 must have seemed at times like "old home week." When the Wolves played the San Francisco Shamrocks, Bill would run into Bill Adamo, George DeFelice, Roy McKay and Doc's brother, Boyd Prentice. Meanwhile, his friend Bill Curik and brother Alex were both playing with the Oakland Oaks. In fact, when the Oaks were in Hollywood for a game near the start of the season, the Barilko brothers spent time together and took in a number of Hollywood sights.

On February 5, 1947, after leaving San Diego en route to Fresno for a contest against the Falcons, a train carrying 14 members of the San Francisco Shamrocks struck a gasoline truck at a crossing near Kingsburg, California, 30 minutes south of Fresno. The truck exploded on impact, and the Southern Pacific San Joaquin Daylight, which was travelling at 85 miles per hour when the collision occurred, proceeded down the track, and engulfed in an inferno, for half a mile. Eight people died in the crash, several players, as well as the coach and trainer of the Shamrocks, were injured. Most seriously hurt was forward Rolly Morrisseau, who suffered burns to his head and face. Coach Al Murray, who had played defence with Tommy Anderson for the New York Americans through the 1930s and had been the bane of Alex Barilko's existence in Galt, seriously burned his hands trying to extinguish the flames in Morrisseau's hair. Roy McKay, who played with the Holman Pluggers when Bill was stick boy, injured his hand badly. Boyd Prentice suffered cuts and bruises, as did Ed Redmond, the father of NHL stars Dick and Mickey.

"The whole train was on fire," remembers Gresko. "All the passengers were jumping out of the train. Some of the boys were burnt pretty badly. Two or three days later, our team happened to be going through there and we stopped in to see them. There were nine or 10 of them involved and four or five of them were in the hospital. One guy [Morrisseau] was burned so badly that all you could see were his eyes. It was awful. It was really, really bad."

Shamrocks owner George Campbell asked Al Leader, the president of the PCHL, for emergency assistance. Two games between San Francisco and Fresno were postponed, and in order to get the Shamrocks through their crisis, each team in the league was asked to send one player to San Francisco until the injured players were released from the hospital. "I was the guy picked from our team," said Babe. "I went up and played two or three games and then went back to Hollywood." Alex Barilko was the Oakland Oak who was designated for the emergency duty.

On the same day that the horrendous collision took place, hockey history of a different sort was unfolding behind the scenes in Toronto.

The Toronto Maple Leafs had been rolling along happily, until Bob Goldham broke his left arm and Garth Boesch suffered a groin injury. The injuries decimated the Leafs' blueline corps. Only rookies Jimmy Thomson and Gus Mortson, as well as Wally Stanowski, were able to play. To fill the gap, Bud Poile was briefly dropped back from forward to help out on defence.

Toronto manager Conn Smythe contacted his farm team in Pittsburgh, intending to promote a defenceman from the Hornets and replace that selection with a Hollywood blueliner. Smythe had his eye on Ernie Dickens, who had played in 15 games with the Leafs the previous season. Now all he had to do was come up with a defenceman of equal quality to fill the gap in Pittsburgh and satisfy the terms of an agreement between the two clubs. Short-staffed, Smythe was reminded of the boy in Hollywood who had impressed him. He called on coach Bob Gracie and veteran Tommy Anderson for a progress report.

It was a good time to ask. The Wolves were in first place at the beginning of February, and Bill Barilko, with nine goals in 45 games, was a primary reason why the team had been doing so well.

Anderson gave a ringing endorsement. "He's pretty green but he's a big boy, not afraid of anyone, bangs 'em around and he learns fast." Smythe asked if Barilko could help for two or three games. "Sure," replied Anderson. "He'll make plenty of mistakes but he won't back down from anyone."

While fans and sportswriters waited to see which defenceman would be promoted from the farm team in Pittsburgh, Smythe made an inspired decision, one he would never have cause to regret. He told Bob Gracie to send Bill Barilko.

Barilko played his last game with Hollywood on Wednesday, February 5, against the rival Los Angeles Monarchs. During the third period, he was told he was being called up to Pittsburgh. Ecstatic, Barilko skated out for the third period as the public address announcer informed the crowd that Bill was to be applauded, as he was leaving the Wolves to play defence for the Pittsburgh Hornets. After taking a moment to give a quick wave to the cheering Pan-Pacific crowd and accept congratulations from his teammates, Barilko ducked into the dressing room to undress, shower and change into his suit. Within two hours, he would be flying across the continent.

43

The Wolves finished first in the PCHL's South Division in 1946–47, leading the entire league with 43 wins and a tie in its 60-game season, allowing only 138 goals through the campaign. By comparison, the cellar-dwelling Shamrocks surrendered 329 goals. The league's most penalized player was Alex Barilko, who accumulated 166 minutes while playing defence for the Oakland Oaks. Although Bill left in February, he still led Hollywood in penalty minutes with 69. His other statistics included nine goals and two assists for 11 points in 47 games.

Although the Wolves finished first overall, it was the Los Angeles Monarchs who would win the league championship, first defeating the Wolves to win the South Division crown, then sweeping the Portland Eagles in four straight games to collect the Henderson Cup.

Bill Barilko's promotion was a timely one. Hollywood folded its franchise after the 1946–47 season. According to *The Hockey News*, "Management of the Pan-Pacific Auditorium felt that 69 games in one season was too much hockey for the Los Angeles area." (The Wolves and Monarchs had each played 30 regular-season games at the Auditorium, plus nine playoff games.) Management decided to drop one of the teams, and the Monarchs survived because, en route to their championship in 1947, they had been a better box office draw. Plans to build a 12,500-seat arena were scuttled, but local sportsmen still held out hope that L.A. would one day host an NHL franchise. It did — but not for another 20 years, when the Kings joined the NHL in the expansion that doubled the league's size.

The Monarchs would continue to be independent, unlike the Wolves, who had been affiliated with the Toronto Maple Leafs and Pittsburgh Hornets. *The Hockey News* reported that "all Wolves players belonging to either of those two clubs have been returned and the remainder of the team was given their unconditional release."

Babe Gresko would play hockey on Canada's east coast the next season. Gus Mancuso moved across the hallway to join the Los Angeles Monarchs. Goalie Pat Boehmer skated into the crease for the Boston Olympics of the Eastern Hockey League. The PCHL's Fresno Falcons benefited most from Hollywood's demise, adding Blink Bellinger, Joe Peterson, Bob Gracie and Doc Prentice. Tommy Anderson, Barilko's mentor, replaced Charlie Conacher as coach of the junior Oshawa Generals.

CHAPTER 6

Dawning of a Dynasty

Sometimes, the darkest hour is just before the dawn, and that was certainly the case for the Toronto Maple Leafs in 1945–46.

The team had scored a surprising Stanley Cup victory in 1944–45 with a lineup patched together with Scotch tape and glue, filled out with university students and a 27-year-old rookie netminder whom the New York Rangers had discarded because of a nervous condition. The Leafs finished a distant third behind Montreal and Detroit, but it was good enough to earn them a playoff berth, and as hockey fans know, anything can happen once the hunt for the Cup begins in earnest.

The Maple Leafs rolled over the first-place Canadiens in six games in the semifinals, then went on a tear in the Stanley Cup finals versus Detroit. Frank McCool, nicknamed "Ulcers," racked up shutouts in each of the first three games of the championship series. Then the Red Wings rebounded, winning the next three and reminding hockey fans of the Leafs great comeback of 1942, when Detroit had led the finals three games to none and appeared certain to cruise to a championship, only to have Toronto rally and win four straight to claim the Stanley Cup. In the seventh game of the 1945 series, however, it was the Leafs who prevailed, clinging to a 2–1 lead to secure the third Stanley Cup title since Conn Smythe took over and rechristened the old Toronto St. Patricks franchise.

With World War II having drawn to a close, the 1945–46 season saw the rosters of each of the six National Hockey League teams replenished with talented veterans whose careers had been interrupted by military service. In Toronto, that meant the eventual return to duty of forwards Syl Apps, Gaye Stewart, Billy Taylor, Bud Poile and Don Metz, defencemen Bob Goldham and Ernie Dickens, plus goaltender Turk Broda. With such fortifications, the Leafs appeared not only to be a much stronger team than the year before, but shoo-ins to repeat as world champions. But a funny thing happened on the way to the Stanley Cup.

Frank McCool, whose four playoff shutouts had backstopped the Maple Leafs to the Cup win in 1944–45, had played in all 50 of the team's regular-season games, tied for the league lead with four shutouts and been awarded the Calder Trophy as the NHL's rookie of the year. But McCool was engaged in a contract dispute with the Leafs, so the new season began with Baz Bastien in goal. Bastien had just returned from two years of military service and was being groomed as Toronto's goaltender of the future pending Broda's eventual retirement. Although he tied the Bruins 1–1 in the season opener, the 26-year-old Timmins native did nothing to impress the Leafs' management through the next four games in which he played. The Leafs dropped like a stone, losing 4–2 to Montreal, 4–1 to New York, 7–4 to Chicago and 4–3 to Boston. Toronto replaced Bastien with 22-year-old Gordie Bell, who had also just returned from two years of military service. Bell fared little better, winning three but losing five. Although he stayed in the Maple Leafs' system for two years, these were the last games Bell would play with the parent club.

McCool had played Russian roulette with Leafs management — and won. He signed for a modest pay raise and was back in goal for the Leafs on December 1, 1945. It was an inauspicious return: McCool leaked like a fork, allowing all eight Blackhawks goals in an 8–2 Chicago landslide. Over the next two months, McCool and the Leafs won 10 games, but lost nine and tied three. On February 3, 1946, at Madison Square Garden, the New York Rangers rebounded from a 6–0 deficit to tie the score. The front office triumvirate of Smythe, assistant general manager Frank Selke and coach Hap Day had seen their team struggle long enough. Turk Broda rolled back into Toronto after completing two years of military service, and although rusty, was thrust into the crease once again. McCool never played another game in the NHL.

The Toronto Maple Leafs' problems weren't restricted to goaltending. Both Ted Kennedy and Syl Apps were injured during training camp. Kennedy returned, but never got fully unwound. Then he suffered a cut tendon and was lost for the remainder of the season. His 1945–46 season was restricted to 21 games, in which the young centre contributed just five points. Similarly, Apps, who had been the Leafs' captain and leading scorer prior to leaving for military service, dislocated a rib prior to the season. Yet, in 40 games, he still managed to score 24 goals and 40 points.

In January, the Maple Leafs were rocked with a bombshell. Babe Pratt, who had been the league's most valuable player in 1944, was suspended for life by NHL president Red Dutton on January 29, 1946, for betting on hockey games. Pratt, a giant of a defenceman at six feet, three inches and 210 pounds, had always been a free spirit. "When he was on the ice, he was a hundred percent team man," Hap Day stated at the time. "But when he was off the ice, you always felt a little dubious about what might be going on." On February 15, Dutton rescinded the suspension, during which Pratt missed only five games, but he was never again the same player. After scoring 17 goals in 1943–44 and 18 in 1944–45, the big blueliner fell off to five goals in 1945–46. It was a slippery slope, and Pratt never regained his footing. He was dished off to the Boston Bruins that summer in return for cash and the rights to Eric Pogue, who never played a game in the NHL. Pratt quickly fell from grace, playing a partial season with the Bruins in 1946–47 before fading into minor-league obscurity and retiring for good in 1951–52.

Although it was predominantly doom and gloom for the Leafs in 1945–46, there were a few reasons to smile through the course of the season. Gaye Stewart and Billy Taylor, both returning from war duty, finished first and second in team scoring. Stewart recorded a league-leading 37 goals and finished second to Chicago's Max Bentley in the regular-season points race. Taylor was solid, too, finishing 10th in the league in scoring. But their efforts were for naught: Toronto finished the regular season in fifth place, a distant five points behind the Detroit Red Wings, who claimed the fourth and final playoff berth. The team's failure to make the playoffs was a bitter disappointment for its fans, and a difficult pill for such veterans as Apps, Sweeney Schriner and Lorne Carr to swallow. But it was absolutely unacceptable for manager Conn Smythe.

※ ※ ※

"When the Maple Leafs were having their long run of success, no one bothered to credit me with any great part in the triumphs," wrote Frank Selke in *Behind the Cheering*. "But now [1946], when we failed to make the playoffs for the first time, I was naturally selected to be the goat." It was the first time the Toronto Maple Leafs had missed the playoffs since the team moved into Maple Leaf Gardens in 1931–32.

Selke had worked diligently behind the scenes for Conn Smythe. He had helped the Maple Leafs develop a farm system, a developmental chain that can be credited with feeding Toronto some of the greatest players ever to skate in the NHL. But ironically, that achievement would help to seal his doom.

While Major Conn Smythe served overseas with the 30th Light Anti-Aircraft Battery during World War II, he left Frank Selke in charge of managing the club, but insisted that he was still to have the final word on any decisions of consequence. "Without question Conn Smythe was the boss at Maple Leaf Gardens," Selke wrote in his biography. "No one wanted it otherwise. Conn was always up to date on everything that was going on in Toronto." Coach Hap Day and acting manager Selke dutifully apprised the Major of all hockey decisions.

But in 1942, Ted Kennedy, a junior phenom in Port Colborne, Ontario, who had been put on the Montreal Canadiens' negotiation list on the recommendation of his coach, the former scoring great Nels Stewart, decided he disliked Montreal. "Montreal doesn't appeal to me. I couldn't be happy there," Kennedy said at the time. Ignoring the risk that his decision might prohibit him from playing in the National Hockey League, Kennedy went home and suited up for the senior Port Colborne Sailors.

The Canadiens realized they weren't going to convince Kennedy to join the *bleu, blanc et rouge*. And they coveted Frank Eddolls, a Leafs prospect who came from nearby Lachine and who had garnered the Habs' attention when he trained with the Royal Canadian Air Force near Montreal. Kennedy, meanwhile, had finished second in the OHA Senior scoring race in 1942–43 and looked like a player who could certainly help the Maple Leafs. With Smythe at war and afraid that the Canadiens might change their minds if there was a delay, Frank Selke constructed a trade in February 1943, and received the approval of two Maple Leaf Gardens directors, Lieutenant-Colonel W.A.H. MacBrien and Ed Bickle. The deal was consummated. "I remember telling sportswriter Ed Fitkin that I thought we might have acquired a superstar," Selke wrote.

Yet, when Smythe found out, he fumed. Selke had made a trade without his permission. Smythe also claimed his right-hand man had been disloyal, and leveled a dubious allegation that Selke had plotted to have him removed as managing director of Maple Leaf Gardens. Never to be crossed, Smythe went on the warpath, at one time chastising Selke for leaving the building for lunch without permission.

Ultimately, the animosity and distrust became more than Selke could stand. In May 1946, he scribbled a note and left it on Smythe's desk. It read, "Lincoln freed the slaves. Goodbye. I quit." Without missing a beat, he was named managing director of the Montreal Canadiens.

★ ★ ★

That summer, Conn Smythe, having recovered sufficiently from war wounds suffered in France in 1944, went to work. He tore the Toronto Maple Leafs apart. "We've got to rebuild immediately," he declared. "There are too many old men on our team. What we need is youth. Fighting youth. Kids with spirit."

Ted Kennedy is quick to support the role that Smythe played in constructing what would become a Maple Leafs dynasty. "There isn't any question in my mind that he was the most influential person towards the success of the team. He was a great inspiration and a very tough boss, but I always felt he was a very fair boss as long as you were trying hard. That was all he requested."

Not only was Babe Pratt traded, but so was Billy Taylor. Taylor had been legendary in Toronto hockey circles since the Leafs' days at the Arena Gardens on Mutual Street prior to their move to Maple Leaf Gardens in 1931. A child prodigy, Taylor had entertained crowds with skating demonstrations between periods at Leafs games. He later starred with the junior Oshawa Generals before joining the parent club in 1939–40. But the smooth-skating Taylor never fully lived up to expectations in Toronto, so he was traded to Detroit for Harry Watson on September 21, 1946. Coincidentally, Taylor would also be suspended for gambling. On March 9, 1948, while playing for the New York Rangers, he was suspended for life by NHL president Clarence Campbell. Through the years, there has been strong conjecture that Smythe was aware of Taylor's betting on hockey, and Pratt's suspension influenced the decision to move him out of Toronto. Taylor's suspension wasn't lifted until 1970.

Lorne Carr, Bob Davidson, Mel Hill and Sweeney Schriner, who had been at the core of the 1945 Cup champions, all retired. Defencemen Moe Morris and Ernie Dickens were sent to the Leafs' American Hockey League farm team in Pittsburgh. Forward prospect Doug Baldwin was traded to Detroit, in a separate deal, on the same day Billy Taylor was traded there. The Leafs therefore had lots of room to inject some youthful exuberance into their lineup.

Smythe's network of scouts, both official and unofficial, did yeomen's work in uncovering prospects after he barked out his blueprint for a successful team: "We want a hard, aggressive team with no Lady Byngers. I'm not interested in hockey players who don't play to win. You can take penalties, but you have to play to win."

Smythe, Day, retired forward Bob Davidson and chief scout Squib Walker traversed North America in search of hockey talent. They found Vic Lynn buried in Buffalo with the AHL Bisons. Garth Boesch was signed after being touted as the best prospect in western Canada. Jimmy Thomson and Gus Mortson were Leaf chattels who had starred with the junior St. Michael's Majors the previous season. Smythe took a well-hedged bet in signing Howie Meeker, who had shown real promise before joining the military but who had nearly lost a leg when a grenade went off in front of him during a training exercise in England. Joe Klukay had played junior hockey with Meeker in Stratford. And former Leafs captain Red Horner tipped Smythe off to a skilled forward named Sid Smith who was playing senior hockey for him with the Toronto Staffords of the OHA.

In goal, the Leafs retained the dependable Turk Broda. "Turk Broda," begins Ted Kennedy, "was a great goalkeeper but he seemed to be able to go up another notch when we went to the Stanley Cup final."

As solid as Broda was, Smythe and Day, who was himself a former defensive stalwart, accurately emphasized strength on the blue line. Nowadays, a team would be ridiculed for overhauling its line-up with rookie defencemen, but that is exactly what Toronto did. Gus Mortson, Jimmy Thomson and Garth Boesch, with five games' worth of NHL experience between them, started the year on the blueline with veterans Wally Stanowski and Bob Goldham.

Conn Smythe's maxim, "If you can't beat 'em in the alley, you can't beat 'em on the ice," was never so evident. "If you got any of them mad or came out of the corner with the puck, you were dead," snorts Meeker.

Hockey pundits often debate the question of the greatest defence corps of history. It is no coincidence that behind the most formidable hockey dynasties, there has been a string of outstanding blueline squads. The Montreal Canadiens of the 1970s boasted the Big Three of Guy Lapointe, Larry Robinson and Serge Savard — all of whom are Honoured Members of the Hockey Hall of Fame. Other historians point to the quartet of Tim Horton, Allan Stanley, Bobby Baun and Carl Brewer with the Maple Leafs of the 1960s. In the latter half of the 1950s, the Canadiens reeled off five consecutive Stanley Cup victories with a unit of Doug Harvey, Tom Johnson, Jean-Guy Talbot and, at least at the start, Butch Bouchard.

But attention should also be paid to the group of defencemen who were the foundation of the Toronto Maple Leafs' dynasty of the late 1940s. Bob Goldham missed all but 11 games to injuries in 1946–47, then was summarily traded to Chicago. Wally Stanowski played a key role in helping develop the young defencemen, but after injuries in 1947, he too was sent packing. That left Jimmy Thomson, Gus Mortson and Garth Boesch, feared and effective blueliners who were prone to mistakes at times but willing to work harder than anyone else on the ice.

And a personnel change made partway through the 1946–47 campaign would make the Leafs blueline corps that much more intimidating. Bill Barilko was called up, not to Pittsburgh, but to the parent club in Toronto. Between them, Thomson, Mortson, Boesch and Barilko would earn 15 Stanley Cup titles as the nucleus of a revamped and revitalized Toronto Maple Leafs franchise.

CHAPTER 7

Planes, Trains and Automobiles (1946–47)

After winning the Stanley Cup in 1945, the Toronto Maple Leafs had missed the playoffs entirely in 1945–46, falling to fifth place, even though their point total over the course of the 50-game schedule (45, compared with 52 in 1944–45) didn't represent a precipitous decline.

But a blue and white wave was about to engulf the National Hockey League, and a terrific crop of first-year players would be riding its crest. Howie Meeker, Joe Klukay and Vic Lynn, who would be joined by Sid Smith later in the season, amended a foundation of forwards Syl Apps, Ted Kennedy, Gaye Stewart, Gus Bodnar, Bill Ezinicki, Bud Poile and Nick and Don Metz, along with Harry Watson, who had just been acquired from the Detroit Red Wings. Meanwhile, on the blue line, rookies Garth Boesch, Gus Mortson and Jim Thomson started the season with veterans Bob Goldham and Wally Stanowski.

"I should have figured it out years ago," sputtered Conn Smythe, the manager of the Toronto Maple Leafs. "Youth is the answer in this game."

When all was said and done, it was the youngest team ever to play in the National Hockey League to that date. Of the 20 players who played a significant number of games in 1946–47, the average age was 24 years, four months. Nick Metz, at 32 years, eight months, was the elder statesman. Only three other players had celebrated their thirtieth birthdays: goalie Turk Broda (32 years, five months), Syl Apps (31 years, nine months) and Nick's brother Don (30 years, nine months). At the other end of the spectrum, Jimmy Thomson was just 19 years, eight months of age. And Bill Barilko, who would join the team later in the season, was a month younger than Thomson.

Conn Smythe enjoyed the exuberance that youth brought to Toronto. The previous season, the Maple Leafs had been the least-penalized team in the NHL, and Smythe insisted that that fact had contributed to Toronto missing the playoffs. "If they start shoving you around, I expect you to shove them right back, harder," Smythe was quoted as saying in the September 27, 1946 edition of the *Toronto Daily Star*. "If one of our players should get injured by illegal tactics of the enemy, I expect the players on our team to see that the man responsible doesn't get away with it."

Smythe needn't have worried about gentlemanly play. Rookies Ezinicki, Mortson, Thomson and Boesch were as feared as they were fearless, and the rest of the lineup had no intention of being pushed around, either. Shortly after the start of the new season, Frank Selke called the Leafs "wrestlers on skates." Toronto immediately rebounded from its dismal showing of the year before.

Through the first two months of the season, the Leafs rolled over the competition, going undefeated in their first six games and losing but once in their first 11 matches. Goaltender Turk Broda earned three shutouts in November, including an 11–0 shellacking of Chicago on the last day of the month.

The Leafs had Chicago's number all year, in fact. In 12 meetings, Toronto won eight, lost three and tied one. Besides the 11–0 shutout, the Blackhawks were on the receiving end of two other significant losses, including the January 8 game in which Howie Meeker, the Stratford rookie, scored five times in a 10–4 cakewalk. And on March 8, the Leafs filled the net with pucks, pounding the Hawks into submission by a 12–4 margin.

Bob Goldham, a defenceman far better known for diving in front of enemy shots than for scoring, earned a $50 savings bond for tallying the first goal of the new season. For Goldham, it was the only good news in a season in which he was to be snake-bitten by injuries (he would only play 11 games all year). First, he was sidelined early on after he tore his knee ligaments, then on December 4 he broke his arm in a collision with the Bruins' Pat Egan.

Garth Boesch also went down with a groin injury, and after a promising start, Toronto began to flag. A 5–4 loss to Chicago on February 1 meant the Leafs had not registered a win in five games. The defence was stretched so thin that skilled forward Bud Poile was being employed back on the blue line. Smythe was forced to react.

In desperation, Smythe called for Sid Smith from the Pittsburgh Hornets and Bill Barilko from the Hollywood Wolves. He had been warned that Barilko was prone to mistakes, but the big, hard-hitting defenceman fulfilled Smythe's mandate of icing an intimidating team. "We've done pretty well with young fellows," he observed. "I'm willing to gamble on another one."

During the Hollywood Wolves' game against the Los Angeles Monarchs on Wednesday, February 5, 1947, coach Bob Gracie received word that Bill Barilko was to fly immediately to Pittsburgh as an injury replacement. There wasn't even time for him to finish the game. A wave to the fans — who were getting the news over the public-address system nearly as soon as anyone else — a round of handshakes for his teammates, and Bill quickly exited for the dressing room. He tore off his equipment, showered, dressed and bolted for the airport. A Wolves game program would later carry an ad wishing Bill much success: "All of us are proud of you, and California'll be rooting you on, up and up — to a top spot in hockey. It was written in the cards."

Barilko left Hollywood just before midnight, under the impression he was going to play with the Hornets. As dawn broke in Pennsylvania, he was met by manager Johnny Mitchell, who informed him he was to continue on to Toronto. "The old man wants you with the Leafs," Mitchell told Bill. "Here's a train ticket to Buffalo. From there, find a cab that'll drive you to Toronto. And one more thing Bill… knock 'em dead!"

Barilko was astonished to discover that he was getting his shot at the big time. He gripped Mitchell's hand with both of his and boarded the train for Buffalo. The weather reports indicated that the Toronto area was being pounded by one of the most severe snowstorms in years. Regardless, Barilko's target was to arrive in Toronto for a 10 a.m. practice at Varsity Arena. (The Ice Follies were in Toronto and using Maple Leaf Gardens that week, so the Leafs were holding their practices at Varsity Arena, on Bloor Street just west of Avenue Road.) Bill stepped off the train in Buffalo and dashed to a waiting taxi. "Can you get me to Toronto? I gotta get there as fast as you can drive!" The cab driver agreed to make the trip and grinned at the prospect of a healthy payday. Bill climbed into the back of the taxi for the long ride. He tried to close his eyes to get some sleep, but between his concern and his excitement about playing for the Leafs, Bill could only sit staring out the window of the cab, daydreaming about wearing the maple leaf on his chest.

When the cab pulled into the parking lot of Varsity Arena, Bill rushed into the dressing room after most of his teammates were already on the ice. "Hey, kid," started trainer Tim Daly. "There's y'r stuff. I advise ya t'get it on. And right quick! Hap hates guys bein' late."

🍁 🍁 🍁

At 10:15 Thursday morning, Barilko stepped onto the ice, exhausted and a stranger to the men executing the drills. He did a few laps around the ice to warm up and stretch his weary legs, then huddled with coach Day, himself a fine defenceman once upon a time. "He made a few mistakes, drifted too wide for rushers, but otherwise fine," Day reported. Bill was paired with veteran Wally Stanowski as the team did line drills on defence pairings. It was only after practice that the two would be formally introduced. With several hundred University of Toronto students watching, Barilko sent Gaye Stewart flying with a hip check.

In spite of the storm swirling around Toronto that morning, once the practice had concluded Bill is reported to have told the assembled scrum of writers, "Brother, the sun is really shining now." Neither Smythe nor Day suffered fools gladly, but the exuberant Barilko came off as confident rather than cocky.

"Smythe said the decision to bring in two untried youngsters [Barilko and Sid Smith] was in keeping with the policy laid down in St. Catharines [during training camp] to rebuild a championship team with young players," reported the *Globe and Mail*. "What Barilko and Smith lack in experience they will make up in enthusiasm and fight."

"We are going to stick with young blood and wind up with the youngest and toughest team in the league," Smythe told the Montreal *Gazette*.

Gus Mortson, one of the seven rookies in the lineup that season for Toronto, was a little dubious about the unknown kid Conn Smythe brought up to play on the Toronto blue line. "If you weren't on the main team, you were playing in Pittsburgh; and if you weren't in Pittsburgh, you were in Tulsa, Oklahoma; and if you weren't in Tulsa, Oklahoma, you were playing out in California. Bill came in from Hollywood. He had an excellent teacher out there — Tommy Anderson. He recommended Bill as a fellow who could help us out. That's how we got Bill — a lack of players — and Bill was welcome to come from California."

Smythe and Day hoped their veterans Goldham and Boesch would return to the Leafs' lineup and that they would only need the 19-year-old Barilko for a short period of time. "He wasn't intended to be there long," remembers Mortson. "They usually give a guy two or three weeks to see if this is what they're looking for. After three weeks, Bill proved that he would be a great help to us. They never looked for another defenceman after that.

"Bill was a very welcome addition, I'll tell you that," Mortson adds. "That year, Bob Goldham had his arm broken and was out for the rest of the year and Garth Boesch always had a pulled groin, so he was seldom playing — and when he did, he'd play one period and that'd be the end of it. So it was really just myself, Jim Thomson and Wally Stanowski. That's all we had, three defencemen. The three of us were rotating all the time."

Although his promotion had been intended to be temporary, Bill had realized a boyhood dream in becoming a Toronto Maple Leaf, and he was determined to do anything in his power to remain one. "This is something I've always dreamed of, and I'm aimin' to stay around."

🍁 🍁 🍁

The Leafs were to rest before boarding a train to Montreal that afternoon. Bill was far too excited to nap, so he decided to send a telegram home to his mother: "Up from Hollywood. Going to play with Maple Leafs. Practised today. Will phone later. Your son, Bill."

"Bill phoned home and said, 'Anne, I'm going to play hockey in Toronto!'" Anne recalls. "I said, 'Why Toronto?' I thought playing hockey in Hollywood was the ultimate. He said, 'I'm going to play hockey with the Toronto Maple Leafs!' He sounded so excited. I didn't know that Toronto was *the* place to play hockey."

"I thought it was a demotion for Bill. I was disappointed that he wasn't going to be playing hockey in California," laughs his sister. "Then he said, 'You'd better send some warm clothes. I don't have any with me.' He gave me an address for his clothing.

"The next day, I was at school and I couldn't figure out why people were making such a fuss about my brother. I asked a friend of mine why playing in Toronto was such a big deal. He said, 'Anne, your brother's going to play with the Toronto Maple Leafs in the NHL!' I said, 'What's NHL?'

"He said, 'Anne, you're going to hear your brother's name on the radio every Saturday night.' I said, 'Oh, *that!*' So I told my mother, 'Mom, Billy's going to play for the team that's on the radio on Saturday nights. We're going to hear our name on the radio!'"

Barilko also dashed off a birthday telegram to Alex in Oakland. Rather optimistically, it said, "Up with Maple Leafs rest season. Brother Bill."

🍁 🍁 🍁

The Leafs convened at Union Station and took the train to Montreal for the Thursday evening contest. The trip would give Barilko a chance to get to know a few of his teammates. Like many of the Leafs, he picked up a newspaper as he eased into his seat on the train. He laughed when he read that he was "expected to add oomph plus socko to the Leafs' heaving defence."

Barilko skated onto the ice at the Montreal Forum for his National Hockey League debut on Thursday, February 6, 1947. Wearing sweater number 21, Bill worked hard, and according to the *Globe and Mail,* was "a bright spot in the Toronto cause with his ability to hit the opposition." Barilko laid thundering checks on both Maurice Richard and Butch

Bouchard. On a hit to Richard, he recorded a minor penalty. "Twice in the last period, he sent big Butch Bouchard flying," reported the *Globe and Mail.*

"He rocked a few of the boys," teammate Harry Watson remembered. "They kept their heads up when he was on the ice." They weren't the only big hits dished out that evening — Elmer Lach of the Canadiens suffered a fractured skull after Leafs forward Don Metz nailed him with a ferocious bodycheck. As Lach was carried off the ice on a stretcher, a flurry of skirmishes broke out across the Forum ice.

Sid Smith, who appeared in his first NHL game that same night, remembered the contest, too. "I'll never forget that first game. We were in Montreal. We lost 8–2." It was the greatest number of goals Toronto would surrender during 1946–47.

The Leafs returned home to Toronto, and on Saturday, February 8, Bill played his first game at the Gardens as a member of the Maple Leafs. It was a terrific thrill for Barilko, who had listened to games originating from Toronto's hockey mecca on the radio every Saturday night since he was a boy.

That night, the Maple Leafs were being challenged by the Boston Bruins, who featured Bep Guidolin, an acquaintance of Bill's from Timmins. "I was getting my game-day rest at the Royal York Hotel and I heard this knock on the door," relates Guidolin. "Who the hell is it but Bill Barilko. I said, 'What are you doing here?' He said, 'They've called me up from Hollywood.'

"He said, 'I'm a little nervous. What am I supposed to do out there tonight?' I said, 'You hit every sonofabitch that moves! And that includes me! When I come across that blue line, I'm going to try and score a goal on your side. If I score a goal on your side, you might have to go back to Hollywood. Do you want that?' He said, 'No. I want to stay.'"

The lightning-quick Guidolin continued. "'You don't hit me along the boards or in the corner. You just tippy-toe in there with me and we'll just hang on to each other. But when I'm coming down the ice, I'm going to be trying to score a goal on you, so you'd better take me out.'

"He said, 'How do I take *you* out, for Christ's sake, the way you can skate?' I said, 'Don't worry, you'll learn quick. I learned quick and I've got it pretty good up here. Just keep those legs moving. But off the ice, you remember, we're still buddy-buddy, and after the game, we have a beer.'

"He said, 'Damn right. And if I beat you, *you* buy the beer.'"

"He was a 19-year-old guy, still wet behind the ears. I wasn't much older than him," mentions Bep. "A few times, I tried to go around him and he took me out into the boards beautifully. But he didn't have great balance on his skates. There were times I'd say to the guys, 'Look, he's going to shoot and he's going to fall down, so just try to get a deflection.'"

The Leafs thumped Bep and the Bruins 5–2 that night, with Bill Barilko scoring his first NHL goal at 16:51 of the third period. "We both got our first NHL goals that night against Boston," remembers Sid Smith. For Smith, it was the first of 186 he would score during regular-season play. For Barilko, the first of 26.

Two games later, on February 16 against the Rangers in Madison Square Garden, Barilko scored again. At 2:34 of the second period, as Toronto killed a penalty, he drilled a high shot from 15 feet out that put the Leafs ahead 2–1, although they eventually lost the contest, 6–2. Bill played a strong game, and also indulged in his first NHL fisticuffs, squaring off with Grant Warwick of New York. After the game and in spite of the loss, coach Day grabbed Barilko coming out of the shower. "Congratulations, Bill," he said, shaking the rookie's hand. "You are now a full-fledged member of the National Hockey League. Good luck to you."

"I'm going to make hockey my career, so I'm sure going to give it everything I have to stay up here with the Leafs," Barilko stated in the *Globe and Mail* at the time. "It's a different, tougher game than any I've ever played, but getting a couple of goals to start sure helps the old confidence."

The *Globe and Mail* hailed the young Barilko's contributions to the Leafs. "Barilko is turning out to be a good man at the pivot on power plays. Also, he has little respect for the opposition behind the blue line and uses his snake hips with damaging effect."

It was those hips that would establish Bill Barilko as a legitimate NHL player. He was fearless on the ice, unafraid of anyone or anything, and his style meshed perfectly with the vision Conn Smythe and Hap Day had for their Toronto Maple Leafs.

Ted Kennedy, who would proudly play on five Stanley Cup championship teams in Toronto, remembers Barilko with great fondness. "Hap Day was our coach then, and I think to this very day he was the most knowledgeable coach that I ever saw operate in the National Hockey League. There wasn't any question about it; there was a 'Leaf system.' There was as much emphasis put on checking as there was on scoring goals."

"When [Bill] first came up from the Hollywood Wolves, he was rambunctious," explains Kennedy. "He went around taking runs at people, and he was out of position most of the time. He was very enthusiastic. When you saw him out there on the ice, you had to pick your head up and watch this big kid.

"He was strong on his skates, and when he got somebody along the boards, he would rub them out. He had a back on him that was huge. You'd see him in the showers and his back was about four feet wide. If the opposing team went into our end and he was on the ice, they had to look out for him as well as try to get the puck and make the play on our net. He attracted a great deal of attention from the opposition.

"I got to know him a little bit on the train trip back to Toronto. He was a very pleasant boy. He was full of confidence, but there wasn't any cockiness in him at all. He was just interested in playing hockey."

Howie Meeker credits the hours occupied by train travel with forging a sense of team unity that is sorely lacking in today's National Hockey League. "There are a lot of wonderful things about playing hockey, but travelling by train and playing cards by the hour — that was one of the best.

"Bill Barilko was always in the middle of anything that was fun. When Jim Thomson had a beer in him, he was a funny bugger. And whenever something happened and nobody could figure out who the hell did it, it was [Turk] Broda."

Meeker turns his attention to the impression Barilko made. "The guy could hit like a ton — did he ever toughen up our defence! At that time, I just did not realize the value of the four tough guys on defence. Thomson was mean with the stick, while Mortson was tough and mean. Garth Boesch was as mentally tough as anyone I ever saw. He was good with the stick and would fight anyone. He played the body all the time and would just punish you.

"Barilko was something else — a hard rock from the north. He just solidified our defence. He made it big, he made it tough and he made it mean. He made it more skilled. One hell of a hockey player! And could he hit? Whoo-hoo!"

Sid Smith, who joined the Leafs the same day as the 19-year-old Barilko, also referred to Bill's size and strength. "Players weren't very big in those days, and he was really a big, well-built guy. He could really bodycheck right out in the middle of the ice."

"Bill was an excellent bodychecker," affirms Gus Mortson. "I've never seen anybody to this day who could hit like Bill. Bill was a little like a football player. If he had somebody lined up to hit, he would get up on the toes of his skates, take three steps and hit somebody. They were clean checks — he wasn't dirty with them. When he hit you, he really took a piece of you. He was solid."

The first image many Toronto hockey fans had of Barilko came in the newspapers after the Boston game. There was the youngster, captured in the act of making a terrific hit on the Bruins' all-star forward Milt Schmidt.

"I figured Bill was going to be a pro hockey player and would play in the NHL but I didn't know it would happen as soon as it did," admits Bill's former Hollywood teammate Babe Gresko. "Next thing I know, I see a picture in the *Globe and Mail* of Bill hitting Milt Schmidt. He stuck with the Leafs ever since."

"One of his favourite guys to hit was Schmidt," Mortson says. "I don't think Milt played more than two-thirds of a season, because he was always injured from Barilko's bodychecks."

Wally Stanowski settles back and recalls his young teammate. "He wasn't that good a skater, but he was a great hitter. If he hit you, he hurt you."

"What else can I do to stay up in the big league?" Barilko asked rhetorically at the time, explaining why his game was so physical. "I'm not much of a skater, not much of a stickhandler and not much of a scorer. I have to be good for something," he laughed.

Bill's sister Anne enjoyed hearing about his hockey exploits in Toronto. "What a thrill! It was so exciting. I'm proud because I'm in high school, my brother's in the NHL and he's the talk of the town." Anne stops for a second, then breaks into laughter. "The funny thing was, we always thought Alex was the better hockey player! Alex was the smooth hockey player and Bill was the rugged one."

Over the course of the remaining two months of the regular season, Barilko made arrangements for both his mother and sister to travel down to Toronto to see him play at Maple Leaf Gardens. "My mother would come down for a game and at a different time, I would come down," recalls Anne. "I can remember saying to Bill, 'I'll have to borrow some luggage because I don't have any,' and he said, 'Go to Marshall Ecclestone [a furniture and hardware store in Timmins] and buy some luggage and I'll pay for it.' I still have one piece of luggage that Bill bought me on that first visit to Toronto in 1947."

It was an exciting adventure for Bill's 16-year-old sister. "I went to Toronto by train, and Bill picked me up at the station and took me to the Westminster Hotel, where he was living at the time. The next day, Billy and I had lunch at Shopsy's Delicatessen on Spadina Avenue, then we went to Niagara Falls. It was breathtaking!"

When Barilko first arrived in Toronto, he had moved into the Westminster Hotel, located in the downtown core on Jarvis Street at Gerrard Street East. From his room, it was a short walk to Maple Leaf Gardens.

"I can still vividly remember seeing Maple Leaf Gardens for the first time, and I was just in awe seeing this magnificent structure in all its glory," Anne says. "And I could hardly wait to see Billy play hockey!"

Anne remembers that everyone attending the games in that era would dress in their Sunday best. "It was furs and fedoras. The men wore suits and the women dressed very elegantly. I was glad that I was dressed quite nicely, too, because my two brothers looked after me very well." Anne stood on Carlton Street, amazed as she watched the bustling crowd file into the main entrance of the Gardens. To the left of the main doors was Dowling's Grill, while McCutcheon's Cameras was to the right.

Alton's Barber Shop was there, too, and the United Cigar Store was right on the corner of Carlton and Church streets. Along Church, Anne noted the other shops that occupied space in the blonde-bricked arena — Connors Beauty Parlour, Crosley Shoes, the Queensbury Athletic Club, the International Brotherhood of Electrical Workers, Tuckett Advertising and Doug Laurie Sports and Cycle.

Anne nervously clutched the ticket her brother had given her and joined the parade entering the hockey edifice. She had never seen so many people in one place before. Games at the McIntyre Arena in Schumacher were certainly never like the one she was now experiencing.

Sporting a Cheshire cat's grin from the moment she first eased herself into her seat, Anne studied the program she had purchased to identify the boys Bill spoke about. "Jimmy Thomson was his best friend, and he also often talked about Wally Stanowski and Gus Mortson," remembers Anne. "Teeder Kennedy was playing, and I heard the chap yell, 'Come onnnnnnn, Teeeeeder!' Actually hearing that at a game was very exciting." During the 1940s, John Arnott's banshee wail from the red seats had become legendary. During stoppages in play, the leather-lunged service-station owner would holler his tribute to Ted Kennedy, much to the delight of the Leafs' faithful.

"I was always so proud of Billy," beams Anne. "I told the people sitting around me, 'That's my brother!'"

It was a short visit for Anne. Saturday night's game was barely over before Bill and his teammates were on the train, headed for their next road game. Anne, who had to be back in school on Monday, would go home on the Sunday. Before he climbed onto the train, Anne's 19-year-old brother had already laid down some rules: "Bill told me not to walk too far. He was very concerned; he was very strict."

In his first months as a Maple Leaf, Barilko also spent time with his aunt and uncle and their family, who had moved to Toronto from Timmins. Nina Weseluck, Bill's cousin, fondly recalls a visit from the newest Maple Leaf. "Bill was still the same old Bill. My father was so proud of him. Dad was very close to the boys after their father passed away. My dad was short in stature and Bill would practically take up the whole doorway. He came into our home and said, 'Hi, Uncle John,' and lifted him up.

"My Dad said, 'Billy, there's something I have to ask you. You're not a rough boy off the ice, but what is this? You're banging people into the boards and they're calling you 'Bashin' Bill' Barilko. I can't understand it.' And Bill said, 'Uncle John, I really have to play the way they want me to. I'm really not that kind of guy.'"

When "Bashin' Bill" was on the blue line, it was rare to find an opposing player on his feet. Coach Hap Day marvelled, "We reach into the bottom of our farm system barrel for a defenceman and we come up with a great, major league prospect who has certainly proved himself so far." Late in the season, Day paired Barilko with Garth Boesch, another big, hard-hitting defenceman and the only player in the NHL who sported a moustache. Boesch and Barilko formed an airtight seal in front of netminder Turk Broda. Together, they created a play dubbed the Maginot Line. As the opposing player was firing a shot, both defencemen would drop to their knees to block the drive. The play took its name from the massive concrete and steel fortification that stretched along France's border with Germany, Luxembourg and Switzerland prior to the Second World War. When it was constructed, the defence was considered impenetrable.

※ ※ ※

When the 1946–47 season was over, the Toronto Maple Leafs had finished in second place with 72 points, trailing only the perennial front-runners, the Montreal Canadiens (with 78). The March 8 trouncing of Chicago represented a shift in the club's momentum; of their last seven games, the Leafs won five and tied one. In his 18 games with Toronto, Barilko had scored three goals and added seven assists for 10 points. He had racked up 33 minutes in penalties, a far cry from teammate Gus Mortson's league-leading 133. As a testament to the Leafs' renewed focus on physicality, they were now the most penalized team in the league with 669 minutes, 108 more than the next most belligerent side, Montreal.

Teeder Kennedy, who was only 20 when the season began, was Toronto's leading scorer with 28 goals and 32 assists for 60 points. That put him fifth in the NHL scoring race, a dozen points behind league scoring champ Max Bentley of the Chicago Blackhawks. Turk Broda played in all 60 games that season after sharing the crease the previous season with Frank McCool, Gordie Bell and Baz Bastien, and was runner-up to Montreal's Bill Durnan in the Vezina Trophy race.

Toronto met the fourth-place Detroit Red Wings in the semifinals. Wally Stanowski was out of the Leafs' lineup with a knee injury, and although he played, Bill Barilko was also on the limp. Still, there was a positive omen: Harry Lumley, Detroit's goalkeeper, was out with a groin injury. Scheduled to take his place was Red Almas, who had appeared in but one regular-season contest.

Game one, which was Bill's first NHL playoff game, was held March 26 at Maple Leaf Gardens. Barilko recorded a minor penalty in the first period of a 3–2 overtime win for Toronto. Howie Meeker scored the winning goal at 3:05 of the extra stanza.

Game two was a debacle, both for the Leafs and the defensive duo of Barilko and Boesch. Like its real-life counterpart, the Maginot Line crumpled; they were on the ice for six goals as the Red Wings drowned the Leafs 9–1. Conn Smythe was livid. "After seeing tonight's game, it's a mystery to me how we even won the first game. I'd have to strain to name three of our players who had played a halfway decent game," he told the scribes.

The third game of the series saw Toronto rebound to a 4–1 victory. Stanowski dressed and played a handful of shifts, but found his knee too tender and retired back to the dressing room. With three minutes remaining and the victory a foregone conclusion, Ted Lindsay struck Gus Mortson over the head like a miner taking a pickaxe to a slab of ore. As Mortson skated off the ice holding his head, he deliberately knocked Detroit's Bill Quackenbush to the ice. Gordie Howe took umbrage to the hit on the mild-mannered Quackenbush, and he and Mortson battled in the penalty box. The fight spread to the crowd, and the police jumped in to try to restore calm. Mortson was hit by a seat hurled by a fan.

Some semblance of peace was restored in game four, a 4–1 win for Toronto in Detroit. Howie Meeker scored twice before taking a slash across the ankle from "Black Jack" Stewart. The sole goal for the Red Wings was collected by Roy Conacher, when both Barilko and Thomson were in the penalty box.

The Maple Leafs wrapped up the semifinal with a 6–1 home victory, eliminating Detroit and garnering them a berth in the Stanley Cup finals against the Montreal Canadiens, who had defeated Boston.

The Canadiens outworked and outclassed Toronto 6–0 in game one, played in Montreal, but the Leafs roared back in game two. The KLM Line (of Kennedy, Lynn and Meeker) began the proceedings, with two goals fired past Bill Durnan while Butch Bouchard was serving a minor penalty. First, Teeder Kennedy scored from Vic Lynn and Bill Barilko at 1:12; then, 24 seconds later, Lynn scored from Kennedy to put Toronto ahead 2–0.

Bill earned a minor late in the first period. Frustrated with the Leafs' early lead, Maurice Richard slashed Vic Lynn over the head and, with Lynn bleeding, Barilko came to his teammate's defence. Lynn was carried from the ice unconscious with blood streaming from a cut above his left eye. While Richard was serving a major, Barilko earned his second assist of the game on a goal by Gaye Stewart. Later in the period, Richard swung his stick again, this time at Bill Ezinicki, who had been goading him all evening. The Rocket was handed a game misconduct for his action, and was subsequently fined and suspended for a game by league president Clarence Campbell. Toronto prevailed 4–0.

The Leafs won game three by a score of 4–2. And the bad blood that lingered after the second game came to a boil at Maple Leaf Gardens in game four. Leaf winger Joe Klukay was taken off the ice on a stretcher after being boarded by Kenny Reardon, after which an endless parade of miscreants beat paths to the penalty box, including Bill Barilko, who continued a feud with Maurice Richard. The dust was finally settled at 16:36 of overtime when Leaf captain Syl Apps scored to give the Leafs a 2–1 victory.

Back in Montreal for game five, the Canadiens won 3–1. Wally Stanowski, who had seen spot duty during the series as he rebounded from an injury, suffered a shoulder separation and was sidelined for the remainder of the playoffs.

The Toronto Maple Leafs won the Stanley Cup with a 2–1 home-ice victory in game six. Ted Kennedy scored the Cup-winning goal when he ripped a hard ice-level shot past Durnan at 14:39 of the third stanza.

The Maple Leafs leapt over the boards in unison to smother Turk Broda in congratulatory embraces. *Les Canadiens* shook hands with the victors in spite of the bitterness that had percolated during the heated battle between the two Canadian franchises. The jubilant spectators littered the ice with hats, programs and anything else they could find, waiting anxiously for the presentation of the Stanley Cup. But that ceremony didn't take place: the trophy had been left in Montreal at the request of a superstitious Conn Smythe, who didn't want to jeopardize his team's chances for victory.

The jubilant dressing room was jammed with well-wishers, including Toronto Mayor Robert Saunders and Ontario Premier George Drew. Frank Selke and Senator Donat Raymond, representing the Canadiens, dropped by the dressing room of the champions to offer congratulations.

Smythe addressed the media and heralded his championship Leafs. "First, there was the coaching of Happy Day, who ran the team and made the decisions. Second, there was the play of the old champions. By that, I mean the veterans of our other great championship teams. Third, there was the play of the kids who wanted to be champions."

Bill Barilko was giddy. Just 19, he had realized a pair of unlikely dreams within the space of two months. Playing in the National Hockey League for the team he had followed since his boyhood was one matter, but being part of a Stanley Cup championship team was beyond comprehension. "I realized a life's ambition. I never dreamed I'd make it so soon, but I knew in my heart some day I'd help the Leafs win a Stanley Cup," he told reporters gathered in the Maple Leafs' dressing room. Painted around the perimeter of the room was the motto Conn Smythe chose to inspire his team: *Defeat Does Not Rest Lightly on Their Shoulders.*

Maurice Richard had been the playoff scoring leader, collecting six goals and five assists for 11 points in 10 playoff games. He also led all playoff performers in penalty minutes with 44. Bill Barilko earned three assists in 11 games, also compiling 18 minutes in penalties.

After the team had showered and dressed, Howie Meeker and Joe Klukay visited Nick Metz, who was recuperating from a chest operation at Wellesley Hospital.

The Stanley Cup was shipped to Toronto for an official championship photograph the next day, Sunday, April 20, at noon. Maple Leaf Gardens hosted a party for the players, management and staff at two o'clock, with speeches by captain Syl Apps, scoring leader Ted Kennedy and Tim Daly, the Leafs' long-time trainer.

Each member of the Toronto Maple Leafs earned $500 for finishing second during the regular season, $1,000 for beating Detroit in the semifinal and $1,000 for winning the Stanley Cup.

Bill made a point of contacting Johnny Mitchell, the Pittsburgh Hornets manager who had first signed Barilko to a contract. "Mr. Mitchell," he blurted, "I'll never be able to thank you enough for all you've done for me and for my family."

A testimonial dinner for the world champion Toronto Maple Leafs, sponsored by the Ontario government, was held at the Training and Re-Establishment Institute on Gould Street on April 22. Premier Drew welcomed the team; CBC radio broadcast the remarks of NHL president Clarence Campbell, Maple Leaf Gardens president Ed Bickle, Conn Smythe, Hap Day, Syl Apps and broadcaster Foster Hewitt. Norman Harris and his orchestra entertained. It was heady stuff indeed for a 19-year-old boy from Timmins, who only two years before had been playing senior hockey in his hometown.

Fifty-seven years later, Anne is still incredulous. "To think Billy played hockey for a couple of months and won the Stanley Cup... Well, who could ever have dreamed something as amazing as that?!"

CHAPTER

8

Second Cup
(1947–48)

"Green as the hills of Killarney but as eager as any beaver, Barilko stepped into the NHL and bodychecked his way to prominence overnight."

That sentence, written in *The Maple Leaf Sports Magazine and Official Programme*, captured the remarkable essence of the Bill Barilko story. In storybook fashion, Bill went from the McIntyre Arena to Hollywood and then to Maple Leaf Gardens. And then, as a late-season addition, Bill was part of a Stanley Cup champion. Three years after he was playing unexceptional juvenile hockey back home, he had become the first Timmins-born player to have his name engraved on the trophy. He was living every boy's dream. And as the 1947–48 season opened, the Toronto Maple Leafs were touting the young defenceman as a candidate for the Calder Trophy as the NHL's rookie of the year.

Barilko was still considered a rookie in 1947–48 because the National Hockey League had adopted a new rule which took effect that season, whereby players who had appeared in 20 or fewer regular-season games in the NHL maintained their rookie status. Barilko had played in only 18 games after joining the Maple Leafs from Hollywood the year before.

Toronto had already boasted an outstanding collection of Calder Trophy winners in the previous decade. Gaye Stewart won in 1943, followed by Gus Bodnar in 1944, Frank McCool in 1945 and Howie Meeker in 1947.

As he had done the previous summer, Barilko returned to his old bedroom in the family home in Timmins. Part of the $2,500 in bonus money he had earned went toward his first car — a beautiful new black Chevrolet he referred to as "Black Beauty." Bill then decided to take care of his mother. "He bought Mom a refrigerator and bought a nice rug for our living room," says Anne. "My Mom had homemade hooked rugs. Bill said, 'Now when I have my friends over, I want to have nice broadloom in our living room like some of our friends.' Bill was very generous to our mother."

Although money had been scarce before her husband's death, Faye Barilko had faced even greater struggles afterward. The Barilko home was still heated by a wood stove, for instance. "We tried to persuade my mother to install a furnace and to buy an electric stove, but she wouldn't think of it because it was more economical to have the wood stove," Anne sighs. Faye continued to rely on the wood stove for heat, hot water and cooking, switching in summer to a two-burner hot plate.

Faye made ends meet by renting out rooms in her home. Apartments both upstairs and in the basement ensured the bills were paid. But she was unable to read or write, and therefore depended on Anne, the youngest child and the only one of the three children still at home, to handle the paperwork. "I started looking after my mother's business affairs as a very young girl," Anne states. Amazingly, Faye later purchased the house next door as an income property, which provided for the family financially. Later, after Steve Barilko's death, Faye bought another piece of property with two houses on it. The rental income eventually paid for the property itself. "Not bad for a woman who could neither read nor write," laughs Anne.

While Bill and Alex were off playing hockey in California, Mrs. Barilko rented out their bedroom. Anne remembers how well it worked out for her mother. "One of my mother's friends, Mrs. Nick Poleyko from Kapuskasing, said, 'That room is empty from four to six months a year. There's a girl in Kapuskasing who wants to attend the Timmins School of Business. Do you think you'd be interested in renting the room to her?' My Mom asked if she was clean and if she would recommend her. When Mrs. Poleyko replied that she would recommend the girl, Mother said, 'Tell girl come see me and she can rent boys' room."

Anne recalls her well. "Her name was Anne Panasuk. She paid $60 a month room and board and my mother did her laundry. She was lovely and cheerful." Anne Panasuk later married Ted Ballantyne. "She still calls me Pun, too," laughs Anne Klisanich."

Anne Panasuk returned to Kapuskasing and got a good job with the Spruce Falls Pulp and Paper Company. Anne Klisanich continues: "My mother said, 'That work out pretty well.' Mrs. Poleyko said, 'Would you let my son, Alex, stay with you? He wants to attend the Timmins School of Business, too.' Up comes Alex and he spends the winter with us." Alex Poleyko later married Lin, a lovely girl from Australia, and landed a good "job at Spruce Falls Pulp and Paper Company as well."

"The third year, Lena Davitsky came to Timmins for the business college," recalls Anne. After graduating, Lena also obtained a terrific job with Spruce Falls. "Her first husband died and she married a gentleman named Fred Davis," Anne adds.

Word travelled quickly that the Barilko household was a dependable place to board in Timmins if you were from out of town. "Lil Sheremeta was a schoolteacher friend of Anne Panasuk's. She got a job teaching at Central School, right near our house, and called my mother about renting the boys' room. Lil was one of my bridesmaids," smiles Anne. "She later married Fred Hurst.

"All four of our boarders came from Kapuskasing. Ironically, when Bill went missing, the search was based at Kapuskasing."

Today, Bill Barilko would have the opportunity to bring the Stanley Cup back to Timmins for 24 hours to celebrate the Leafs' victory with his friends and those in the community, but during the summer of 1947, no such arrangements existed. In fact, there was no special celebration for Bill in his hometown that summer at all. "My brother was so modest. You wouldn't even know he was a celebrity. He simply loved the game and he loved the guys on the team. He never looked for individual glory," mentions Anne. "My mother thought they should have done something in Timmins for Billy, but he said, 'Oh Mom, it's all okay.'"

Still, folks in the Porcupine were immensely proud of their most popular export. Carlo Cattarello, a coaching legend in Timmins, says, "Once Bill was a Leaf, I don't think we ever missed a game, listening on radio."

Bill *was* the guest of honour at the Porcupine Juvenile Hockey League's Fourth Annual Hockey Banquet in the McIntyre Auditorium. He was joined there by Leafs trainer Tim Daly, who said of Barilko, "He's a real gentleman. He's young and willing to learn and he's got all the guts in the world. If he lacks anything now, he'll gain it with experience." When it was Barilko's turn to speak, he told guests that dreams really do come true and thanked his Timmins coaches, including Carlo Cattarello, for their help through the years. He concluded with, "Stay in shape all summer long. I'll do the same and I'll be in there plugging with the Leafs again next season."

Bill was true to his word. He skated through the summer months at the McIntyre Arena in Schumacher. Barbara Ann Scott, who was Canada's female athlete of the year in 1947, was skating at the same arena that summer in preparation for the 1948 Winter Olympics in St. Moritz, Switzerland.

Hap Day, an outstanding defenceman in his day, had worked painstakingly with Barilko throughout the latter half of the 1946–47 season. Bill was a motivated learner, and his efforts at the McIntyre rink that summer paid dividends. His skating improved to the point that *The Hockey News* called him one of the best skaters on the 1947–48 edition of the Toronto Maple Leafs. "He wasn't a smooth skater," Allan Stanley observes. "He was more of a runner on skates. But he could skate backwards faster than anybody in the league."

Frank Mahovlich, who would go on to win six Stanley Cup championships himself, remembers being a youngster and seeing Bill Barilko during the summer of 1947. "I was living in Timmins at the time and I must have been about nine years old," recalls Mahovlich, who is now a member of Canada's Senate. "I was walking along and my mother mentioned, 'There's Bill Barilko.' He had this big, beautiful car and he was driving by. That was the first time I saw him.

"Our family used to go to a lot of festivities every Sunday night up in Schumacher at the Croatian Hall. He was Ukrainian, but his sister married a Croatian. Anne and the Klisaniches used to belong to this organization called the Croatian Fraternal Union. That's where we did a lot of partying. A lot of weddings took place there. I would see Bill Barilko there occasionally.

"I remember around 1947, Father Les Costello and Bill Barilko were on the ice at the McIntyre Arena. They used to go practise by themselves during the summer months. There they were — the two of them were on the ice and Costello would go down the boards trying to get around Barilko, but Bill was a great backwards skater and he laid into Costello, and Costello went right over the boards and into the stands. That was the last time I saw Bill Barilko."

Bill spent most of the summer with his friends, including Allan Stanley. "We ran together then. Those were the years we were closer. There were the Curik boys, there was Bill and a few others in there," explains Stanley. "I went back to Timmins every year until I got married in 1958 — the year I went to Toronto."

The boys did everything together. "We called ourselves the Personality Club Boys and quite often went to Doc Hudson's cabin on Watabeag Lake," recalls Leo Curik. "Bill loved it. We did a lot of fishing out there."

"There were only one or two married of the six or eight of us then," adds Allan. "We went on fishing trips. I think we went for the outing rather than catching the fish. One fishing trip we went on, there were four of us. Bill was there with me and the Curik boys. We were fishing off the shore about 20 miles out of Timmins at Watabeag Lake. The four of us were standing maybe 20 feet apart. Everybody was pulling fish up, except me. Every time the other boys put their line in the water, they pulled up a fish. Bill was next to me and he was pulling fish. I'm standing next to him and I can't even get a bite. I said to Bill, 'Do you wanna trade positions? I can't catch anything.'

"He stood in my spot and I stood in his and he started pulling fish out and I couldn't get a bite there, either. So I said, 'Bill, will you trade fishing rods with me?' And we traded fishing rods and he pulled fish out of the water and I still couldn't get a bite." Allan laughs heartily. "I'm not a fisherman, that's all there is to it."

The "hockey boys" socialized with Lou Hudson, a local doctor who had been a terrific hockey player once upon a time and, in 1928, was part of the Varsity Grads hockey team that handily won a gold medal at the Winter Olympic Games in St. Moritz. Hudson lived in a large home on the Mattagami River and owned a couple of cottages on Lake Temagami, about 100 miles southeast of Timmins. Hudson often invited the boys to bring their friends to the cottage for a weekend. "We used to go Saturday night and come back Sunday night with our girlfriends," reports Stanley. "It was a beautiful sunny day and about six of us got in the outboard boat and went across the lake. It was quite a way across, then up the river, because some of us hadn't seen too much of the lake before and wanted to go for a little ride on a nice day. Up north there, at times, the temperature can drop 40 degrees. When that front moves in — oh boy! We were all in shorts; no one had on anything warm at all — it had been too nice a day. We had a drink up there on the creek and we started heading back, when the front moved in and it dropped 40 degrees and we were freezing.

"We got a couple of minutes out in the lake and the motor conked out. We all took turns pulling the motor trying to start it. Nothing worked. Bill got on it and he pulled that thing so hard I thought he was going to rip it right out. He pulled it so often and so hard, but we couldn't get anything going. The weather closed right in on us. It was misty, and you couldn't see anything out there at all. We were a mile or two away from the island. We stopped pulling [the cord on the outboard motor] and who do we see but our friend, Lou Hudson. It was his island and his cottage, and who's coming across the lake out of the mist and fog but Lou in a canoe. The canoe was full of blankets and jackets and everything. That was the most pleasant sight we ever saw. We got all covered up and got back to the cottage. It was a very large cottage. He had army bunk beds all around the great big living room and dining room. He had a big wood stove. We sat around that wood stove for a long time to get warm."

Allan, Bill, Gaston Garant and the Curik boys also spent a lot of time each summer at the Victory Hotel. "That was our hangout," snickers Allan. The Victory was owned by the Curik family. "There were three Curik brothers — Lawrence, Leo and Bill. If the Curiks ever got stuck, we'd fill in serving beer. Some nights when we were having a good time, to liven things up, we'd get the music going and we'd dance with all the elderly ladies in there to get them motivated. They had a ball! They thought that was the greatest thing. It was a real fun place for us. They were wonderful friends.

"The only boys [amongst Bill's friends] who worked were the Curiks and they worked at the hotel. I didn't really work. A couple of summers

I sold cars. My Dad kept telling me that the Ford dealer needed some help. I hadn't been working, so I said, 'You sure he needs help?' My Dad said, 'Yes, he needs help.' I went there and worked for the summer.

"That's when I bought my first car. It was a 1947 black Chevy. Another summer, my Dad told me the Plymouth dealer needed help. I said, 'You're sure, eh?' I think he was just trying to get me working. He said, 'Yeah, he needs help.' So I went and worked a summer down there. I sold my Dad a car that year. That was the extent of my summer working experience."

Gaston Garant was an anomaly among the young men who spent the summers together in Timmins in that he didn't play hockey. "When Bill would come home in the summer from Hollywood, we'd ask him what kind of year he had. It was just that. He was just hoping he'd play in the National Hockey League. He dreamt that someday he'd play in the NHL. I was very excited to hear that Bill was going to play with the Toronto Maple Leafs. We had quite a celebration when he came home after his first year with the Maple Leafs. All his buddies got together at the Victory Hotel, the hotel the Curiks had. When I listened to *Hockey Night in Canada*, I used to like Bep Guidolin — he was a very good player — and Real Chevrefils was a fantastic player," Garant recalls. "Pete Babando from South Porcupine, too."

Garant talks of his friend with great affection. "Bill Barilko never changed, even though he played for the Toronto Maple Leafs. He was really comical. We used to have a lot of fun together."

When Bill went home that summer, his sister Anne showed him the scrapbook she had been compiling. "Bill was playing hockey for the Toronto Maple Leafs and his name was in the paper, his picture was in the paper and the kids at school were bringing me in their newspapers. I began to cut out the newspaper clippings and started a scrapbook. When Billy came home that summer, I showed it to him. It contained his school days and then the 1947 season with the Toronto Maple Leafs. He was flabbergasted that I was doing that. I can still picture him saying to me, 'Anne, will you keep doing that for me? If you will, next year when I come back to Timmins, there's going to be a fur coat for you and one for mother.' He bought me a beautiful muskrat coat. He bought Mom a black Persian lamb coat at the same time! I wore that coat with great pleasure and pride.

"Billy was very humble. He didn't expect too much from others. He gave a lot of himself. I admired him and I enjoyed working on the scrapbooks because I was so proud of him."

🍁 🍁 🍁

That autumn, the Tulsa Oilers severed their working relationship with the Toronto Maple Leafs. Gus Marker, who had coveted the Barilko boys, was fired as coach. And while Bill was preparing for his second season as a Toronto Maple Leaf, Alex was trying out with the Atlantic Seagulls of the Eastern Amateur Hockey League. Bill and Alex both dreamed of one day playing together on the blue line for the Toronto Maple Leafs.

🍁 🍁 🍁

The NHL Board of Governors had met during the spring of 1947 and decided that an All-Star Game would take place that fall in Toronto, with one-third of the gross gate receipts going to a Toronto charity chosen by the Maple Leafs and the other two-thirds to the Players Emergency Fund. In a subsequent meeting in September 1947, attended by the team governors and three player representatives (Syl Apps of the Leafs, Glen Harmon from Montreal and Detroit's Sid Abel), the attendees decided to put the players' cut towards a pension plan that had been newly initiated for the players' retirement. The Leafs designated the Community Chest of Greater Toronto for the other third of the proceeds.

The game, played on October 13, pitted the Stanley Cup champion Toronto Maple Leafs against the dozen players who had been named to the NHL's First and Second All-Star Teams after the 1946–47 season, supplemented by five additional players selected from the five other NHL teams. The All-Stars, coached by Dick Irvin of the Canadiens, comprised Bill Durnan, Butch Bouchard, Kenny Reardon and Maurice Richard from Montreal (all of whom were selected to the First All-Star Team as well); Frank Brimsek, Milt Schmidt, Bobby Bauer and Woody Dumart of Boston (Schmidt had also been selected to the First Team); "Black Jack" Stewart, Bill Quackenbush and Ted Lindsay of the Red Wings; Bill Mosienko and Max and Doug Bentley from the Chicago Blackhawks (Doug Bentley rounded out the First Team selections); and Tony Leswick, Grant Warwick and Edgar Laprade of the New York Rangers.

Each member of the 1946–47 First All-Star Team was awarded an engraved gold puck, while a cornucopia of gifts awaited the members of the Maple Leafs. Each player received a gold medallion that served as a lifetime pass to Maple Leaf Gardens as well as a silver watch chain from Conn Smythe, gold cufflinks from the government of Ontario, gold watches from the City of Toronto, silver serving trays from the National Hockey League, team photos from Lou and Nat Turofsky at Alexandra Studios, coats from Eaton's, hats from Simpson's, ties from Sammy Taft Hats, cigarette cases from Maple Leaf Gardens, table lighters from Birks, golf balls from CCM and pocket knives from Dowling's Grill, the restaurant inside the Gardens.

Barilko and the Leafs played a spirited game. Bill Ezinicki picked up a goal, an assist and three minor penalties, while Harry Watson earned a goal and an assist in a losing cause as the NHL All-Stars edged the Leafs 4–3. Syl Apps also scored for the Leafs while Max Bentley, his brother Doug, Grant Warwick and Maurice Richard scored for the Stars.

The 1947–48 season began five days later, on October 18, with the Stanley Cup champions opening at home against the Detroit Red Wings and tying the game two-all. Barilko wore sweater number 21, just as he had done in 1946–47. Toronto entered November having lost but one of its first five game. "We got a real break when Barilko came up to us last spring," Conn Smythe observed. "He's been our best defence player so far this season."

Barilko was skating better but had lost none of his bodychecking prowess. Smythe loved the rambunctious attitude of his rookie rear-guard. "It was just like running into an anvil," says Howie Meeker, shaking his head. "He loved to do what he did well, and that was to hit. He wasn't dirty — never went after you with the stick. He usually played the left side, and I felt sorry for all the right wingers in the league. If he hadn't died, but kept on playing and acquired the mental finesse that comes with it, I can safely say that Bill would have been a First Team All-Star from the ages of 27 to 32." Meeker pays Barilko a supreme compliment: during the period he refers to, the trio of Doug Harvey, Red Kelly and Bill Gadsby jockeyed for the defence slots on the NHL's First All-Star Team. That would place Bill in rarefied company indeed.

Emile Francis, who was a netminder for the Chicago Blackhawks during the mid-1940s and later was inducted into the Hockey Hall of Fame as a builder, recalls Bill Barilko. "The best bodycheck I ever saw was right in Maple Leaf Gardens over there at the visitors' bench," he said, pointing across an empty ice surface. "I was playing goal for Chicago. Charlie Conacher was our coach. We had this fella, Alex Kaleta. We called him 'Killer Kaleta.' Bill Barilko corked him one. He was down on his hands and knees trying to pick up the blue line. Conacher was yelling at him to get off the ice. Kaleta said, 'Okay, coach, but I can't get hold of my goddamned stick here!'"

In a 1948 radio interview with Toronto radio station CFRB, Barilko recalled the best bodycheck he ever delivered. "[Milt] Schmidt was coming up the boards. He had deked one of our men, then he deked [Joe] Klukay, both times feinting for the middle of the rink and going through on the boards. I figured he'd try the same thing on me, and he did.

"It was a terrific check, and I got a penalty. Schmidt twisted his ankle somewhere in the deal."

Bill credited Bob Gracie and Tommy Anderson of the Hollywood Wolves for aiding his physical game. "Bob Gracie had me work on my backwards skating, which in turn helped with my bodychecking. There aren't too many trying to go through the centre on me now. That cuts down their chances and makes me look better," Barilko laughed in a January 1948 interview with the *Toronto Daily Star*.

A physical game is often accompanied by time in the penalty box, and Bill Barilko was no stranger to the sin bin. "I don't mind getting a penalty when I have it coming," he admitted in an interview with the *Star*. "Now I think the referees are watching me too closely and are giving me chippy penalties. That's the only trouble about being the league's bad man. That won't stop me, though. I like it here in Toronto."

Even if Bill was cavalier about the matter, his sister Anne was concerned about how aggressive her brother's play had become. "I said to Billy, 'You better smarten up. You want to stay in Toronto, don't you?' He was getting too many penalties. We didn't want them to send him to Pittsburgh."

Bill didn't reserve his punishing bodychecks for the opposition. Gus Mortson chuckles as he recalls that, "In practice, he'd give a little signal to keep your head up and then he'd take you out." Carry the puck across the blue line and you'd hear "beep, beep," then be thundered to the ice by Barilko's shoulder. It didn't matter that the puck carrier was wearing blue and white — the difference was that a teammate got a warning, while opponents did not. Howie Meeker remembers being on the wrong end of a Barilko shoulder. "He hit me one day in practice — he could have killed me! I was looking down to get a pass. I heard 'beep, beep' and I looked up and he just ran into me nice and easy, but I ached for a week. It hurt! He was like an anvil no matter where you touched him, even on the cheek of his ass."

Ted Kennedy laughs when he thinks about Barilko's warnings during practices. "Bill would never warn the opposition that he was coming, but he would warn the boys during scrimmages. He could hurt you not just by running at you or taking a couple of steps to hit you — all he had to do was rub you out against the fence and he'd hurt. He realized that and he didn't want to hurt any of his teammates during a practice, so he would go 'beep, beep, beep' to let us know that he was coming and was going to take us out. But it hurt when he took you out. Your whole upper body was twisted."

"There was no malice attached to that boy," Teeder hastens to add. "None whatever. He loved the bodychecking and making an important play defensively."

Allan Stanley, who was a member of the Holman Pluggers back home in Timmins when Bill was their stick boy and who would make his own NHL debut with the New York Rangers in 1948–49, remembers reading about his friend and listening to Leafs games on the radio. "When he came into the league, he was one crude hockey player. He was an unpolished gem. If you went around his outside, if he missed you with his hip, he'd swing his right leg around, and if he missed you with that he'd turn around — and he used a 25-ounce stick, which was heavy in those days — and he'd chop you down like a tree."

"[The Leafs] had four guys at the blue line or even a fifth coming back to check," explains Stanley. "It was like going through a meat grinder every time you played them. Bill just stood there and bashed them."

Elmer Lach, the Montreal Canadiens star, didn't get the benefit of a warning and told the press at that time, "He's the hardest hitter in the league. When he hits you, he hurts you."

Bill could be tough and aggressive on the ice, but that wasn't his way in his civilian clothes. "Bill was a very outgoing person. He was very likeable. He never had a bad thing to say about anyone else. He got along with everyone," mentions Gus Mortson.

The season was still young, but manager Conn Smythe wasn't pleased with the composition of his Maple Leafs, who were 3–2–2. "We have two great centres in Syl Apps and Ted Kennedy," he said. "If we could get one more, our strength down the middle would make us the best." On November 4, 1947, Smythe and Bill Tobin of the Chicago Blackhawks orchestrated one of the most significant trades to that date in NHL history. Toronto sent an entire line plus a pair of defencemen to the Hawks in return for Max Bentley, who had led the league in scoring the previous year.

The Flying Forts Line, so named because all of its members hailed from Fort William, Ontario (now part of the city of Thunder Bay), had been part of the previous spring's Stanley Cup championship team. The young, quick and skilled trio of Gus Bodnar, Bud Poile and Gaye Stewart was bundled up and sent to Chicago along with the highly regarded Bob Goldham and a member of the 1942 Stanley Cup champions, Ernie Dickens. In addition to Bentley, the Hawks threw in a minor-league prospect, Cy Thomas.

All five of the traded Maple Leafs were popular with fans and management alike, but in order to pry a player of Max Bentley's calibre away from Chicago, a steep price had to be paid. And although Smythe had a wealth of talent in Pittsburgh, waiting for a break, the deal was still a sizable gamble. Should Bentley get hurt or lose his scoring touch, Toronto would be in trouble.

Acquiring Bentley gave Toronto not only three of the best centres at that time, but three of the finest centres ever to play the game. Apps, although near the end of his career, was an outstanding leader who contributed significantly to the Leaf offence. Ted Kennedy would one day replace Apps as Leaf captain, and his feisty play made him one of the most desired players in the NHL. And Bentley gave the Leafs a third outstanding centre on which to base their attack. Bentley would also play the point during power plays, a strategy that gave the Leafs incomparable firepower whenever they had a manpower advantage.

Bentley and his brother Doug had been the keys to Chicago's offence. Partnered with Bill Mosienko, the three comprised the dynamic

Pony Line, which had been one of the league's best in the 1940s. In 1942–43, Doug led the league in scoring, while Max finished third. In 1943–44, Doug finished second and Mosienko came in eighth. The next season, Mosienko tied for fifth. In 1945–46 it was Max's turn to win the scoring title, while Mosienko again tied for fifth. In 1946–47, all three finished the regular season in the top 10 — Max first, Doug sixth and Mosienko ninth.

The trade left Hawks fans devastated. "Why did they let him go?" asked the *Chicago Tribune*. "The answer is simple. They couldn't win with him. In other words, no matter what he did, the team wasn't good enough."

The trade was hard on both Bentley brothers, too. Doug had broken in with Chicago in 1939–40, and Max joined him in 1940–41. They were exceptionally close, both on and off the ice.

Smythe was delighted but surprised. "I really didn't think I could get Max," he later admitted. The deal captivated the city of Toronto. Throughout the city, fans argued about which club had done better in the five-for-two deal.

"No club in the history of hockey ever had four centres like that," boasts Howie Meeker. "We had Apps and Kennedy at centre. Max Bentley, who won the scoring championship the year before, was the third-line centre. Nick Metz was the backup. We were the best hockey team that year by a country mile." Apps, Kennedy and Bentley were all eventually inducted into the Hockey Hall of Fame.

Although the lineup was blessed with a surfeit of scoring prowess, coach Hap Day still maintained a conservative, defensive strategy. "I liked to carry the puck, but Hap Day used to hold the defence back," explains Gus Mortson. "He'd say, 'As soon as you get to the blue line, pass it.'"

When Max Bentley joined the Leafs, he and Bill became very good friends in spite of a seven-year age gap. In a 1982 *Toronto Star* article, Bentley recalled his teammate: "Bill loved the New York Yankees. He loved movies, nickel and dime poker games and, now and then, the horse races."

Leafs trainer Tim Daly would regularly joust with Barilko in the dressing room for fun, a practice that would keep the players loose and often in hysterics. In John Melady's book *Overtime, Overdue*, Max Bentley recalled one exchange between the two. "Bill used to kid Tim, saying he was always drunk. 'Barilko,' Daly would say, 'You think you're a Hollywood star but you sure can't play hockey! You should be back in the bushes where you came from!'"

On December 6, Toronto blasted the Hawks 12–5. Max Bentley scored a hat trick against his old mates.

Gaston Garant spent New Year's Eve with his pal Bill Barilko, later cheering him on in the New Year's Day game against the Canadiens, which Toronto won, 2–1. "Bill got me tickets to Maple Leaf Gardens three or four times. The first time, he brought me into the Toronto Maple Leafs' dressing room. Turk Broda was in the nets and was upset that the Canadiens had spoiled his shutout. He said, 'Those Frenchmen caught me with my pants down.' I'll never forget that."

Hockey worlds converged in New York in mid-January for Bill and his brother Alex. On January 18, Bill and the Leafs faced the New York Rangers at Madison Square Garden, skating away with a two-all tie. That same day, Alex was in town as his Valleyfield Braves doubled the New York Rovers 6–3 in a Quebec Senior Hockey League contest. After the game, Alex joined his brother and several of the other Leafs for an evening of dinner and drinks at the Harem Club.

The season had gone well for Toronto. As with any good trade, both teams benefited. The Maple Leafs finished the season first overall, securing top spot with back-to-back wins over the Red Wings to close the season. It was the first time since 1934–35 that Toronto had finished first. Max Bentley finished the regular season fifth in scoring. His brother Doug finished third, while former Leafs Poile and Stewart finished fourth and sixth respectively. What the trade could not accomplish, however, was to lift the Blackhawks out of the basement.

In his first full NHL season, Bill Barilko's totals included five goals and nine assists for 14 points in 57 games. His 147 penalty minutes led the league.

🍁 🍁 🍁

June Thomson, the widow of Leafs defenceman Jim Thomson, remembers how close all the players and their partners were during that time. "We did practically everything together," she recalls. "It was like a fraternity. The boys liked to be together, and of course they talked hockey. The girls got to be real close too. For instance, when Jim and I were getting married, Lil Watson [Harry's wife] had a shower for me, and all the girls were there at her house in Leaside. We sat around and listened to the hockey game!"

The group often congregated at the Watson home in Toronto's east end. "Lil had three small children, so it was easier for people to go to her house rather than her having to get babysitters all the time. But they really enjoyed having the company, too," explains June. "Sometimes we played cards, but mostly, we sat around and talked. Turk and Betty Broda, Gus Mortson and Sheila, Garth Boesch and his wife, Lil and Harry Watson, Cal Gardner and his wife Mary. Ted and Doreen Kennedy occasionally came. They were very friendly but didn't often come. Bill [Barilko] always came. He was happy-go-lucky. He made everybody feel good because he always had a big smile. I'm sure he must have had some serious moments, but he was always the life of the party. Bill and Jimmy were very good pals. We only knew Bill for about four years, of course. Before Bill started seeing [girlfriend] Louise [Hastings], he brought different girls. Jim lived with the Hastings family until we got married. That was his home. He used to call Mr. and Mrs. Hastings Mom and Pop."

"The boys were on the road a lot," June continues. "They went by train, and a trip to Boston, for instance, might be five days. When the boys came home and said, 'Hey, let's get together,' we'd go out to the Old Mill. It seemed to be one of the special spots we all went to. As a matter of fact, that's where Jim and I went on our first date."

* * *

First-place Toronto was matched against third-place Boston in the opening round of the playoffs. The Leafs had finished 18 points better than the Bruins through the regular season. Barilko was his usual spirited self through the series, knocking down Bruins like bowling pins.

Toronto won the first game 5–4 in a seesaw battle that saw the Leafs come from behind three times before Nick Metz scored the winning goal at 17:03 of overtime. Game two saw Toronto outscore Boston again, this time 5–3. Ted Kennedy was the star, recording a hat trick.

The series moved to Boston for game three, a 5–1 Toronto victory marred by wild fisticuffs both on and off the ice. During the first period, Bill Barilko scored the Leafs' second goal, an unassisted tally after he intercepted a clearing pass by Grant Warwick. Two Boston fans took swings at Barilko as he left the ice. Late in the third, a fight between Warwick and Bill Ezinicki spawned a bigger bout pitting Murray Henderson, a tough Bruins defender, against big Harry Watson, traditionally a pacifist. But Watson's well-aimed jab to Henderson's nose left him bleeding badly and doctors were forced to set the busted beak. As the teams left the ice after the final buzzer, the real trouble began. Spectators swarmed onto the ice and lunged at Garth Boesch and Hap Day. Boesch was struck on the head and knocked unconscious, while Wally Stanowski jumped in to assist his coach. Weston Adams, the Bruins' president, raided the Toronto dressing room after the game, so Conn Smythe ordered him ejected.

After dropping a 3–2 decision to the Bruins, the Maple Leafs clinched their berth in the Stanley Cup final, winning the game 3–2 and the series 4–1 back in Toronto. During the second period of this match, Barilko served a minor during the second period.

In the meantime, Detroit had pushed aside the New York Rangers, advancing to the final. The Leafs and Red Wings had finished one-two during the regular season.

The series began with Toronto pulling out a 5–3 win at Maple Leaf Gardens. Barilko picked up two minors in the first period, but played a strong game. Late in the second period, having just scored the Leafs' fourth goal, Gus Mortson broke his leg and was rushed to Toronto's Wellesley Hospital after he and Jimmy Thomson sandwiched "Black Jack" Stewart. Wally Stanowski stepped in beside Thomson to replace the injured Mortson on the blue line.

Toronto doubled the Wings 4–2 in game two. At the end of the first period, Barilko and Fern Gauthier participated in a spirited dust-up that saw both whistled off the ice for five minutes each for fighting. Bill picked up a minor in the third to pad his penalty total. At the buzzer, the two goaltenders, Turk Broda and Harry Lumley, staged a boxing match in venerable Maple Leaf Gardens, and both were assessed 10-minute misconducts for their actions. The scrap represented a renewal of hostilities between the two netminders, who had staged a bout on December 10 earlier that season.

The series moved to Detroit for game three, and the press had a field day when they learned that Bill had packed five suits and 67 ties for the series. He always wanted to be well appointed, but sartorial splendour was of no value on the ice. He again visited the penalty box, in the first period. The Leafs, backed by a Broda shutout, won the game 2–0. "If this team wins the Stanley Cup, I will say it is the best Maple Leaf team we have ever had," boasted Conn Smythe.

Before the fourth game, Toronto Mayor Hiram McCallum sent Smythe a telegram that read, "Please convey best wishes to Maple Leafs for success in game for Stanley Cup tonight. If they win this game and are returning during day on Thursday, we shall be glad to extend a civic welcome at City Hall." Smythe refused to read the telegram to his team. He had no intention of jinxing them.

The Leafs completed their sweep of the finals with a 7–2 victory at the Detroit Olympia to claim their second consecutive Stanley Cup championship. The Detroit fans were gracious, loud and appreciative of the Maple Leaf win. Coincidentally, Toronto had become the first back-to-back champion since Detroit in 1935–36 and 1936–37. Former Leaf stars Charlie Conacher and Baldy Cotton were on hand to witness the festivities. Conacher had spent the season coaching the Chicago Blackhawks, while Cotton was scouting for the Boston Bruins.

That night, April 14, the Stanley Cup was not presented. The superstitious Smythe was again responsible. Not one to toy with the fates, he had asked that the Cup not be brought to the Olympia.

The victorious Leafs hooted and hollered every step of the way from the ice surface to their dressing room. Howie Meeker dumped a bottle of Coca-Cola down Broda's sweater, but just as Turk was about to reciprocate, Detroit general manager Jack Adams arrived to congratulate the champions. Smythe later hosted a party for his team at the prestigious Penobscot Club in downtown Detroit.

No other Toronto hockey team had ever won both the league title and the Stanley Cup in the same season. "It was strength down the middle that paid off," boasted Conn Smythe. "There is no doubt about it, this is far and away the greatest of the Toronto teams. They never failed to do what we asked. Not once did this bunch require a pep talk. They keyed themselves to rise to every occasion."

Ted Kennedy led all playoff performers with 14 points. In nine games, he scored eight goals and added six assists. Bill Barilko scored a goal in Toronto's nine contests. His 17 penalty minutes were second only to teammate Vic Lynn for the playoff lead.

The train bearing the conquering heroes arrived from Detroit the next day. The Queen's Own Rifles band led the Leafs in a parade from Union Station, north on Bay Street towards the old City Hall at the corner of Queen Street, playing "For He's a Jolly Good Fellow" as they went. The inhabitants of the office buildings along the route showered the victors with ticker tape and paper.

At City Hall, the players and management were met by Mayor Hiram McCallum and 10,000 well-wishers. After the mayor made his speech, Conn Smythe took to the microphone and told the crowd, "This is the greatest team our organization has ever had!" The throng screamed its approval. Hap Day, Syl Apps and Ted Kennedy all said a few words, then the boys signed the City Hall guest book. The name of Gus Mortson, who was still recuperating from a badly broken leg at Wellesley Hospital, was added to the guest book in absentia. Then the team left for a party at Maple Leaf Gardens, where wives, family and friends awaited them.

Jimmy Thomson's wife June remembers the Leafs' celebration that year. "I didn't know Jim when they won the Stanley Cup in 1947, but in 1948, Colonel MacBrien, who was a director at Maple Leaf Gardens, threw a party at his big, beautiful home. The parties were always very elaborate — blue and white cake and the flowers dyed blue and white, too. Later on, we'd all go to the Old Mill to celebrate. We usually partied for a few days. It was a lot of fun!"

On April 16, the day after the celebrations, the Toronto Maple Leafs had their official Stanley Cup portrait photographed on the ice at Maple Leaf Gardens. Gus Mortson was transported to the arena by ambulance, helped into his uniform and, standing in the back row, was included in the group shot.

Each of the Leafs received a $3,000 bonus from the National Hockey League — $1,000 for finishing first and $2,000 for winning the Stanley Cup. Finally, with smiles as wide as Bay Street itself, each of the players left for the summer. Turk Broda took part in an NHL barnstorming tour through western Canada. Vic Lynn planned to get married that summer. Garth Boesch and the Metz brothers returned to their respective farms in the west.

"Our Aunt Anne (Kozloff) asked Billy if she could borrow $2,000 of his Stanley Cup money to open a textile centre in Kirkland Lake," remembers anne. "She paid my brother back, and that store was open for more than twenty years."

Although Bill Barilko had enjoyed a strong season, he did not win the Calder Trophy. That honour went to Jimmy McFadden of the Detroit Red Wings. Timmins native Pete Babando was runner-up. "Though he joined the Leafs at the tail-end of the 1946–47 season and helped them win the Stanley Cup, Barilko was still eligible for the Calder Trophy last winter but probably fell victim to the fact that no defenceman has ever been picked as the top first-year performer," hypothesized *The Maple Leaf Sports Magazine and Official Programme.*

The next Leaf to win the Calder Trophy would be Timmins-born Frank Mahovlich, who earned the rookie award in 1958. In 1948, the 10-year-old Mahovlich was in his bedroom, listening to the Stanley Cup exploits of his favourite Toronto Maple Leaf players. "We had a radio, and Foster Hewitt used to describe the hockey games at that time — Syl Apps, Ted Kennedy, Max Bentley and Bill Barilko."

CHAPTER 9

Three Times Lucky (1948–49)

After winning their second consecutive Stanley Cup championship and attending the resultant celebrations, the Leaf players fanned out to attend to their various responsibilities over the summer of 1948. For most of the family men, summertime meant a second job — an essential for most players, given the salaries they earned in those days. But there was time for other pursuits: Bill Ezinicki played golf, a passion that rivalled hockey for the rambunctious winger, and Gus Mortson strengthened the leg he broke during the playoffs by water-skiing on Crystal Lake near his hometown of Kirkland Lake.

And for Bill Barilko, life couldn't get much better than it was in the summer of 1948. He had been in the NHL for less than two seasons and had already been part of two Stanley Cup championships. And for the next three months, he would relax by the many lakes found in the Porcupine area.

Gillies Lake was terribly dirty from the sludge from the local mines. The Mattagami River had a beach, but the river was fast-flowing and too dangerous to enjoy. On the Buffalo Ankerite Mine property on the outskirts of Timmins was McDonald Lake, and for young people in the Porcupine, *this* was the lake of choice.

"We used to go there to swim in the summertime," reminisces Gaston Garant, Barilko's childhood friend. "A whole bunch of us would go — Leo Curik, Bill Curik, Bill Barilko, Allan Stanley — the whole gang. Bill had a convertible Model A Ford. I think it was a 1925, if I'm not mistaken. We used to go riding in that car all over the place. Then I got married — I was 21 years old. I kept my friends even though I was very young when I got married. They used to come to my home quite often and they'd put empty beer bottles on the posts of my fence at four o'clock in the morning. We never drank to get drunk. We drank for pleasure. I was the first one to get married. The rest of the boys were single seven or eight years after I got married. The boys used to come to the house and my wife would make dinner. We had a great time."

That summer, Bill met Helen Hegedus, an 18-year-old beauty from Schumacher. "I was at McDonald Hill. There's a small lake there where everybody went on Saturday afternoons. Allan Stanley and Bill Barilko and a few of the other hockey players who used to hang around there were at McDonald Hill one day. That's where we met — on the beach."

As they got to know each other, Helen and Bill started to date. At first, there were casual meetings at Hollinger Park. "It was a nice community. Everybody seemed to know each other," remembers Helen. She and Bill went to the Fern Cottage Restaurant for dinner, then started to see each other more frequently. Many of the dates incorporated sporting activities. On Friday nights the couple would go ice skating at the McIntyre Arena. "Bill used to like the songs on the hit parade, but there's one particular one that we always skated together to," smiles Helen. "It was 'Cruising Down the River on a Sunday Afternoon.' That was kind of a special song." Bill often left the slower-skating Helen to go at her own pace while he raced around the rink.

On Sunday afternoons, Bill took Helen to baseball games at the Hollinger ballpark, staying afterwards for the band concerts held there. Occasionally, the couple went up to the dance at the McIntyre Arena. "Bill was a good dancer," remembers Helen. "Of course, we danced differently at that time than they do today."

"My background is Hungarian and he was Central European, so we both liked cabbage rolls and perogies," Helen recalls. When she visited the Barilko home, Helen was introduced to beet borscht for the first time. "I liked it," she admits.

Several NHL players visited Timmins for a benefit hockey game that summer that pitted the Maple Leafs against the Porcupine All-Stars. The Leafs iced the better portion of their lineup, although Barilko, Tod Sloan and Sid Smith dressed for the All-Stars. Proceeds went to Ontario Crippled Children, one of Conn Smythe's favoured charities. "I met a few of the Maple Leaf players at the McIntyre Arena," remembers Helen. "After the game, Bill had all of them over to his mother's house for food and drinks." Faye Barilko was the genial host, adored by all the boys. The Leafs played another charity contest the next day, with the NHL All-Stars facing off against the American Hockey League All-Stars.

"We dated for two years," Helen says. Memories of Bill Barilko are distant, but very pleasant. "Bill and I just parted," she adds matter-of-factly. In 1950, she moved to Toronto to work for the Canadian Imperial Bank of Commerce. "I was not in contact with Bill when I moved to Toronto. He was going all over playing hockey. You don't make a really strong connection. You don't know which way your life is going to go or how you're going to end up." Helen does remember Bill as being very thoughtful. "He'd give you the shirt off his back. I remember one time he went fishing and he brought all his fish over to my parents' house. He'd go and catch fish just to give them to people. That's the kind of person he was. He didn't even eat fish himself."

Fishing was an all-consuming passion for Bill, and any opportunity he had to drop a line in the water was enthusiastically accepted. "We used to go fishing with Dr. Lou Hudson," says Garant. Hudson, a local doctor, was an avid sportsman, as was his brother, Dr. Henry Hudson, who was a dentist in Timmins. "Dr. Lou Hudson had a cottage on an island in Watabeag Lake, which was 30 or 40 miles from Timmins. We used to get pickerel there — all kinds of pickerel."

Henry Hudson's dental practice was above Dalton's Bus Lines, which neighboured the Victory Hotel at 91 Cedar Street South. "That's how we all got to Watabeag Lake with Dr. Hudson," explains Gaston Garant. "We would have been in our early twenties and hanging out at the Victory, which was owned by the Curiks. Dr. Lou Hudson knew a lot of the hockey players, but he never talked much about hockey with us."

Bill was back and forth between Timmins and Toronto several times that summer. In June, Leafs star Ted Kennedy married Doreen Dent at the Knox College Chapel in Toronto, and most of the Leafs — including Bill, who drove down from Timmins — took time from their summer hiatus to witness the special event.

After a summer of fishing and swimming, Bill was ready to report when training camp beckoned in September. The big defenceman gathered some clothes and drove to St. Catharines for the commencement of camp. Checking into the Welland Hotel, he ran into a few of his teammates in the lobby. "Hey Dum Dum, I hear you've got a fan club," they teased. He laughed, "Yeah, pretty funny, eh?" Although Bill chuckled and feigned discomfort, he was in fact very proud to be the subject of the Bill Barilko Fan Club, run by Noretta Lawrunson of Kingston, Ontario.

A popular feature of training camp was the annual Blue and White Game. Players and prospects were divided into two squads and, in front of an appreciative local crowd, battled for bragging rights.

Alex Barilko was to play with the Toronto Marlboro seniors that season, and was elevated to play for the Leafs' White team, while brother Bill played for the Blue squad that September day in 1948. It was as close as the Barilko brothers would ever get to playing together on the Toronto Maple Leafs.

The Senior Marlies had a fine team in 1948–49. Coached by former Leafs great Joe Primeau, the team boasted a roster that included future Leafs captain George Armstrong, as well as Johnny McCormack and Alex Davidson — the brother of former Leafs captain Bob Davidson, who was both manager and a defenceman for the Marlboros. The Timmins area was well represented, too, not only by Alex, but by Johnny McLellan and Chuck Blair from South Porcupine and Ray Hannigan from Schumacher. Doug Harvey's younger brother Howard was the netminder, although he would be forced out of hockey after developing severe allergic reactions. "Howard was touted as the man who would replace Turk Broda in the Toronto net," wrote William Brown in *Doug: The Doug Harvey Story*. "After a game, Howard's face and hands would be so swollen, he looked more like a boxer than a hockey player. Maple Leaf doctors suspected he was reacting to the material in his hockey equipment."

❄ ❄ ❄

When Conn Smythe embarked on his rebuilding program after the Leafs' disappointing 1945–46 season, the goal was to have a team that could compete for the Stanley Cup by 1948–49. Instead, Toronto had succeeded immediately, and the autumn of 1948 saw the team striving not only for a title, but its third in as many years.

The team that competed for that third Cup in a row would be different from the one the year before. After 10 exemplary seasons in blue and white, Syl Apps had played his final game on March 21, 1948. He was only 33 years old and had just enjoyed the finest season of his NHL career. Teammate Sid Smith felt that Apps still had a lot of great hockey left in him. "I'm sure he could have played another five or six years," he said, with a note of incredulity.

At one time, it looked as though he might return. Leafs boss Conn Smythe did convince him to relent and suit up for 1948–49, but when Apps learned that he would not be resuming his captaincy, which coach Hap Day had awarded to Ted Kennedy, he decided not to report.

At the Stanley Cup Victory Dinner at the Royal York Hotel on September 18, 1948, Apps spoke to the appreciative crowd. "I do want to thank, very sincerely, the many fans in Toronto and throughout Canada for the wonderful support they have accorded me during my years with the team," he began. "I can ask nothing more than that they give the same support to the player who has been chosen to take over my duties." With that, Apps reached over and shook the hand of his successor. "Good luck, Teeder!" With that, Ted Kennedy was anointed the captain of the Toronto Maple Leafs.

Nick Metz played his final NHL game the same night as Apps. He announced his retirement on April 22, and returned to farming.

Also in April, the Leafs sent defenceman Wally Stanowski to New York for forward Cal Gardner and defencemen Bill Juzda and Frank Mathers. The Leafs brain trust hoped that the newly acquired Cal Gardner would step into the void left by Apps's retirement.

Squib Walker and the Toronto Maple Leafs' scouting staff would play a role in filling the vacancies. They did an incomparable job during the 1940s, turning up four Calder Trophy winners (Gaye Stewart, Gus Bodnar, Frank McCool and Howie Meeker) in five years from 1942–43 through 1946–47. "The secret of their success is an open secret," pronounced one local newspaper. "More players than anybody else, younger players than anybody else, faster players than anybody else and better conditioned players than anybody else."

"I believe that if you don't put three or four new players on your club every year, you'll go down the chute," opined Conn Smythe. "There are three or four players on the Pittsburgh club who are ready for the Leafs. There are at least three on the Marlboro seniors who are primed for Pittsburgh, and there are four or five ready to move from junior to senior ranks."

The new faces who would debut for the Maple Leafs that fall included Ray Timgren, who had played junior hockey with the Toronto Marlboros, and two recent graduates of the Memorial Cup–winning St. Michael's College Majors — Tod Sloan (a member of the 1945 champs) and Les Costello (who played on Cup winners in 1945 and '47).

Les Costello, from South Porcupine, was a very familiar face to Bill Barilko. Costello had played on the Holman Pluggers team that had won the provincial juvenile title in 1943–44. "My Dad wanted me to stick with education, so naturally, the only place for a good Catholic boy was St. Mike's College [in Toronto]," laughed Costello in the book *Life After Hockey* by Michael A. Smith. "I was influenced at the time by Dave Bauer. He said there were a lot of things to do in life besides hockey, but at the time I wasn't paying too much attention to him." Bauer had been an exceptional junior prospect who answered a higher calling, becoming a priest. Father Bauer went on to coach the St. Mike's juniors to a Memorial Cup championship in 1961, then oversaw the development of Canada's national team.

Costello had actually debuted as a Maple Leaf during the 1948 play-offs, scoring two goals and two assists in five games and getting his name engraved on the Stanley Cup. In 1948–49, Les played 15 games with Toronto before he was sent back to Pittsburgh. "I had been thinking about the priesthood," Costello admitted. "Smythe and the guys were very surprised. It wasn't that I had anything against hockey. It's not that I didn't appreciate the game. There was just something lacking — something tugging at my heart to give something else a chance." Costello joined the seminary in May 1950, and later went on to St. Alphonsus Church in Schumacher, with which he was associated for close to a quarter of a century.

During a dinner for the Flying Fathers, a team of hockey-playing priests Costello co-founded in 1963, Father Les told several of his fellow clergymen about his decision to leave hockey to answer his vocation. "He told us it was a great experience, but he was surprised that once he got to the NHL and won the Stanley Cup, he didn't feel better about it," Father Tim Shea told the *Toronto Star.*

Before his death on December 10, 2002, Father Les was asked about the difference in hockey between the Leafs' dynasty years and the current day. "There were a few who could really skate and shoot in my day, like Ken Reardon, Rocket Richard and Bill Barilko, but now all the players can do it. Is it dirtier? Rougher? Debatable. Who's tougher or stronger than Gordie Howe, Ted Lindsay or Gus Mortson? There were some dirty bastards in our day. I think one thing that has disappeared from the game is bodychecking."

The 1948–49 season opened on October 16, with Boston facing Toronto at Maple Leaf Gardens. Prior to the initial face-off of the season, National Hockey League president Clarence Campbell presented the Vezina Trophy to Leaf netminder Turk Broda, who had registered the lowest goals-against average among NHL goalies in 1947–48. The Bruins beat Toronto 4–1, and Barilko's defence partner Garth Boesch started the season on a sour note by pulling a groin muscle.

In an era when a player's sweater number was tied to his standing on the team, Barilko was assigned number 19 after having worn number 21 in his first two seasons in the league.

Bill played in his second All-Star Game on November 3, in Chicago — by this time, the regular season was already into its third week. The format was the same as the year before: the Stanley Cup champion Leafs again faced a team made up of the NHL's postseason All-Stars. Turk Broda, the First All-Star Team's goalie in 1947–48, remained in the Leafs' lineup, however, his place taken by Bill Durnan of the Canadiens. The other First Team Stars were defencemen "Black Jack" Stewart and Bill Quackenbush, both of Detroit, while Detroit's Ted Lindsay and Maurice Richard and Elmer Lach of the Canadiens occupied the forward line. The balance of the All-Star side that night included Gordie Howe from Detroit; Frankie Brimsek, Milt Schmidt and Woody Dumart of the Bruins; Doug Bentley, Gaye Stewart and Bud Poile of Chicago; Butch Bouchard and Kenny Reardon from Montreal; and Neil Colville, Edgar Laprade and Tony Leswick from the New York Rangers.

Before the game, Syl Apps, now the president of the NHL Pension Fund, announced that $23,018 had been raised for the players' retirement fund.

As they had done in 1947, the NHL All-Stars beat the Maple Leafs, 3–1. All of the game's goals were scored in the second period. Max

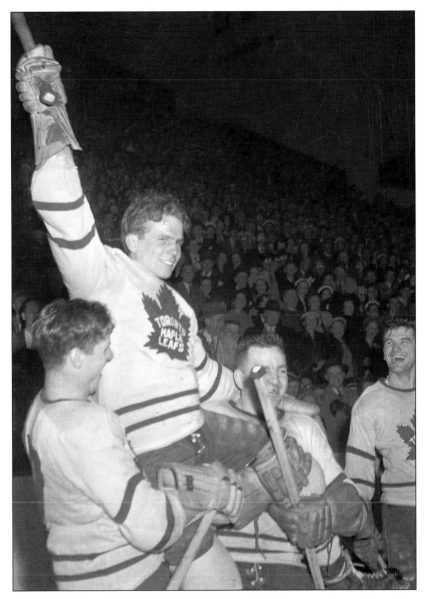

Moments after scoring the deciding goal on April 21, 1951, Bill Barilko was lifted onto the shoulders of teammates Cal Gardner (*left*) and Bill Juzda (*right*). A beaming Harry Watson (*far right*) looks on.
(Imperial Oil-Turofsky/Hockey Hall of Fame)

Three weeks after arriving in Timmins from Poland, Feodosia Karpinchuk married Steve Barilko on January 18, 1925.

(Anne Klisanich collection)

Steve and Feodosia, now known as Faye, welcomed to the world Alexander (*standing*) in 1926 and William (*on his mother's knee*) in 1927. A third child, Annie, was born in 1930.

(Anne Klisanich collection)

Faye Barilko boasted about her little Billy's weight as a baby. That same bottom would later prove devastating to opposing forwards, as Bill used his hips to great effect in halting oncoming rushes.
(Anne Klisanich collection)

The Barilko family managed to get by on Steve's meager income, but Bill (*left, in this 1931 photograph*), Anne (*centre*) and Alex (*right*) never did without because of the indominatable spirit of their mother.
(Anne Klisanich collection)

Thirteen-year-old Billy (*left*) stands with his mother and dapper, older brother, Alex, on a winter's day in 1940.
(Anne Klisanich collection)

Although the siblings are beautifully attired, Anne remembers that these clothes were borrowed for this 1942 photograph. Twelve-year-old 'Pun' stands between Alex (*left*) and Bill (*right*).
(Anne Klisanich collection)

In 1946, Bill (*centre*) and Alex (*right*) were playing in the Pacific Coast Hockey League. Anne (*left*) was still in high school in Timmins, enjoying clothes her brothers brought back for her from California.
(Anne Klisanich collection)

In 1948, Bill (*right*) was starring with the Toronto Maple Leafs and Alex (*left*) with the Toronto Marlboros Seniors. Eighteen-year-old Anne was in Toronto for a visit with her brothers.
(Imperial Oil-Turofsky/ Hockey Hall of Fame)

The Holman Pluggers, Ontario juvenile champions of 1942-43, included Roy McKay (*front, 3rd from left*), Pete Babando (*front, 7th from left*), Eric Prentice (*front, far right*), Bill Barilko (*back, 3rd from left*), Alex Barilko (*back, 4th from left*) and Allan Stanley (*back, 8th from left*). Coach Carlo Cattarello Senior is in the back at the extreme right while mascot Carlo Jr. kneels behind the trophy.

(Hockey Hall of Fame)

Bill truly honed his hockey talents as a member of the Timmins Canadians. Pictured left to right for the juvenile club are coach Wink Wilson, Leo Curik, Rusty Aiken, manager Charlie Arnot, Frip McGonegal and Barilko.

(Anne Klisanich collection)

The newly-signed Barilko attended the training camp of the American Hockey League's Pittsburgh Hornets in 1946. No one dreamed that the raw-boned defenceman would be playing in the NHL within a few months.

(Hockey Hall of Fame)

Bill's development took a quantum leap under the tutelage of Tommy Anderson with the Hollywood Wolves of the Pacific Coast Hockey League.

(Anne Klisanich collection)

Bill indulges in one of his favourite passions prior to joining the Maple Leafs. Even while playing in the NHL, Bill spent his summers in Timmins, fishing whenever he got the opportunity. Ironically, Bill wouldn't eat fish.

(Anne Klisanich collection)

(*below*) Bill relaxes in a rubber dinghy on one of the many lakes that dot the Porcupine's landscape.

(Anne Klisanich collection)

Through 252 regular season contests, Bill Barilko scored 26 goals and added 36 assists for 62 points, while serving 456 penalty minutes. He contributed 5 goals, 7 assists and 12 points, as well as 104 minutes in penalties, in 47 playoff games.

(Imperial Oil-Turofsky/ Hockey Hall of Fame)

Bill Barilko began his minor hockey career as a bespectacled goaltender. By the time he joined the Toronto Maple Leafs during the 1946-47 season, Barilko was a feared defenceman sporting contact lenses.

(Imperial Oil-Turofsky/Hockey Hall of Fame)

On February 6, 1947, Bill Barilko debuted in a Toronto Maple Leafs uniform. That same night, Sid Smith (*left*) was summoned from Pittsburgh and joined Barilko in the Leafs line-up versus Montreal. The Canadiens whipped Toronto that evening, 8-2.

(Imperial Oil-Turofsky/Hockey Hall of Fame)

When Bill was summoned from Hollywood, he was initially paired on the Maple Leafs blueline with veteran Wally Stanowski (*right*).

(Imperial Oil-Turofsky/Hockey Hall of Fame)

Friends opened the newspaper following Bill's first game in Toronto as a Maple Leaf on February 8, 1947 and caught a glimpse of their pal upending Boston's Milt Schmidt with a tremendous bodycheck – something he did frequently when Toronto met the Bruins.
(Imperial Oil-Turofsky/Hockey Hall of Fame)

Sporting Hollywood good looks, Barilko was the frequent target of celebrities who visited Toronto, including figure skating legend, Barbara Ann Scott, who trained in Schumacher's McIntyre Arena during the 1940s.
(Imperial Oil-Turofsky/
Hockey Hall of Fame)

Bill Barilko was no stranger to the penalty box, leading the Maple Leafs in penalty minutes in 1947-48. The Red Wings Gordie Howe is standing behind Barilko in the sin bin.

(Imperial Oil-Turofsky/ Hockey Hall of Fame)

During Barilko's era, penalized players from both teams curiously were placed in the same penalty box. Bill looks up at the photographer while teammates Jimmy Thomson (*far left*), Gus Mortson (*standing*) and Bill Ezinicki (*behind Barilko*) sit out as well. Boston's Ed Harrison (*left*), Clare Martin (#19) and Murray Henderson (#8) are also serving their time during the 1947-48 season.

(Imperial Oil-Turofsky/Hockey Hall of Fame)

The Barilko brothers both found themselves in New York City on January 18, 1948. Alex's Valleyfield Braves defeated the New York Rovers 5-3 while Bill's Leafs tied the Rangers 2-2. Pictured at Nat Harris' Harem are (*left to right*) Howie Meeker, Don Metz, Gus Mortson, Joe Klukay, Alex Barilko, Bill Barilko, Max Bentley, Sid Smith and Garth Boesch.
(Anne Klisanich collection)

Maple Leafs teammates celebrated the wedding of Ted Kennedy to Doreen Dent on June 12, 1948. Standing in the foreground are (*left to right*) Bob Davidson, Bud Poile, Howie Meeker, Gus Bodnar, Tim Daly, Kennedy, Sid Smith, Wally Stanowski, Syl Apps and Turk Broda. The back row shows (*left to right*) Bill Barilko, Gus Mortson and Harry Watson.
(Imperial Oil-Turofsky/Hockey Hall of Fame)

After the retirement of Syl Apps, Ted Kennedy was selected as captain of
the Toronto Maple Leafs beginning with the 1948-49 season. Bill Barilko
holds the captain's sweater while Jim Thomson (*left*), Ted Kennedy
(*centre right*) and Bill Ezinicki (*far right*) look on.
(Imperial Oil-Turofsky/Hockey Hall of Fame)

March 18, 1949 was declared 'Timmins Night' at Maple Leaf Gardens.
Local lads Bep Guidolin of the Blackhawks (*left*) and Bill Barilko (*centre*)
are presented with traveling bags by Tony DelMonte (*center left*), MP Karl
Eyre (*right of Bill*) and Timmins mayor Leo DelVillano.
(Imperial Oil-Turofsky/Hockey Hall of Fame)

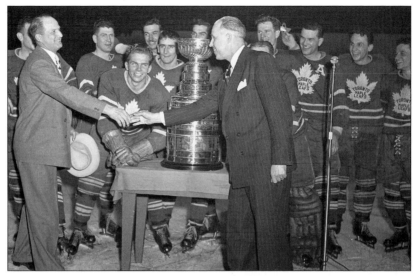

NHL president Clarence Campbell shakes the hand of victorious coach, Hap Day, after the Leafs captured the Stanley Cup in 1949. Barilko leans in, grinning, to the left of hockey's Holy Grail.
(Imperial Oil-Turofsky/Hockey Hall of Fame)

Barilko Brothers Appliances officially opened on June 2, 1949, drawing more than a thousand fans plus Turk Broda (*left*), Harry Watson, Bill Barilko (*holding ribbon, left*), Faye Barilko, coach Hap Day (*cutting ceremonial ribbon*), Alex Barilko and Jimmy Thomson (*holding ribbon, right*).
(Imperial Oil-Turofsky/Hockey Hall of Fame)

Partners on the ice and friends off, Bill Barilko (*left*) and Garth Boesch (*right*) formed a feared pairing on the Leafs blueline before Boesch's retirement in 1950.

(Imperial Oil-Turofsky/ Hockey Hall of Fame)

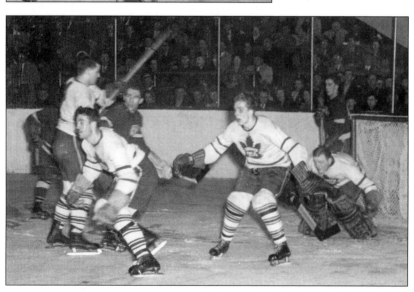

Despite both being stickless, Garth Boesch (*left*) and Bill Barilko (*centre*) protect crouching netminder, Turk Broda. Between 1946-1950, the pairings of Barilko with Boesch plus Jim Thomson with Gus Mortson allowed the Maple Leafs to boast one of the most formidable defence corps in NHL history.

(Imperial Oil-Turofsky/Hockey Hall of Fame)

Bentley's marker for Toronto was sandwiched between goals by Ted Lindsay and Woody Dumart on one side and Gaye Stewart on the other.

The regular season reconvened with the Maple Leafs hosting the Rangers on November 6. It was the first NHL game that Bill would play against his boyhood friend Allan Stanley, who was just breaking in with New York. "I was chasing the puck down the ice going across the blue line, and Bill was playing left defence and he stepped into me and knocked me down. When the play was finished, he skated up to me and said, 'Sorry, Allan.' I looked at him, and I think he was serious. That's how different the game was then to now. Can you imagine anybody saying they're sorry because they knocked you down out there today?"

"We didn't fraternize," Stanley emphasizes. "The policy was that you don't fraternize with the enemy — the other five teams. The very odd one did — it wasn't anything in public and wouldn't be lengthy. Even on the train: we'd travel from Chicago, and maybe Montreal would be on the same train; we'd have to walk through the Montreal car to get to the dining room, and you might nod your head just a touch. Now it's quite different. There were times back then that you'd pass through a car and guys would start fighting."

Stanley's comments are illustrated by a letter Clarence Campbell, the league president, sent to all six NHL teams in November 1948. "It has come to my attention several times recently that there has been a considerable increase in fraternizing between the opposing teams on the ice before the start of the game and occasionally between periods and that, in addition, there has been a considerable amount of fraternizing in public places between competing teams before and after the game.

"There is no specific rule or by-law in our league which prevents this practice, but I am convinced that this is a development which is definitely bad for the welfare of the game and it only breeds suspicion in the minds of the public as to the genuineness of our competition and this is a risk which we certainly cannot afford to take.

"I think the interests of the league and the clubs will be best served by a strict prohibition against these types of fraternizing by the players."

There was certainly no fraternization during the Leafs' November 25 contest against the Canadiens. Gus Mortson of Toronto and Kenny Mosdell of Montreal used their sticks on each other in a vicious fencing match. Maurice Richard leapt onto Mortson's back, and Howie Meeker joined the melee to wrestle Richard. All four were assessed major penalties, but no sooner had play begun again than Kenny Reardon and Joe Klukay began swinging their sticks at each other. Barilko jumped in and fought Reardon, while Klukay took on Billy Reay. Garth Boesch and Hal Laycoe paired off in a side match. Ten majors in all were handed out in this 2–0 Leaf victory.

On New Year's Day, fans experienced a sense of déjà vu. With Montreal visiting Toronto, another stick-swinging incident occurred. Cal Gardner and Kenny Reardon viciously attacked each other with their sticks, and the two were fined and suspended for the next game between the two teams. The fight was at the core of an animosity that simmered through the two players' entire careers, and in fact the hard feelings would last for decades.

From the first of December until Christmas Day, the Leafs won but three of their nine contests. And their situation went from bad to worse on December 26 when, during practice, Howie Meeker cut in front of the net, stepped on Bill Ezinicki's stick and went crashing headfirst into the boards. Meeker broke his collarbone and missed most of the remainder of the season.

Not only were they losing with a consistency that worried the hometown faithful, but they were losing manpower at an alarming rate. By mid-January, the entire KLM Line was on the sidelines — Ted Kennedy with a bruised back, Vic Lynn with a shoulder separation and Howie Meeker still recuperating from his fractured collarbone.

A bright spot for the slumping Leafs occurred on December 5, when Turk Broda earned a 2–0 shutout against the Blackhawks in Chicago. It was Broda's third shutout in his last six games. The win was accompanied by a comedic interlude after a Chicago fan, who had smuggled a rabbit into the Stadium, let it loose on the ice; in a scene reminiscent of a Keystone Kops movie, the players chased the frightened hare, but it was Barilko who caught the rabbit.

In a hotly contested game between the Leafs and Wings on February 12, a fan shouted to Max Bentley, "Hey Maxie, if you score on this shift, I'll give you a horse!" An astonished Bentley cocked his head and looked back to where the fan was seated. It was Charlie Hemstead, whom Max knew from the racetrack. Bentley smiled — he loved the ponies. Twenty seconds into that second-period shift, with the game tied at one, Max fired the puck past Harry Lumley. He grinned at Ray Timgren and Joe Klukay, his wingers on the Three Feathers Line, then skated over to Hemstead, who was sitting at ice level. "Thank you, Charlie," Max laughed, shaking his hand. "George McCullagh promised me a horse, too."

McCullagh, who had just purchased the Toronto *Telegram*, was a part owner of the Toronto Maple Leafs and he sat on the Maple Leaf Gardens board of directors. McCullagh and his family lived on a 100-acre estate north of Toronto, where they kept horses.

Bentley's two racehorses, Royal Hem from Charlie Hemstead and Filalo from George McCullagh, were both later claimed on him.

All that season, the ill will between Montreal and Toronto was palpable, and such was the case for their game on February 17. *Les*

Canadiens targeted Barilko, who had put both Ken Reardon and Normand Dussault out of action — both Habs were carried off the ice on stretchers after finding themselves on the wrong end of Barilko hits. The Montreal *Herald* chastised Barilko and the Leafs, writing, "When in one game, two hockey players can receive crippling injuries through being tossed into the boards with no penalties being meted out in return, it's time to do a little inquiring into what goes on here." Maurice Richard took a run at Barilko later in the game and was handed a charging penalty, but nothing more transpired.

Then, three nights later, Vic Lynn was carried off the ice on a stretcher after he was cracked over the head by Red Hamill of the Blackhawks. Hamill was suspended for one game and handed a fine of $250. That same night, Meeker returned to the Leafs' lineup after a six-weeks absence, only to take a slash from Ralph Nattrass that broke a bone in his foot. Meeker's *annus horribilis* had come to a disappointing conclusion.

While his team was battling to earn a playoff spot, Bill Barilko was playing his best hockey since entering the National Hockey League. King Clancy, the Hall of Fame defenceman, was an NHL referee during the late 1940s. During the playoff drive, he gave credit to the Maple Leafs' catalyst: "As goes Barilko, so goes the Leafs," he stated.

During an interview with Wes McKnight of CFRB radio in Toronto towards the end of the regular season, Barilko was asked to name the toughest forwards he had faced. "Why, I'd have to say Maurice Richard, Doug Bentley and Jimmy Conacher, who I haven't caught yet." There weren't many who Barilko didn't catch. Sportswriters called it "getting Barilkoed," and Milt Schmidt certainly knew what the term meant. He was hit so hard so many times by the Leafs defenceman that Fern Flaman, who was a teammate of both Schmidt and Barilko during his career, recalls: "Bill was one of the more devastating body checkers. He used his hip an awful lot. He used to own Milt Schmidt at the time. Milt was one of the great players, but Milt could never get around him, and Billy kind of enjoyed that."

Had the New York Rangers and Chicago Blackhawks not finished the season so dismally, Toronto — with a record of 22 wins, 25 losses and 13 ties for 57 points over the 60-game schedule — might very well have missed the playoffs in 1948–49. As it was, they claimed a playoff spot by finishing fourth. Despite the injuries that had marred the lineup for the better part of the season, the Maple Leafs limped into the postseason.

The Leafs' season was not devoid of bright spots. Harry Watson, who led the Maple Leafs in scoring with 26 goals and 45 points, placed seventh in the league's individual scoring race and tied for second overall in goals. Even competitors recognized Watson's talent. Kenny Reardon of the Canadiens said, "Watson's speed, weight and skill are always a handful." And amazingly, given the violence that marked many Leafs' games, Watson got through the entire campaign without drawing a single penalty.

Watson, Max Bentley and defencemen Gus Mortson, Jimmy Thomson and Bill Barilko each played in all 60 games in 1948–49. Bill scored five goals and assisted on four others for nine points. His 95 penalty minutes were second on the team to Leafs — and league-leader, Bill Ezinicki, who collected 145 minutes in penalties.

※　※　※

As the playoffs arrived, it was readily assumed that the first-place Detroit Red Wings would break Toronto's Stanley Cup streak. But the feisty Leafs had other ideas.

Toronto faced the second-place Boston Bruins in the opening round. Although Boston finished nine points ahead of the Leafs in the standings, the teams had been a fair match for each other during the regular-season series. In 12 games, the Leafs had won six times, Boston five, and there was one draw.

In the final game of the regular season, the Bruins had walloped the Leafs 7–2, but when the playoffs opened two nights later on March 22, Toronto was all over the Bruins like ugly on an ape, shutting out the Bruins 3–0 in Boston. Harry Watson stepped up and fired two goals, while Max Bentley picked up the third and playoff veteran Turk Broda recorded the shutout.

In game two, also at the Boston Garden, Harry Watson again scored a pair of goals as the Leafs edged Boston 3–2.

The series shifted to Toronto for the third game, but the Bruins wouldn't lie down. Both teams exploded offensively, and when the dust cleared, Boston had prevailed, 5–4. Boston's Woody Dumart scored the overtime winner — his second goal of the game — at 16:14.

Sid Smith was summoned from Pittsburgh to add some spark to the Leafs' line-up for game four. After scoring 55 goals and 112 points with the Hornets in the AHL, he was inserted beside Ted Kennedy and proceeded to score twice and assist on a third goal in a 3–1 Leaf win. In the book *Come On, Teeder*, Ed Fitkin called Smith "lightning on skates; a darting, devilish will o' the wisp." Fans called him just what the doctor ordered.

The Maple Leafs eliminated the Bruins on March 30 in Boston with a narrow 3–2 victory. During the third period, the Bruins' fans littered the ice to the point that both teams were sent to their dressing rooms for close to 20 minutes while the ice surface was cleared.

Next up was Detroit — the league leaders would tackle the defending Stanley Cup champions to see who would lay claim to the World Championship in 1949.

The series opened April 8 at the Olympia in Detroit. Although it took 17:31 of overtime to lay claim to the win, Toronto edged the Red Wings 3–2. Ray Timgren outbattled the Wings for the puck and rifled a goalmouth pass to Joe Klukay, who put the puck in the net.

Game two could have been called the Sid Smith Show. The team's sole Toronto-born player, who had appeared in just one regular-season game with the Leafs, scored all three goals in a 3–1 Leafs win. Nicknamed "Muff" by his mates, Smith scored all three of his goals on Toronto power plays. On the second goal, he deflected a shot by Barilko past netminder Harry Lumley.

Games three and four were to be played at Maple Leaf Gardens. Toronto won the third one, again by a 3–1 margin. Gus Mortson was masterful, hitting everything that moved and adding an insurance goal in the second period. Then, Mortson and his defence mates held the Red Wings to just four shots in the third period.

In the final game of the season, April 16, 1949, Detroit coach Jack Adams brought canisters of oxygen to the Wings' bench, hoping the infusion of O_2 would perk up his deflated Detroit squad. Instead, "the Leafs just skated and hammered their rivals into the pipes," according to the *Toronto Star*. The Maple Leafs swept the Wings in four straight games, registering a third consecutive 3–1 victory. Cal Gardner scored the Stanley Cup–winning goal at 19:45 of the second period.

With the victory, the Toronto Maple Leafs became the first team in the storied history of the National Hockey League to win three successive Stanley Cup championships. In fact, only Detroit (1935–36 and 1936–37) and the Montreal Canadiens (1929–30 and '30–31) had even won back-to-back Stanley Cup championships.

As the third period ended, the band began playing "Happy Days Are Here Again." "Black Jack" Stewart led the Wings over to congratulate Toronto. A table was carried to centre ice and the Stanley Cup was placed upon it — that the Cup was present in the building was a notable break from the tradition of the past two springs. League president Clarence Campbell congratulated Conn Smythe, Hap Day and the Toronto Maple Leafs on their accomplishment. As is customary, the winning captain stepped forward to receive the Cup. "I don't know what to say," Ted Kennedy mumbled. "This is one of the greatest thrills of my life. We owe a great deal to Mr. Smythe and Hap Day for being here and to you fans for standing by us. There was a time earlier in the season when it looked like we might not even make the playoffs. But here we are — and there's the Cup. That's all I can say." The Toronto faithful responded with an outpouring of verbal appreciation, and Teeder's teammates surrounded him, patting him on the back as they ran their hands over the Stanley Cup. Tim Daly, the Leafs' trainer, laughed heartily. "I don't know why you guys are so excited at winning the Stanley Cup. We do it every year!"

"That was really a thrill, to be able to hold the Cup," Kennedy recalls today.

The fans began to chant, "We want Meeker! We want Meeker!" Howie hobbled out onto the ice surface and waved to the fans. Later that evening, Howie and his wife Grace hosted a party for the players at their apartment on Avenue Road in Toronto's downtown core. "We must have had 150 to 200 people there," Meeker related in his biography *Golly Gee — It's Me!* "At 5 a.m., we ran out of beer and the police there said 'no problem' and made a phone call. A few minutes later, a police van pulled up and out came some 250 beers, so that kept the party going."

Anyone with even a loose connection to Maple Leaf Gardens was in attendance at the Meekers' party. Hap Day, a teetotaller, opted for "a nice cold glass of milk" rather than champagne or beer, but he and Syl Apps were the only abstainers. During the festivities, the family dog got out and ran away; a quartet of policemen arrived at the door half an hour later with the pet in tow.

This was Day's fifth championship as a coach. He had been behind the bench for victories in 1942, 1945, 1947, 1948 and 1949 — an impressive run of five in eight years. Day had also played on a Stanley Cup champion as part of the crew that won the Maple Leafs' first Cup in 1932. Day's son Kerry, the club's mascot, had also been part of the three championship seasons.

"Everybody on the team was just elated, knowing that we were the first NHL team to win three Stanley Cups in a row," Gus Mortson recalls. "The funny thing is, most of the boys on the team were under 25 and went on to win another Cup in 1951."

Indeed, of those who played on all Cup-winning teams, Turk Broda was the elder statesman at 35. The rest of the club's core was very young. Garth Boesch was 27 and Joe Klukay 26. Both Bill Ezinicki and Harry Watson were 25. Captain Ted Kennedy was just 24, as were Vic Lynn and Gus Mortson. Sid Smith and Howie Meeker were only 23. And the two youngest Leaf stalwarts were also two of the toughest — both Jimmy Thomson and Bill Barilko were just 22 years of age.

"Broda was the best playoff goaltender I've ever seen," exclaimed Howie Meeker. "He was 70 percent of the reason we won that third Cup." Ted Kennedy agreed. "Turk was a great goalkeeper but he seemed to be able to go up another notch when we went to the Stanley Cup final."

Teeder Kennedy had collected eight playoff points to lead the Leafs, while Harry Watson and Max Bentley both tallied four goals apiece. Gordie Howe of the Red Wings led all playoff performers, totalling 11 points on eight goals and three assists in 11 games. His teammate, "Black Jack" Stewart, led the penalty parade with 32 minutes. The battling Bills — Barilko and Ezinicki — tied with 20 minutes each to lead Toronto. In nine games, Barilko recorded one assist.

The Toronto Maple Leafs gathered for their official Stanley Cup team photograph 36 hours after winning hockey's most prized trophy. The city hosted a reception for the champions, and Controller Allan Lamport stated, "We owe these young Canadians our heartiest congratulations on their success. They are a tribute to the type of athlete Canada is producing!"

Besides winning the Stanley Cup, each member of the championship Maple Leafs team collected $150 for finishing fourth in the standings, $1,000 for defeating Detroit in the semifinal and an additional $1,000 for winning the Stanley Cup. In addition, each of the Maple Leaf players received a sterling silver platter, a sterling silver rose bowl, a cigarette box and tabletop lighter, an engraved gold wristwatch, a water pitcher and a Stanley Cup ring.

The awarding of a championship ring did not originate in the 1940s, but it certainly gained in popularity at that time. The Leafs had begun the tradition with the 1947 Stanley Cup title. Because the Leafs won the Cup in three consecutive seasons, management did not award new rings each time; instead, with each subsequent victory, the owners took the rings back long enough to replace the diamond with a larger stone.

Asked years later to name the greatest team with which he had ever been involved, Leaf owner Conn Smythe didn't hesitate. "The 1948–49 squad — that was the greatest Maple Leaf team ever."

"The Maple Leafs were a glittering national treasure; as Canadian as prairie wheat fields and lonely northern lakes," wrote William Houston in *Inside Maple Leaf Gardens*. "They symbolized excellence and a winning tradition. In English Canada, they were the country's most popular team — in any sport."

No team in the history of the National Hockey League had ever won three consecutive Stanley Cup championships before the Toronto Maple Leafs. What was to have been a rebuilding phase had produced three seasons of winning hockey's most prized trophy. The players were still young, but they had gelled sensationally and, all things being equal, looked unstoppable for several years to come. And with the farm system producing outstanding prospects, there was no imagining how long the string of championships could extend.

But reality tends to get in the way of dreams.

CHAPTER
10
Heartbreak
(1949–50)

"Gus Mortson and Bill Barilko of the Maple Leafs will fly into Northern Ontario bushlands in search of uranium at the conclusion of the Stanley Cup playoff," reported the *Globe and Mail*. The plan for the two northern Ontario defencemen during the summer of 1949 was to prospect in the vast Canadian northland. Mortson had been prospecting during the off-season for several years. Barilko had no experience.

"Gosh," said Barilko in the *Globe* article. "I hope we don't get lost."

"You think you're going to look for uranium," interjected Leafs netminding prospect Baz Bastien, "but if you take Barilko, you'll be looking for him all the time!"

As it turned out, the summer would hold a different adventure for Bill Barilko.

* * *

Traffic along Toronto's Danforth Avenue was crawling by the inch on Thursday, June 2, 1949 — much to the aggravation of drivers trying to escape downtown for the city's east end, but to the absolute delight of Alex and Bill Barilko. That evening was the official opening of Barilko Brothers Appliances at 167 Danforth Avenue.

The store's grand opening was a huge event in Toronto, as several members of the Stanley Cup champion Toronto Maple Leafs attended to support their teammate's new venture. Coach Hap Day cut the ceremonial white ribbon to officially open the store, while Jimmy Thomson, Harry Watson, Turk Broda and Gus Mortson looked on.

Faye Barilko came down from Timmins for the opening of her sons' store. Bill's girlfriend, Louise Hastings, and Jimmy Thomson's girlfriend, June McKinnon, were there, too. "We were all there on opening night," recalls Louise. "We sat on wooden chairs lined up in a row." More than a thousand visitors spilled onto the street, elbowing their way through the throng to get a better glimpse of the hockey players. Each visitor went home with a small souvenir cardboard hockey stick printed with "Barilko Bros., 167 Danforth" and the phone numbers, Riverdale 2491 and 2492.

Tagged "The House of Champions," Barilko Brothers' storefront was 25 feet wide and 100 feet deep. The store sold refrigerators and stoves, radios and records, some of Toronto's earliest television sets, as well as sporting goods, including shotguns and — naturally — fishing tackle. The store was painted grey and wine with a white ceiling, and the walls were papered in a floral pattern.

Prior to the Barilkos' endeavour, the shop on Danforth Avenue had housed Mayfair Radio, and before that, 167 Danforth had been the long-time home of the Globe Slicing Machine Company and Artcraft Signs.

Earlier in the year, Ed Whittaker, a vice president of Admiral Appliances, had approached the Barilko boys about becoming involved in a store that would carry the Admiral line of appliances. Bill and Alex discussed the venture between themselves, then agreed to put their money on the line and their names on the business. They would be as involved in the day-to-day operations as two hockey players who were on the road seven months a year could be. A partnership was formed between the Barilko boys, Ed Whittaker, his brother, Art, who took on the role of store manager, and George Ellies, who became the assistant manager. Dorothy Patry was brought on board to oversee the record department. "Bill had met a couple of hockey fans in the appliance business. He and Alex opened Barilko Brothers store," Gus Mortson recalls. "Alex was playing for the Marlboro Seniors and Bill was with the Leafs. There were two fellas who really ran the store for Bill [Ellies and Whittaker]. Bill would go up to the store quite often to help them."

Bill moved into a rented room on the second floor of the Eton Hotel at 710 Danforth, a few blocks east of his appliance store. He promised to do whatever he could to ensure the store's success.

An advertisement from that time vowed the participation of the Barilko Brothers:

> SPORTS FANS!
> If you're in the market for any kind of electric appliance, radio or even a television set, why not visit our store and let us see if we can accommodate you.
> Either Alex or myself are usually on hand to look after you. Incidentally why not let us install a television

set in your home for a free 3-day trial demonstration.

Hope to see you soon.

Sincerely,
Bill Barilko

Bill guaranteed his teammates that any Leaf who registered a hat trick would receive an Admiral television set. Turk Broda called out, "Hey, what about me? Don't I get a chance at a television set?" Barilko laughed. "Yeah, sure. I tell you what: I'll give you an Admiral TV with every shutout!"

That season, Broda blanked the opposition nine times! He took just one television set from Bill, collecting his prize after an October 27 shutout over Montreal. Harry Watson received a TV for a three-goal performance in the very next game — an 8–1 romp against Boston on October 29.

Towards the end of the summer, Bill boasted of two summer victories. "Yes, I signed my contract this week and also sold Mr. Smythe a television set and a refrigerator." The store even sponsored the pro hockey players' softball team that summer.

Not everyone was excited about the business venture. "Alex got Bill involved in that store against our mother's wishes," states the boys' sister, Anne. "My mother said, 'Why you no ask me first?' She wondered why the boys were getting into something they knew nothing about. She said, 'You play hockey. That's enough! Who going to run store?'

"My mother had no education, but she had a great deal of common sense. She said, 'No, I no want you should open store. No sign nuttink.' But much to her dismay, they said, 'Mom, we've already signed the papers. We thought Anne would come down and run the store.' I was only 18 or 19; Mother thought I was too young to move to the big city to run my brothers' store.

"It was frightening for me even to think about. I had a good job back home — I was the secretary to the mayor of Timmins. I was very happy in the field of work I was in. Mother wasn't happy. I remember her asking, 'Why you sign and no ask me?' I told them, 'You've got hockey and you should concentrate on that.'"

"I don't know why, but they opened that appliance store," says Louise Carley, Bill's girlfriend at that time. "I have no idea. It didn't last very long. They just weren't around to run it properly."

The brothers ran the store for a couple of years, but after Bill's death it became a source of much heartache for Anne and Mrs. Barilko. "When Bill died, we were so upset, we didn't care what happened to the store. In fact, we didn't want anything to do with the store."

In 1953, two years after Bill's disappearance, the sign on the front of the store was changed from "Barilko Brothers" to "Koury Television and Appliances."

❦ ❦ ❦

During that summer of 1949, Bill Barilko spoke at a number of gatherings. "First off, you've got to stay healthy," he told several groups of boys and young men. "Smoking and drinking are not good for your body." He talked about hockey skills, too. "It is important to skate well. I was not a very good skater myself when I was young, but I worked at it — hard — and it really has made a difference." Barilko spoke about developing good stickhandling skills and the benefits of a hard shot. He then urged young players to "use your head when playing. You can play an effective game without being sent to the penalty box." The appreciative crowd laughed at Bill's suggestion, knowing how much time he had spent watching his teammates from the Leafs' penalty box.

Turk Broda, Harry Watson and Jimmy Thomson joined Bill at the YMCA for three weeks to prepare for training camp. Bill reported to camp weighing 190 pounds — his heaviest playing weight yet. Both Mortson and Thomson arrived heavier, too, but the Leafs' management were pleased that all three young defencemen had added bulk. Conversely, there was concern that Bill Juzda, who arrived at camp heavier than anyone else, might be carrying too much weight.

As had become tradition, training camp was held in St. Catharines. It was not a tame affair, as established players laboured mightily to get back into playing shape while others were hell-bent on earning a roster spot. On September 19, in the very first practice of the 1949 camp, goaltender Baz Bastien was struck by a puck and was blinded in his right eye, ending his playing career.

Naturally, Bill was dead serious about training camp. He spared no one, not even his teammates, from being "Barilkoed." Cal Gardner remembers an exhibition game of shinny during Leafs camp: "Bill was skating backwards, and when I shifted by one guy, he turned around and hit me straight up with his forehead. It broke my cheekbone."

The summer had been a busy one for former Maple Leaf bachelors, as Bill Ezinicki, Ray Timgren and Joe Klukay all got married. And on September 30, just days before the season opener, Gus Mortson also took a bride. Bill Barilko was one of the few eligible Leafs remaining on that young squad.

❦ ❦ ❦

On October 10, 1949, Bill Barilko played in what was to be his third and final All-Star Game. For the third year in a row, the game would see the

Maple Leafs, as defending Stanley Cup champions, face off against the NHL All-Stars, led by First Team All-Stars Bill Durnan of Montreal in goal; Bill Quackenbush and "Black Jack" Stewart, both of Detroit, on defence; and a forward line of Roy Conacher (Chicago), Maurice Richard (Montreal) and Sid Abel (Detroit).

Bill, again wearing number 19, opened the scoring at 15:22 of the first period; it would prove to be Toronto's only goal of the contest. It was also the sole point Barilko earned in his three All-Star Games. The NHL All-Stars, meanwhile, countered with tallies by Bob Goldham, Paul Ronty and Doug Bentley to finish with a 3–1 win.

❧ ❧ ❧

As the Maple Leafs embarked on the 1949–50 regular-season schedule — to which the league had added 10 games for a total of 70, the longest to that date in NHL history — the roster was virtually identical to the one that had skated off with the Stanley Cup the previous spring. The few changes included the trading of Tod Sloan and Harry Taylor to the Cleveland Barons of the AHL, while Les Costello and Frank Mathers spent the season with Toronto's AHL club in Pittsburgh. Over the course of the season, Fleming MacKell and Rudy Migay would be introduced into the Toronto lineup.

The October 15 home opener began, as it traditionally did, with an on-ice appearance by the 48th Highlanders, who performed "The Maple Leaf Forever." Once the ice surface was cleared of pipers and drummers, the puck was dropped and Chicago and Toronto fought to a 4–4 tie.

Through the first month and a half of the season, the Leafs looked solid, although certainly not spectacular. One bright spot was the play of goaltender Turk Broda, who earned three shutouts in the first full month of the 1949–50 season. But then the Maple Leafs' fortunes sank. On November 16 in a game against Montreal, Cal Gardner broke his jaw for the second time that season when he was hit by archenemy Kenny Reardon.

Despite playing an aggressive, physical game, Bill Barilko had been largely free of injury to that point in his career. But he tore knee ligaments hitting defenceman Clare Martin in a game against Detroit. The check, which the *Toronto Daily Star* reported "folded Martin like a camp cot," cost Barilko three weeks on the injured list.

Pentti Lund, the second Finn to play in the National Hockey League (Albert Pudas was first, with Toronto in 1926–27), had a strong couple of seasons with the New York Rangers in 1948–49 and 1949–50. The slick, playmaking winger who won the Calder Trophy as the NHL's top rookie in 1949, later was a sportswriter with the now-defunct *Times-News* in Thunder Bay. He described Bill Barilko's on-ice performance as "rampageous," an outstanding adjective that is defined as "characterized by violence and passion; unruly."

The Chicago Blackhawks beat Toronto 6–3 on November 27. At this point, the Leafs hadn't won a game since a 1–0 shutout of Montreal on the 16th, losing five times and tying once. During the slump, the Maple Leafs were forced to take a backseat to the football Argonauts, who were monopolizing the sports pages. To regain his team's place amongst local sports fans, Conn Smythe responded with the famous "Battle of the Bulge" campaign. "Apparently, we're running a fat man's team," the manager told the Toronto *Telegram.* Smythe zeroed in on defenceman Garth Boesch, forwards Vic Lynn, Howie Meeker and Sid Smith, and especially goaltender Turk Broda. "Get rid of those excess pounds if you have to hack them off with a carving knife or suffer the consequences," Smythe warned. "If I can't get the good players to improve, I'll bring up the young ones and at least give the fans the enjoyment of seeing them improve.

"Broda weighs 197 pounds. I'm taking him out of the nets and he's not going back until he shows some common sense," Conn Smythe scolded. Broda had played 244 consecutive games for Toronto since returning from his military service and was now being ordered to drop seven pounds. "He's not getting any younger," continued Smythe. "He should know his reflexes are going to slow faster when he's carrying all that excess weight."

Although Smythe, with tongue planted firmly in cheek, was known for pulling pranks via the local press, it appeared that this time he might be more than a little serious. The mercurial manager summoned goaltender Gil Mayer from the Pittsburgh Hornets and purchased another netminder, Al Rollins, from the AHL's Cleveland Barons. Smythe announced that Mayer would play the next game and remain in net until Broda lost the required weight. "I don't care if we lose 500–0, although I don't think we will," stated Smythe. The physical contrast between Broda and Mayer couldn't have been greater; Mayer, nicknamed "The Needle," weighed a mere 130 pounds.

The press had a field day with the story. Readers submitted recipes that might aid the "corpulent" Broda in shedding the excess avoirdupois. The Turofsky Brothers snapped staged shot after staged shot of Turk at the dinner table, about to lunge into a meager meal while his beautiful, slim wife Betty and their little girls all ate heartily.

In spite of the hoopla, Gil Mayer played just one game, a 2–0 loss to Detroit on December 1, 1949. Broda returned on December 3, weighing in at a svelte 189 pounds, and promptly shut out the Rangers 2–0. But the ploy had had its effect, and in fact it set the stage for the goaltending platoon system that Smythe would inaugurate in 1950–51.

Outside the sideshow spotlight, Bill Barilko was enjoying an excellent season, playing alongside Bill Juzda on a more regular basis after an injury to Garth Boesch. Juzda and Barilko became the Leafs' best defence pairing that season, and upon his return Boesch ended up relegated to fifth on the team's blueline depth chart. The Juzda-Barilko tandem was likely the toughest in the National Hockey League. The *Toronto Star* considered Bill's game against the Red Wings on January 22 "the finest performance of this semester." Using his body effectively and regularly, Barilko helped the Leafs win 1–0 that evening.

Although he hit everything in sight in his own zone, Bill occasionally lent his skills to the offence, too. In a 9–1 demolition of the Blackhawks on January 28, Barilko scored on a long ice-level slap shot on the goalie's glove side. He scored again on February 5, this time potting the winning goal in a 2–1 victory over the Bruins. Barilko sent a long, drifting shot towards the Bruins' net late in the second period. The puck found its way through a maze of players in front of goalie Red Henry, then found the back of the net. As Barilko shot, a Bruin slashed him on the hand, numbing it temporarily, but there was no further damage.

As fierce a competitor as he was on the ice, Barilko could be an equally cool customer away from the rink. An ice show was being staged at Maple Leaf Gardens in January 1950, so the Leafs held their morning skates at Varsity Arena. One morning, Bill was standing in the shower after practice, singing his own parodied words to popular songs, when a firecracker was thrown into the dressing room. While his teammates ran and ducked for cover, Barilko barely missed a beat, finishing his song as he rinsed the soap off his chest.

Early in the first period of a February 19 game at Madison Square Garden, Howie Meeker tussled with Rangers goaltender Charlie Rayner in front of the net. Jimmy Thomson skated in and got into a shouting match with Rayner, and during the first intermission, the two began to fight in the corridor that led to both teams' dressing rooms. Gus Mortson jumped in, but coach Lynn Patrick cold-cocked him with a fist to the face, cutting Mortson's lower lip. Meeker grabbed Patrick, who rewarded Howie with a punch to the side of the head for his trouble. Then Mortson and Patrick went at it; it took six stitches to close the gash to Patrick's fist. Even spectators heading for the corridors got into the midst of the scrap.

"I guess our tempers were a little hot," admitted Jimmy Thomson afterwards.

Late in the game, with the Rangers ahead 2–1, coach Hap Day pulled goalie Turk Broda in favour of an extra attacker. New York's netminder, Charlie Rayner, snagged the loose puck, skated with it up to the blue line and fired at the empty net, missing by inches. Had his shot found the net, he would have been the first NHL goaltender to score a goal. As it was, it would be another 30 years before a netminder earned that distinction. On November 28, 1979, in a game between the

Colorado Rockies and New York Islanders, a delayed penalty was called against the Islanders. The Rockies pulled their goalie. Deep in Islanders territory, Colorado defenceman Rob Ramage fired an errant pass towards the point, and it sailed the length of the ice into the empty net. Goaltender Billy Smith had been the last Islander to touch the puck, so he was credited with the goal.

Bill Barilko earned the only penalty shot of his career on March 1, 1950, against the Boston Bruins. Facing the Bruins' rookie netminder, Jack Gelineau, he skated in from centre ice, dropped his right shoulder in a deke, then fired a goal in a 5–2 Leaf win. It was Bill Barilko's third goal in just over a month.

In mid-March, the Leafs and Blackhawks played a home-and-home set. In the first game, played March 15 in Chicago, Frank Brimsek shut out Toronto 4–0. Three nights later in Toronto, the Leafs edged Chicago 2–1 to gain some manner of revenge. That evening was Timmins Night at Maple Leaf Gardens, and 200 fans from the Porcupine rode buses south to Toronto and descended on the Gardens for the event. Native sons Bill Barilko of the Leafs and Bep Guidolin of the Hawks were presented with overnight valises by Timmins Mayor Leo del Villano, Tony Delmonte from Timmins and Karl Eyre, a member of Parliament from Cochrane. It was a proud night for Bill's sister, Anne, and Guidolin's two married sisters who made the excursion. "There was a nice ceremony before the game and Mr. Eyre presented both boys with travelling bags. Bill was quite a standout that night," remembers Anne, who two weeks later was crowned Queen Esther at the prestigious Purim Ball at the Riverside Pavillion in Timmins.

Bill Barilko enjoyed a career season, with seven goals and 10 assists for 17 points — his most productive season in the NHL. He had also cut his penalty minutes back substantially, drawing only 85 minutes, his lowest total since his 18-game debut in the NHL. Teammate Bill Ezinicki again lead the NHL's penalty parade with 144 minutes.

At the conclusion of the regular season, the Detroit Red Wings proved to be the elite of the NHL, recording 88 points, a healthy 11-point margin over the runners-up from Montreal. It was the second year in a row that the Wings had captured the regular-season crown. Toronto was third with 74 points, and the New York Rangers, who had not seen postseason activity since their first-place finish in 1941–42, were fourth. As a result, the Rangers challenged Montreal while the Maple Leafs would try to overtake the strong Red Wings.

❦ ❦ ❦

The first- and third-place teams met on March 28 at the Olympia in Detroit for game one of their semifinal series. The teams had fared comparably on defence — the Wings allowing 164 goals to Toronto's 173 — but Detroit boasted the league's most potent offence in 1949–50, with 229 goals, 53 more than the Leafs. Leading the way were the three members of Detroit's famed Production Line — Ted Lindsay, Sid Abel and Gordie Howe, who had claimed the top three spots in the individual scoring race, in that order. By contrast, Toronto's top scorer, Sid Smith, had come in 15th.

It was also destined to be a rugged series; a strong rivalry existed between the two teams, who had met in the Stanley Cup finals four times in the 1940s, and the Red Wings were as tough as they were skilled (an image reinforced, perhaps inadvertently, by Jack Adams's decision to trade All-Star defenceman Bill Quackenbush, the 1949 winner of the Lady Byng Trophy for sportsmanship and gentlemanly play, prior to the regular season).

At the 11-minute mark of the first period, Barilko tussled with Gordie Howe, and both were dispatched to the penalty box for two minutes.

Just 10 seconds into the second period, Joe Klukay scored for the Maple Leafs, assisted by Barilko and Bentley. The rough play continued, and with Ted Lindsay on the penalty bench for roughing Toronto goalie Turk Broda, Barilko scored at 8:49 to earn his second point of the night. He also drew an interference penalty at 12:20. Roughly three minutes later, Howe and Bill Juzda went at it hammer and tongs, and both were sent off with fighting majors.

Going into the third period up 3–0, Toronto continued to capitalize on Detroit's overly aggressive play. But the game was clearly overshadowed by a serious third-period head injury to Gordie Howe. The Detroit star suffered a broken nose, broken cheekbone, fractured skull and scratched eyeball when he crashed into the boards at 8:41. Carried from the ice on a stretcher and immediately rushed to Harper Hospital — accompanied by his brother Vic, Detroit coach Jack Adams and club owner James Norris — Howe underwent emergency surgery to relieve pressure in his brain. The operation was successful, and Gordie was wheeled out of surgery at 2:30 that morning.

On the ice, meantime, the Wings immediately ganged up on Ted Kennedy, whom they blamed for injuring their star forward. Howe's linemates Sid Abel and Ted Lindsay both slashed and tripped the Leafs captain, who was already limping after crashing into a goalpost in the second period. Toronto coach Hap Day pulled Teeder off the ice. The game was already in the record books as a Toronto victory when ruffians Ezinicki and Barilko squared off against Steve Black and "Black Jack" Stewart of the Wings at 18:47. The game ended in a 5–0 Leaf road win.

Detroit tried to exact revenge on Toronto in game two, both for the loss and for what the players felt had been a deliberate attempt on

Kennedy's part to injure Gordie Howe. Although it was considered a draw in terms of physical play, the Wings tied the series with a 3–1 victory. Toronto *Telegram* sportswriter Bobby Hewitson wrote, "What the 14,297 fans saw at the Olympia last night was not hockey, the fastest sport in the world. If it was, then it wasn't just rough hockey. It was plain dirty hockey — the kind that has no place in sport."

Detroit was up 3–0 in the last minute of the second period when Ted Kennedy was knocked down by Detroit's Lee Fogolin, then cross-checked by Ted Lindsay. The incident only served to pour gasoline on a smouldering fire. While Lindsay mauled Kennedy near the boards, Leo Reise struck Teeder with his stick. Meanwhile, a fan pounded Kennedy in the head with his fist. Jimmy Thomson charged over to even the sides and had his eyes blackened when Reise's stick struck him in the face, causing a five-stitch cut over his left eye. A bleeding Thomson left the game, and was unable to return. Kennedy and Reise left for their respective dressing rooms, both suffering from facial gashes. Order was temporarily restored, but there were still 20 minutes of hockey to complete.

Fleming MacKell broke Harry Lumley's shutout bid just past the five-minute mark of the third, but it was clear that neither side cared about the score at that point. Bill Juzda and Jimmy McFadden fought early in the period, followed shortly thereafter by McFadden and Meeker. Then, with less than a minute until the final buzzer, a donnybrook broke out. Ted Lindsay and Bill Ezinicki threw haymakers at each other, which prompted a further battle between Steve Black and Bill Barilko. All four earned minors for roughing and were sent to their respective dressing rooms. As he was leaving the ice, Lindsay coldcocked Bill Juzda, and the two combatants engaged in a flurry of fists. Gus Mortson and Lee Fogolin joined the fray, while Detroit's Sid Abel rushed to assist his mate. The game ended in a 3–1 Wings victory; a furious Conn Smythe spat, "The Lord and 12 apostles couldn't have kept the Red Wings under control tonight."

Game three took place in Toronto on April 1, and little of the foolishness associated with the second game was transported to Maple Leaf Gardens. After Howie Meeker high-sticked Lindsay at the 54-second mark, the teams settled down to hockey and the game resulted in a 2–0 Leaf win, with the Toronto defence giving Broda terrific protection en route to his second shutout of the playoffs.

Detroit and Toronto swapped goals in the first period of game four, also played at Maple Leaf Gardens. The game was chippier than its predecessor, with Barilko and Fogolin drawing roughing minors and Steve Black and Bill Juzda being assessed fighting majors in the last minute of the first period.

The game was deadlocked after regulation time. Then, late in the first overtime period, Bill Barilko was charged with slashing Lindsay and was penalized. Thirty-eight seconds into the second overtime period, while Barilko looked on sullenly from the penalty box, Leo Reise fired a shot that deflected off Mortson's leg and stick and found the back of the net behind Broda to give the Red Wings a 2–1 win. The *Toronto Daily Star* reported that "Barilko's penalty wasn't any more obvious than some others which preceded it." Nonetheless, the series was deadlocked at two games apiece.

Back in Detroit on April 6 for game five, Turk Broda earned his third shutout of the series, blanking the Wings 2–0. Ted Kennedy and Max Bentley generated all the offence the visitors needed. Barilko took minor penalties in both the second and third periods.

Game six, back at Maple Leaf Gardens, saw Detroit exact a measure of revenge on the Leafs by stoning them 4–0. Barilko was victimized twice in the first period. With Garth Boesch already in the penalty box, Barilko was thumbed for an infraction and sent to join his colleague. With a two-man power play, Marty Pavelich scored to put Detroit ahead 1–0. Then, at 19:40 of the first, Bill was serving a questionable minor for tripping Lindsay when George Gee scored to give Detroit a 2–0 lead. "The puck-carrying Lindsay jumped just as Barilko came in to check him at the Toronto defence," alleged the Toronto *Telegram*. "Barilko went under him, lifted him and he hit the ice with a crash and stayed there. [Referee Georges] Gravel waited longer than usual before blowing the whistle for a penalty. Lindsay arose just as soon as Barilko was settled in penalty row."

The Red Wings scored a goal in each of the second and third periods to knot the semi-final series at three games each.

The seventh and deciding game was fought with extraordinary passion on April 9, 1950. Through three periods, the game remained scoreless. Then, at 8:39 of overtime, the Detroit Red Wings eliminated the defending Stanley Cup champions. Leo Reise fired a shot that glanced off Bill Barilko's leg and squeezed between the post and Broda's pad to end the longest Stanley Cup reign in NHL history. "I don't know how it went in," sighed Broda. "In fact, I didn't know it until the [red] light went on." Jimmy Thomson was close to tears when he commented that Broda "was like a pitcher hurling a no-hitter for 10 innings and then losing on an error." The aging Turk was as sharp as ever in 1949–50, earning three shutouts in the combative series after collecting nine to lead the NHL through the regular season.

The Red Wings met the New York Rangers — who had upset the Canadiens — in the Stanley Cup finals and proceeded to win the series in seven games. Ironically, although the Leafs had been eliminated, the Gardens would be pressed into service during the finals. The Ringling Brothers and Barnum & Bailey Circus had been booked into Madison Square Garden for its traditional April residency, leaving the Rangers unable to play at home. Arrangements were made for games two and three of the finals to be played in Toronto, while the balance were scheduled for Detroit's Olympia.

Pentti Lund of the New York Rangers scored six goals and five assists for 11 points to lead all playoff scorers in 1950. Teammate Gus Kyle served 30 minutes in penalties to lead the playoffs. Bill Barilko collected a goal and an assist as well as 18 penalty minutes through the seven playoff games Toronto played.

The Maple Leafs received $850 in bonus money from NHL — $350 for finishing third and $500 for losing to the Red Wings in the semi-finals. But the game wasn't about money at that time — it was about pride. The Maple Leafs were bitter, knowing that with a bounce in their favour, they could have won a fourth consecutive championship.

The Leafs had entered game seven of the Detroit series poised and confident. Then, a shot from a distance drifted towards the Leaf goal, hit a body, and went in, ending the dynasty. And on its way in, the puck had struck Number 19: Bill Barilko.

After the game, as he shook hands with each of his combatants, Conn Smythe stated: "It's been a long reign. You've been a great team for four years and you went out like champions. I'm proud of you."

A disconcerted Sid Smith later said, "In '49–50, Leo Reise, who didn't score two goals all year [he actually scored four that season], got two overtime goals. With any luck at all, we could have won five [championships] in a row. Detroit went on to play the New York Rangers, and I'm telling you, we had the Rangers' number all year. We could have won five in a row."

CHAPTER 11

The Struggle
(1950–51)

Bill Barilko spent the majority of the summer of 1950 managing his store, but got away for a month to fish and hunt in northern Ontario. Early that summer, Bill announced that his friend and teammate Max Bentley had joined the ownership group of Barilko Brothers Appliances.

While in Toronto that summer, Bill was an occasional visitor to Club Indigo, a sophisticated jazz night club that had just opened in the Barclay Hotel in downtown Toronto. The club was the brainchild of Fred Maddalena, a veteran restaurateur who had started out as a busboy at the King Edward Hotel. The greatest entertainers of the era performed at Club Indigo — including Harry Belafonte, Tony Bennett, Sophie Tucker and Sarah Vaughn. "Bill was a very debonair guy. He went first class and did everything with flair," remembers teammate Johnny McCormack. "He dated a girl named Lois Pettit from time to time. She was gorgeous and was a Miss Toronto," he recalls. Lois Pettit later married Eric Pogue, another player in the Leafs system at the time.

❋ ❋ ❋

Conn Smythe, the president and general manager of the Toronto Maple Leafs, had a business-related announcement of his own to make in May 1950: that he was relinquishing some of his duties and had elevated Hap Day from coach to assistant general manager. One of Day's principal roles was to evaluate talent for the Maple Leafs. In today's parlance, Hap Day would be director of player personnel.

Day was a longtime Leafs employee who had proven his considerable merit over his multifaceted career in Toronto. He and Ace Bailey had starred with the Toronto St. Patrick's when Smythe bought the team in 1927. Hap was the first captain of the Maple Leafs, proudly playing that role from 1927 until he was sold to the New York Americans in 1937. During his tenure as captain, Day led the Leafs to their first Stanley Cup championship in 1932. After playing one season with the Americans, Day retired, but rejoined the Leafs organization as coach on April 17, 1940. In 10 years as coach, Hap was behind the bench for five Stanley Cup championships.

Smythe installed former Leafs great Joe Primeau as the new head coach to replace Day. Primeau had spent seven seasons with the Leafs, most notably as centre of the Kid Line with Charlie Conacher and "Busher" Jackson. Like Day, Primeau and the Kid Line had also been part of the Cup championship in 1932. Primeau had already coached the St. Michael's Majors of the Ontario Hockey Association to Memorial Cup titles in 1945 and 1947, and he was behind the bench with the Toronto Marlboro seniors when they won the Allan Cup in 1950.

On September 10, 1950 Anne Barilko, married Emil Klisanich in what was the social event of the year in Timmins. Bill Barilko was best man at his sister's wedding.

"Bill asked, 'What are you going to do for a honeymoon?'" Anne recalls. "I said, We've got three weeks planned. We're going to rent a car and drive to Niagara Falls, then cross over to the States and visit New York and Atlantic City.' Billy said, 'Don't rent a car,' and lent us his black Chevrolet. He said, 'On the way back, drive to St. Catharines. I'll be there at training camp. Then, I can drive you home.' So we did," smiles Anne.

September once again brought together the Maple Leafs for training camp in St. Catharines. The boys rolled into town from all over the map and checked into the Welland House hotel, where the lobby was filled with laughter as teammates greeted one another, kibitzing and slapping each other on the back.

Max Bentley had been given permission to report late to training camp. The "Dipsy-Doodle Dandy" was tending to his 320-acre farm in Delisle, Saskatchewan, building a new home on the property and looking after his recently acquired two-horse stable.

Johnny McCormack, who had played the better part of 1949–50 with the Leafs and become a regular in 1950–51, remembers the relationship between Barilko and Bentley. "Bill's closest friend on that team was Max Bentley. Max was quite a bit older than Bill, but age was no barrier. Max used to like to bet on the horses or World Series. Bill used to say, 'If Max bets on it, I want it, too.' They would always go together on their bets. They car-pooled going to practice or going home."

Fern Flaman, who joined the Leafs later that season and partnered with Bill on the Leafs' blue line, adds, "He got quite chummy with Max Bentley. They were like two peas in a pod — wherever Max went, he took

Bill with him. Max used to like the horse races, and on off-days he got Bill involved in that. There was nothing the matter with that." He adds, "Bill Barilko was a fine young man."

* * *

The 1950 training camp was no less strenuous than others had been. Players were called at 6:45 in the morning and reported to the hotel lobby in casual attire. The team ate breakfast as a group at 7:30, then had a half-hour off-ice instructional session. At 9:00, they worked out with an instructor.

Each morning at 10:30, Leafs and prospects alike stepped onto the ice. After a workout, they showered and changed for lunch. Then, at 2:00, it was back on the ice again. The group golfed each afternoon at 3:15, then, with military precision, returned for dinner at six o'clock, dressed in business suits. There was free time after the evening meal, but the lights were turned out at 11.

"We called Bill at training camp from our honeymoon," adds Anne. "Bill had told Turk Broda that Emil worked for a beer company. Turk asked Emil to bring him a case of beer on the way to St. Catharines. 'We are not allowed to have beer during camp,' Broda said.

"Emil brought Turk his beer, and before we knew it, Turk had downed three bottles so fast, we could barely believe it. 'Emil, you're a hell of a beer salesman,' Turk said, and Billy, Emily and I laughed so hard," Anne chuckles.

The revamped line-up had some serious challenges to overcome. Turk Broda was going into his 13th season tending goal for Toronto. Although he was still a vital component of the Leafs roster — in 1949–50 he had led the NHL with nine shutouts, the best total of his Hall of Fame career — at 36 he was considered ancient. The Leafs decided to employ a platoon system in goal, making them one of the first NHL teams to experiment with using two netminders on an ongoing basis. Twenty-four-year-old Al Rollins was brought in to work alongside the aging Turk. The two were affectionately played off one another in print — Broda, at five feet, nine inches and nudging 200 pounds, was tagged "The Fat Man" by the press. Rollins, at six foot two and 175 pounds, was naturally called "The Thin Man."

The blueline corps was a greater source of concern. Garth Boesch had retired after the 1949–50 season, deciding to return to his parents' wheat farm. The dapper Boesch had been quite an anomaly over his four-season NHL career. Teamed on the Leafs blue line with Barilko, he played with a real sense of style. The two were very aggressive and had perfected their on-ice partnership, including their wildly popular and highly effective "Maginot Drop," whereby the two of them would simultaneously drop to their knees to block shots. But Boesch stood out in another way. His hair was always beautifully groomed, slicked back using Oliveon, a popular olive oil–based hair product in those days. And, he was the only NHL player of his era to sport a moustache.

Originally the property of the New York Americans, Boesch was unable to leave Canada to attend the Americans' training camp in September 1941 due to wartime travel restrictions. He made his NHL debut with the Toronto Maple Leafs in 1946–47. In four NHL seasons, he was an integral member of three Stanley Cup championships. Leafs management entertained hopes that Hugh Bolton, a six-foot, three-inch Toronto-born defenceman who had played a couple of games for Toronto in 1949–50, would slip efficiently into the retired Boesch's spot in the line-up. Barilko, for one, was confident. "We should have a better balanced club all the way around," he stated. "Despite the loss of Garth Boesch, I think our defence will be as good as last year. Bill Juzda and I proved we could work well together and Hugh Bolton will help considerably." Unfortunately, Bolton was injured during training camp.

In a statement that could easily have been made 50 years later, Day said, "Kids don't show much enthusiasm nowadays. There are probably too many diversions now." Nevertheless, forward Danny Lewicki cracked the veteran-laden Leaf line-up, while Tod Sloan rejoined the Leafs after spending a season with the Cleveland Barons of the AHL.

With Brigadier General John Rockingham dropping the puck for the ceremonial season-opening face-off, the Leafs' 1950–51 campaign came to order at home on October 14. In the third game of the young season, Barilko hurt his left leg in a collision with Paul Ronty of the Boston Bruins. In their search for emergency help, the Leafs looked to their affiliate in Pittsburgh, where Tim Horton, Frank Mathers and John Ashley were biding their time, but none was called up. Nor did St. Mike's or the Marlboros have anyone ready to step into the line-up. To fill the gap, Johnny McCormack was temporarily moved back to defence from his spot at centre, while Bobby Hassard was brought up from the Hornets to fill the vacated forward slot. Hugh Bolton lined up on defence whenever he wasn't sidelined by injuries of his own.

The situation was desperate enough for Conn Smythe to put out a call to 31-year-old Bobby Copp, the lanky defenceman who had last played in the NHL in 1942–43, when he was working towards his degree in dentistry at the University of Toronto. "I loved Toronto," Copp admits. "If it hadn't been for Happy Day at that time…" His voice trails off. Copp's experience and offensive abilities would seemingly have meshed beautifully with the Maple Leaf teams of the mid–1940s, but Copp would rather play for the Ottawa Senators of the Quebec Senior Hockey League.

"I would have gone back if it hadn't been for Happy Day. I liked playing for the Leafs," Copp states. Although Day had proven himself a winning coach, not everyone appreciated his heavy-handed tactics. "Day was terrible," fumes Copp. "I was doing everything at that time. I was taking COTC [Canadian Officers' Training Corps, a compulsory military training course for university students during the Second World War], I was in my last year of dentistry and I didn't have a car. We never had a skate on the day of a game, but we had a meeting at the Gardens. One Saturday, I was one minute late and he locked me in the dressing room and said, 'You'll be here on time the next time or you won't be here again.'

"Another time, I scored two goals. I scored the winning goal and we won, 3–2. He called me into his office the next morning and said, 'You play another game like that and you won't be here next week.' I couldn't believe it!

"The worst one was, we played on a Tuesday night and I was writing my final exams. He wouldn't give me the time off. That Saturday, my Mom and Dad and sister came up from New Brunswick to see me play. Three o'clock that afternoon, he said, 'You're not playing tonight but you're playing tomorrow.' I said, 'That's what you think. That's the last game I'm going to play for you.' So I didn't play anymore.

"That's the kind of guy he was. The sportswriters wrote about how bad he treated me, but that was one of the reasons I never went back."

In 1946, when Babe Pratt was suspended for gambling violations and the Leafs were in need of a defenceman, they called on Copp. "They wanted me to go back in 1946 and they offered me $5,000. But I was getting paid $200 a game to play amateur in Ottawa, and I had just bought my practice to get started [as a dentist]. I had just bought a house in Ottawa, too," recalls Copp.

Still, the Leafs kept Copp on their voluntarily retired list, which meant that they retained his NHL playing rights. And in 1950–51, Bobby finally relented. "Bill Barilko was hurt and [Conn] Smythe, Happy Day and Joe Primeau tried Hugh Bolton on defence, but he wasn't good enough. So all of a sudden they decided, 'Let's call Ottawa and see if we can get Bobby Copp.' I wouldn't have gone back, except that Joe Primeau was coaching so I didn't have to see Day very much that time."

"They had to get permission from National Hockey League president Clarence Campbell for me to play," continues Bobby. Under NHL rules, amateurs were allowed three-game tryouts without having to sign a professional contract. "They called me up on Saturday morning and flew me to Toronto. Smythe and Joe Primeau met me at the airport in Smythe's limousine. They took me down to the Gardens, and I stayed there from noon hour on. I didn't go to a hotel or anything because we were playing two nights in a row." After Saturday night contests, the Maple Leafs traditionally boarded a train and travelled overnight to their next destination for a Sunday evening match.

For the rest of the players, the end of the team meeting meant a return trip home, where they packed for the train and napped before the game that evening. Bobby, with nowhere else to go, remained downtown. "After the meeting on Saturday, I hung around Maple Leaf Gardens," he remembers. "I went over to Yonge Street. They were building a subway at that time and I watched them. I was all alone, so I didn't see any of the other players."

"We played the game Saturday night [October 21] against New York and we won that game, 5–0," remembers Copp. The *London Free Press* reported, "Playing on the Toronto defence for the first time since 1943 and looking right at home in the NHL again was Bobby Copp, replacing Bashing Bill Barilko."

"Then, after the game, we got right on the train to Chicago. We won that next game [5–3]. I was partnered with Bill Juzda. Then I went back to Ottawa to finish the season with the Senators."

The team had changed dramatically from the one Copp played with in 1942–43, although there were a couple of familiar faces. "Teeder Kennedy was a big shot then. Turk Broda was still playing goal. I played with both of them when I was up with the Leafs in '42–43," Copp recalls.

His injuries healed, Barilko returned to the lineup, which meant Copp's stay with the Leafs consisted solely of those two weekend games. "That was the end of that. After that, I said to my wife, 'Let's go to Toronto,' so I sold my practice and went down to Toronto in August. I went to see Smythe and he said, 'You know, you're 33 years old. You're getting pretty old, but if you want to come out and practice with the Leafs, we'll pay you so much a week.' I forget what it was. So I said, 'Okay, I'll do that for something to do.' I went down; I didn't play that year, but I spent the whole year practising with the Leafs. They flew me back to Ottawa a few times to play a couple of games with the Senators, but at the end of that season I decided to go back to Ottawa. I ended up finishing the rest of my career with the Senators. But it was quite a thrill to play two games with the Leafs at that time."

A more permanent solution to the Leafs' defensive shortfall was needed, so on November 16 the club pulled the trigger on a sizable deal with the Boston Bruins. Toronto shipped Bill Ezinicki and Vic Lynn to Boston, receiving veteran Fernie Flaman as well as Phil Maloney, Kenny Smith and junior prospect Leo Boivin in return. Flaman was a hardnosed battler from Dysart, Saskatchewan, renowned for two things during his days as one of the top stay-at-home NHL defencemen: his legendary battles with such tough guys as Rocket Richard, Ted Lindsay and Lou Fontinato, and his fanatical devotion to clearing the area in front of his team's goal.

Both Ezinicki and Lynn had been playing in Pittsburgh for the American Hockey League at the time of the trade. "Neither one of them fit into our plans for the future, but we never keep a major league player in the minors so, when [Boston general manager Art] Ross suggested a deal for them, we were willing to dicker," explained Conn Smythe at that time.

Including three years with the Boston Olympics of the Eastern Amateur Hockey League, Flaman had been in the Bruins' system since 1943. "Boston was my home," says Fern. "I was quite disappointed." The Toronto papers liked Flaman, though. The *Telegram*'s assessment was that the stay-at-home defenceman was "rough and unpolished but was a good policeman and could hit like a pile driver."

"I got some good advice from the newspaper people [in Boston]. They said, 'Look, don't burn your bridges. You don't know what will happen,' so I never said too much. I just thought I'd go to Toronto and work hard as heck, but Toronto had a different idea. It was quite a shock. I had been in the league three and a half years. I thought I was doing pretty well. [The Leafs] sent me to their farm team in Pittsburgh and I was there for a month." After 11 games, the Maple Leafs used Flaman's experience to solidify their blue line. "They brought me up and I stayed up for four years with the Leafs," says Flaman.

⁂

Through his four NHL seasons to that point, Barilko had become feared for his thunderous bodychecks. "Bashin' Bill" was as solid as granite, and not afraid to use his body to make the opposition take that fraction of a second to see where he was on the ice at all times. During the dying moments of the November 16 contest against the Rangers, with Toronto ahead 5–4, New York pulled goaltender Charlie Rayner for an extra attacker. The Rangers' Jackie McLeod chased a puck that a Leaf had shot back into his end. Barilko was on McLeod's heels in hot pursuit, and just as McLeod touched the puck, Bill slammed him face-first into the boards, and the young Ranger crumpled to the ice in a heap. McLeod was taken away on a stretcher and diagnosed with a broken collarbone. No penalty was called on the play. Rangers coach Frank Boucher commented, "I don't think the Toronto fans themselves liked it!"

Bill was using his body as confidently and effectively as he ever had. Ted Kennedy remembers, "When it came to bodychecking and going down to block shots on his goal, Barilko had no peer during my time."

In a 1950 interview, Max Bentley recalled a damaging bodycheck dispensed by his good friend Bill Barilko. "I was bothering [Bill] Gadsby [of the Chicago Blackhawks] and I looked up just in time to steer away before Barilko let go. If I ever got mixed up in that collision, I'd still be sailing through the air. I'm a paperweight compared to those guys."

"Barilko smashed him to the ice with the most terrific check this reporter ever has seen," said the *Toronto Daily Star*, covering the November 22, 1950, contest. Gadsby lay sprawled on the ice while his teammates circled referee Bill Chadwick, barking about the inequity of the check. When the Hawks protested that Bill should have been given a penalty, referee Bill Chadwick responded, "That's the best check I've ever seen." It was the worst check Gadsby *never* saw — he suffered a shoulder separation that bothered him throughout the rest of his lengthy career. Toronto beat the Blackhawks that night, 5–2.

Gadsby was a tough player in his own right, but he remembers the hit. "The toughest injury I ever had came when I had my head down and ran into Bill Barilko of the Maple Leafs. We were both knocked out. When I got to the dressing room, I couldn't raise my arm. The trainer had to cut off my uniform and my undershirt to see what was wrong. A bone was sticking through my skin up by the shoulder."

When Toronto faced Detroit on November 23, Barilko and George Gee earned major penalties after getting into a scrap. Blueline partner Bill Juzda came to Bill's rescue and faced Bob Goldham in a separate tussle. Juzda then went at Gaye Stewart. Barilko, Juzda, Gee and Goldham all drew majors, and Barilko was also assessed a minor for high-sticking. Less than a minute later, Toronto's Gus Mortson earned a holding penalty. Marcel Pronovost of the Red Wings was then whistled for tripping, followed four seconds later by Ted Lindsay. At one single time, seven players were seated together in the penalty box.

"Bill was a tough, hard-hitting guy," states Johnny McCormack. "Goose" had also played with Bill's brother, Alex. "I played senior with the Marlboros for three years. At that time, I was going to university, and that's where I played with Bill's brother, Alex. We had a pretty good club with the likes of George Armstrong. Alex was one of our defencemen and he was a great skater. Alex was a much stronger skater than Bill."

But Bill had other tools in his arsenal besides his aggressive play. Earlier in the season, he had started using a slap shot. "It's a deadly shot mainly because it's low and hurried," he told the press. But coach Primeau had other thoughts. "The slap shot is more of a fad than anything else," he pronounced. "Its popularity is gradually fading out. I asked a number of players from last year's [Allan Cup–winning] Marlboro Seniors why they used the slap shot. Most of the players couldn't give me an answer, and I suggested they return to straight shooting. They did, and the results proved more satisfactory."

A scrap between Barilko and the Canadiens' Butch Bouchard on November 30 seemed to take some of the wind out of Bill's sails. "[Bouchard] cooled out The Basher with some well-directed wallops. Barilko hadn't reckoned on such heavy treatment," wrote the Montreal *Daily Star*.

On December 2, Chicago and Toronto battled to a scoreless tie. At 6:50 of the second period, Al Rollins was hit over the left eye by a puck shot by Ernie Dickens and had to leave the game on a stretcher. Twelve stitches closed the gashes above and below the eye. The game was delayed 15 minutes so that Turk Broda could dress and get onto the ice. Then, at 16:03, a puck fired by the Leafs' Harry Watson caromed off the stick of Harry Lumley and broke the nose of the Hawks netminder. To give Lumley time to have his nose repaired, the second intermission began early and the remaining four minutes of the second period were added to the third. Lumley was able to finish the game. In one of hockey's great oddities, the three netminders — Rollins, Broda and Lumley — were named the three stars of the scoreless game.

Around that time, Bill's sister, Anne visited him in Toronto for what would prove to be the final time. "I stayed with one of Bill's friends on the Danforth — her name was Norma Jabour, and she and her mother Adele shared an apartment across the street from the store. Adele treated Bill like a son; in fact, she wrote to Bill and signed her letters 'Mom Jabour.' They were very good to me."

Bill's final Toronto address was the room in the Eton House Hotel at 710 Danforth Avenue. Bill kept his eye on Anne. "Bill was very protective of me," Anne Klisanich explains. "'Don't go past that bridge because it's not safe,' he cautioned." At that time, there was a public washroom on the south side of Danforth just west of Broadview, and Bill had heard stories that the area was not to be trusted at night. "But Billy knew I was safe with the Jabours during my short stay," Anne continues. "One or two nights was all it was. The Leafs were on the train right after the Saturday night game and on their way to the next city for their game Sunday night."

Train travel helped to galvanize teams in those days before airplanes became the primary mode of transport. John McCormack credits the time spent riding the rails with the strength of the bond that existed between teammates at that time. "We were thrown together and found that we liked each other. It was as simple as that," McCormack says. "Today, they just hop on a plane and go somewhere and get back. There isn't a lot of time spent together. We didn't have agents and consultants to talk to and hold our hand. We just learned to lean on each other."

Bill was clearly struggling on the ice as the year 1950 wound down to its conclusion. In a 4–3 loss to Detroit on December 13, readers of the *Toronto Daily Star* were told, "That's two in a row Barilko — uh, I mean Detroit — have beaten the Leafs and no other team can make that claim this season. Bill Barilko and Bill Juzda produced their worst effort of the season." The rival *Telegram* cast the beam of blame more broadly: "The way the Leafs have performed at home is inadequate. Their fans would be justified in accusing them of high treason."

Bill was often chastised by Primeau for straying too far into the opponent's end. Primeau, like Day before him, viewed a sound, defensive effort as the surest way to win games. "Bill had his ups and downs. Primeau used to get on him," states Johnny McCormack. "But he was just such a bright spirit, you couldn't stay mad at him."

The January 6, 1951, edition of *The Hockey News* told the tale: "Bill Barilko has been a big disappointment this season. His play has fallen a way off and he's been riding the bench in a number of Leafs games of late."

Something was distracting Barilko, and the elements of the game that had made him so effective earlier in his career were not being employed with the same enthusiasm. "This has been one of Barilko's poorer seasons," *The Hockey News* continued. "He hasn't been hitting the players in his meanest manner and it has drawn comments from all corners of the hockey world."

His teammates sat him down one afternoon and discussed their concern. "Bill, the old man [Smythe] is going to send you to Pittsburgh if you don't smarten up," one warned. It wasn't an idle threat. Smythe didn't tolerate ineffectiveness, and the franchise was too deep in talent to show much patience. Besides which, Tommy Anderson, Bill's Hollywood mentor, was coaching the Pittsburgh Hornets in 1950–51 and would dearly have loved to get Barilko into his AHL line-up.

Although Bill was always kidding with his teammates, Gus Mortson sensed there was an element of sobriety when it came to the prospect of being sent to the minors. "After one game where he didn't feel he had played up to par, I remember Bill saying, 'Here I come, Pittsburgh!'"

Early in the new year there was move that delivered a serious jolt to team morale and illustrated just how real the threat of demotion could be. Popular Maple Leaf John McCormack tells the tale. "I got married during the [regular] season," says McCormack, who wedded Margaret Gordon on January 31. Conn Smythe greeted the newlyweds with a special gift: two tickets to Pittsburgh. "I was sent to the minors. I guess it must be because I got married without first talking it over with Leafs management." McCormack had been playing well for Toronto, which reinforces the perception that his performance on the ice wasn't the issue that prompted Smythe to send him down. "I wasn't even aware that that wasn't normal. Gus Mortson had been married the year before and Ezinicki the year before that — both during the season." Howie Meeker punctuated the indignity of Smythe's move in *Golly Gee — It's Me!* "The demotion sort of rocked us all a bit, but it didn't shock us," he said. "That was the sort of crap he threw at his players. That was Conn Smythe." It was a prime example of how NHL owners held all the power during this era.

In Barilko's case, the intervention had its intended effect. His game turned itself around. On February 16, he played a strong game defensively and contributed a goal in a 2–2 tie with Montreal. He scored two goals in a 6–2 drubbing of the Bruins on February 24, and *The Hockey News* chimed in, "Playing a vastly improved brand of hockey, Barilko seems to be coming out of what, up until now, has been termed a rather disappointing season." The *Globe and Mail* concurred: "From a Toronto viewpoint, the steady improvement in the play of Bill Barilko was noticeable. Barilko scored both his goals through alertness. His mind was on the game, something that didn't appear to be happening earlier in the season." For the week ending March 3, 1951, Bill Barilko was named *The Hockey News*'s Player of the Week.

Bill's noticeably improved play seemed to act as a catalyst for Al Rollins, Cal Gardner, Bill Juzda and Fern Flaman, all of whom found a new gear. Having come over recently from one of the league's doormats, Flaman was well aware that there was a different work ethic in the Leafs organization in general. "At Boston, we practised maybe twice a week and had a lot of time on our hands," he said at the time. "Practice makes perfect and I think that's a big point in the Leaf system and is what makes them the best-coached team."

Cal Gardner spoke of the bond between the players. "The Leafs are together so often, they're like one family. They get to know each other, both on and off the ice. That's good."

"When we were on the road, we'd sometimes go out after a practice instead of staying around the hotel," adds Fern Flaman. "We would go down the street to some delicatessen and have something to eat. In Toronto, we were a pretty close group. There was one place we used to congregate at with our wives so we all got to know each other pretty well. Bill was not married, but he was a big, handsome guy so he was never without a date."

Gus Mortson further explains how the team bonded throughout the course of the season. "Saturday nights we played at home in Toronto and Sunday, on the road someplace. On Wednesday, we played in Toronto and Thursday, out of town again. Those were the nights we played. We would get together on Monday nights, and we brought our wives. Generally speaking, we went to the Old Mill. We had dinner there and everybody chipped in. There was always music there and we'd have a dance.

"We enjoyed ourselves there. It was far enough from the game Wednesday that if you had an extra beer, it wasn't going to hurt you. We were always able to go there and not be bothered." The Old Mill, still a very popular location for fine dining today, is located on the Humber River in Etobicoke, now part of Toronto's west end.

"It was a good bunch," adds John McCormack. "We got along well. We were all different personalities and Bill just blended in with them all."

McCormack points to another reason why the team got along so well. "Before I got married, I used to live with Gus and Sheila Mortson.

But on the road, we didn't have hard and fast roommates. Hap Day or Joe Primeau would just pair you up. The defence would more or less be kept together and the forwards the same. But we'd have different roommates and that way we didn't form cliques. I think that was part of the strategy. I roomed with everybody under the sun, from Harry Watson to Teeder — you name it. It made for great camaraderie."

With the team having fun and playing well, the Maple Leafs' record improved. When Turk Broda played on March 3, it was the first action he had seen since January 9, Rollins having assumed the chores exclusively in the interim. With a solid shell surrounding him, Turk earned a 3–0 shutout against the Chicago Blackhawks. But Toronto lost two stalwarts on defence during the game: Mortson was suspended for deliberately attempting to injure Adam Brown, while Barilko twisted his knee and looked to be out of commission for several games.

After missing two games, Bill returned to the Leafs dressing room, bringing his joie de vivre with him. "Bill Barilko rejoined the team in practice yesterday and injected a lot of pep into the proceedings," said the *Toronto Daily Star*. "Bashing Bill may not be the smoothest character in the NHL but I doubt if any player gets more fun out of playing than the hard rock from Timmins."

The Toronto Maple Leafs posted a record of 41 wins against 16 losses and 13 ties for 95 points in 1950–51. In most years, they would have topped the league standings with room to spare, but the Detroit Red Wings were even better, with 44 wins, 13 losses and 13 ties for what was then an all-time NHL high of 101 points. The league was really a two-horse race in 1950–51: Montreal was a distant third with 65 points, while the final playoff spot went to Boston, who with 62 points edged out the Rangers by one point. Far behind those three were the dismal Chicago Blackhawks, who picked up just 36 of a possible 140 points for a winning percentage of .257.

Gordie Howe led all scorers with 43 goals and 43 assists for 86 points, 20 more than second-place Maurice Richard. Max Bentley was the most productive Leaf, contributing 21 goals and 41 assists to Toronto's attack. Tod Sloan led the club in goal scoring with 31. When the Leafs had the man advantage, coach Joe Primeau could call upon a fearsome and highly effective power-play unit of Ted Kennedy, Tod Sloan and Sid Smith up front, Jimmy Thomson as the lone defenceman, and centreman Max Bentley playing the point. Despite injuries, Bill Barilko played in 58 games that season, collected six goals and six assists, as well as 96 penalty minutes. Teammate Gus Mortson earned 142 minutes in penalties to lead all regular-season combatants in that category.

With five championships in eight seasons, the Toronto Maple Leafs might be considered the NHL's dominant team during the 1940s. It is interesting to note, however, that the team is noticeably under-represented on the postseason All-Star teams of the era. Conn Smythe and others close to the Leafs camp squawked that the Professional Hockey Writers' Association, whose members chose the teams, was biased against Toronto. Viewed another way, the lack of individual accolades might have been a tribute to the club's strong emphasis on teamwork — in Toronto, no one player stood out above the rest, while there were many who played integral roles in the team's success.

Turk Broda was the goalkeeper selected to the First All-Star Team in 1947–48, while two years later — in a season when Toronto did not win the Cup — defenceman Gus Mortson made the First Team and Ted Kennedy was the Second Team's centre. After the 1950–51 campaign, the voters were a bit more generous, naming Jimmy Thomson, Ted Kennedy and Sid Smith to the Second All-Star Team.

Meanwhile, Al Rollins, the Leafs' rookie netminder, was awarded the Vezina Trophy. He had started 40 of the team's 70 games in 1950–51, with an eye-popping record of 27 wins, five losses and eight ties. The Leafs' platoon of Rollins and Broda allowed 138 goals, just one fewer than the Detroit Red Wings, who were backstopped by another outstanding rookie, Terry Sawchuk. In fact, the race went down to the wire, as Rollins chalked up shutouts in two of the Leafs' final three regular-season games to claim the Vezina (he blanked the opposition five times in all that season).

But while the Vezina Trophy would come to be shared by netminding tandems of the 1960s, '70s and '80s, Turk Broda's name does not appear on the award as a co-winner in 1950–51. Goaltending platoons were still a novelty in the NHL; at that time, therefore, the trophy went to the principal goaltender on the team that had allowed the fewest goals. A decade or so later, the Vezina would evolve into more of a team award with the advent of two- and three-goalie rotations, before morphing once again into an individual honour akin to baseball's Cy Young Award in 1981–82.

Though his playing time had been curtailed, Broda turned in some fine performances of his own. He collected six shutouts in his 31 appearances, including the December 2 game against the Blackhawks when he relieved the injured Rollins just past the halfway mark after his partner had been cut. That game ended in a scoreless tie.

Rollins finished the season with a goals-against average of 1.77, while Broda's average of 2.24 was also outstanding. Detroit's Sawchuk finished with a 1.99 average, while yet another first-year netminder, Gerry McNeil of the third-place Canadiens, came in with a 2.63 average. The NHL's rookie of the year in 1949–50, Jack Gelineau of the fourth-place Boston Bruins, allowed 2.81 goals per game, followed closely by Chuck Rayner of New York at 2.85. Harry Lumley of the sad-sack Chicago Blackhawks — who were generally lax in their attitude towards backchecking — struggled to keep things from getting too far out of hand, posting a 3.90 average.

Though they had ultimately performed admirably, the Toronto Maple Leafs' roller-coaster ride of 1950–51 was far from over. The struggles of the regular season would prove to be a mere foreshadowing of what lay in store during the playoffs: a pair of series that, for Toronto sports fans, would encompass what ABC television's *Wide World of Sports* would later describe as the gamut of sporting emotions — "the thrill of victory and the agony of defeat."

CHAPTER 12

Sudden Death

"What you accomplished during the season is all out the window," Leafs coach Joe Primeau told his charges in the spring of 1951. "This is the final examination and everyone must go all out."

The Detroit Red Wings, with their record-breaking 101-point season, were the odds-on favourite to collect the Stanley Cup. General Manager Jack Adams tagged his Red Wings squad "the greatest team I've ever had." In the semifinals, Detroit was to meet the Montreal Canadiens, who had finished third with 65 points, far behind the Red Wings and Maple Leafs. Toronto's second-place finish, meanwhile, meant it would oppose the fourth-place Boston Bruins in the first round.

Boston had not won a game at Maple Leaf Gardens all season, but the Bruins shocked the hometown team and its fans in game one on March 28 by shutting out the Leafs 2–0. Harry Watson had been scratched from the lineup with a shoulder separation. Al Rollins got the start in goal, but during the first period he came out of his crease to chase a loose puck and tore both his pads and his knee ligaments in a collision with Boston's Pete Horeck. Pundits worried whether Broda could step in and backstop the Leafs, but the veteran played like the Turk of old, eventually eliminating the Bruins with his exemplary goal-tending.

In one of the oddest twists in playoff history, game two on March 31 ended in a 1–1 tie — the first playoff tie in the NHL since 1927. Bill Barilko had scored at 3:47 of the first period, while Johnny Peirson replied for the Bruins midway through the second. There was no further scoring in regulation time, and a full overtime period was played without resolving anything. But a Toronto municipal bylaw against Sunday sports prohibited games from continuing past 11:45 p.m. on Saturday night.

To comply with the bylaw, the game was terminated and the one-all tie stood as a meaningless result, though the scoring statistics were incorporated into the record book.

Game two was vicious. "Actual hockey was of secondary importance as players of opposing teams skated out with but one thought in mind: to soften the other fellow up," said the *Globe and Mail*. Leaf captain Ted Kennedy was cut for five stitches over his eye, but the Bruins fared worst. Peirson fractured a cheekbone and Murray Henderson was cut for three stitches. Dunc Fisher suffered a 12-stitch cut to his scalp after being boarded by Barilko, and Pete Horeck took 10 stitches over his left eye after fencing with Bill.

Boston coach Lynn Patrick was so incensed by the play of the Leafs that at one point he leaned over the boards and punched Jim Thomson in the face. Barilko was charged with 21 minutes in penalties — three minors, a major and a 10-minute misconduct. "Barilko was a smashing threat all evening," reported the *Globe and Mail*. "He made five trips to the penalty bench but was still one of the most effective 'softeners.'" The misconduct was assessed when Bill protested one of referee Red Storey's decisions by gesticulating with stick in hand.

Conn Smythe punctuated the game's result, stating, "The Leafs never lose in the playoffs when the other team gets rough."

Game three took place the next night in Boston, but both teams settled down somewhat and stuck to hockey. Turk Broda and his Leafs shut out the Bruins 3–0 on goals by Max Bentley, Cal Gardner and Fern Flaman, the last of whom had started the year as a Bruin. Barilko earned an assist on Max Bentley's goal in the third period, after being chased for interference late in the first. Midway through the second period, Pete Horeck was sent to repent for high-sticking Barilko. And over the course of the game, Boston's star centre, Milt Schmidt, banged up both his knees.

Game four, played April 3 at Boston Garden, resulted in a 3–1 Leaf victory. Schmidt struck Barilko in the face with his stick in the first period, drawing a penalty — and blood from Barilko's lip — but the Toronto defenceman stayed on to play the rest of the game. Dunc Fisher opened the scoring for Boston, but that was the only goal for the Bruins. Sid Smith, Max Bentley and — at 14:08 of the third period — Bill Barilko, cemented the win for Toronto. Barilko also picked up a minor penalty for tripping in the third period. The Leafs defence tandem of Barilko and Flaman was outstanding. "Barilko, top Toronto man tonight and most other nights in this series, is the top Leaf scorer with two goals," reported the Toronto *Telegram*.

In a bid to alter the momentum of the series, Boston replaced netminder Jack Gelineau with Red Henry for game five in Toronto on April 7, but the move was to no avail. Joe Klukay scored twice and

Fleming MacKell and Ted Kennedy added one each to give Toronto a commanding 4–1 win. Bill Ezinicki scored late in the third to foil Broda's shutout bid.

Smelling blood, the Leafs pounced on Boston in game six, closing out the series with a decisive 6–0 spanking in a penalty-free game in Boston on April 8. Kennedy, MacKell, Smith and Tod Sloan each collected a goal, while Klukay had his second consecutive two-goal game and Broda registered his second shutout of the playoffs. Bill Barilko earned an assist on Joe Klukay's first-period goal.

Winning four games to one versus Boston, Toronto earned the right to compete against the Montreal Canadiens, who had upset the defending Stanley Cup champion Detroit Red Wings in seven games to set up an all-Canadian final for the Stanley Cup. Astonishingly, it was only the second time the adversaries had met for the hockey championship. In their previous meeting, in the 1947 Stanley Cup finals, the Leafs won the best-of-seven series four games to two.

The confident Maple Leafs wanted to avenge the previous season's heartbreaking loss to the Detroit Red Wings in the semifinals. It also looked to be the last playoff series of the incomparable Turk Broda's career, so there was a great incentive to send him off as a winner. No one realized it would be the final series for Bill Barilko, too.

❋ ❋ ❋

The 1951 Stanley Cup final series is considered by most hockey historians to be the greatest ever. "The Canadiens were our biggest rivals back then," said Harry Watson. "We hated them, especially Maurice Richard. There were other teams we wouldn't get as up for, like the Chicago Blackhawks and the Boston Bruins, but Richard's Canadiens — we were always ready for them."

It's peculiar how destiny works. Bill Barilko, whose regression through the regular season had almost caused his demotion to the AHL's Pittsburgh Hornets, would be a dominant factor in all five contests against Montreal in the finals.

For the only time in NHL history, every game in the Stanley Cup final was decided in overtime. The teams battled ferociously for supremacy. The goaltenders, Gerry McNeil for Montreal and the tandem of Rollins and Broda for the Leafs, were, in a word, extraordinary. McNeil had just emerged from a brilliant series against the vaunted Red Wings. "It was like running into one-hit pitching your first time out," muttered Detroit manager Jack Adams. "The greatest goalkeeping this team has ever faced." Toronto was strong top to bottom, with two strong goalkeepers, an outstanding defence and offensive firepower. *The Hockey News* wrote, "The cash customers couldn't have asked for any more in the way of thrills and drama than they got in these five evenly contested games."

🍁 🍁 🍁

The teams faced off for game one on April 11 at Maple Leaf Gardens in Toronto. "Everyone knew the series was going to be close, but I don't think anyone had any idea it was going to be as tight as it really was," mentioned Harry Watson. He returned to the Toronto lineup after missing the Boston series with a shoulder injury, but only managed a handful of shifts. Meanwhile, Montreal's Bernie Geoffrion had hurt his knee against Detroit in the semifinals, and was skating gingerly.

Sid Smith fired up the Gardens faithful by opening the scoring at the 15-second mark of the game. Maurice Richard tied the game at 15:27 when he knocked down a Barilko pass intended for Fern Flaman, danced around Bill and scored against Broda with an off-balance shot. "I tried to clear the puck but Richard knocked it down," admitted Barilko. "I should have made sure I got it out of there." The Leafs exacted revenge 15 seconds later when Tod Sloan banged in a rebound off a Gus Mortson shot to put Toronto up 2–1 at the end of one period.

Paul Masnick of Montreal tied the game early in the second period, and the 2–2 score held through regulation time. The Leafs thought they had scored the go-ahead goal at 7:56 of the third, but Mortson's marker was disallowed because Cal Gardner was in the crease. Regulation time ended with the teams deadlocked at two.

Early in overtime, Bill Barilko deprived Montreal of a win by diving between an open goalmouth and Maurice Richard and deflected the Rocket's blistering shot — and certain goal — harmlessly over the net. "If the diving Barilko hadn't reached that scorcher, it was home," said the *Toronto Daily Star*. Later, Sid Smith skated in from the corner and flicked a backhand over Gerry McNeil at 5:51 to give Toronto a 3–2 over- time win and one victory towards the four needed to win the Stanley Cup. It was Smith's second goal of the contest.

The Hockey News praised Number 5 of the Leafs: "Bill Barilko has been a tower of strength to the Leafs. He's thrown himself in front of several hard shots that might have slipped into the Toronto goal."

Harry Watson explained why Rocket Richard was so dangerous. "He would circle all the time, just trying to get some daylight. Then all of a sudden he would dart in toward the net like an arrow. And he had a great shot. He would hardly ever miss the net."

Three nights later, on April 14 at Maple Leaf Gardens, Montreal reversed the decision of the opening game with a 3–2 overtime win of its own over the hometown Leafs. Masnick opened the scoring for Montreal at 2:18, putting the puck behind Broda in the Leaf net. In the second, Billy Reay's goal put the Canadiens up 2–0, but Sid Smith, with his third goal of the finals, pulled his Leafs within a goal with a power-play marker at 15:31. Fern Flaman injured his groin late in the second and would miss the next two games nursing his injury.

In the third period, Leafs captain Teeder Kennedy passed the puck to Tod Sloan, whose shot rebounded off McNeil's pads, hit Kennedy on the knee and bounced into the net. The Canadiens argued vehemently that Kennedy had kicked the puck in, but the goal stood. Bill Tobin, acting as supervisor of the series, ruled that the puck had gone into the net after bouncing off Kennedy's knee. The tying goal was scored with Richard in the penalty box, and it set the stage for a second consecutive overtime decision.

As the Leafs changed lines early in overtime, Richard scored a brilliant goal to win the game for Montreal. The Rocket took a pass from Doug Harvey, stepped around a defenceman, pulled Broda out of his crease and fired the puck into a gaping net at 2:55 to give Montreal the win. The Canadiens sat in their dressing room singing a boisterous version of "Alouette."

The teams travelled to Montreal for game three on April 17. It was Canadiens netminder Gerry McNeil's 25 birthday, and Toronto ruined the celebration with a 2–1 overtime win. After splitting the first two games with the veteran Broda between the pipes, Leafs coach Joe Primeau and majordomo Conn Smythe played a hunch and inserted rookie goaltender Al Rollins in goal for the Leafs. He would play each of the remaining games in the series.

The Rocket scored just over two minutes into the opening stanza while Sloan served a holding penalty. Sid Smith cradled a drop pass from Max Bentley, then fired a missile past McNeil for a power-play tally at 5:58 of the second to tie the score. The Canadiens argued to no effect that the play was offside. The third period was relatively uneventful, other than a misconduct awarded to Howie Meeker of the Leafs in the early going. Later in the third, Richard fired a blast that Rollins was only able to get a piece of, but Barilko was there to sweep away the rebound.

Astonishingly, the game would be decided in OT for a third straight time. Calum MacKay went to clear the puck from Montreal's end, but was intercepted by Sloan, who dished the puck to Kennedy. Teeder made no mistake, whistling the puck past the birthday boy at 4:47 of the extra frame to give the Maple Leafs both a 2–1 win on the night and a 2–1 lead in the series.

Before game four on April 19 in Montreal, Ted Kennedy read his Toronto teammates a telegram he'd received: "As Stanley Cup hockey is reducing studying time for all important final examinations next week, request immediate elimination of unworthy opposition. Signed, Three hard-pressed McGill students."

Two of the game's greatest goaltenders, Toronto's Turk Broda and Bill Durnan of the Canadiens, observed the game together from the press box, chatting amiably throughout the contest.

Many Forum patrons were just settling into their seats when Sid Smith scored his fifth goal of the finals at the 38-second mark of the opening period. The Rocket countered later in the first to tie the score. The teams went into the intermission deadlocked.

Howie Meeker scored just over a minute into the second period, while Elmer Lach scored in the third to tie the game at two. The Montreal faithful rained the ice surface with programs and newspapers, delaying the game for several minutes while the maintenance crew scrambled out onto the ice to clear the debris.

Fans never seem to tire of overtime hockey, and for a fourth consecutive contest they would be rewarded with sudden-death action. This time, it was Harry Watson of the Leafs who broke the impasse. "There was a line change coming up, so I jumped on the ice because no one else was moving," he recalled. Max Bentley had stolen the puck from "Boom Boom" Geoffrion and fed it to Watson, who put a low, hard shot past McNeil to give Toronto the victory and a 3–1 lead in the incomparable series that *The Hockey News* labelled "tight as bark."

As improbable as it might seem, there was yet another overtime goal to be scored in the series, one that would earn its scorer, Bill Barilko, a permanent place in the mythology of hockey.

CHAPTER 13

The Goal

Through its first four games, each of which was decided in sudden-death overtime, the 1951 Stanley Cup final series had been spectacular, filled with the highest levels of suspense and excitement. The nation was gripped by the confrontation. And as a crowd of 14,577 filed into Maple Leaf Gardens on the evening of Saturday, April 21, 1951, the fans were abuzz with the possibility, unlikely though it might be, of yet another overtime thriller.

For the hometown Leafs, who led the series three games to one, the opportunity to win the Stanley Cup on home ice was on the line. Coach Joe Primeau rallied his charges. "We have to go out and give everything we have and a little more," he barked.

Faye Barilko sat halfway up the west side of Maple Leaf Gardens that night, watching, but not totally grasping, all the on-ice happenings. "I so nervous, I could not watch," she recalled in a 1982 *Toronto Star* article. Bill had called her during the week. "Mom, I've got a ticket to the game Saturday night for you. Find a ride and come see me," he requested.

Mrs. Barilko knew that when the puck was put into the Montreal Canadiens' net, that was good for her Billy and his team. And she was quick to let those around her know that the player wearing sweater number 5 for the Toronto Maple Leafs was her son. "That my Billy, that my Billy," she'd boast excitedly, pointing to the big, blond defenceman. Those seated nearby smiled, charmed by a mother's pride.

Anne Klisanich, meanwhile, was at home in her Schumacher apartment, listening intently to Foster Hewitt's play-by-play on her new Spartan radio. "There was no television in those days," Anne explains. It was a wonderful time in Anne's life — she and husband Emil were expecting their first child in June. "I was pregnant at the time. That's why I didn't go to the game."

Emil was working at the Pearl Lake Hotel in Schumacher, which was owned by his mother. Built in 1932, it was the first hotel in Schumacher. The beverage room, restricted solely to men in those days, was packed that night.

"On the night of a hockey game, it was a very busy night at the hotel," says Emil, who was tending bar while he kept one ear on the results of the Leaf game. And on this evening, Emil would have been paying special attention to the radio, since his brother-in-law was at Maple Leaf Gardens, competing for hockey's most cherished trophy.

Emil met Anne in 1948, and the couple had married on September 10, 1950. Alex was an usher and Bill served as best man.

"The customers at the hotel were well aware that I was married to Bill Barilko's sister," laughs Emil. "Bill used to visit me there at the hotel."

Frank Bonello watched the game from the standing-room section at the top of Maple Leaf Gardens. Bonello, who is today the Director of NHL Scouting , was a Toronto boy playing in the Maple Leafs organization in 1951. "I had played with the Marlboro midgets back then. We used to practise at Maple Leaf Gardens, albeit kind of early in the morning, but there was nothing wrong with that. It was always a big thrill to be there," states Bonello. "I used to get down to a lot of games. You paid 65 cents for a standing-room ticket up behind the greys. You'd be one of many standing in the lobby by the big iron gates at the entrance inside Maple Leaf Gardens. They'd swing open this big gate, you'd hand the usher your ticket, then run like hell all the way up the stairs. You wouldn't even pause; you ran up there until you got a spot behind the last row of greys and you stayed right there. If you had to go to the washroom, you got someone to stand there for you or asked a couple of guys to spread out but to keep that spot for you."

Hockey Night in Canada commentator Harry Neale was also at the game. "My Dad and I took the streetcar down from North Toronto — this was before the subway. I always wanted a hot dog and a Coke; I'm not sure that was what my father wanted," smiles Neale. "My Dad worked for Imperial Oil, so every once in awhile, he got tickets. We sat in the south-end blues, just off to the right a bit. We were in the fifth or sixth row, so they were good seats for a young guy. You never had to stand up to watch the play, sitting on the end, and that was the end that Barilko scored the goal in, so it was a little easier to see exactly what happened."

During the early '50s, photographer Nat Turofsky traditionally perched himself at ice level in the northeast end of the rink, affording him a terrific view of plays near the goal. There were times, such as in the instance of a fight, when Turofsky would hop the boards and shuffle quickly out onto the ice to capture a moment, but his seat along the boards usually afforded him a perfect vantage point from which to capture the action. The Turofsky brothers, Nat and Lou, had been the official photographers of the Toronto Maple Leafs since 1928.

Referee Bill Chadwick dropped the puck between the two rival centres to start game five. "Drama and suspense gripped the Toronto fans in an icy clutch before the game was half a minute old as Teeder Kennedy was carried off the ice on a stretcher," reported the *Globe and Mail*. The Leafs' captain collided with Montreal rookie Paul Meger and crashed into the boards. The crowd held its collective breath, waiting to determine the extent of their captain's injury. Whispers between rows talked of a back injury, but moments after leaving the ice surface in obvious pain, Kennedy returned to his familiar centre-ice position. "C'monnnnn, Teeeeederrrrr!" hollered John Arnott, a season-ticket holder since 1936 well known by Gardens crowds for his roaring benediction to the Toronto workhorse. The partisan crowd joined in an ovation for their captain.

At the end of one period, there were no goals on the scoreboard. The game summary shows only that Bobby Dawes, a former Leaf, was charged with slashing at 27 seconds, while Bill Barilko took a charging minor at 16:04.

Early in the second, Dawes tried to stop Ted Kennedy and awkwardly slid into the boards, fracturing his right leg and ending his season on the spot. Maurice Richard opened the scoring at 8:56 of the second period on a spectacular solo rush. As the Rocket cut across the front of the net past Leaf defenceman Jimmy Thomson, he backhanded the puck past netminder Al Rollins, who had committed himself early.

Tod Sloan replied for Toronto at the 12-minute mark, scoring even though Doug Harvey was draped over him like a blanket. Near the end of the period, with the score deadlocked at one, Barilko collided inadvertently with Montreal goalie Gerry McNeil. McNeil took his paddle and swatted Bill on the backside as he scurried to get back into the play. It wouldn't be the last time the two faced each during this game.

Paul Meger put the Canadiens ahead 2–1 in the third, backhanding a Harvey rebound that deflected off Joe Klukay's stick at 4:47. McNeil was brilliant in the Canadiens' cage, snaring a Barilko slap shot obscured by a crowd of players in front of him. Bob Hesketh of the *Telegram* reported, "Barilko making some razzle-dazzle dashes." McNeil made fine stops on Smith, Meeker and Barilko again through the third. Aggressions between the teams were held in check until 10:36 of the period, when Barilko and Tom Johnson of Montreal were sent off with matching roughing minors. Then Billy Reay of the Canadiens was handed a 10-minute misconduct for shoving linesman Bill Morrison.

With 1:33 to play in the third period, and Montreal leading 2–1, the Leafs pulled netminder Al Rollins in a valiant attempt to tie the score. Coach Primeau sent out six attackers: Ted Kennedy, Tod Sloan, Sid

Smith and Harry Watson, with Max Bentley and Gus Mortson on the point. Montreal countered with Kenny Mosdell, Floyd Curry and Eddie Mazur, with Tom Johnson and Butch Bouchard on defence in front of Gerry McNeil.

With Toronto applying pressure in the Montreal end, the Canadiens cleared the puck. Mosdell took off after it, corralled it and was in the clear with an empty net. The crowd groaned, but Watson cut across the ice at the Leafs blue line and took the puck from Mosdell, circled the net and carried the puck up the ice, having thwarted a certain goal.

With 61 seconds remaining and a face-off outside the Montreal blue line, Rollins skated back into the crease, but as soon as Kennedy won the draw and moved the play into the Canadiens' end, Rollins raced for the bench. The puck was jammed up against the boards and the whistle blown. Another face-off, this time with 39 seconds remaining in regulation.

Montreal coach Dick Irvin put Billy Reay, Bert Olmstead and Maurice Richard on the ice along with Bouchard and Harvey. Leaf coach Joe Primeau took a gamble, leaving the same six skaters on the ice — Rollins on the bench and Kennedy, Sloan, Smith, Watson, Bentley and Mortson on the ice. He played a hunch and rolled the dice.

"Now we've got the face-off in their end," remembers centre Ted Kennedy. "We're down a goal and we've pulled our goalkeeper. The fellow who's coming in to face off with me for the Canadiens is Billy Reay, and I think, 'Uh oh, I'm in trouble, because he's one guy I've had a lot of trouble getting the draw from. I'll be a son of a gun, but Dick Irvin pulls Reay out and puts Elmer Lach in. One guy I hadn't had all that much trouble with was Elmer Lach. I thought, 'I've got a chance.'"

"Teeder was the greatest face-off guy in the league, without question," maintained Sid Smith. "We had Max Bentley on the point, so Teeder's job was to get the puck back to Max, and we were just told to take a man — don't let anybody get out there."

Bill Chadwick dropped the puck between Kennedy for the Leafs and Lach for the Canadiens. Ted Kennedy relives the play-by-play: "I got it clean back to Bentley and Lach disentangled himself with me and rushed right out to Bentley. Max gave him the double shuffle, walked in about three strides, and let fly."

There was a sea of bodies in front of Gerry McNeil in Montreal's net. "Max shot and it either hit my leg or the referee's," said Smith. "It popped down beside me and I shot it through. I could see it hit the post and I thought, 'Oh my God, it didn't go in.' And then all of a sudden, the light went on. What happened? It deflected across to Sloanie, who was on the right side, and he batted it in and that saved our bacon right there."

Primeau's gamble had paid off. Tod Sloan scored his second goal of the game at 19:28 to knot the score at two. The goalmouth scramble meant that it took the illumination of the red goal light for the fans to realize that the Leafs had miraculously tied the game and the game was all but certain to go into overtime. The capacity crowd let out a magnificent roar of celebration. "Seldom have fans in Maple Leaf Gardens gone so completely joy-crazed," wrote Ed Fitkin in *Max Bentley: Hockey's Dipsy Doodle Dandy*. Programs were heaved onto the ice in a spontaneous show of appreciation, and it took several minutes to clear the ice surface so that the third period could be concluded. As the maintenance crew collected the debris strewn on the ice, the band started to play.

Years later, Canadiens coach Dick Irvin defended his choices. "They were the best five players I had. What more could I do? I was hoping Richard or Olmstead would get hold of the puck and whip it down the ice."

The Gardens thundered and, sensing possible victory, started chanting, "We want the Cup! We want the Cup!" This rolling, roaring accompaniment sustained itself through the intermission into the overtime frame. Moments earlier, sensing defeat, the Toronto faithful had been resigned to the prospect of game six in Montreal. Now they realized that the Leafs could go into overtime and collect the win — and the prize that went with it.

"I figured we had it after we tied it up in the final minute," Jimmy Thomson later admitted. "It took the heart out of them." Howie Meeker adds, "We knew right then and there that one of us wearing a blue and white sweater was going to get the overtime winner."

Both teams were also aware of the 11:45 p.m. curfew, and the need not only to end the game but to do so as quickly as possible. Turk Broda, who watched game five while Al Rollins defended the Leafs goal, made a prophetic observation. "I felt that Barilko or Mortson, the way they were going, would break in and settle the whole thing."

❦ ❦ ❦

In the corridors of Maple Leaf Gardens, Lou and Nat Turofsky met for a smoke and discussed Sloan's last-minute goal. Lou lit a cigar while his chain-smoking brother reached for the match and lit his cigarette. Every conversation between the brothers was animated, and their discussion of the tying goal was no different. After taking one final drag from his cigarette, Nat crushed the butt onto the Gardens' floor and shuffled to grab his camera from its spot in the ice maker's room. The Turofsky brothers owned Alexandra Studios on King Street West, from which they supplied hockey photos to the *Globe and Mail*, the *Telegram* and the *Daily Star*. For this overtime, Nat was hedging his bets. He was loath to lose a sale and, knowing that his clients would want the game-winning goal, he found a stool along the boards at the south end of the rink, hoping for a Toronto goal on McNeil that would play on the front pages of Monday's newspapers (there being no Sunday papers in Toronto in that era). He was taking a gamble: if he guessed wrong and Montreal scored, he would be at the wrong end of the rink and somebody else's photographs would grace the daily papers.

From the opening face-off of the overtime period, the Leafs applied pressure. Early in the period, Rocket Richard shook loose from the Leafs defenders and was on a breakaway. He deked Al Rollins out of position and was about to tuck the puck into the wide-open cage to end the game... until, out of nowhere, a body materialized in front of the net and deflected the puck away. It was Bill Barilko, who resurrected Toronto's hopes by foiling Richard on the play.

The Leafs worked the puck over the Canadiens' blue line. Slightly two minutes into the extra stanza, Harry Watson of the Leafs collected a rolling puck in the Montreal zone and passed it across the front of the net to Howie Meeker. Meeker lost control of the puck but corralled it and went in behind the Canadiens' goal. Nat Turofsky trained his Speed Graphic camera on goaltender Gerry McNeil as the puck went in behind the net. Meeker attempted a wraparound. Gerry McNeil seemed to slip as he went to guard the right post. Meeker got the puck back and was chased behind the goal by Montreal defenceman Tom Johnson. The Leafs' Watson was standing in front of the net, watched by Butch Bouchard. Meeker tried to get the puck out to Watson, who swung at the pass, but it glanced off Bouchard's skate and bounced out to the face-off circle. Barilko charged in from the blue line, narrowly avoiding teammate Cal Gardner. Goaltender McNeil started to regain his feet, but in one motion, Bill Barilko drilled the puck on his backhand as he sailed through the air to the right of Montreal goaltender McNeil.

Nat Turofsky clicked the shutter. It was 11:07 p.m. as the flash ignited, capturing the puck as it wired over McNeil's right shoulder into the Montreal net. The image captured by Turofsky is extraordinary. Barilko is suspended in mid-air above the ice surface; suspended in mid-air for eternity. Immortalized. The timing of the shot is so perfect that the goal light has yet to be turned on, and the Gardens faithful therefore have yet to recognize that the game has concluded. A split-second later the Gardens was to erupt in a fashion neither heard before nor since. One journalist called it a moment that will be remembered "as long as hockey is recalled." Never before in the history of Stanley Cup competition had five consecutive games gone into overtime, and it hasn't happened since.

Barilko watched the puck enter the net as he flew through the air. He bounded to his feet as he crossed the red goal line and leapt up, throwing both hands in the air. His magnificent goal at 2:53 of the first overtime period had earned the Toronto Maple Leafs the Stanley Cup!

Seconds earlier, Bill's sister Anne had leaned forward, straining so as not to miss a word of the play-by-play being described by Foster Hewitt. Her brother Bill had been on the ice in overtime and Hewitt's voice had reached a crescendo with excitement. "Skating down the left wing into the corner. Shoots and hits the side of the net. Here's right in front to Meeker. Meeker went by the net. Centres out in front. McNeil fell. In front again. Watson shoots. He shoots, *he scores*! Barilko! Barilko has won the Stanley Cup for the Leafs! Barilko shoots it into the net while McNeil was left all by himself. The Toronto Maple Leafs are world champions!"

Anne could scarcely believe her ears when she heard the call of her brother's legendary goal. "I can still vividly picture my brother scoring the winning goal and Foster Hewitt's famous words, 'He shoots, he scores.' I was gasping with excitement.

"It was such a glorious moment. We lived in a small apartment building. My neighbours came running down the hallway. Kay Currie, the manager of the coffee shop at the McIntyre Arena, came running to the apartment. So did my neighbours Millie and Bill Hartling.

"I couldn't even offer them a drink — we didn't have anything in the apartment. Kay said, 'I do. Come on down to my apartment!' We went down there, then I went down to the Pearl Lake Hotel and continued the celebration with my husband and everybody at the hotel. It was a very exciting night!"

🍁 🍁 🍁

While almost three million Canadians listened to Foster Hewitt's radio play-by-play, there were 14,577 pairs of eyes witnessing the game from within Maple Leaf Gardens. But none watched as intensely as Faye Barilko. She was a nervous wreck. It didn't really matter to her who was on the ice at that moment; all that mattered was that her Billy had skated out to his familiar position at left defence. As the play veered into the Canadiens' end, a man seated in front of Mrs. Barilko stood up, so she quickly leaned to her right to avoid losing sight of her boy. In a 1982 *Toronto Star* interview, Faye revealed more about those final moments of overtime. "I close my eyes. I squeeze them shut. I ask man beside me, 'Is it over yet?'" The crowd exploded, and Faye jumped to her feet when she realized who had won the Stanley Cup for the Toronto Maple Leafs. "Billy score! Billy score!" she remembered screaming to no one in particular. Her voice was almost lost in the cacophony. "I could not believe it. My Billy score!" Faye threw both arms up in the air in triumph, just as her son did on the ice below, as his teammates streamed over the boards to congratulate the hero of the 1951 Stanley Cup finals.

Barilko had gambled, straying from the blueline post he had promised his coach he would not leave. Ted Kennedy remembers the irony.

"Joe Primeau was our coach and Bill Barilko was a free spirit. He could be coached, and for the most part he did what he was supposed to do, but there were times when he'd break rank and do things on his own. Barilko would take chances and Primeau was having a great deal of difficulty keeping him back in his defence position. It got to the point where he was saying, 'Bill, when the puck is in their end, you've got to make sure you take up your position.'

"Shortly before that overtime goal, he said, 'Bill, I'm going to get a big hook and I'm going to throw it out there when you're out of position. I'm going to hook you back to your spot.' Now, Bill saw the loose puck, skated up and fired it into the top of the net to win the Cup for us. Everybody's out there on the ice. Everybody's congratulating Bill. When Joe congratulated him on the ice after the goal, Bill said, 'You didn't want a hook on me that time, did you, Coach?' Then they both laughed."

"I can remember this just as plain as day," starts Howie Meeker. "I'm home free and I haven't got much room to put it in along the ice. As usual, I hit the outside of the post. I go behind the net and Tom Johnson's coming back at me. I just throw it in front. I don't see anybody. Just as Barilko put it in, Tom Johnson puts his hand on the back of my head and the other on the middle of my back and jams me into the fence. I turn around and I'm gonna give him a shot right across the head, but the red light goes on.

"I said, 'There you are, you big SOB,' and we looked at each other, laughed, shook hands and it was over. I looked around then and I saw Gardner and Juzda with Barilko on their shoulders, so I knew Bill scored the goal. I went over to him and said, 'Great shot, big guy.'"

"I can still see Bill Barilko scoring the winning goal," remembered Cal Gardner. "The puck came back and he was flying through the air when he let it go and it went over McNeil's right shoulder up in the top corner." He told the *Globe and Mail:* "The puck came real close to me, but if you look at the famous photograph of the goal, you'll see me skating in the direction of a Montreal player. It was the Rocket. I had my attention on him, not on the puck. The thing was, Barilko had left his defence spot open. If he hadn't scored, the puck could easily have come out to Richard. So I was just doing my job, putting a guard on Rocket Richard." In a *Toronto Star* interview, Gardner added, "Smythe said I should have got the goal, and I probably could have picked the puck up and scored, but I had a good reason not to. I figured I had to watch the Rocket, or Smythe would have been on my back."

Harry Watson also had a perfect view of the winning goal. "We got an early jump in the overtime and worked the puck into their zone. I hit Meeker with a pass and he took a shot that hit the outside of the net and then settled behind the goal. Meeker went behind the net with Tom

Johnson battling for the puck. Meeker won the battle and threw it in front, hoping someone would be there. I took a crack at the puck, but I missed it. That's when Barilko spotted his chance.

"Barilko was supposed to stay on the blue line, but he saw the puck coming out, so he just roared in and took a slap at it. He made contact and sent it toward the goal. McNeil had gone down on the ice, and Barilko was on his way, too. He tripped over Gardner's skate as he took the shot and his momentum carried him toward the goal. He put his arms out and was totally horizontal above the ice, bracing for the fall. We picked Barilko up off the ice and began to celebrate our victory."

"There have been a lot of great overtime goals in the history of the NHL but to me, Barilko's was one of the best," Watson said. "Barilko's goal was a perfect ending to a tremendous series. It's just a shame that it was also the end of a great man's career, too."

Fern Flaman was Barilko's defence partner through much of the season, and was on the blue line with Bill when the winning goal was scored. "Whatever he missed, I caught. Or whatever I missed, he got. We did well. Bill was a little more offensive than I was. I was always a stay-at-home defenceman. Bill used to like to gamble once in a while. He did that the night we won the Stanley Cup against Montreal. Instead of hanging back at the blue line when the puck was in their zone, the puck came out about halfway and he skated in as hard as he could and just snapped the puck. When he did that, he just flew in the air and thank God the puck went in — otherwise I was there all alone. When I saw the red light go on, I took my stick and threw it in the air," Flaman laughs. "The monkey was off everybody's back. The tension was so devastating because they were all overtime games; they were all close games both in Toronto and in Montreal. We all hugged each other. It's a feeling I can't even describe. It was tremendous!"

Montreal captain Butch Bouchard stood helplessly in front of his net as Barilko's shot sailed over Gerry McNeil's shoulder. "I couldn't do a darned thing because I had to cover somebody in front on my side," he sighed.

"Most goals, you have a sense of it coming some way and you get ready but this one just happened," mused McNeil. "I don't know what happened. I had to look at pictures afterward. It surprised me — I didn't know how that puck got in. But there was Barilko. It was just a shocker."

Maple Leafs manager Conn Smythe was ecstatic. For much of the team it was their fourth Stanley Cup championship, but for Smythe, this was number seven. He had a special fondness for Barilko, and saw him not only save a goal by throwing himself across the net to thwart a Maurice Richard shot, but score the Cup-winner shortly thereafter. "We wouldn't be feeling so good right now if it hadn't been for Barilko," Smythe told his charges. "That was really the old college try."

Longtime season ticketholder Tom Gaston was at the game, and in his book, *A Fan for All Seasons,* he remembered, "The crowd went crazy! It may very well be the loudest I ever heard Maple Leaf Gardens."

"I was crying when Bill scored the goal," recalls his girlfriend at that time, Louise (Hastings) Carley. "I was jumping up and down. It was hours before I could get near Bill."

Frank Bonello screamed with the rest of Maple Leaf Gardens. "The celebration was bedlam. Of all teams, the Montreal Canadiens! And with all these overtime games — the suspense all series was unbelievable. The fans went crazy when that puck went in the net. You never expected Bill Barilko, a defenceman without a lot of puck finesse, to score the goal. If Bentley or Kennedy or Sid Smith got the puck, you might look for a goal, but you certainly weren't thinking about a goal being scored when Barilko was shooting it."

Bill's childhood friend, Gaston Garant, was at home in Timmins, listening to the game with his wife. "It was almost unbelievable. That was a wonderful thing for Bill. And you know what, it didn't affect Bill at all. Bill was always a very modest person."

Harry Neale's bird's-eye view of the Stanley Cup–winning goal gave him an outstanding perspective on Barilko's play. "It wasn't just that the overtime goal won the Stanley Cup, it was how he scored it," Neale explains. "He roared off the blue line, and I think he was off his feet when he shot the puck. So it was a timely goal, but it was a spectacular one, too. I can still remember it like I went to the game yesterday, and every time I see that picture of Barilko scoring, I just think that I was about 50 feet from it. I always say overtime goals that win the Stanley Cup — you can't beat that!"

When the Hollywood Wolves folded, Barilko's former teammate Babe Gresko returned to Toronto and met his wife-to-be. "I'll always remember the day Bill scored the winning goal: April 21, 1951," beams Gresko. "That's the day I got married."

"I was playing with Pittsburgh and we were in Cleveland that night," remembers John McCormack, who had started the season with this Stanley Cup–winning squad. "We lost that night, and they won that night with Billy scoring the goal. I was very pleased for him." In 2002, McCormack was given a Stanley Cup ring for his contributions to the 1950–51 championship season.

Nina Weseluck, Bill's cousin, didn't get to the game herself, but her sister did. "My sister Leda is the middle child in our family, and Bill was the middle child in my Aunt Faye's family. Leda had worked in the office at the Dome Mine in South Porcupine, and when we moved to Toronto she got a job with the Hydro. When one of the workers from the Dome came into Toronto, he had an extra ticket for the hockey game. He didn't know anybody in Toronto, so he called Leda and asked her to go.

She came running home and said, 'You're not going to believe it, but I've got a ticket for the game!' When Bill scored, she screamed, 'That's my cousin!' She had a seat up high, but she went all the way down [to the dressing room] and had a sip out of the Stanley Cup. Bill's mom was there with my sister Leda. Billy put his arm around her and said, 'This is my cousin.' She used to say, 'I'll never forget that game.'"

Faye Barilko had made her way through the screaming throng to congratulate her boy. She didn't get near the dressing room for some time, as the celebrations spilled from the inner sanctum into the corridor. Finally, an usher was able to guide Mrs. Barilko into the dressing room. By then, Bill had showered and dressed in one of his many suits. "Hey, Ma!" shouted Nat Turofsky. "Ladle some champagne from the Cup into Billy's mouth for a picture, will ya?" The players and their wives gathered around to watch the photo opportunity.

"I was with the Rangers when Billy Barilko scored the goal. We were finishing early those days, you know," laughs childhood friend Allan Stanley. "New York and Chicago were fighting for last place all the time. We had a long summer. I was back home." This was the second year in a row that one of Stanley's friends would score the goal that won his team the Stanley Cup championship. "I didn't have any pride when [Pete] Babando scored the Stanley Cup–winning goal in 1950. I was on the ice! But with Bill, we were out of it, and if anybody was going to get it, it's got to be one of us Timmins boys. I was really, really happy for him." As he reminisces, the affection that Stanley still has for Barilko is evident. "When Bill did something, he did it all out. You can see it in the picture. It shows the energy that was there — the spirit and the heart. He put everything he had into that shot. That's the effort he always put into the game."

    ❧ ❧ ❧

"All the excitement, all the thrills and all the drama that can come out in hockey were crammed into the last three minutes and 24 seconds of the game," wrote *The Hockey News*. "During that stretch, there didn't seem to be a sane person among the 14,577 witnesses. A seasoned and cynical reporter, unable to make himself heard above the din to his next-door neighbour in the press box, scribbled on a piece of paper, 'If the man from Mars were to walk in here, what would he think?'"

Nat Turofsky, camera in hand, climbed over the boards and half-shuffled, half-slid across the Gardens ice as the Maple Leafs swarmed the Stanley Cup hero. Joe Primeau was one of the first over the boards when he saw the goal light go on, and he arrived at the Montreal net at the same time as Al Rollins, who skated from his crease at full speed, dropping his goalie stick along the way. Bill Juzda and Cal Gardner hoisted Barilko onto their shoulders, and Nat fired shot after shot of the conquering hero.

The crowd's roar reached a deafening level when Turk Broda stepped onto the ice arm-in-arm with Conn Smythe. The immensely popular Leafs goaltender had not dressed for the final three games of the series. "We made the change because, over the season, our figures show that Rollins is a better performer than Broda by one goal," Smythe explained later. "That edge undoubtedly is the difference in their ages. We have found that Broda, when he starts to let in a few goals, invariably goes on and lets in more. This is taking nothing away from Turk, who has been marvellous."

The defeated, crestfallen Canadiens stood still. "I seemed to be lost," says Gerry McNeil. "I was separated from my team some way or other. My team was all over the place. I was alone on the ice, trying to get to the exit." Then, in the spirit of sportsmanship, the Canadiens gradually skated over to congratulate the winners before heading to their dressing room.

The Stanley Cup was carried out and placed on a table at centre ice. NHL president Clarence Campbell presented the trophy to Leafs captain Ted Kennedy. "Thank you very much, Mr. Campbell," started Teeder, calming the Gardens crowd only slightly. "First off, I want you all to show your appreciation to Captain Butch Bouchard and his Canadiens, who went down fighting all the way." Kennedy then proceeded to honour his coach, stating, "If any one person deserves credit more than any other, it's our coach, Joe Primeau! If you think it was tough for me to succeed Syl Apps as captain, think what a tough job it was for Joe to succeed a man like Hap Day as coach!" The crowd roared its approval. Day, incidentally, was not in attendance for the celebration at Maple Leaf Gardens. He was in Pittsburgh, watching the Cleveland Barons defeat the Hornets, Toronto's AHL farm team, for the Calder Cup.

Primeau took his turn at the microphone. "It has been a wonderful season, and winning the Cup is a thrill I never dared to dream of. I've never had a finer bunch of fellows to work with!" The former Maple Leafs star had accomplished an amazing feat as coach: he had led St. Michael's to the Memorial Cup championship in 1945 and 1947, and in 1950, he coached the Toronto Marlboro seniors to the Allan Cup championship. The Stanley Cup win on this night meant that Primeau had completed a coaching triple play.

"The celebration wasn't nearly as choreographed as it is today," mentions Harry Neale. "Clarence Campbell came out very quickly and presented the Stanley Cup. There was no Conn Smythe Trophy winner back then, of course."

Frank Bonello adds, "Now, everybody takes the Cup and goes around the rink, and we see children of the players coming on the ice. But back then, it was quite orderly. Clarence Campbell would walk out and they'd gather at centre ice and present the Cup. They'd pat each other on the back, shake hands with their opponents and skate off to the dressing room."

The victorious Leafs retreated to their dressing room to sip champagne from Lord's Stanley's treasured bowl. Howie Meeker was the first Leaf to reach the room, arriving without his stick, which someone had grabbed from him on the ice surface during the celebration. Archie Campbell, Toronto's assistant equipment manager, stood by the door and collected the sticks as they bounded into the dressing room. Inside, Leaf teammates gave Barilko three cheers as the photographers snapped off shot after shot.

As the last of the Maple Leafs left the ice surface for the dressing room, the stands emptied quickly — but not quietly. "I do remember that when I was going home, everybody was honking their horn and people leaving Maple Leaf Gardens were chanting, 'Go Leafs Go!'" recalls Harry Neale.

The three stars of the game were Bill Barilko, Tod Sloan and Gerry McNeil. Barilko was also named Player of the Week in the April 28 edition of *The Hockey News.*

There was no doubt in anyone's mind that Gerry McNeil had starred through the intire series. The *Telegram* wrote that McNeil "fell on 'em, kicked and smothered shots with uncanny precision." Toronto had outshot the Canadiens 41 to 19 in game five.

Hockey is a game measured in inches and fractions of seconds. With Barilko's winning sudden-death goal, the game came to a crashing halt for the Canadiens. Maurice Richard and Gerry McNeil sobbed in the Montreal room while the Leafs' jubilant celebration continued. Bill Durnan, who was McNeil's predecessor, reassured the despondent netminder that he could have done nothing more. "It was a tough one to lose," he said. "It's not your fault. You played a swell game."

Al Rollins, meanwhile, took his time undressing, peeling off his sweat-soaked equipment. "Right now, I feel like an old man after just one season," said the rookie, who had turned 24 at the beginning of that season. "Boy, there was a lot of tension!"

In the ensuing celebration, held in a large room adjoining the dressing room, the champagne corks popped and rebounded off the walls as players, their wives, team officials, reporters, photographers and well-wishers crowded in. The Stanley Cup was filled with champagne and the players took the first celebratory sips. Faye Barilko ladled champagne into the smiling mouth of her boy hero.

There had been whispers during the season that Barilko was going to be traded to Montreal, and Frank Selke had often mentioned how much he coveted the Leafs defenceman, but the rumours were extinguished quickly when Bill scored the winning goal.

"It was a long time coming. It is something I've dreamed about doing all my life," admitted Barilko. Forgotten was the midseason slump and the fears that Smythe would send him to Pittsburgh. And in fact, Barilko's famous goal was scored while nursing a broken nose, the result of a third-period collision with Bert Olmstead. "That Barilko must be the toughest hombre in hockey." wrote Milt Dunnell in the *Toronto Star*. Bert Olmstead tripped him into the boards so hard, he moved the Gardens six inches along Carlton Street. Barilko should have been a stretcher case — you have proof he wasn't."

While enjoying the celebration, the Maple Leaf players were informed that each would receive a $2,500 playoff bonus — $500 for finishing second during the regular season, $1,000 for eliminating Boston in the semifinals and $1,000 for their victory over Montreal. Each of the Canadiens, meanwhile, collected an $1,850 bonus.

"After the game, we went out to a restaurant. You don't always know exactly when you're going to win so you can't really plan things ahead of time," June Thomson, wife of Leafs defenceman Jimmy, reminisces. "After the restaurant, some of the players and their wives had gone home, but a few stragglers went back to a friend's home after. Bill was there. We called a radio station and told them that Bill Barilko was celebrating scoring the winning goal and winning the Stanley Cup and we wanted to dedicate a song to him. I can't remember what song it was."

Looking back on the remarkable series, *The Hockey News* stated, "The cash customers couldn't have asked for any more in the way of thrills and drama than they got in these five evenly contested games." Leafs president Conn Smythe had watched the Montreal Canadiens battle his Toronto Maple Leafs and declared, "The difference between those teams is the width of a hair."

The fact that four different Leafs scored game-winning goals during the series bears witness to the balance within the lineup: Sid Smith scored the overtime marker in game one, Ted Kennedy in game three, then Harry Watson and Bill Barilko. By an incredible coincidence, each of the goals was the only overtime goal any of the four men would score during their NHL careers.

"It was a great, great hockey series," Howie Meeker reminisces. "Certainly the most exciting I was ever in."

❦ ❦ ❦

Al Rollins had started four playoff games for the Leafs, allowing just six goals for a minuscule 1.50 goals-against average. Turk Broda started seven and relieved Rollins at 16:41 of the March 26 game, giving up just nine goals for an average of 1.12. He also posted two shutouts.

Max Bentley and Maurice Richard tied for the playoff scoring lead, each collecting 13 points in 11 games. The Rocket had nine goals and four assists, while Bentley dipsy-doodled to score two goals and add 11 assists. Sid Smith, a 30-goal scorer during the regular season, led the Leafs in playoff goals with seven.

In 11 playoff games, Bill scored three goals and two assists for five points. He scored both the first and the last goal for the Leafs in the finals against the Canadiens. Billy was assessed 31 penalty minutes as well, second only to Jimmy Thomson's 34. But really, the only statistic that mattered was the goal scored on April 21, 1951.

The Toronto Maple Leafs of 1946–1951 were the first dynasty in the National Hockey League's 34-year history. Four Stanley Cup championships in five years is an extraordinary accomplishment in any era, and unprecedented at the time. A sizable core of Leafs, of whom Bill Barilko was only one, participated in all four championships; the others included Turk Broda, Teeder Kennedy, Joe Klukay, Howie Meeker, Gus Mortson and Jimmy Thomson.

"We should have won the Cup in 1950, too," says Mortson. "We lost [that seven-game semifinal] series by two overtime goals. It was just the luck of the draw that we were on the short end of both, or we would have won five Stanley Cups in a row."

"We were as tough as anybody in the league," declares Howie Meeker. "We had the best system by far. We had the best coach in the league in Hap Day and the best goaltender in Broda. We expected to win. Cripes, we should have won five in a row!"

✤ ✤ ✤

On Sunday morning, April 22, Bill Barilko received a telegram at his room in the Eton House Hotel: "Congratulations on win tonight scoring the winner. Wish I had been there. Was listening and will never forget it. Give best to Mom and hope you have good time and rest. You deserve it. Don't forget what you want in contract for next season. Pay me visit. Home in fall. Alex Barilko."

Monday morning arrived, and the newspapers touted the biggest story of the weekend. "Leafs Win Stanley Cup in Dramatic Climax," screamed the *Telegram*. The *Star* blurted, "Bashin' Bill Barilko's Blow Kills Canadiens." "Jubilant Crowd Hails World's Hockey Champions after Last-Minute Victory," read the *Globe and Mail*.

"Emil, listen to this," implored Bill's sister Anne back home in Timmins. "The *Daily Press* headline says, 'Timmins' Bashing Bill Stanley Cup Hero.'" It was the second year in a row that a Timmins boy had turned the trick. Pete Babando had scored the Stanley Cup–winning goal for Detroit in overtime in the spring of 1950. Although raised in Timmins, Babando was born in Pennsylvania.

Bill bought the *Toronto Daily Star* on his way to Maple Leaf Gardens, where the team's official Stanley Cup portrait was to be taken. "Hey, you're Bashin' Bill Barilko," the astonished cashier said. "Let me shake the hand that scored the greatest goal in Toronto Maple Leaf history! Your money's no good here with me today. Go on, the paper's on me!"

Bill beamed like the butcher's dog. It had been an incredible 36 hours since his backhand eluded the mitt of Gerry McNeil. He drove west along the Danforth past his store and across the Prince Edward Viaduct to Church Street, where he turned left and proceeded south to Maple Leaf Gardens. The boys were all starting to gather, kidding each other as they pulled on their uniforms one last time before breaking for the summer.

Nat Turofsky and Conn Smythe situated the members of the Leafs. "Teeder, put the Cup right in front of you," Smythe instructed. At 11 o'clock on Monday, April 23, there was certainly no need for Turofsky to implore the boys to smile. "Say, 'Stanley!'" The Leafs laughed and grinned.

It was the last official moment that Bill Barilko would spend with his teammates. It was the last time he would officially pull on his Maple Leafs sweater. His equipment was packed away for the summer with that of the rest of the team. No one dreamed that it would sit in Barilko's dressing room stall, unworn, the following October.

🍁 🍁 🍁

There was a parade in Toronto the Saturday following the Maple Leafs Stanley Cup victory. Except, surprisingly, it wasn't to honour the Toronto hocley club — it was for cowboy film star Hopalong Cassidy. The city's parade started at Union Station at 9:30 the morning of April 28 and proceeded up Bay Street to City Hall.

CHAPTER
14

Victim of Victory

Bill Barilko never hesitated to gamble. On April 21, 1951, his roll of the dice resulted in a huge payoff. Spotting a loose puck at the face-off circle and ignoring the mandate from Leafs coach Joe Primeau that he not step into the Canadiens' zone, Barilko darted in and fired the goal that secured his place in hockey history. But for every victory, someone has to lose.

In 1950–51, Gerry McNeil became the regular goaltender for the Montreal Canadiens, a position he would maintain through an all-too-brief interregnum between the Hall of Fame careers of Bill Durnan and Jacques Plante. The Canadiens had last won the Cup in 1946 and made their last appearance in the finals a year later. Such legends as Durnan, Toe Blake and Ken Reardon had since retired, while Buddy O'Connor had been traded; Butch Bouchard and Elmer Lach were now in their thirties; and the generation of stars who would supply the foundation of the late-1950s dynasty — Jean Beliveau, "Boom Boom" Geoffrion, and Dickie Moore — were still on the horizon.

Throughout a sub-.500 season, no one could question the fight put up by the little man — five foot seven, 155 pounds — who tended the Habs goal and was a standout during the 1951 Stanley Cup playoffs. But for more than 50 years, Gerry McNeil's name has been indelibly linked to that of Bill Barilko. One is regarded as a hero, while the other is remembered for surrendering the goal that created the hero.

"It's been my claim to fame," Gerry McNeil sighed in his Montreal-area home. "I still get a lot of mail from that goal — people asking me to autograph their picture of the Barilko goal."

McNeil died in Montreal on June 17, 2004, at the age of 78. The unwilling victim of a goal that has taken on mythic status, he should be remembered for his superb netminding. In fact, McNeil's name made news again during the 2003 playoffs — this time because of his proficiency at stopping shots. That spring, the Mighty Ducks of Anaheim rode the uncanny netminding of Jean-Sebastien Giguere all the way to game seven of the Stanley Cup finals. In the Western Conference finals against the Minnesota Wild, the almost-unbeatable Giguere did not surrender a goal until 4:37 of the first period of game four — which snapped a streak of 217 minutes, 54 seconds of shutout hockey. It was the longest such display since Montreal's McNeil posted a run of 218:42 — ironically, during the playoffs of 1951. McNeil's career regular-season goals-against average, a sparkling 2.36, matches that of his predecessor Durnan, while Plante finished with a 2.38 average. In playoff action, Plante carried a career average of 2.16, while Durnan's was 2.07. Gerry McNeil posted a superior mark of 1.89.

McNeil was part of Montreal Canadiens' teams that won the Stanley Cup in 1953 and 1957, and he played in the All-Star Game in 1951, '52 and '53.

※　※　※

Gerry McNeil began his hockey career as a goaltender in his hometown, Quebec City. "There was a guy in our neighbourhood who made an outdoor rink in an open field by himself," Gerry recalled. "He watered it and we helped him shovel. There were no boards — the puck was always in the snowbanks. I played goal so that I could be on the ice all the time. I hated to sit on the snowbank."

Mike McMahon, a defence prospect for the Canadiens, was at training camp in 1943 and told general manager Tommy Gorman about Gerry McNeil. "He said, 'There's this young goalkeeper in Quebec you should look at.' Tommy Gorman called me and asked me to go to the Canadiens training camp," said Gerry, who was just 16 years old at the time. Although Bill Durnan was locked into the netminding role with Montreal, McNeil played exceptionally well through the training camp and preseason games. "The year before, I was going to St. Pat's High School and I couldn't even make that team, and here I was in goal for the Montreal Canadiens!" Gerry chuckled.

In an era of multimillion-dollar contracts, McNeil laughed when he recalled his first professional contract. "They offered me $3,200 for the season. They'd put me up at the Queen's Hotel (owned by Canadiens owner Senator Donat Raymond). All my room and board, meals and laundry would be paid and they'd register me at a Catholic high school. But I wasn't interested in a contract. It wasn't about the money at all. I was lonesome, so I went back home. Tommy Gorman called the house and talked with my dad, who was an employee of the Anglo-Canadian Pulp and Paper Mill. My Dad came to me and said, 'You'd better think this over, Gerry, because here's my paycheque for the week,' and he showed me a cheque for $19.75."

Although the Canadiens weren't about to replace their star netminder with an untried 16-year-old, Gerry did sign a contract with the Habs and would practice with the parent club while playing with the Montreal Royals of the Quebec Senior Hockey League.

"I got quite friendly with Bill Durnan," remembers Gerry. "I didn't want to take his place." McNeil made his NHL debut with two games as an injury replacement for Durnan during the 1947–48 season. It would be two years before he donned the pads for the Canadiens again — this time for six games, during which he recorded his first NHL shutout. McNeil also played two playoff games in 1949–50, and a headline in *The Hockey News* read: "Habs Sub McNeil Outdoes Old Master Durnan." That spring, Durnan, who often felt tremendous anxiety playing goal, succumbed to the pressure of playoff hockey. The call went out to McNeil, who, remembering his loyalty to the Canadiens' starter, declared, "I will play only if Bill wants me to."

Durnan, a Hall of Fame netminder, played only seven NHL seasons, yet he was a First Team All-Star and Vezina Trophy winner as best goaltender in six of those campaigns. But the stress he felt during the 1950 playoffs convinced him it was time to retire. In 1950-51, McNeil stepped into the crease for Montreal on a full-time basis and, as an NHL rookie, played in all 70 regular season games and each of the 11 playoff matches the Canadiens took part in.

While the Toronto Maple Leafs were dismissing the Boston Bruins in one semifinal series, Montreal met the Stanley Cup champion Detroit Red Wings in the other. "The Red Wings were shoo-ins at the time," admitted McNeil. The first-place Wings had finished 36 points ahead of third-place Montreal and had dominated the Canadiens during their 14 regular-season meetings.

Game one, played in Detroit on March 27, was deadlocked at two going into overtime. Just over a minute into the fourth overtime period, Maurice Richard stripped the Red Wings' Leo Reise of the puck and fired the game-winner past Terry Sawchuk. "We ended up winning that first game in Detroit, so it gave our team a little lift. From then on, we thought we could win," Gerry recalled.

In game two, again played at the Olympia in Detroit, the teams were locked in a scoreless tie after regulation time. At 2:20 of the third overtime period, the Rocket again scored on Sawchuk to give Montreal a 1–0 win and a two-games-to-none advantage in the series. "Those were long, long games," remembered McNeil without a hint of understatement. "And we won both of them."

The series shifted to Montreal for games three and four, won 2–0 and 4–1 by the Red Wings. Although his streak of more than 200 blemish-free minutes was snapped in the third game, McNeil was brilliant in net through both contests. Detroit simply outplayed Montreal in tying the series. It was a tough semifinal in other ways, too: when McNeil ventured out of his crease during the fourth game, Ted Lindsay dumped him and was quickly greeted by the fists of Doug Harvey for his efforts.

Back to Detroit on April 5, and Montreal again won on the road, outscoring Detroit 5–2. The combatants returned to the Forum for game six on April 7. Through two scoreless periods the teams went at each other, although it is remarkable that no penalties were called. In the third, the game was broken wide open: five goals were scored in the 20 minutes, with Montreal emerging on top 3–2 to eliminate the Red Wings.

That paved the way for the final series against Toronto, who had eliminated the Bruins. Again the Canadiens would have their work cut out for them — their regular-season record against the Leafs in 1950–51 was 2–10–2, and the Habs had been held to seven goals in their last five meetings. Yet all five games of the series went into overtime — in fact, seven of Montreal's 11 playoff matches required extra time — and Gerry McNeil was the sole reason Montreal was so competitive. "When you look at it now, you think, 'That must have been a lot of tension,'" noted McNeil.

Game one was tied at two after 60 minutes, before the Leafs won it at 5:51 of overtime. The second game was decided at 2:55 of OT, this time with Montreal emerging on the winning end of a 3–2 score. The third game, tied 1–1 after regulation, took an additional four minutes and 47 seconds before the Leafs won it. Toronto potted the winner in game four at 5:15 of overtime, defeating Montreal 3–2.

Game five, played in Toronto on April 21, 1951, shouldn't have been as close as it was. Toronto outshot Montreal 41–19. "When I saw the footage of the last two minutes of the game plus the overtime, there was just no question that the Leafs were going to win," states David McNeil, Gerry's proud son and an associate professor of English at Halifax's Dalhousie University. "They were all over the Habs at that point. Everything I've come across says my dad was great in net."

Then, 2:53 into overtime, Bill Barilko scored the Stanley Cup–winning goal.

"Barilko's shot was not that difficult for me," admitted Gerry McNeil. "I just simply missed it. You have a sense on most goals of the puck coming and you get ready, but on this one, I don't know what happened. I had to look at pictures after. It surprised me — I didn't know how the puck got in. At the time, I didn't even know who shot it — I never knew who scored most of the goals that were scored against me. But there was Barilko. He was right at the face-off circle.

"It was just a shocker. It was an awful disappointment."

As the jubilant Maple Leafs emptied their bench to circle the hero of the moment, Gerry McNeil stood isolated, just a few feet away.

"Of all the memories I have in hockey, that is one which I'll never forget," stated Gerry. "Each game was so close that there was never any let-up on either of the goalies in the series. It was tough on everyone's nerves."

The Hockey News, headlining the article "McNeil Greatest Hero Even in Habs Stanley Cup Defeat," said, "In defeat, Gerry McNeil, a little bit of a guy with a heart a thousand times his size, whom the experts predicted would never do, outshone, outworked and performed as magnificently as any goaler ever performed down the glorious Stanley Cup road. In defeat, this little guy was a hero."

"I still feel bad that we lost the Stanley Cup that year, but I'm proud of the fact we had beaten the Red Wings and then went with five straight games against the Leafs in overtime. That is an achievement in itself," said McNeil, years later. "And with that photo of the winning goal scored by Barilko, I will always have that as a reminder of the whole series."

Gerry McNeil has another reason to remember that game. When reporters manoeuvred their way through the throng in the visiting team's dressing room to get McNeil's reaction to Bill Barilko's goal, they found the netminder on the bench, sobbing. Most assumed it was out of disappointment. In fact, he was elated. "We were playing in Toronto and my wife was in the hospital in Montreal. My oldest daughter, Karen, was born that night," smiled Gerry. "She always remembers, too," he added. "The Barilko goal has something to do with her."

David McNeil agrees. "For the family, whenever the Barilko goal comes up, we think fondly of the fact that that was also the night our sister Karen was born. If you were to meet my sister, you'd discover what a wonderful person she is. For us, we don't care who won the Stanley Cup that night — that was the night Karen was born."

"All these years, I've seen my Dad at various public functions and he's always been very proud to be a Montreal Canadien and has had only a positive feeling about his career," beams David. "Dad was so proud of being so competitive."

After his stellar performance in the heartbreaking 1951 playoffs, Gerry McNeil went into 1951–52 with a new confidence. "You felt that you fit in. You knew that you could do it," Gerry said.

The Canadiens improved from 65 points to 78, and finished second in the standings in 1951–52. McNeil's 34 wins were second only to the 44 victories chalked up by Detroit's Sawchuk. After an exhausting and physically punishing series with Boston — during which the Bruins took a 3–2 lead in games and were ahead 2–1 late in game six — Montreal was defeated in four consecutive games against the Detroit Red Wings, who won the Cup in the minimum eight games that spring.

In 1952–53, McNeil — who led the league with 10 regular-season shutouts — finally got to experience a championship of his own, when Montreal defeated Boston four games to one, capturing the Cup with a dramatic 1–0 overtime win in game five. "I came off the ice and Dick Irvin said to me, 'What are you smiling about?' He said, 'Take that smile off your face. You stopped every shot the wrong way!'" McNeil was incredulous as he retold the story.

Then, as if McNeil hadn't been victimized enough for one career, in game seven of the 1954 Stanley Cup finals against the Red Wings, Montreal lost 2–1 at the 4:29 mark of overtime. Detroit's Tony Leswick fired a routine shot at the Canadiens' net and was astonished to discover the puck had made its way past McNeil in the Montreal goal. "Leswick was near centre ice and he flipped it up in the air. The puck was coming down four or five feet in front of the crease. Doug Harvey put his hand up to bat it down and head up ice, but the puck hit the side of his glove and went right in the net."

McNeil had been preparing to catch the puck and couldn't react in time as it changed direction, went over his left shoulder and into the net just under the crossbar. "That was the most disappointing goal I ever let in," Gerry admitted.

Goal. Game. Series. Cup. Gerry McNeil again was the victim of victory.

Gerry McNeil didn't play hockey during 1954–55. "I almost quit playing because things weren't working out with Dick Irvin." But then, the Canadiens made a change and hired former star Toe Blake to coach the team. "Toe came to my house and said 'Gerry, I have [Jacques] Plante, who is a great goaltender, but I'd be so happy if I could have you in the wings." Gerry joined the Montreal Royals of the Quebec Hockey League for 1955–56 and promptly won the league's top goaltender award. When Plante was debilitated by asthma attacks during the 1956–57 season, Gerry stepped in and played nine games for Montreal. Although that was the extent of his on-ice contribution to the Canadiens that season, McNeil earned the right to have his name engraved on the Stanley Cup a second time.

Although Gerry McNeil played just four full NHL seasons, all with the Montreal Canadiens, he made a sizable contribution and has his name attached to some of the most famous moments in hockey history. When asked if he had any regrets about his NHL career, the delightful McNeil had a quick response. "My biggest regret is not being a few inches taller. I keep thinking about that," said the 5'7" McNeil. "If I had been six foot, I could have gotten a few more of those pucks. It would have been easier to reach the other end of the net."

CHAPTER 15

Forever Young

Within the remarkable collection of photographs that are respect-fully and lovingly archived within the Hockey Hall of Fame, there is one that is requested more often than any other. It is the incomparable photograph of Bill Barilko firing the shot that eluded goaltender Gerry McNeil at 2:53 of the first overtime period of game five of the Stanley Cup finals, played on April 21, 1951. This shot, captured for eternity by the precise timing of a shutter's click, has preserved a high point in Toronto Maple Leaf history — and the legacy of Bill Barilko.

The image, captured by Nat Turofsky, is exceptional, and is a tribute to the photographer's extraordinary timing. Barilko, falling forward, is captured in mid-flight, his neck craned as he watches his shot fly over McNeil's right shoulder into the Montreal goal. As Andrew Podnieks noted in his book *Portraits of the Game: Classic Photographs from the Turofsky Collection at the Hockey Hall of Fame*, when the photo was snapped, the red goal light had yet to been turned on, and the fans had yet to recognize what had occurred. Captured in black and white is that final exquisite split-second before the crowd erupts in a fashion never heard before or since at Maple Leaf Gardens.

Few images so concisely encapsulate an entire story. The only other hockey photograph that conveys a similar sense of drama while also capturing an historically important moment is the one of Bobby Orr's incredible Cup-winning goal for the Boston Bruins on May 10, 1970. There are some remarkable parallels between the two: both depict Stanley Cup–winning goals, both of which were scored in overtime (Orr's came at the 40-second point of the extra frame). Both goal scorers are defencemen, and both are flying through the air as they score. Barilko appears to have dived merely to get his stick on the puck.

Orr is in flight as the result of being tripped by St. Louis Blues defenceman Noel Picard.

🍁 🍁 🍁

Turofsky's photograph is one of three extraordinary photographs, each taken by an equally extraordinary photographer, from three different vantage points.

Nat Turofsky traditionally shot Maple Leafs games from the north end of Maple Leaf Gardens, but he gambled that Toronto would score the winning goal against Montreal and moved to the south end, near the Montreal blue line, where he trained his Speed Graphic camera on Gerry McNeil in the Montreal goal. Seated several places to Turofsky's left, closer to the goal line than the blueline, was Harold Whyte of the Toronto *Telegram*. Whyte's shot, a little tighter on Barilko and McNeil, is no less vivid, though much less frequently seen. The shot was taken a fraction of a second after Turofsky clicked his shutter, and Bill has landed on the ice and is sliding towards the goal line. His head is up, and he has watched the puck strike the net behind Gerry McNeil. A ghostly reflection can be seen in the recently cleared ice surface.

The third was taken from the opposite side of the arena by Michael Burns, a freelance photographer who at one time had worked for Nat and Lou Turofsky at their Alexandra Studios. Taken from the west side of the arena, almost directly across the ice from Harold Whyte (in fact, in the right-hand side of Burns' shot, you can clearly see Whyte holding his camera), the image is arguably more spectacular than that of Turofsky. Taken a millisecond later, Barilko is still in flight, but he is apparently aware he has scored because a smile traces the lips that will soon be sipping champagne from the Stanley Cup. McNeil is glancing behind himself to see the puck. To the left, Butch Bouchard can be seen watching the puck's trajectory, while Maurice Richard, caught in the glow of Burn's flashbulb affixed to the glass above the boards, casts an eerie shadow on the east-side boards.

In 1951, the chance that a historic hockey moment would be captured by one photograph is extraordinary. The fact that *three* photographers would beautifully chronicle the same moment is nothing short of astounding. Although all three were outstanding photographers, it would be an understatement to say that the era wasn't conducive to hockey photography. Cameras were large and cumbersome, for one thing. And in a game as fast as hockey, focus and composition are always challenging — fast films and strobe lighting would become invaluable aids, but these were still years away. The Speed Graphic camera used plates, so there was no second chance should the first opportunity be missed. Flashbulbs, set up on the glass by the photographers before the game, had to work in perfect tandem with the camera. With precision and patience, all three photographers — Nat Turofsky, Harold Whyte and Michael Burns — captured the greatest goal in the history of the Toronto Maple Leafs.

Before his death on December 20, 1956, Nat Turofsky, along with his brother Lou and their Alexandra Studios, made a fair bit of money selling the Barilko photograph to newspapers and books. But it was not Nat's favourite shot. That honour goes to a photograph of the Leafs leaping over the boards on April 19, 1947, after they had defeated the Montreal Canadiens 2–1 to win the Stanley Cup.

❄ ❄ ❄

Michael Burns, who was elected to the Canadian Horse Racing Hall of Fame in 1997, is known worldwide for his classic photography. A shot of Northern Dancer hangs on the wall in his office on the grounds of Woodbine Racetrack in Toronto. He has been photographing "the sport of kings" for 50 years, and yet, even though he shot hockey for only five or six years, it is the Barilko goal for which he is best known. "Yes, it is my most requested shot," Burns states. "I don't remember anything about that game, though. And I don't really know anything about Barilko, either. I used to see him before the games and probably said hi to him, but that was it."

"I liked hockey, but it was a job for me," he continues. "I sat in the seat I always sat in, with executives from Imperial Oil right beside me. The *Toronto Star* guaranteed me they'd use one shot from every Leaf game, but I hustled my photographs wherever I could. The *Telegram* had staff photographers, so I never had much success there, but I got shots picked up by newspapers and magazines. A chewing gum company bought my photographs, too.

"Most Saturdays, I would photograph the [Toronto Argonauts] football game, then hurry over to Maple Leaf Gardens so I could set up my lights on the boards for the game that night. As soon as the game was over, I'd rush back to my little office and develop the photographs through the night. Then I'd sleep in Sunday, then have to go to the papers to show them what I had so they could go to press with Saturday's story in Monday's paper." A half-smile creeps over Michael's mouth. "It was difficult. I had a wife and family, and I'll bet I was at Maple Leaf Gardens just about every night of the week. There were usually two hockey games, plus I shot the wrestling matches, so I'd be at the Gardens for that. There was always something going on."

❄ ❄ ❄

Despite the parallels between Nat Turofsky's photograph of Barilko and the iconic shot of Bobby Orr in 1970, there is a significant difference. The Barilko photo depicts the entire play in microcosm. It takes only a modicum of imagination to determine not only *what* has happened, but *how* it transpired. Clearly, he has lunged in from his prescribed post on the blue line. We see McNeil on his backside in the crease, and can surmise that he has just made a save that left him out of position to face Barilko's shot. Behind the net, Habs defenceman Tom Johnson has delivered a punishing bodycheck to a slumping Howie Meeker, while his partner, Butch Bouchard, seems to be covering Harry Watson. Leaf skaters outnumber Canadiens four to three — indicating that the Leafs are fully committed to the attack and that Barilko is gambling, and hinting at a defensive lapse on the Canadiens' part. But most remarkable is being able to observe the flight path of the puck from Barilko's stick into the netting behind McNeil's shoulder. By comparison, the Orr shot simply shows us the result. No matter how long we study the photograph, we cannot tell how the play developed.

"The [Turofsky] photograph itself would have made Barilko famous forever, but his death, the way it happened, and the way they found him by chance, solidified the fact that Bill Barilko will never be forgotten," agrees author James DuPlacey, who wrote the text on Barilko's famous hockey card that inspired the song "Fifty Mission Cap" by The Tragically Hip.

* * *

As early as 1944, Conn Smythe had insisted that each Maple Leafs home game be filmed so that he could analyze plays and evaluate players. The man who committed those early games to film was Donald "Shanty" McKenzie, who had played with the Toronto Argonauts of the Canadian Football League before and after the Second World War, captaining the 1950 squad that won the Grey Cup. In 1941, Shanty joined Conn Smythe's Sportsmen's Battery as a sergeant-major, and upon his return to Toronto, Smythe hired him to film Leafs games, a position he held until 1968, even after being named building superintendent of Maple Leaf Gardens.

Smythe's use of film was revolutionary for hockey, and Smythe was scoffed at by his contemporaries. Three decades later, when such visionaries as Roger Neilson began to study videotapes of games, they too were mocked. Neilson, who coached the Maple Leafs between 1977 and '79, earned the less-than-complimentary nickname "Captain Video." These days, the practice is virtually universal.

Paul Patskou is a Toronto-based broadcast historian who specializes in hockey. His private collection includes thousands of hours of games dating from the earliest known films to the most recent contests and interviews.

Paul was not only able to discover footage of Barilko's Stanley Cup–winning goal, but in an unprecedented — and miraculous — find, the rest of the game shot by Shanty McKenzie on April 21, 1951 — including film that hadn't been seen by anyone since that date.

"I had been trying to find any 16-millimetre hockey films not catalogued and simply referred to as 'unknown hockey' at the National Archives in Ottawa. The assumption would be that most of that type of footage would be unimportant pieces of film put aside because they had little if any significance. No one had paid the slightest bit of interest to any of these films since they were sent to the Archives."

Paul arranged to have the contents of these 16-millimetre reels transferred to VHS videotapes so that he could view them. "When I received copies of the films, I watched the silent action and looked for any clues that might help me identify the footage. As I watched, I noted the players on each team, the officials, and other specifics that indicated the game was shot at Maple Leaf Gardens. Shortly into the film, I was able to pinpoint that the game was a Toronto Maple Leafs home game against the Montreal Canadiens from 1950–51.

"The goals had been physically edited out of these reels," he notes. Before the advent of videotape, the producers of newscasts or, later, *Hockey Night in Canada* would have isolated the goals for replay purposes.

"I started to realize that this was no ordinary game," says Patskou. In fact, he was quickly able to deduce through the players involved and the line combinations coaches were putting onto the ice that he had stumbled upon game five of the 1951 Stanley Cup finals. "As I neared the end of the tape, I was astounded to discover that, although the overtime goal was cut out, the entire post-game celebrations on the ice were on this footage. No one, other than the people there, had ever seen what was on this footage!" exclaims Paul, incredulously. "It was just outstanding. It is the most lengthy postgame on-ice Stanley Cup presentation and celebration ever filmed up to that time."

Realizing that the source of the pictures was Maple Leafs game film shot by Shanty McKenzie, Paul was surprised at the camera position. "I had thought that McKenzie filmed from the greens, but this looks like a lower angle, closer to the ice."

Thanks to his collection, Paul also knew that Shanty McKenzie's film of Bill Barilko's overtime goal had been shown only once before — on *Hockey Night in Canada* on April 11, 1964.

But what he had discovered was only the last half of the 1951 Stanley Cup championship game.

"A year or so later, I located other unidentified films in a completely different collection," continues Patskou. "On one, I knew right away that it was the first half of that 1951 game.

"Although the goals are cut out, this is one of the earliest complete hockey games ever. Fortunately, three of the goals from that game exist on other footage," smiles Patskou.

If not for Patskou's curiosity and diligence in identifying the footage, this game would never have been discovered. "The discovery of this Shanty McKenzie film at the National Archives is one of the best I have ever made," Paul states. The mystery remains as to why this particular game was separated into two distinct parts, housed in two different collections, and further how it had come to be labelled as "unidentified."

While Patskou stumbled upon the rest of the game, there are actually *three* versions of Bill Barilko's overtime Cup-winner that have been discovered through the decades. Paul continues: "The National Film Board has about five minutes from that game, including Tod Sloan's tying goal late in the third period plus most of the overtime, including Barilko's goal. It was shot from a high angle — presumably up in the greys [the highest level of seats at Maple Leaf Gardens]. They have also captured much of the on-ice celebration.

"Newsreel companies routinely sent cameramen to any potential Stanley Cup championship games at that time. The newsreel film includes Rocket Richard's goal earlier in the game, plus Barilko's overtime goal from an angle similar to that of the National Film Board. The newsreel has a voiceover describing the action."

Patskou took the time to watch (and re-watch, over and over again) the Barilko goal from various angles. His observations are fascinating:

> The play is started by Harry Watson, carrying the puck over the Montreal blue line, being chased by Tom Johnson with Emile "Butch" Bouchard also in pursuit. Watson is ridden into the boards by Johnson in the corner to the right of goaltender Montreal goalie Gerry McNeil. The puck squirts loose behind the red line, and Watson beats Bouchard to the puck and sends a hard pass out to the front of the Montreal net where Howie Meeker, who was trailing on the play, comes streaking in from his right-wing position. The puck goes right past Leaf winger Cal Gardner, who was to the right of McNeil at this time.
>
> Meeker takes the pass but can't handle it, then pursues the puck behind the Montreal net. Meeker then skates behind the Montreal net, passing teammate Gardner going the other way, and tries a wraparound in an attempt to score on McNeil. But the netminder has moved over and covered the other side of the net. In making the save with his feet, Gerry McNeil falls into a sitting position on the goal line.

Meeker takes the puck after the failed wraparound and, from behind the net on the goalie's right-hand side, throws a backhand pass to Harry Watson in front of the net. Watson is positioned in front of Gerry McNeil, having come from the corner.

Bouchard is checking Watson as Harry one-times the pass towards the Montreal goal. Tom Johnson of the Canadiens has ridden Meeker into the boards in back of the Montreal net at this point. McNeil is still in the sitting position inside his goal. Maurice Richard has skated into the area, backchecking, and Cal Gardner has arrived in the slot position.

Watson's pass appears to hit Bouchard's skate and it caroms to the right of the goal, where Bill Barilko, having come from his point position, backhands the rebound. At that moment, Cal Gardner is also in position to get to the puck after it went off Bouchard. Gardner had completed a full circle, having arrived almost at the same point he was when he didn't take Watson's original pass from the corner.

Gerry McNeil, still on his behind, has shifted over to his left side, anticipating the failed shot from Watson, and he can't get back to the other side of the net where Barilko had shot the puck. McNeil lifts his right leg a little to try to block the shot that goes over his right shoulder. He never gets the opportunity to get up.

Many people seeing the photo for the first time wonder why McNeil was in a sitting position when Barilko shot the puck. The play happened very quickly, and McNeil, by shifting to the left side of the net for Watson's shot, missed his only opportunity to get to his feet.

Barilko has to have been cheating from the blue line a little in order to be able to get to the bottom of the face-off circle to backhand the pass in the lunging motion we see in the Turofsky photograph. Perhaps Barilko has seen the play develop and rushed in after Watson's shot hits Bouchard and rebounds out to the bottom of the face-off circle. He must have been moving very quickly.

It is apparent that, if his gamble fails and Barilko misses the shot, he, Watson, Meeker and Gardner would all be trapped deep in the Montreal zone.

Richard, who is in the vicinity of Barilko, would pick up the puck and, with Bert Olmstead turning around, would go up ice with linemate Elmer Lach [presumably] on a three-on-one break with Leaf defenceman Fernie Flaman the lone man back. Only Cal Gardner would have any chance of getting back on the play. [The only players not shown in the video footage are Lach from the Canadiens and Toronto's Flaman.]

Montreal's left winger, Bert Olmstead, ends up halfway between the goal and the blue line directly in front of the net when Barilko's goal was scored. Rocket Richard has come back into the Montreal defensive zone, but not in time to block Meeker's pass to Watson in front of the net. Richard then turns away and is unable to check the lunging Barilko.

The question begs to be asked: Where is Elmer Lach? Usually, the centre's responsibility is to hang down low in the slot. But he isn't there. This was not a great defensive line, as they make a few mistakes on the goal.

The Leafs' Cal Gardner is also in the Montreal zone to McNeil's right as Watson initially passes the puck through the front of the net, but Gardner doesn't try to take the pass. Gardner then circles around the back of the Montreal goal, passes Meeker going the other way behind the net and actually ends up in front of the Montreal goal. Gardner is mere steps away from Barilko when he scores.

It is possible that Gardner could have shot the puck if Barilko hadn't moved up, but Bill beat him to the loose puck as Gardner was not moving very fast.

🍁 🍁 🍁

More than 50 years after his tragic death, hockey fans still talk about the remarkable story of Bill Barilko. And the reason is magnificently, yet simply, due to the remarkable good fortune of a seasoned photographer, who with a precision honed by years of experience, clicked the shutter of his camera to capture an image that has kept Bill Barilko, the handsome 24-year-old hero of April 21, 1951, forever young.

CHAPTER 16

Hudson Brothers

A smile traced Barilko's lips as he walked briskly up Danforth Avenue from the room he'd been renting at the Eton House Hotel to his appliance store. Usually, when Bill glanced up at the sign that bore his name, it made him proud, but the pressures of the business had been mounting lately. Nonetheless, it felt good to know that he wasn't able to take more than a few steps before another fan greeted him with a handshake or a slap on the back. "Way to go, Bill. Hell of a goal. Hell of a series!" A carload of teenaged girls drove by, waving as they giggled and shouted, "We love you, Bashin' Bill!" It had been the same all summer. "It's great to play hockey in Toronto," Bill thought.

"Those of us who grew up listening to Foster Hewitt on the radio every Saturday night knew that Maple Leaf Gardens and fame and fortune were far away for kids like us growing up in Timmins," explains Vic Power, the mayor of Timmins. "And here was somebody from our town who was actually there and doing very well. Bill Barilko was a local hero. When he would return to Timmins for the summer, I remember everybody warmed up to him when they saw him driving around in his shiny new car."

Mayor Power adds, "I can't say that I knew him personally. I only talked to him once. But in 1951, I was working at the old Riverside Pavilion, a famous dance spot which no longer exists. I was working there on weekends and I remember the night Bill Barilko scored the goal. I went up to the bandleader, Henry Kelneck, and told him, 'Bill Barilko has scored the winning goal in the Stanley Cup final!' He announced it to the people at the dance at the Riverside Pavilion and there was a loud cheer. It was quite a story."

Bill's sister, Anne, and her husband, Emil, were expecting their first child, so Bill drove up to Timmins in June to be there when the baby was born. "It was a special time for our family," grins Anne. "The baby would be the first grandchild for my mother."

"When Billy arrived home, he said, 'Anne, now that you're married and expecting a baby, I guess you're old enough to go to Tony Sandrelli's Spaghetti House. You're supposed to be 21, so don't say anything to anyone, but I'd like you and Emil to come with me. Alex is going to be there. The whole gang is going to be there — Leo Curik, Allan Stanley, Gaston Garant. All of them.' Tony Sandrelli's place was up on Cook's Lake, and Bill swore it served the best spaghetti he had ever eaten. Tony sold alcohol but he didn't have a licence. The favourite drink there was a gin collins."

The baby arrived on June 6, 1951. "Bill was extremely proud to become an uncle to our newborn son, Frank. When I had the baby, Bill sent two dozen roses to the hospital. I remember the nurses saying, 'We've seen a dozen roses before, but we've never seen *two* dozen roses!' Bill was a very thoughtful and generous person."

When the Klisaniches brought their newborn home, Uncle Billy was a frequent visitor. "I remember Bill saying, 'Every time I come here, Frank is either sleeping or you're feeding him,'" recalls Anne with a giggle. "I said, 'Well, Bill, that's what babies do!' But Bill was such a proud uncle. He would say, 'Well, we're going to make a hockey player out of this little guy.'" The baby, Frank Klisanich, was just over two months old when his Uncle Bill disappeared. "If I had had any idea what was ahead, I would have named him 'Billy,'" Anne says sombrely.

While Bill was back home, he made a number of public appearances — in Timmins, South Porcupine, at the McIntyre Arena; put simply, anywhere he was asked to appear. Fans were thrilled to meet the home-town hero who had scored the Stanley Cup–winning goal.

Back in Toronto towards the end of July, Bill was trying to sort out the affairs of his store. His best friend, Leo Curik, says, "Business wasn't going too well, so I invited him to drive down to Springfield [Massachusetts] with me to see Dorothy [Curik's future wife]."

"I can't, Leo. The store's taking up too much of my time," Barilko responded, adding with a sigh, "I wish I never got involved in it." But Leo had an idea that he knew would sway his pal. "Bill, come on. We'll drive down to Springfield, then whip over to New York City to see DiMaggio and the Yankees."

Bill hesitated, but agreed. "All right, Leo, let's go," he said. "I've got to clear my head anyway." Leo decided he would drive, and picked Barilko up in Toronto on the way from Timmins to Massachusetts.

"We went to Yankee Stadium to see DiMaggio play during his last season," Curik recalls. "We tried to meet him, but it didn't happen. Bill was a huge Yankees fan, y'know."

The trip to the States was a pleasant diversion for Barilko, and it provided a temporary respite from matters both confusing and confounding at the appliance store. Curik continues, "I drove back to Timmins on a Saturday night, but Bill went back to Toronto. He didn't stay long, though, because he surprised us by coming up on Monday."

Bill needed to get away for a while — let the world slow down for a few days. He drove home, dropped off his bag and kissed his mother, then met the boys at the Victory Hotel. "The Victory Hotel was the hang-out for Bill and his friends, because the Curiks owned the hotel," mentions Anne. The word had spread that if you wanted to see Bill Barilko when he was in town, you had to go to the Victory. "Some of the other hotel owners said, 'I sure wish you'd come and visit our hotel while you're in town, too,' and Bill always tried to accommodate all the requests."

As the boys talked and laughed over a few beers, the conversation swung around to another regular topic — fishing. Bill loved to fish when he was home, and he and his friends would often drown a few worms just southeast of Timmins at Watabeag Lake. There, nestled among the jack pines, Bill and his friends would usually catch suckers, although from time to time they would reel in a trout, perch, pike or pickerel. Occasionally, they would be the guests of Dr. Lou Hudson at the cottage on Watabeag Lake nicknamed "The Gluepot" because visitors seldom were able to leave.

Lou's younger brother, Dr. Henry Hudson, had spoken to several of the boys about flying up to James Bay for one final fishing trip that summer. Rangers defenceman Allan Stanley, who was also home for the summer of '51, was one of them. "Henry Hudson was my dentist — Bill's, too. When I went to see him, he said, 'Next trip, I'll take you.'" But that week, Stanley was out of town and the trip was planned without him.

"I had a dental appointment on the Friday morning with Henry, but I had heard that he was going on this trip without me, so I said to him, 'You were going to take me!' He said, 'You weren't here when we planned the trip so I've made arrangements to take Lou,'" Stanley relates. "Henry said, 'Next time, if you're here, we'll take you,' and they left for the weekend."

Leo Curik remembers Henry Hudson inviting his brother Bill for an end-of-summer fishing excursion, too. "My brother Bill was scheduled to join Doc Hudson to go fishing near Rupert's Bay, but when Bill [Barilko] unexpectedly arrived, plans changed," says Leo. "You can go anytime," Barilko told Bill Curik. "Let me go."

Helen O'Neil, who was then known as Helen Ferrari, was Henry Hudson's receptionist. "The trip that Dr. Hudson took with Bill Barilko was quickly arranged. I wouldn't have scheduled any appointments that day if I had known about it," she recalls.

"When Bill came in [to the office] out of the clear blue sky, he asked if he could talk with Dr. Hudson and I said, 'As soon as he's finished with his patient.' When Dr. Hudson was through, Bill asked him if he could finally go fishing with him. There had never been a good time for both of them to get together. Dr. Hudson said, 'Yes, we'll do that for sure,' and turned around to me and said, 'Cancel the appointments for the end of the week and cancel Monday. I don't know whether I'll be back Monday or Tuesday.' I said 'Fine.'"

Helen efficiently went to work. "I quickly got on the phone and cancelled all our appointments."

"When things got too hectic, Henry would leave the office via a washroom and leave Helen Ferrari to handle the patients," optometrist Dave Wigston related. Others who knew Henry attest that the story is not uncharacteristic.

"Although I was only in my early twenties, I'd been working for Dr. Hudson for years," says Helen. "I knew Bill because we were about the same age and he was a friend of mine. Everybody knows everybody else in Timmins. Bill Barilko would have known Dr. Hudson for a while. He wasn't a patient, but he was a good friend."

O'Neil remembers that Lou Hudson was supposed to accompany his brother and Bill. "As a matter of fact, he had everything all packed and they were ready to go, but the plane wouldn't take off. Dr. Hudson had a Fairchild 24, which seated four people, but the plane couldn't lift off with the weight of all the equipment. So Lou said to his brother, 'I'll stay home so you and Bill can go.' And that's what he did."

✹ ✹ ✹

The Hudson brothers, Lou and Henry, were well-known and well-respected Timmins citizens, as highly regarded for their sporting exploits as for their medical practices. Dr. Lou Hudson was a physician and surgeon, while younger brother Henry was a dentist.

In sporting circles, Lou was the better known of the brothers. Born in Toronto on May 16, 1898, he attended Humberside Collegiate, from which he graduated in 1917. He then attended the University of Toronto, following in the footsteps of his father. Lou originally studied dentistry for two years before moving his studies to medicine.

Lou played hockey with the Aura Lee juniors, a Toronto team that also featured Hall of Fame defenceman Lionel Conacher, before joining the U of T Dentals in 1919. Between 1920 and 1926, Lou Hudson was a forward for the University of Toronto Varsitys, a senior team, coached by Conn Smythe, that was nothing short of outstanding. Lou captained the team in 1923–24 and 1925–26.

The U of T seniors went undefeated in intercollegiate play in 1924–25; they also competed in the Ontario Hockey Association, where they finished third. In the spring of 1925, the Varsitys went all the way to the Allan Cup finals, playing for the senior hockey championship of Canada. The series, held in Winnipeg, pitted the Varsitys — as eastern Canada's champions — against the Port Arthur Bearcats, the top team in the west. Port Arthur won both games.

In 1925–26, Smythe moved Hudson from left to right wing, and Lou found great success at the new position. Again that season, the Varsitys easily captured the intercollegiate crown, first beating Queen's University from Kingston, then Montreal's McGill University. Toronto then handily defeated Dartmouth, the U.S. intercollegiate champions, at the newly built Madison Square Garden.

The Varsitys then faced their nemeses from the previous season, the Bearcats, in a best-of-three series for the Allan Cup. The first two games were played in Montreal, with Port Arthur winning the first and Toronto the second. The deciding game was played at Arena Gardens in Toronto, most often referred to as the Mutual Street Arena. At the end of the first period, the Varsitys were ahead 3–0, but by the end of regulation time the teams were tied three-all. After three 10-minute overtime periods, the score was still 3–3. Another deciding game was played, but it, too, ended in a tie, this time 2–2. Finally, in the second overtime period, Port Arthur scored to defeat Toronto and capture the Allan Cup for a second consecutive season. The University of Toronto's *Torontonensis* called the series "the greatest championship series ever played in Canada."

During the summer of 1926, construction began on Varsity Arena. The rink, tucked off Bloor Street just west of Avenue Road on the U of T campus, was completed that December, giving the school's teams liberal access to ice for practices.

Almost to a man, the Varsitys' members graduated from the University of Toronto in 1926. Not ready to abandon their amateur sporting careers just yet, they put together an unofficial team of budding doctors, lawyers and others. This alumni team, led by Lou Hudson and coached by Smythe — who was part of a group that would purchase the NHL's Toronto St. Pats in February 1927 and rechristen them the Maple Leafs — was given official status by the Ontario Hockey Association and called itself the U of T Varsity Grads. The Grads' season began December 22, 1926, and they went undefeated through the entire campaign. The Grads went on to win the John Ross Robertson Trophy as senior hockey champions of Ontario.

After steamrolling the Quebec champions, the Varsity Grads travelled west to Vancouver to face the Fort William Thundering Herd for the Allan Cup. Departing from Union Station on St. Patrick's Day 1927 with a rousing send-off from followers, the team won two games, tied one and lost just one to win the national title. The University of Toronto was finally vindicated.

At that time, the Allan Cup champions represented Canada in Olympic competition, and so the Varsity Grads made their way to St. Moritz, Switzerland, to wear Canada's colours at the 1928 Winter Games. Coach Conn Smythe was unable to attend due to his commitments to the Toronto Maple Leafs, so he sent William A. Hewitt and Harold Ballard in his place.

While in Europe, the Grads gave a number of hockey exhibitions that amazed fans. They also won the gold medal handily, drubbing Sweden 11–0, Switzerland 13–0 and Great Britain by a 14–0 margin. Their closest competitor in the tournament was Sweden, who scored seven goals and allowed 12. Observers called the Grads the greatest hockey team ever seen in Europe. "We never had a goal scored against us, but the other teams didn't know much about the game," Hudson admitted later.

Besides Lou Hudson, there were a number of notables on the gold-medal squad. Netminder Joe Sullivan used his influence to get his brother Frank on the team, threatening to sit out himself unless Frank was added. Joseph Sullivan went on to become a distinguished ear, nose and throat specialist, and was later named to the University of Toronto's board of governors, the U of T's Sports Hall of Fame and, in 1957, the Canadian Senate.

Hugh Plaxton went on to play with the Montreal Maroons in 1932–33. He, too, lobbied successfully to get his brothers added to the team, and Bert and Rod also represented Canada in St. Moritz in 1928. Dave Trottier joined the Maroons after the Olympic Games and spent 10 years with the team before concluding his career with a season as a Detroit Red Wing.

A monstrous crowd awaited the Varsity Grads' triumphant return to Toronto. A parade led the team to City Hall, where they were met by Mayor Samuel McBride and members of the city council.

Conn Smythe called Lou Hudson "one of the greatest hockey captains I ever had." Reflecting some decades later, Smythe stated, "I've had some great captains in my day — men like Syl Apps and Ted Kennedy — and he [Hudson] sits right alongside them."

Lou Hudson never did turn pro, deciding to pursue his medical career instead. He moved to Timmins in the mid-1930s, where he opened a practice at 35½ Third Avenue. While there, Lou got involved in a number of sporting endeavours, including curling and fishing. "We would have been in our early twenties and Dr. Lou would have been in his forties by then," says Allan Stanley. "He knew a lot of the hockey players of course, but he never talked much about hockey with us."

Lou's brother, Albert Henry Hudson, was also born in Toronto, in 1902. Known by his middle name, he followed in the footsteps of his older brother, attending Humberside followed by the University of Toronto, where he studied dentistry.

Although he never achieved the same athletic proficiency as his brother, Henry was a fine athlete in his own right. While at U of T, Henry was a defenceman on the Dentals hockey team for three years. Amateur teams in the 1920s consisted simply of a principal forward line and one defence pairing plus a couple of substitutes. In 1926, Henry was a sub on the Dentals junior team. The University of Toronto yearbook *Torontonensis* reported that "Hudson and Mahaffy were hard to keep off the regular line-up, and did not weaken the team any when they were used."

Henry was also on the swimming team for three years, wrestled for two years and not only played on the rugby team all five years he was at the University of Toronto, but captained the team in his third season (1926–27). He was also president of the Intercollegiate Rugby Association one year. *Torontonensis* mentioned that "Hudson starred with his broken field running" in 1925–26, and that in his final season (1929), "Hen. Hudson [was] the most dangerous man on the team. He takes a chance on anything and fights to the last ditch."

Henry Hudson was also an avid outdoor sportsman who loved to fish and hunt.

After graduating in 1929 from the Faculty of Dentistry, Hudson set up a part-time dental service at Toronto General Hospital. He practised in Toronto for several years, but moved to Timmins in 1935. His former assistant, Helen O'Neil (then Helen Ferrari), remembers Henry's arrival in Timmins. "When things were so bad in Toronto during the Depression, things weren't so bad up north. Timmins had the mines and the men were working. That's why Henry came up north."

After the move, the likable dentist became very involved in community activities and grew to be extremely well known and well liked in the north. He was president of the Timmins Kinsman Club in 1940, and that same year was secretary of the Council of Service Clubs of the Porcupine. In 1943–44, Henry was president of the Porcupine Dental Society, and at the time of his tragic disappearance was secretary-treasurer of the Northern Ontario Dental Association.

But it wasn't all business with Henry. He was very social, recognized as the life of a party who could often be found leading a sing-along. The ladies at these social gatherings enjoyed Henry's spontaneous sense of fun, and he made them titter with his bawdy songs like "Three Old Ladies Locked in the Lavatory":

> Oh, dear, what can the matter be?
> Three old ladies locked in the lavatory.

They were there from Monday to Saturday
Nobody knew they were there

The first one's name was Elizabeth Porter
She went in to get rid of some overdue water
And she stayed there far more than she ought to
And nobody knew she was there.

Henry, like his brother, Lou, also enjoyed curling. His involvement in that sport was to put him at the centre of a most curious situation.

The Ontario Curling Bonspiel was taking place in mid-February of 1942 at the Royal Canadian Curling Club on Broadview Avenue near Queen Street in Toronto's east end. The initial matches, one of which saw a team from Timmins compete against Toronto's High Park squad, took place on February 17.

The Timmins skip was Dr. Lou Hudson, who was about to play his last stone in the 10th end with the score tied 8–8, when his brother and teammate Henry shouted, "I've been shot!" The other members of the Timmins team tried to stop the bleeding in Hudson's thigh, while other curlers ran up to the arena's balcony, thinking the shot might have been fired from up there. The police were called immediately, and upon their arrival, every locker, bag and curler was searched, but no evidence could be found that a shot had been fired.

"I don't know how it happened," stated the 40-year-old Henry afterwards. "I was curling with the team and was leaning over with the broom. I felt a sharp pain like a sting on my thigh. I didn't know it was a bullet then. It sort of spun me around."

Detective James Ledbe, as perplexed as anyone, commented, "The only answer we can see to it right now is that the gun was accidentally discharged. There were a lot of men from the north country and many of them were wearing their north country mackinaws and windbreakers. It's quite possible that one of them forgot he had a gun in his pocket. It could have been discharged in half a dozen different ways." Another policeman, Inspector Charles Greenwood, reported, "The shot was fired by someone standing on the level of the ice; not above or below. It travelled fast enough to lodge in the thigh muscle. The course of the bullet was straight."

Dr. Henry Hudson was driven to Toronto General Hospital. "It just came out of the blue," he said. As he patted his thigh, he noted, "It's still in there." The .22-calibre bullet had entered the dentist's right thigh and lodged against an artery on the inside of his leg. After several days, the bullet was removed, and Henry had returned to his Timmins dental practice by the end of that month.

The mystery of where the bullet came from — and more perplexingly, why it was fired — has never been solved. "They never found out anything about who shot him," says Helen O'Neil. There has been much conjecture over the years, but circumstances about the shooting remain obscure.

❆ ❆ ❆

Archie Chenier accompanied Dr. Henry Hudson on fly-in fishing trips for many years. He remembers his good friend as a dynamic man who loved life. "He was a poor man's Ernest Hemingway," Chenier told North Bay journalist Ken Pagan. "He was a real doer."

Chenier, who describes Hudson as "cavalier," was proficient at carpentry, and Henry often hired him to do repairs on the cottages or his docks. Archie was nicknamed "Minou" by Hudson, and recalls a memorable trip taken with the Hudson brothers. "Henry and Lou and I were driving back to Timmins from Lake Temagami and we stopped for a beverage at Goddard's Hotel in Temagami." An argument broke out between the Hudsons and a group of local boys, and a fight ensued. Although 15 to 20 years older than the boys, Lou and Henry were fit and robust and had no trouble bringing a quick conclusion to the melee. "Henry said to Lou, 'I'll stand them up and you knock them down.'" Chenier laughs as he adds, "I stayed out of the altercation."

"He had no fear when it came to judgment while flying," Chenier continued in his interview with Ken Pagan. Although Archie never flew with Henry Hudson to Seal River, he remembers one adventure in which Hudson's Fairchild 24 ran frighteningly low on gas. Approaching Cochrane, Chenier said, "Let's put her down, Henry." Henry replied, "No, we're okay," but Archie repeated, "Henry, let's put her down."

The plane ran out of gas, and Hudson was forced to land at Lillabelle Lake, three miles north of Cochrane and not far from where Hudson's plane would crash in 1951. Even though the area was remote, Hudson and Chenier could hear bulldozers working in the distance. Stranded, the friends worked their way over to where the construction sounds originated and were able to convince the crew to give them some gas.

In 1949, Archie Chenier had another scare with Henry Hudson in the same plane that eventually took the dentist and the hockey player to their deaths. In early October, Hudson attempted to take off on Lake Temagami, but the weight of the plane, which included spare batteries and pop bottles, made the load heavier than usual. The plane struggled to achieve flight and then, at about 200 feet, the engine burst into flames. The plane immediately lost elevation, but Henry was able to safely land the plane back on the lake and extinguished the fire. Employees of the Ministry of Lands and Forests arrived and towed

Hudson and Chenier to shore. The engine was badly burned, and Archie remembers a new engine being ordered and installed.

In early August 1951, Chenier and Hudson were fishing together at Radisson Lake when the dentist told his companion of a plan for the two of them, along with Henry's brother, Lou, that would involve flying in to Seal River to fish during the latter part of the month. Within a few days, Chenier landed a construction contract with Abitibi and was forced to cancel his participation in the adventure. "I told him, 'Henry, I can't go, I've got to work,'" Chenier said. "Naturally, he had to find someone to fill my place; someone who wasn't working."

Hudson found Bill Barilko.

Archie Chenier believes that with Barilko on the trip, Henry Hudson may have taken risks he would never ordinarily have attempted. "Had you been there, it wouldn't have happened," Chenier remembers Henry's wife, Phyllis, commenting later.

✳ ✳ ✳

"Dr. Henry Hudson was a really nice guy," comments Helen O'Neil. "He never came up the steps when he wasn't whistling. Always."

Hudson's office was in the Killeen Building, on Third Avenue. "There was only one floor up above. We had Dr. Connor in one office and Mr. Wigston, the ophthalmologist. At that time, we had a government office for immigration. There was a chartered accountant. Downstairs, Killeen Electric sold refrigerators and stoves.

"Henry and his wife, Phyllis, didn't have children. They always had dogs. They had a beagle named Jester and a basset hound named Susie when I worked for him. I looked after the dogs whenever they went away anywhere. I'd bring them to the office with me and take them home at noon when I went home for lunch."

"Dr. Hudson was doing very well with his practice," she recalls. "They lived across the [Mattagami] river in a beautiful home. They didn't want to leave the house unattended, so I looked after their house while they were away."

"Henry took up photography and developed his own photographs. Back then, nobody did that. He had a beautiful camera on that plane [when they disappeared]. He took a lot of pictures. I never heard what happened to that camera," Helen says.

"Dr. Hudson used to be my dentist," mentions Allan Stanley. "He was a very nice man. He used to bring the boys along to go fishing." Dr. Henry Hudson was well known to all in the community, and in the loosest sense could be considered the family dentist for the Barilkos. "The only time we went to Dr. Hudson was when we had a toothache. We never had regular checkups. That would be too expensive," states Anne.

In addition to their home on the river, Henry and Phyllis Hudson owned two cottages on Lake Temagami, 100 miles to the southeast. Dr. John Shaw notes that Henry owned a 31-foot inboard launch named *Slowpoke* that could outrun any OPP boat on Lake Temagami. "It could reach speeds of 55 knots," mentions the Timmins dentist. "Lake Temagami has a number of rocky areas. One time, Henry went over to visit a neighbour and backed the boat over a rock." Archie Chenier, Hudson's longtime friend, remembers, "There was just a round ball of copper for a propeller."

The Hudson brothers left an indelible mark on those they touched. As medical practitioners, their circle of patients was vast, but it was as solid citizens and fun-loving sportsmen that Lou and Henry Hudson will best be remembered. And, of course, Henry's name lives in infamy, tied intrinsically to the epic saga of Toronto Maple Leafs champion Bill Barilko.

✦ ✦ ✦

In the earliest years of the 17th century, it was the great hope of western Europe's seafaring nations to discover a more efficient route to the Orient, one that would eliminate the need to sail south through the Atlantic and around the southern tip of Africa, before looping eastward through the Indian Ocean to Asia. The English explorer Henry Hudson was one of several sea captains willing to sail in search of a Northwest Passage, guided by maps that were based more on conjecture and fiction than hard data, as to that point the Arctic was almost entirely unexplored.

After three unsuccessful voyages — during which he explored Chesapeake, Delaware and New York bays, as well as the river that bears his name — Hudson was hired by a syndicate of British merchants and provided with a ship called *Discovery*, aboard which he set sail in the spring of 1610. Three months later, *Discovery* reached a body of water, later called the Hudson Strait in his honour, that led to what he believed was the Pacific Ocean. In fact, it was Hudson Bay, also later to be named after him. Hudson spent the months of August through November sailing aimlessly into and around what is now James Bay, and was horrified to discover he was not in the Pacific. The icing up of the bay forced Hudson and his crew to spend the winter on the frigid, barren tundra of northern Quebec, suffering from hunger, disease and severe cold.

The crew of *Discovery* shared neither Hudson's belief nor his commitment. In June 1611 they mutinied, setting Hudson, his 12-year-old son John and seven severely ill crew members adrift in a small boat on the frigid waters of James Bay. Hudson and his party disappeared without a trace, never to be seen again. The remaining crew sailed back to England, yet their report gave continued hope that there was indeed a passage that existed between Hudson Bay and the Pacific Ocean. Continued exploration of that region led to the establishment of the Hudson's Bay Company, a fur-trading firm, in 1670.

One of many waterways in the vicinity of James Bay is Seal River, located in northern Quebec, 400 miles north of Timmins. It is a desolate spot, all but untouched by humankind's attempts at progress. The harsh, frigid air has ensured that little has changed through the centuries, other than the continued regeneration of spruce, caribou and fish.

Much of this area is inaccessible. The rock and muskeg that comprise most of the region host dense stands of spruce, balsam fir and tamarack punctuated by innumerable streams, ponds and lakes. Because of its location in Canada's north, away from prying eyes and eager fishermen, the Seal River and its neighbouring waters produce hearty fish that have plenty of time to multiply freely and grow to magnificent sizes. The small rivers and lakes on the east side of James Bay stay cool even through the summer months, rendering the waters conducive to walleye, trout and Arctic char.

To those who appreciate the taste of fish, Arctic char is considered a delicacy. A branch of the salmon family, its flesh is a deep orange and very tasty, though it spoils quickly. It thrives in the pure, cold waters of Canada's north — in fact, Arctic char makes its home farther north than any other freshwater fish.

Seal River held a romantic lure for Dr. Henry Hudson. He spoke excitedly about the quantity and quality of fish that thrived in the area. He had made the trip several times before and had never been anything but enthusiastic about the results of his trips. When he talked to the hockey boys, they were as eager as he was to bring back a feast of northern fish.

🍁 🍁 🍁

Anne Klisanich recounts a story she has told countless times through the years. "On Thursday, August 23, Bill went to our mother and said, 'Mom, I'm going on a fishing trip and I'll need a hundred dollars.'" Bill had always handed his paycheques over to his mother for safekeeping. "That's the way she trained him," Anne explains. "Mom would say to Bill, 'When you need money, come to me.' He was always very good about giving Mother quite a bit of his money to invest. She would help him with that, although by that time there was also a lot of money put into the store.

"My mother said, 'Why you need hundred dollars for fishing?' And when he told her he wanted to go to James Bay, she was very angry.

Mother pleaded with him not to go. 'Billy, why go so far fishing? Not on Friday. Your Papa die on Friday. I no like Fridays.'" Steve Barilko had died on a Friday five years before. Bill's mother demanded, "No go, Billy. No go."

"My mother was superstitious about Fridays," states her daughter, shaking her head. "She'd say, 'Oh, I no like doing t'ings on Friday.'

"My mother tried to talk Bill out of going and I tried to talk him out of going," Anne says emphatically. "It wasn't the weather. It was just the distance and that he had so much on his plate. He said, 'Gee whiz, Dr. Hudson makes this trip two or three times a year. There's nothing to worry about.'"

Faye Barilko had a premonition that something was going to happen. "Me so mad," she said through gritted teeth. "Billy, no go fishing in wild bush!"

Bill then approached his sister to lend him the money for the trip. "He asked me if I would lend him a hundred dollars. That was a lot of money in those days. I said, 'Why do you need a hundred dollars?' He said, 'I'm flying to James Bay with Dr. Henry Hudson and I have to pay the expenses, like fuel for the airplane.'

"I guess that's how Dr. Hudson did it — whoever went with him to James Bay on a fishing expedition would pay some of the expenses.

"I was angry, too. I said, 'Bill, why do you want to go so far?' I was flabbergasted! To think that Billy would want to go on a fishing trip so far north. He said, 'I don't know why you're making such a big fuss about this fishing trip! Mom won't give me the hundred dollars I need and now you're giving me a hard time. Why? If I can't get the money from you'll, I'll get it from my friends.'

"I said, 'That's an awful long way to go to get fish, and you don't even like to eat fish!' He said, 'It's the joy of fishing!' I reminded Bill that he had to drive to Toronto for some scheduled autograph sessions and personal appearances at the CNE [Canadian National Exhibition] the next week."

Anne told her brother, "You've got all these things to do in Toronto and you have to drive there." At that time, the highway to Toronto had only two lanes and the road was often rough. "You'll be tired," Anne warned. "Don't worry," Bill replied. "I can handle it. We're leaving Friday and we'll come back on Sunday. I'll be just fine. I'll leave for Toronto on Tuesday or Wednesday.'"

Anne fumes as she continues her story. "I said, 'Okay, I'll lend you the hundred dollars,' but I just didn't like the idea that he was going so far away to catch fish. Then he said, 'Will you make a lunch for me?'

"'Good gracious!' I said. 'Why do you need a lunch?' Bill said, 'Well, we're leaving very early Friday morning, and it'll be a couple of hours before we get to our destination and we'll need a sandwich in the plane.'" Anne was annoyed at her brother, but Bill could be stubborn, and it appeared there was no way to dissuade him from the fishing trip.

🍁 🍁 🍁

Dr. Henry Hudson was a licensed pilot who was in a position to own his own small aircraft — a Fairchild 24, a three-passenger plane very popular with wealthy sportsmen in the 1930s and '40s. Hudson owned the Deluxe model, which featured wing flaps, roll-down windows, plush upholstery, extra instruments, electric fuel gauges and a hand-rubbed finish.

Between 1933 and 1946, when production ceased, approximately 1,500 Fairchild 24s were produced, all in the United States. By the end of the Second World War, the cost of the aircraft had dropped to levels that were comparable to purchasing a car. Dr. Hudson likely bought his plane from one of the many airfields that had been built in Ontario during World War II.

The interior of the plane was renowned for being "car-like." The craft was designed for light transport, so although it *could* hold four people, space was usually restricted to the pilot, a passenger and their gear. The Fairchild 24 had a range of 750 miles and could reach a top speed of 117 miles per hour.

The small plane could be equipped with tires, skis or pontoons. The pontoons and tires were easily interchangeable, comparable to putting snow tires on a car.

Helen O'Neil, who worked for Hudson at the time of his disappearance, recalls the Fairchild 24 very well. "It was a beautiful plane," she starts. "He had had it for a little while and he had put in a new engine. He did a lot of work on it. He really took care of it.

"Dr. Hudson had flown for a number of years. He used to enjoy flying down to the World Series with his wife each year. He also used to fly to Toronto to see his mother and father — Henry had a lot of friends in Toronto. And he flew to his cottage in Temagami for the weekend. It was astounding at that time. He was the only one we knew who could do that."

Helen only flew with Dr. Hudson on one occasion. "I just went for a trip around the area. We didn't stay up long. I didn't like flying in a small plane," she remembers.

Anne Klisanich also got an aerial tour of the Porcupine area. "I can vaguely remember Bill driving me out to South Porcupine Lake, where Dr. Hudson kept his plane. Bill introduced me to Henry, and he asked me if I'd like to go for a ride. I said, 'Sure,' so I actually rode in that very plane that Billy died in. Henry took me up for about 10 minutes. I can remember looking down and seeing the cars and saying, 'Everything down there looks so tiny!' That was my very first time in a plane. That was quite scary."

But when her brother told her of his fishing plans, it was another matter. "I remember saying, 'You want to go to James Bay in *that*?' To me, it seemed very fragile, like the model planes Billy used to make as a child. There were no windows — there was a clear vinyl that snapped or tied on somehow, but no windows!"

* * *

Many Timmins residents who knew Dr. Henry Hudson regarded the dentist as a carefree flier. Correspondence from Catherine (Morten) Sorley, a Timmins neighbour whose husband hunted and fished with the Hudson brothers, reads, "Bill was such a fine fellow. While he was home in Timmins, we often met him on the street and he wanted to get us tickets for a Maple Leaf game. Henry Hudson was a real nut. He would go on those [fishing] trips and on the way home, he would swoop over Schumacher three times to let his wife know he was home again."

Gossip circulated around the Porcupine, questioning how Henry could live such an extravagant life, owning a beautiful home, several cottages, a boat and a plane, on a dentist's earnings. For a decade, there were whispers that Hudson was high-grading gold out of northern Ontario and smuggling it into the U.S. for sale.

* * *

Bill went to the Klisaniches' apartment in the Korson Block in Schumacher to pick up the money he was borrowing — and his lunch. Anne remembers, "I made him a cheese sandwich. He said, 'Thanks, Anne. Now I'm going to go down to the Pearl Lake Tavern to have a beer with Emil.'"

Emil Klisanich, Anne's husband, was working that evening. It was about 10 o'clock or 10:30 on Thursday night when Bill arrived at the Pearl Lake Tavern to enjoy a beer with his brother-in-law. "They were good pals," says Anne. "Emil actually knew my brother Alex better than Bill. Alex and my husband were closer in age and they played ball together in 1943. That was long before Emil knew either Bill or me," Anne laughs. "But Bill was later the best man at our wedding."

The next morning, Friday, August 24, Bill was up shortly after five o'clock. A stretch, a yawn, and Bill swung his legs over the side of his bed. There was a terrific adventure ahead, and Barilko was ready to embark on his journey.

He inched towards his mother's room and peeked inside to see whether she was awake so that he could say goodbye. Whispering, Bill asked, "Mom, are you awake?" His mother didn't respond. "Mom? I know you're up. I just came in to say goodbye." An angry Faye pretended to be asleep so as to register her irritation with Bill. "'Bye, Mom," Bill said a little louder. "I'll see you Sunday night."

Those were the last words Faye Barilko heard from her son. It was the first time she hadn't said goodbye to Bill, the first time she didn't kiss him and send him on his way with a hug. Tragically, it was also the last.

"My mother was so angry that Bill was going on that fishing trip that she never said goodbye to him," says Anne. "Mom always talked about that. She'd cry, 'I no say goodbye to my Billy.' She never forgave herself for that." It was a decision she'd regret for the rest of her life.

🍁 🍁 🍁

Allan Stanley was sitting outside the Victory Hotel on the Saturday morning when he got quite a jolt. "It was a beautiful day. I was downtown around 10:30 and I was waiting around for an appointment in half an hour. I talked to Leo and Bill Curik, and who comes walking by but Lou Hudson with a packsack on his back. I said, 'I thought you were supposed to go up there [fishing with Henry Hudson and Bill Barilko].' He said, 'I was.'

"They'd got to South Porcupine, about seven miles away. It was a dead calm morning and the plane wouldn't take off with the weight they had in the plane. They even had another plane taxi in front of them to create an air disturbance. But the plane still couldn't take off, so Lou Hudson had to stay home."

Bill Curik was the last of his friends to see Bill Barilko alive. "Bill laughed and hit me on the shoulder just before getting on the plane," Curik told the *Toronto Star* in 1982. "He said, 'If I don't come back, be sure to send me some daisies.'

"I'll never forget that until the day I die."

CHAPTER

17

"Why My Billy No Come Home?"

On the morning of Friday, August 24, 1951, Bill Barilko flew off to Seal River in Dr. Henry Hudson's Fairchild 24. It was a nice weekend — an ordinary weekend in the Porcupine area.

"We told Bill, 'Make sure you're back Sunday because we're going to have a farewell party for the hockey boys at Mr. and Mrs. Carmichael's place,'" recalls Leo Curik. "We wanted to say goodbye to the hockey players who were going to their various training camps. Allan Stanley was off to the New York Rangers; Bill was, of course, going to the Maple Leafs camp; Mike Narduzzi and I played with the Springfield Indians the year before, but they didn't have an AHL team in '51–52. The franchise moved to Syracuse and became the Warriors."

❋ ❋ ❋

An orange moon hangs over James Bay, its light dancing over the water's still surface the way a ballerina might jeté across a stage. The light illuminates the area with an eerie glow. It is both haunting and resourceful.

Early on that August morning in 1951, Hudson's small plane lifted off gingerly from Porcupine Lake. It was a humid, windless summer day — perfect conditions for a weekend of fishing. The dentist and the hockey player chatted animatedly, both anxious to reach Seal River and the cache of Arctic char that awaited them there.

❋ ❋ ❋

In 1950, 18-year-old James Crawford was working for Sangamo, an electrical company in Leaside, a suburban community in Toronto's east end. Not surprisingly for a young man of his age, he was looking for an adven-

172

ture. A help-wanted ad in *The Globe and Mail* seemed to offer it. "I was born and raised in the Queen and Bathurst area of Toronto and was a little tired of the electrical work, so believe it or not, I left a job that paid me $140 a week to take a job with the Hudson's Bay fur trading department up on James Bay for $140 a month!

"I had to sign a contract on the understanding that if I left their employ at any time, I had to give them three months' advance notice or forfeit three months' pay. I didn't think too seriously about that at the time, but it did come back to haunt me at a later date."

Crawford enjoyed travelling up and down the coastline of James Bay on behalf of the Company of Adventurers. "I got to meet a lot of Canada's native people; I was transferred from a posting at Moose Factory, Ontario — I was there for a period of months — to a post at Rupert's House, Quebec, which was further up the east coast of James Bay. I was quite happy there. I met the staff and the manager — they didn't call them managers; to this day, they're known as 'factors.' Part of my duties included looking after any visitors coming by plane or boat to extend the welcome of the Hudson's Bay Company."

Rupert's House, now known by the Cree name Waskaganish and home to fewer than 2000 residents, was a very significant place in the Hudson's Bay Company's lengthy history. In 1668, the French explorer Médard Chouart des Grosseilliers, in the employ of English merchants, landed here and established a post called Fort Charles. Two years later, the Hudson's Bay Company was incorporated, and Fort Charles was its first trading post. It came to be known as Fort Rupert or Rupert's House, and the company would have a presence there as recently as 1987, when the Bay's Northern Stores division was sold off. Coincidentally, Rupert's House is likely also the spot where explorer Henry Hudson spent the winter of 1611.

🍁 🍁 🍁

Rupert's House was a routine stop for bush pilots who needed to refuel as they made their way further north into the Canadian wilderness. "I got to know many of the bush pilots," says Crawford. "I was a young lad who liked a cold beer. If you wanted a barrel of beer flown in, then it paid to have a contact with a bush pilot who flew in or out of Rupert's House."

James Crawford, already a sizable six feet, four inches and 240 pounds, was with the Hudson's Bay Company when he had the occasion to meet Bill Barilko and Dr. Henry Hudson during the summer of 1951.

"Dr. Hudson flew a Fairchild, bright yellow in colour," recalls James. "I went down to the dock to meet the incoming plane and its passengers, and that's where I first met Bill Barilko. Dr. Hudson was as much a stranger to me as Barilko was. I wasn't really a Toronto Maple Leaf fan until later years."

The three men made small talk while Crawford refuelled Hudson's plane. "They were on their way north to a fishing spot that I'd never been to before, although I'd heard it was an exceptionally fine place for fishing. It was a place called Seal River — much further up the [eastern] coast of James Bay."

The inquisitive Crawford asked Hudson and Barilko about the kind of fish they were likely to find. "Barilko said, 'We're going to fish for Arctic char,' and he asked if I'd ever tasted one. I said, 'Never, but I'd love to.' He then said, 'When we come back to refuel again, we'll see to it that you get one of the Arctic char. We'll be gassing up at your place on the way back from Seal River.'"

Barilko and Hudson flew directly from Rupert's House to Seal River, looking out over a desolate area, treeless except along the banks of slow-moving rivers and stagnant ponds. The Fairchild 24 found a place to touch down, and after Henry and Bill set up a temporary camp they were fishing almost immediately. The fish were plentiful, and the two would joke that it almost wasn't sport to be able to catch so many large, beautiful specimens with so little effort.

As scheduled, Barilko and Hudson packed up their belongings and flew out of Seal River on Sunday, bound for their refuelling stop at Fort George. At one o'clock that afternoon, Mrs. J.C. Shepherd, the wife of Reverend Canon H.S. Shepherd, an Anglican missionary stationed at Fort George, welcomed the two Timmins men. "They both seemed happy enough," Mrs. Shepherd recalled. "I asked Dr. Hudson up to the house for a cup of tea, but he said he didn't have time — they had to be back at Timmins for supper that night."

Bill kidded with John and Ted Shepherd, the children of the canon and his wife. The boys remembered Barilko as being very happy and friendly, and they were offered tickets to a Toronto Maple Leafs game should they ever get down to Toronto. Dr. Hudson, meantime, expressed some mild concern over the gusting winds, reaching 40 miles per hour, that had kicked up as he flew.

The plane was too heavy and the pair needed to get rid of anything expendable in order to continue their flight home. Barilko and Hudson unloaded two tents, two sleeping bags and some cooking utensils to lighten their load and asked Allan Thorburn, the manager of the Hudson's Bay Company outpost, if they could leave the items there until they returned the next year. "They were away again in 10 minutes," states Mrs. Shepherd.

Three hours later, they landed at Rupert's House. Dan Wheeler, a clerk at the Hudson's Bay Company, refilled the Fairchild 24. "Dr. Hudson looked tired," mentioned the 23-year-old at the time. "He said he had a rough trip from Fort George. He took the lid off one of the compartments of a pontoon to look at his fish and said he had to get back to Timmins that night or they would spoil. There was about 150 pounds of fish in the pontoons."

Standing nearby was Eva Williams, the wife of another Anglican missionary. "You must like it up in this country!" she hollered to Bill. "I sure do," he answered, laughing.

James Crawford noted Dr. Hudson's small yellow Fairchild flying overhead and hurried over to the dock. "It was obvious that they were fairly heavy, the way the plane came in," recalls Crawford. "Being inquisitive and looking for my Arctic char as promised, I asked them how their fishing trip went. Barilko said it went exceptionally well." Hudson and Barilko undid the circular caps on the pontoons to reveal 60 or more large Arctic char. "It was the first time I had seen fish kept in the pontoons of an aircraft," says Crawford.

Bill delved into the pontoon and was searching for a large fish to give James as he had promised. Crawford remembers Dr. Hudson getting annoyed with Barilko, admonishing him, "Don't give him a big one; give him a smaller one." But Barilko said, "No, I promised this young lad a good-sized Arctic char and that's what I'm going to give him!"

"It was a beautiful fish; one of the nicest fish I ever tasted," smiles Crawford.

The sky had darkened to an ominous grey and there was no doubt that a storm was about to settle into the region. A radio report from Moose Factory indicated that weather south of the area had turned bad. "The whole sky was blackening," recalls Crawford. "I commented to both Doc Hudson and Barilko that, under the circumstances, I didn't think they should fly in this weather. I could put them up at the Hudson's Bay lodge and told them they were welcome to stay here at Rupert's House. Any Hudson's Bay post up and down the coast had extra rooms in case they needed to accommodate somebody coming in — it wasn't an advertised attraction. But they were anxious to continue on. It was Doc Hudson who said, 'We have to get these fish back to Timmins and into cold storage before too long so they don't spoil.'"

Little time had passed before Henry Hudson climbed back into the yellow plane ready for the final leg of the expedition.

The Fairchild struggled to gain altitude. "They were having trouble climbing. The wings were wavering back and forth. It was obvious that they were having difficulties even at that stage," says James. "I watched them for a long time until they were completely gone out of sight. I thought, 'I guess they're all right; I guess they're going to make it." He continues, "I was no flyer, but if it had been up to me, I wouldn't have been up in that plane that day.'" Some residents remembered Dr. Hudson having trouble taking off after a similar fishing trip the month before. His small plane had been overloaded with fish and had gone through similar motions before righting itself and becoming airborne.

The wind was gusting at 55 miles per hour at 2,000 feet. Although the plane's cruising speed was 80 miles per hour, the headwinds would have limited it to 25 miles per hour. Hudson and Barilko carried 50 gallons of gasoline and because the Fairchild burned between nine and 11 gallons per hour, the plane wouldn't have been able to reach Timmins without refuelling. Those at Rupert's House believed Dr. Hudson would likely stop in Moose Factory, where he could get gasoline as well as ice for his fish.

"I didn't learn just how famous Bill Barilko was until a little while later," says James Crawford. "I think I got that from the police personnel and the air force personnel who told me just how well he was admired in hockey circles as a member of the Toronto Maple Leafs."

* * *

Just before dusk that evening, Joseph Koostachin and Dave Okimowinue of Moosonee reported to George Field of Brownrigge Section House that they had observed a plane travelling northwest whose engine had cut out three times. Neither man was wearing a watch, but they agreed the time had been between five o'clock and 5:15. The sky was overcast and the coming evening made it impossible to discern the colour of the small plane seen a half-mile away.

A ham radio operator at Rupert's House relayed the observation to another radio operator in Moosonee, who sent a subsequent telegram to Austin Airways in South Porcupine. The story was corroborated by both Reverend A.C. Williams, an Anglican missionary, and Father R. Grenon, a parish priest, both of whom lived in Moosonee. Both noted that the plane had had difficulty taking off. Even more telling was that both men had noted the plane's colour as yellow and clearly remembered seeing the number 24, which identified the aircraft as belonging to Dr. Hudson.

Inspector I.R. Robbie of the Ontario Provincial Police in Timmins questioned eye witnesses for additional details and wrote, "They claimed that the plane taxied back and forth for some time before it was finally able to leave the water. After it had taken off, all said that it had at first rocked back and forth from wing tip to wing tip and that its nose lifted into the air. It stalled time after time in this position but pushed off out of sight with its nose up and its tail down."

It would have been extremely dangerous for any aircraft to take off in the James Bay area on the day the Fairchild 24 was last seen, reported Jim Hobbs, a pilot for Austin Airways. He had made a trip to Moosonee along the same route Dr. Hudson was assumed to have taken. "I was aided by a high ceiling, but before reaching Moosonee, the ceiling was so low that I could hardly see the water in landing," he stated. "Headwinds in the region that afternoon were 58 to 60 miles per hour."

🍁 🍁 🍁

Allan Stanley knows the north well and remembers that Hudson would have had two potential flight routes available to him. "They had a choice of going down the west side, where all the water was, or coming down the east side where they could follow the train tracks. They decided to follow the tracks."

Dr. Lou Hudson knew his brother's flight patterns well and was himself an experienced pilot. "My brother knows the area like the back of his hand," he told newspaper reporters. Lou believed that his brother would have flown the Fairchild from Rupert's House to Lake Kesogami, then to Porcupine Lake near Timmins. "If they ran up against heavy [bad] weather, and there was a low ceiling Sunday, they would most likely follow the Ontario Northland Railway Line between Cochrane and Moosonee," predicted Dr. Lou Hudson.

Lou Hudson hoped that his brother and Barilko would make radio contact, but the Fairchild 24's radio equipment had not been in working order.

🍁 🍁 🍁

Back in Timmins on Sunday evening, Leo Curik and the rest of the hockey gang waited for Bill Barilko to arrive. "Bill was supposed to be there at four in the afternoon," remembers Leo. "We waited until one or two in the morning and just thought, 'You know Bill, wanting to get a little more fishing in.'" But the next morning at nine o'clock, he received a phone call from sportswriter Bunny Morganson of the Toronto *Telegram*. "He said, 'Leo, I hear Bill is lost.' I told him he was wrong and that Bill just probably stayed an extra day because the fishing was so good, but he said, 'No, Leo. They can't find the plane!'"

Dr. Hudson's plane didn't return on Monday, either. The friends feared the worst.

"On Monday, August 27, I got a call from Leo Curik, Bill's best friend," recalls Bill's sister Anne. "This was about 10 o'clock in the morning. Leo said, 'Anne, I just want to let you know that Doc Hudson and Billy didn't come home last night.' I said, 'Oh, my God!' But Leo said, 'Don't worry. Henry does this so often. They probably had a problem with the weather, but they'll be home today.' But right away, I was thinking, 'We didn't want him to go, and now maybe something has happened!' That was my initial instinct. I said, 'Leo, I don't like what you're telling me!' He said, 'Don't worry, they probably just ran into some bad weather or decided to do some more fishing. They should be home this afternoon, but you should probably tell your mother.'"

Allan Stanley was downtown for a dental appointment on that Monday morning. "It was 10 o'clock and the nurse said, 'They're not back yet.' I said, 'Okay, I'll come back later.' I went over to the Victory Hotel, Leo Curik's hotel. There was a nice bench there and it was a nice sunny morning and I was sitting out there outside. It was just 12 noon and the nurse came walking by. I said, 'Are they back yet?' She said, 'No, they're not, and we're starting to get worried.' Later on that day, I phoned in again and she said, 'Allan, they're still not back.'"

Anne Klisanich picks up the narrative. "I said to my husband, Emil, 'We better drive over to Timmins and see Mother. This is not something I want to tell her on the phone.' My mother would have known that Bill hadn't come home because he was staying with her, but maybe she had forgotten what time Bill said he was coming back — she didn't call me to say, 'Bill didn't come home last night.'"

Anne and Emil drove over and told Faye Barilko about the call from Leo Curik. "Billy say he be back Sunday if nice weather," Faye reminded them. "If bad weather, they stay 'til weather nice."

"I said, 'Mom, don't worry. Maybe they're still fishing.' Of course, she was getting angry. Her voice got higher and higher — 'I tell him no go fishing!' She was devastated. None of us wanted Bill to go on this trip in the first place. It was horrific news for us." Faye Barilko sobbed uncontrollably. "Billy! My Billy! I tell him no go!"

Extraordinary anxiety was accompanied by anger and tears. "Why my Billy no come home? Why they no come home when they say?"

Anne tried to calm her mother. "'Mom, he'll be home this afternoon,'" Anne recalls saying to placate her mother. "Leo said that Henry went on these fishing trips to James Bay quite often and occasionally was late in returning. We spent all day at my mother's home waiting for some news of the airplane," Anne says haltingly. "I was fearing the worst."

The seconds felt like hours as Anne, Emil and Faye waited for Bill to come through the door. It never happened. "There was no sign of him," Anne says. The three grew more certain that something was wrong. "There was a rainstorm in our area on that Sunday, so we thought they had encountered bad weather," remembers Anne. "Within 24 hours, they decided they were going to start an air search. When Mother heard that, she was hysterical."

The story broke in the media the next day — "Barilko Vanishes in North," screamed the *Toronto Daily Star* on Tuesday, August 28, 1951.

With that, the search for Bill Barilko and Dr. Henry Hudson had begun.

CHAPTER
18

Courage

It was on the morning of August 27, 1951, that Anne Klisanich received a phone call telling her that her brother, Bill, and his friend Dr. Henry Hudson had not returned from Seal River as scheduled the night before. "At first, I was in a state of disbelief. We were devastated when we heard this shocking news. It was a horrible time for our family."

"2 Timmins Men Lost in North," trumpeted the Timmins *Daily Press* the next day. Word spread like wildfire to every corner of Canada, including the hockey world.

Harry Neale, the former National Hockey League and World Hockey Association coach who is recognized as one of today's best television commentators on hockey broadcasts, was an aspiring hockey prospect when he heard the news. "Like most Toronto kids do, I went to the Canadian National Exhibition, and I'll never forget the boy from the Toronto *Telegram* yelling, '*Telegram! Telegram!* Get your *Telegram!* Bill Barilko vanishes in north!' As a young Leaf fan — I was about 13 or 14 then — I can still remember being devastated that something like that could happen."

June Thomson, the widow of Bill's friend and teammate Jimmy Thomson, recalls hearing the devastating news. "Every summer, we went out to Winnipeg, to Jim's mother's home. We were in Winnipeg when we heard the news. We packed up fast and hurried home — not that we could do anything, but we just wanted to be closer to where the news would be. That was so shocking!"

"I was in Timmins when I heard Bill was missing," reflects Bep Guidolin, who was getting ready to return to the Chicago Blackhawks that fall. "I used to go back to Timmins during the summers to be with my Mom and Dad. It was a quiet summer. I never went fishing; I was a golfer. If I loved fishing like Billy did, I might have been in that plane.

Doc Hudson was a great guy — we loved him. He was our dentist. He was a real down-to earth, ordinary guy."

Johnny McCormack had played with Bill on the Leafs for parts of the previous four seasons. "I can remember that day very well. I played baseball with Turk Broda's All-Stars. That was a misnomer because there wasn't an all-star ball player among us, but we would barnstorm around, playing hither and yon. We were going to play a game at Kew Beach Park in the Beaches area of Toronto. I went to the game, and I heard it on the radio. It's one of those things you can remember, like where you were when John F. Kennedy was shot. It was a real shocker. All we could do was say a prayer and just hope that they landed somewhere else."

Gus Mortson, Barilko's colleague on the blue line, remembers that day as well. "I was living out in Oakville at the time. We used to play exhibition softball games for charity, and the news came out that Barilko was missing. The fellas on the team laughed and said, 'There's Bill looking for publicity again.' It never struck us that Barilko could have had an accident."

"I was playing ball at Trinity Bellwoods Park [in Toronto's west end] and we were playing against the NHL Old-Timers," relates Babe Gresko, a teammate of Barilko's with the Hollywood Wolves. "I remember Sid Smith coming by and saying, 'Babe, did you hear that we lost one of our buddies?' He knew I had played with Bill."

Fern Flaman was Barilko's defence partner through the better part of the 1950–51 season and was on the blue line when Bill scored the Stanley Cup–winning goal. He was in New England when he heard the news. "I always kept my home in the Boston area. It's a town called Westwood, about 25 minutes out of Boston. When I was in Toronto in the winter, I used to rent my house out to a hockey player, then I'd come back in the summer and the player who had been renting the house would go back to his home, wherever that might be. My summer job was with Budweiser. You had to take a summer job back then. I got a job on one of the big beer trucks, throwing kegs around. It kept me in pretty good shape."

A number of the Maple Leafs, including Howie Meeker, were at the Shopsy's Delicatessen booth at the Canadian National Exhibition in Toronto when they heard that their friend and teammate had disappeared. "We knew we'd lost a big part of our defence. And a big piece of our heart."

Ted Kennedy was golfing in a foursome with Conn Smythe on August 28. "Mr. Smythe and his childhood friend Bob Murray — he was a very fine man, a dentist at Broadview and Danforth Avenue — and Jack Amell, a jeweller, had invited me to play golf up at Rosedale golf course. After our game was over, we went into the locker room and were sitting there relaxing. The locker room steward came up and said, 'It's too bad about Barilko.' Mr. Smythe said, 'Why, what happened to Barilko?' The steward said, 'He was out fishing and was on a private plane and he's missing. They can't find any trace of him.'

"So Smythe looked down at the floor and said, 'Another one of your publicity stunts, eh, Smythe?' And Dr. Murray looked up and said, 'Conny, what do you mean by that?' Mr. Smythe said, 'That's what they'll say. They'll say I'm pulling a stunt.' And Dr. Murray said, 'No, no, Conny. They'll never think that!' Mr. Smythe said, 'Oh no? Just you wait and see.'

"Well, sure enough, there was one story saying this was just one of Smythe's publicity stunts. Mr. Smythe understood that. It wasn't unusual for somebody to try to twist something that Mr. Smythe did so that it included publicity for his hockey team. But that's how I found out about Bill Barilko's plane going down."

Smythe immediately went into action and used his influence with Ontario Premier George Drew to involve the military in finding Barilko and Hudson. Search and rescue operations were set up at Kapuskasing Airport, about 100 miles northwest of Timmins, under Flight Lieutenant G.J. "Rusty" Ruston of Hamilton, Ontario. By the conclusion of the search, which was dubbed "Operation Hudson" by the military, it was to escalate into the largest rescue mission in Canadian aviation history, encompassing 38 Royal Canadian Air Force planes carrying 270 members of the air force, flying for 1,354 hours over bush and water at a cost of $285,000. Many private planes added to the search, aided by hundreds of civilians, trappers and native guides.

Dr. Hudson's wife, Phyllis, had been through this scenario before. "Two years ago, Henry was flying in the same area on a similar fishing trip and he was lost four days in the bush," she told *Timmins Daily Press* in the mid-sixties. "His plane had battery trouble and he was forced to land on a lake and wait it out. He lived off the land for four days by himself until a rescue craft spotted him. They flew in repairs, and Henry was able to take off and return to Timmins in his own plane."

Phyllis was concerned but tried to remain optimistic. "I hope they just ran out of gasoline. The aircraft fuel tanks held just enough to make a trip to the fishing spot on Hudson Bay and return. They might just have landed on some little lake somewhere." She added, "Henry has been flying for five or six years [he purchased the plane in 1947] and goes on fishing trips nearly every weekend when it's nice." Other northern Ontario flyers familiar with Hudson classified him as a careful pilot.

Gus Mortson, who was born and raised in northern Ontario and lives there today, was also confident that the boys would be found. "There are a lot of small lakes on which they could land and the route they'd travel isn't too far from the T & NO railway. For that reason, I don't think they'd lose their way. They both had been over the route previously."

The airport in Kapuskasing served as the base of operations for the search for Barilko and Hudson. The two had last been seen at four o'clock on the afternoon of Sunday, August 26, when they left Rupert's House on James Bay for Porcupine Lake near Timmins. A blanket search was initiated, in which hundreds of tiny islands and lakes were observed over and over again. The desolate territory that was searched is made up of thousands of acres of muskeg, winding rivers and scrub. In case signs of the plane or the missing men were found, para-rescuers were prepared to jump down into the unforgiving terrain to retrieve them. Military planes were aided in the effort by private planes and commercial craft from Northland Aviation Ltd. They carried extra gasoline on the chance that the Fairchild was intact and merely out of fuel.

Tommy Cooke of the Department of Lands and Forests directed the search from headquarters on Porcupine Lake and cautioned anyone from panicking too quickly. "The men can stay in that kind of country for at least a week if they crash landed as long as they have no serious injuries." On Tuesday, August 28, he zigzagged along the course he believed Hudson had flown. There were no signs of the yellow Fairchild 24, and finally darkness forced him to abandon the search that day.

Although Kapuskasing was 120 miles from Timmins and the Klisaniches didn't own a car, Faye Barilko insisted on journeying there. "My mother said, 'I go Kapuskasing,'" states Anne. "So, Mom, Emil and I drove to Kapuskasing with Alex, who had a car. We spent five days there, waiting for the search planes to bring us some news. It was just heartbreaking. Every time the planes would come back, there was no news.

"My mother, Emil and I stayed with Mr. and Mrs. Poleyko, who were friends of my mother's. They might even have been distant cousins. Alex stayed at the Kap Inn, a nearby hotel, so he could be closer to the airport in case there was any news from the pilots." The historic Kapuskasing Inn, built in 1921 by the Kimberly-Clark paper company for men working in the pulp and paper mills of the area, was used as headquarters of the search for the lost sportsmen. "The pilots all stayed there," adds Anne.

✴ ✴ ✴

By Wednesday, August 29, RCAF crews were scouring areas most likely to have been travelled by Dr. Hudson. A severe electrical storm that day curtailed some of the search activities, mostly those carried out by private planes. That day, word reached the searchers that a possible sighting had been made on Sunday. Smoke had been observed coming from an area 10 to 12 miles west of Coral Rapids, but men at an Ontario Hydro survey camp located near there reported that they had not heard any aircraft flying overhead that day.

The popular Barilko meets contest winners from Timmins in the Leafs dressing room at Maple Leaf Gardens. With Bill are (*left to right*) Roger Poulin, John Oreskovich and Edward George.

(Imperial Oil-Turofsky/ Hockey Hall of Fame)

During the 1951 Stanley Cup final, arch-rivals Montreal and Toronto took all 5 games to overtime. Maurice Richard (*centre right*) scored an O/T winner for Montreal, while Sid Smith, Ted Kennedy, Harry Watson and Bill Barilko (*centre left*) scored winners for the Leafs.

(Imperial Oil-Turofsky/Hockey Hall of Fame)

The most requested photograph in the expansive Hockey Hall of Fame archives is this outstanding shot taken by Nat Turofsky at 2:53 of the first overtime period on April 21, 1951. The goal earned the Maple Leafs their fourth Stanley Cup championship in five seasons. (Imperial Oil-Turofsky/ Hockey Hall of Fame)

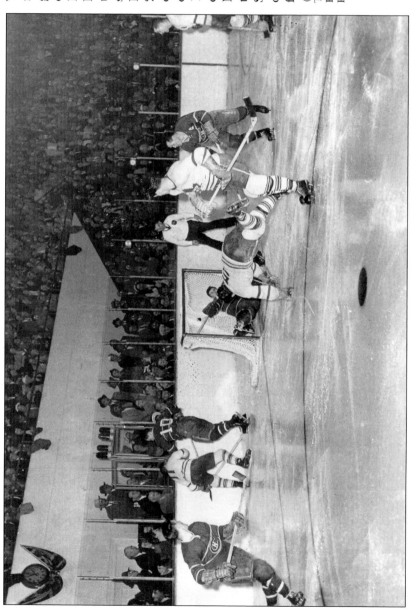

This exciting angle of the famous Barilko goal shows Bill mid-air, but clearly realizing the puck has eluded Montreal goaltender Gerry McNeil for the overtime winner.
(Michael Burns Photography)

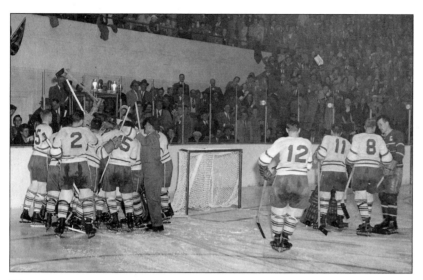

Victorious teammates leapt over the boards to mob Stanley Cup hero,
Bill Barilko.
(Imperial Oil-Turofsky/Hockey Hall of Fame)

The evening's hero is congratulated by coach Joe Primeau (*centre left*)
and manager Conn Smythe (*centre right*) as teammates Fleming MacKell
(*far left*) and Al Rollins (*far right*) look on.
(Imperial Oil-Turofsky/Hockey Hall of Fame)

Following the presentation of the Stanley Cup, a beaming Bill Barilko and his Maple Leafs teammates retired to the dressing room to continue their celebration.
(Imperial Oil-Turofsky/Hockey Hall of Fame)

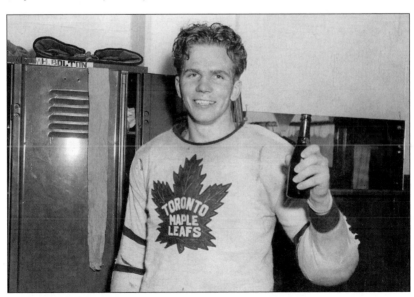

Certainly no one could have imagined that the 24-year old Barilko had played his final hockey game. Four months later, Bill and Dr. Hudson disappeared while returning from a fishing trip on James Bay.
(Imperial Oil-Turofsky/Hockey Hall of Fame)

TORONTO MAPLE LEAFS 1950-51
CONN SMYTHE (PRES MAN) C H DAY ASS'T MANAGER
C G McCULLAGH (V PRES) J Y MURDOCH KC (V PRES)
J BICKELL DIRECTOR E B BICKLE DIRECTOR
THOMAS DALY TRAINER E D FITKIN PUB DIRECTOR
A CAMPBELL (ASS TR) T NAYLOR (ASS TR) G E WALKER CH SC
BILL BARILKO MAX BENTLEY HUGH BOLTON
WALTER BRODA FERN FLAMAN BOB HASSARD
CAL GARDNER BILL JUZDA TED KENNEDY
JOE KLUKAY DANIEL LEWISKI FLEMING MACKELL
HOWARD MEEKER GUS WORTSON JOHN McCORMACK
ELVIN ROLLINS TOD SLOAN SID SMITH
JIM THOMSON RAY TIMGREN HARRY WATSON
J PRIMEAU COACH W A H McBRIEN CHAIRMAN

The 1950-51 Stanley Cup champion Toronto Maple Leafs, engraved in perpetuity on the Stanley Cup. (Dave Sandford/ Hockey Hall of Fame)

A proud mother ladles champagne for her heroic son following his clinching goal on April 21, 1951. It would be several years before Faye Barilko could watch another hockey game.

(Imperial Oil-Turofsky/ Hockey Hall of Fame)

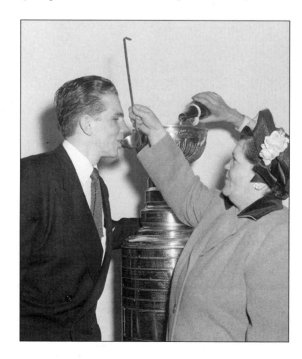

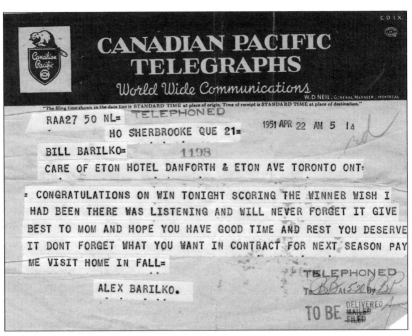

The brothers Barilko remained close through their entire lives. Alex, intensely proud of his brother's accomplishments, sent Bill this telegram the morning after the Stanley Cup was won by the Leafs.
(Anne Klisanich collection)

Now showered and dressed, the triumphant Toronto Maple Leafs toast a fourth championship in five seasons. Standing front and centre are (*left to right*) Conn Smythe, Bill Barilko, Joe Primeau and Howie Meeker.
(Imperial Oil-Turofsky/Hockey Hall of Fame)

The Stanley Cup champions of 1951 – the Toronto Maple Leafs.
(Imperial Oil-Turofsky/Hockey Hall of Fame)

Bill with the girl he left behind – Louise Hastings (*now Carley*) at a cottage on Lake Simcoe during the summer of 1948.

(courtesy of Louise Carley)

They called themselves the Personality Club Boys, and were inseparable during summers when Bill was home from playing hockey. Here, at Lou Hudson's lodge on Watabeag Lake in 1946 are (*left to right*) Lawrence Curik, Mel Richards, unidentified child, Bill Curik, Bill Barilko, Leo Curik and Dick Richards.

(courtesy Dorothy and Leo Curik)

During August 1951, best friends Bill Barilko (*left*) and Leo Curik (*right*) drove to Springfield, Massachusetts to visit Leo's girlfriend, Dorothy. Within weeks, Bill had disappeared without a trace.

(courtesy Dorothy and Leo Curik)

One of the last known photographs of Bill Barilko shows the well-dressed Leaf standing in front of Allan Stanley's car during the ill-fated month of August, 1951.

(courtesy Dorothy and Leo Curik)

The Allan Cup-winning Toronto Varsitys of 1927 featured captain Lou Hudson, back row, second from the left. The team competed for Canada at the 1928 Winter Olympics in St. Moritz, Switzerland, winning the gold medal. Observers called them "the greatest hockey team ever."
(Hockey Hall of Fame)

Dr. Henry Hudson is relaxing aboard his boat *Slowpoke* during a fishing trip on Lake Temagami with his friend Archie Chenier, taken during the summer of 1950.
(courtesy Archie Chenier)

On June 6, 1962, eleven years after disappearing while returning from a fishing trip, the crash site of Hudson's yellow Fairchild 24 plane was discovered, obscured by dense forest, just north of Cochrane, Ontario.
(Department of Lands and Forests (Ontario))

Pilot Gary Fields caught a glimpse of yellow and what he believed were pontoons in the dense woods of Northern Ontario. It turned out to be the yellow, four-seater, pontoon plane with registration CF–FXT belonging to Dr. Henry Hudson. The skeletal remains of both men were still strapped into their cockpit seats.
(Department of Lands and Forests (Ontario))

On June 15, 1962, family and friends laid to rest the long undiscovered remains of Bill Barilko. Facing the camera are pallbearers Allan Stanley, Mel Richards and Steve Denisavitch, while Harry Watson, Leo Curik and Gaston Garant have their backs to the photographer. Behind and to the right are Bill's mother, brother and nephew, Frank.

(Anne Klisanich collection)

Under the family surname on Barilko's tombstone is a photo of Bill wearing his Toronto Maple Leafs sweater. Carved into the stone is "Wm. (Bill) Barilko, 1927–1951." Beneath the dates of his lifeline are the years in which Bill contributed to winning the Stanley Cup: 1947, 1948, 1949 and 1951.

(Anne Klisanich collection)

On October 17, 1992, the Toronto Maple Leafs officially retired the numbers 5 and 6. Anne Klisanich, assisted by Ted Kennedy, helped hoist her brother's number 5 banner to the rafters. Simultaneously, Joyce Bailey and Ron Ellis raised Ace Bailey's number 6. These are the only two numbers to be retired by the franchise – never to be worn again.

(Anne Klisanich collection)

Bill Barilko's legacy was ensured with The Tragically Hip's song, "Fifty Mission Cap." Since being released on the band's *Fully Completely* album in 1992, the song has gone on to be one of the most played songs in Canadian radio history. Anne met The Hip at the Hershey Centre in Mississauga, Ontario on February 19, 1999. Left to right are Gord Sinclair, Gord Downie, Anne Klisanich, Paul Langlois and Johnny Fay. The band's Robby Baker is absent.

(Anne Klisanich collection)

The Klisaniches, Bill Barilko's closest family members, congregated for a family portrait. Anne, Bill's sister, is married to Emil Klisanich. Their children are Frank and Barry. Frank is married to Chris, and the couple has three children – John, Caroline and Michael. Left to right, John, Caroline, Frank, Anne, Emil, Chris, Barry and Michael.

(Anne Klisanich collection)

Anne and Emil Klisanich met Wayne Gretzky at an event held in his Toronto restaurant. When introduced to Anne, The Great One exclaimed, "Bill Barilko! That's all my father ever talked about! Bill Barilko!"

(Anne Klisanich collection)

Bill Barilko's final contract was signed prior to the 1950-51 season for $9,000.

(courtesy of Allan J. Stitt)

STANDARD PLAYER'S CONTRACT

National Hockey League

The _____

of _____

WITH

I hereby certify that I have, at this date, received, examined and sealed of record the within Contract, and that it is in regular form.

Dated _____ 19__

President National Hockey League

IMPORTANT NOTICE TO PLAYER

Before signing this contract you should carefully examine it to be sure that all terms and conditions agreed upon have been incorporated herein, and if any has been omitted, you should insist upon having it inserted in the contract before you sign.

NATIONAL HOCKEY LEAGUE

STANDARD PLAYER'S CONTRACT

This Agreement

BETWEEN: _____ MAPLE LEAF GARDENS LIMITED _____
hereinafter called the "Club",
a member of the National Hockey League, hereinafter called the "League".

—AND— _____ WILLIAM BARILKO _____
hereinafter called the "Player".

of _____ TIMMINS _____ in (Province) of _____ ONTARIO _____ (State)

Witnesseth:

That in consideration of the respective obligations herein and hereby assumed, the parties to this contract severally agree as follows:—

1. The Club hereby employs the Player as a skilled Hockey Player and agrees to pay the Player for the season of 19.50-51 ("season" meaning the period commencing the date on which the Player reports to the Club at its training camp or other place designated by the Club, and ending on the completion of the Club's games in the National Hockey League Championship Schedule, Play-off and Stanley Cup Series) a salary of

_____ --Nine Thousand Dollars--- _____ Dollars ($ 9000.00.

If the player B. Barilko makes the Second All Star Team, will receive bonus of $500.00

If the player B. Barilko makes the First N. H. L. All Star team, he will receive a bonus of $1000.00

Payment of such salary shall be in semi-monthly instalments following the commencement of the regular League Championship Schedule of Games or following the date of reporting, whichever is later. Provided, however, that if the player is not in the employ of the Club for this entire period, then he shall receive such proportion of the salary as the number of days of actual employment bears to the total number of days in the said period.

17. The Club agrees that it will on or before October 1st next following the season covered by this contract tender to the Player personally or by mail directed to the Player at his address set out below his signature hereto a contract upon the same terms as this contract save as to salary.
The Player hereby undertakes that he will at the request of the Club enter into a contract for the following playing season upon the same terms and conditions as this contract save as to salary which shall be determined by mutual agreement. In the event that the Player and the Club do not agree upon the salary to be paid the matter shall be referred to the President of the League, and the parties agree to accept his decision as final.

18. The Club and the Player severally and mutually promise and agree to be legally bound by the Constitution and By-Laws of the League and by all the terms and provisions thereof, a copy of which shall be open and available for inspection by Club, its directors and officers, and the Player, at the main office of the League and at the main office of the Club.
The Club and the Player further agree that in case of dispute between them, the dispute shall be referred within one year from the date it arose to the President of the League as an arbitrator and his decision shall be accepted as final.

19. The Player agrees that the Club's right to renew this contract as provided in Section 17 and the promise of the Player to play hockey only with the Club, or such other club as provided in Section 2 and Section 11, and the Club's right to take pictures of and to televise the Player as provided in section 8 have all been taken into consideration in determining the salary payable to the Player under Section 1 hereof.

20. The Player hereby authorizes and directs the Club to deduct and pay, and the Club hereby agrees to deduct and pay, to the National Hockey League Pension Society, out of the salary stipulated in Section 1 hereof on behalf of the Player the sum of Nine Hundred Dollars ($900.00) or such lesser proportion thereof as the number of days' service of the Player with the Club under this contract bears to the number of days of the League Championship Schedule of games, and to obtain from the National Hockey League Pension Society a proper receipt for such sum in the name of the Player.

21. It is severally and mutually agreed that the only contracts recognized by the President of the League are the Standard Player's Contracts which have been duly executed and filed in the League's office and approved by him, and that this Agreement contains the entire agreement between the Parties and there are no oral or written inducements, promises or agreements except as contained herein.

In Witness Whereof, the parties have signed this _____ Eighth _____ day

of _____ August _____ A.D. 19 50

WITNESSES:

MAPLE LEAF GARDENS LIMITED
By _____ Club
_____ President
_____ Player
63 Sixth Avenue, Timmins, Ontario
Home Address of Player

Another report came in that a yellow plane with pontoons was sighted crashing near Hannah or St. John Township by a railway foreman. In fact, he had seen a plane similar to Dr. Hudson's, that was merely flying low over the treetops and that had not crashed at all. "The plane which a section man said he thought he saw crash in the bush must have been mine," said Tommy Cooke. "I was flying across that area at about 1,000 feet about the time of the report. It seemed to be a case of hunting for myself, but no possible clue can be ignored." Both aircraft were yellow and about the same size, although Hudson's was a Fairchild 24 and Cooke's plane was a Beaver.

Later that day, Phyllis Hudson heard an airplane "buzzing" her house and ran out, assuming it was her husband returning from the Seal River expedition. But again, it was Cooke's small plane, circling the town for a landing, that had been mistaken for the missing Fairchild 24.

On August 30, the RCAF found that the search was getting cumbersome and excluded private planes from the hunt. Various friends of Barilko's, including Bep Guidolin, kept vigil at the South Porcupine airport. A number of former teammates, including Roy McKay from the Holman Pluggers, also helped in the search. Carlo Cattarello Jr., the mascot for the 1942–43 Pluggers, also remembers following the search for Barilko. "We'd walk down to the lake every day, hoping we were going to get some news about what happened. It was really hard."

Allan Stanley grows quiet as he remembers the painful days that followed the disappearance of Barilko. "It was unbelievable. I flew up to Kapuskasing for four or five days. They had big cargo planes from the air force, but they had to fly too high and too fast and you couldn't see anything. Then, Leo Curik and I flew in a float plane with Dr. Lou Hudson. It flew lower and it flew slower. Lou was quite a bush man — he knew all the signs. We'd be sitting there looking for yellow spots or anything else that might be their plane, and we'd say, 'Look at that, Doc. There's a yellow spot,' and Lou would take one glance and say, 'That's a beaver dam.' He knew all the signs.

"We flew four or five days, and then training camp was starting so I had to get there, but they had a lot of help there and a lot of people for sighting."

The Timmins *Daily Press* headed their August 31, editions with the headline, "Refuse to Lose Hope, Weary Eyes Seek Signs of Life."

Twelve air force planes, summoned from the Trenton, Centralia and Rockcliffe bases in Ontario, scoured vast areas of northern wilderness. A Lancaster Bomber, two Mitchell Bombers, a Canso flying boat and four Dakota transports were included in the early days of the search.

Searchers thought they might have uncovered a lead when a flash of yellow was spotted during the search, but closer inspection proved that it was nothing more than a yellowed poplar tree.

Sergeant Bill Farr, with the para-rescue squadron from Trenton, Ontario, said, "If the plane crashed and burned Sunday, it would be almost impossible to find it. This is hopeless." Another on the para-rescue team was Corporal Cliff Lockett, also of Trenton, who grew up in Timmins and attended Timmins High and Vocational School with Anne Barilko.

※ ※ ※

The flying armada was increased to 19 planes and 125 men on September 1, while an additional 12 long-range planes were requested from the air force base in Trenton. Additional equipment, including bunk beds, was secured from lumber camps in the Spruce Falls area. Six Lancaster Bombers from the North Atlantic Squadron flew into the area from Greenwood, Nova Scotia, to assist in the search.

Eight trucks, each carrying a 2,200-gallon load of gasoline, made repeated trips to Kapuskasing from either North Bay or Toronto to ensure that the search aircraft had a steady supply of fuel on hand. Two men manned each truck, taking turns driving while the other slept in order to maintain the continuous deliveries. In addition, a pair of railway tank cars, each carrying 6,800 gallons of gasoline, also arrived in Kapuskasing, and they returned every second day for the duration of the search.

Weary eyes continued to report possible sightings. A canvas lean-to, resembling a tent, was sighted near Normetal, Quebec, but it turned out to be a prospector camping in the area. Spotters noted moose, deer and beavers, but no sign of the missing Timmins men.

On September 2, a Lands and Forests ranger, Henry Huneault, was walking through the dense bush at his farm in Lowther, 25 miles northwest of Kapuskasing, when he discovered two pieces of Plexiglas that together formed a complete window. One of the pieces was lying flat on the ground while the other was upright, stuck in the ground about one hundred yards away. Dr. Lou Hudson brought recent photos of his brother's Fairchild 24, with good views of the aircraft's windows, for comparison. Excitement turned to disappointment when it was realized that the window couldn't have been from Hudson's plane. "Windows have been known to drop out of planes on numerous occasions, but that is definitely not a window from the Hudson plane," announced Flight Lieutenant Ruston.

A Welland businessman named Ed Ahr, who was also an experienced bush pilot who knew the region well, joined the search on September 5. Ahr lived most of his life in the Timmins area and founded the Algoma Air Service, the first of its kind in the vicinity, in 1924. That same year, he also initiated the Porcupine Flying Club. Dr. Henry

Hudson was one of the first to join the club and was a longtime friend of Ahr's, who was also an experienced bush pilot and knew the area well.

This wasn't the first hockey-related rescue in which Ed Ahr had been involved. In the spring of 1936, a light plane carrying two Timmins men and several from Toronto was returning from watching the Maple Leafs take on Detroit in the playoffs. The plane crashed in the bush south of Timmins in 15-degree-below-zero weather and was lost for three days. Ed took one of his planes and within three hours had located the crashed plane on a small nearby lake. Joined by a doctor and Karl Eyre, who later became a Member of Parliament for Timmins, Ahr landed on the ice surface and made 12 trips in order to rescue all the men, several of whom were severely injured.

Flight Lieutenant Ruston reported that the trail was "cold as a mackerel" but reinforced that the rescue operation had not yet reached its peak. Several friends and family members took roles as spotters in the planes involved in the search. Bill's brother, Alex, his brother-in-law, Emil, and friends Leo Curik and Allan Stanley all took turns as spotters. Each would crane their necks for a glint of yellow in the dense, unforgiving forests of northern Ontario while the pilot maneuvered just above the treetops.

"We stared into bush for six hours straight at a time," Emil Klisanich remembers. "It was bush, bush, bush everywhere. By the second week, we were losing all hope." Emil was familiar with flying as he had been in the RCAF.

"Day after day after day, I and many others took part being observers with binoculars going up and looking to see what we could see," tells James Crawford, one of the last to see Barilko and Hudson alive. "We thought that with the plane a light yellow, it wouldn't be hard to spot. You have to know the bush in that area — it's the type of bush that once you come down, the whole bush would just close around and no one except somebody searching on the ground would be able to see it. Certainly no one from the air."

The RCAF contended that 60-mile-an-hour winds might have carried the small plane farther north than originally believed, so on September 5th the search area was extended to the east side of James Bay where it widens into Hudson Bay and, in a westerly direction, to the Albany River.

🍁 🍁 🍁

Conn Smythe kept in regular contact with Faye Barilko during the ordeal and showed great concern at the disappearance of his star defenceman. "Mr. Smythe wrote my mother a lovely letter saying he was there if there was anything he could do," acknowledges Anne Klisanich.

"After five days, Mother said, 'We go back home.' I had a baby — Frank was only two and a half months old. My mother-in-law couldn't look after the baby because she had to run the hotel. Our neighbours, Millie and Bill Hartling, looked after our baby while we were in Kapuskasing. They were the most generous and kind people; having them there gave me peace of mind that Frank was okay. They had a little girl, Tina. To this day, Tina calls me and we talk about my brother, Bill," Anne nods.

A photo-plane was brought into the area on September 6 to take aerial photos. The film was then rushed to Trenton, processed and inspected under a microscope in hopes that something might be picked out that the naked eye had been unable to detect.

Tragedy was narrowly averted on September 7 when a Dakota 427 rose six feet off the runway in Kapuskasing, then came down almost immediately, plowing about 100 feet of ground at the end of the runway. Frost on the wings was blamed for the crash, and minor injuries were suffered by the pilot and the radio-navigator. The left engine was snapped in two, the right wing was pierced by a small tree, and the nose of the aircraft was crumpled. The crew was out of the plane within seconds, and the co-pilot, Flight Officer Johnny Aikens, who crawled through the hatch in the roof, returned to the plane when he discovered that the pilot had not left the aircraft. He returned to find that Flight Officer Don Lewis had his foot caught between the controls. Lewis was treated for a sprained ankle while Aikens broke three fingers and suffered lacerations to his face and hands. Nine others were treated for shock or a battery of cuts and bruises.

Alex Barilko had been scheduled to be on that plane as a spotter, but had failed to appear, thereby avoiding being on board the crashed Dakota. "I overslept and when I got down to the airport, I saw the wrecked Dakota," confessed Alex. "I guess I was lucky."

Although hope was beginning to fade, Squadron Leader W.A.G. MacLeish of Trenton went on record as stating, "The search is by no means over. The end isn't even in sight."

❀ ❀ ❀

On September 10, Mrs. Henry Huneault, on whose farm the Plexiglas window had been discovered earlier in the search, went out to place a flag in the dense bush where her husband had discovered the windows. On the return trip, she got confused and headed off in the wrong direction. When she didn't return, her husband and son went out to look for her and, while searching the woods, became separated. The son returned home and informed neighbours that his parents were lost. Inspector I.R. Robbie called in 12 trained men from the Department of Lands and

Forests to search for the couple, but just as they were about to embark on the search, the Huneaults' daughter ran over and informed Robbie that her parents had just returned safely. Henry had followed his wife's footprints through mud left by a cold rain and found his wife wandering aimlessly around a bush camp seven miles from their home.

✹ ✹ ✹

Anne Klisanich continues: "When the search started for my brother and Henry, Lou Hudson got in touch with my mother and me and said, 'I want to go to Kapuskasing to assist in the search, but I don't have a car.' He lived in an apartment on the main street in Timmins, so he didn't really need one. When he needed transportation, his brother, Henry, or friends looked after him. Lou asked, 'Can I drive Bill's car to Kapuskasing?' We said, 'That would be fine,' so he drove the car to Kapuskasing. We were there for five days and then it was time to go home."

Amidst the anxiety and fear of Bill's disappearance, Anne was forced to learn to drive as well. "Alex decided to stay behind in Kapukasing while the search continued and asked us to drive his car back to Timmins," recalls Anne. "Lou Hudson also planned to stay, and said, 'You'd better take Bill's car back. I'll get a ride with Leo Curik or one of the other hockey players.' My husband, Emil, said, 'Well, I'll drive Alex's car back, but how are we going to get Bill's car back?' And I said, 'Well, I don't know how to drive!'"

Despite her protests, it was decided that Anne was the only one available to drive Bill's car home to Timmins. But who would give her the driving lessons she needed? "My brother said, 'Well, I'm not teaching you,' and Emil said, 'No way I'm going to teach you.' So I talked to Alex Poleyko. We were staying at his house while we were in Kapuskasing, and he said, 'Anne, I'll give you a crash course in how to drive.' In one hour, I learned how to drive a car.

"Emil drove Alex's car behind me and said, 'You just keep your foot on the gas pedal and keep changing the gears and stay on the right side of that line.'" With her mother, Faye, in the car providing support, Anne made the journey successfully.

✹ ✹ ✹

Turk Broda, the primary goaltender for the Leafs through the five seasons Bill Barilko played with Toronto, announced on September 14 that he was organizing benefit softball games, the proceeds of which were to be earmarked for the search for Barilko.

The next several days raised several false alarms. One spotter reported seeing pontoons in a remote clearing, but they turned out to be logs resting side by side. Two flares, "like Roman candles," were sighted near Blacksmith Rapids on the Abitibi River, but authorities in Kapuskasing reported, "The missing Fairchild was not equipped with emergency flares. Nevertheless, all reports are closely checked by our aircraft."

The search suffered another setback when an RCAF helicopter, carrying three men involved in the search, crashed near Rupert's House on September 17. The helicopter's engine failed, but fortunately, no one was hurt. The three were forced to camp in the bush for a day until the waters in the river had calmed enough to allow a floatplane to land and rescue them.

Hope was dwindling by September. "There are many, including the missing men's brothers, Alex Barilko and Dr. Lou Hudson, and a group of Bill's teammates, who feel that only a ground search will provided a definite clue to the fate of the popular fishermen," reported the Timmins *Daily Press* on September 18. Nonetheless, a fund was initiated by associates of Bill Barilko, including Turk Broda and Ted Kennedy of the Maple Leafs and Art Whittaker from Barilko Brothers Appliances, where employees at the store had expected Bill back on Thursday, August 30.

August and September passed without any good news. After 17 days of intense searching, the air force ceased its operations and left the area.

On October 30, 1951, Toronto Maple Leafs president Conn Smythe, hoping to urge searchers to continue looking for the lost sportsmen, put forward a reward: "Maple Leaf Gardens Limited offers the sum of $10,000 to the person who finds William Barilko, professional hockey player, or recovers his body. This offer expires on the first day of January, 1952. Should there be more than one claimant for the reward, it will be apportioned as the President of Maple Leaf Gardens Limited deems appropriate."

On that same date, Conn Smythe sent Bill's mother, Faye Barilko, the following letter: "I have been instructed by the Board of Directors of Maple Leaf Gardens to advise you of the following resolution which was passed at our meeting on October 24th. It was unanimously resolved that the President convey to Mrs. Barilko the best wishes of the Board in the search for her son, their confident hope for its success and their sincere sympathy during the anxious period of waiting for news."

At Faye's suggestion, Bishop R.J. Renison — speaking in Cree — broadcast an appeal over radio station CKGB in Timmins for First Nations listeners to report anything they had seen or knew.

🍁 🍁 🍁

Bush pilots continued to search for the missing men, but nothing came to pass in October, either. Then the snow started to fall, making it impossible to continue the search. Periodically over the years, a possible sighting was reported, but the leads all turned into dead ends. Everyone gave up hope. Everybody but Faye Barilko.

"My mother never gave up hope," declares Anne. "I said to her, 'Mother, you're not going to like what I'm going to tell you, but we have to be realistic. If Bill was alive, he and Henry would have made a fire and they would have been found.'

"She said, "I no give up hope 'til I get proof.' She kept thinking that maybe he had amnesia, that he could be around somewhere and he'd be coming home. Mom said, 'My Billy come back.'

"And do you know that every spring my mother would take out Billy's suits and his sport jackets and hang them on the clothesline so they'd be aired out and fresh for when Billy came home?" A meek smile crosses Anne's lips. "Mom made sure all his shirts were kept up. She just did everything as if she was expecting Bill to walk through the front door at any time."

"Mother also kept Billy's car for three or four years," Anne mentions. "A gentleman from Timmins approached my mother and asked her what she was going to do with it. He said, 'I'd like to buy it and I'll give you fair value. I'd be so proud to own Bill Barilko's car.' We discussed it and agreed to sell it.'

"Through the years, we got so many beautiful letters expressing sadness for Bill and sympathy for what my mother was going through. Many of the letters were simply addressed, 'Mrs. Barilko, Timmins, Ontario.' The post office made the deliveries," says an astonished Anne.

"There were rumours that Bill might have been teaching hockey in Russia," she continues. "There weren't too many smiles on my mother's face for a long, long time, I can assure you, but she would smile when she heard that rumour. She said, 'If story true, Billy alive!'" During those days, Faye's tears seldom subsided. "As soon as you talked about Billy, there would be tears," says Anne. "It was very hard. It was heartbreaking."

Timmins Mayor Vic Power remembers the melancholy that hung over the region. "At the end of 1951, the mayor at that time, Wilf Spooner, was interviewed by the Timmins *Daily Press* and asked 'What was the most important event in Timmins this year?' He said, 'Well, the tragic disappearance of Bill Barilko, because it brought sadness to the whole community.'"

"It was just devastating to think that such a young boy at the peak of his hockey career and with so much to live for — that this could happen," says Anne, wiping a tear from the corner of her eye.

🍁 🍁 🍁

Helen O'Neil, who ran Dr. Hudson's office, wasn't overly concerned about the disappearance at first. "I just kept cancelling the appointments from day to day, expecting that he and Bill were going to come back. I was thinking, 'Maybe they just got lost.' They weren't far off course, you know." Eventually, as days turned to weeks, Helen gradually lost hope that Dr. Hudson and Bill Barilko would be discovered alive. "We kept holding on to hope. Nothing happened to Dr. Hudson's practice for a year. We were in constant contact with Dr. Lou Hudson, Henry's brother. He would let me know if there were any developments."

"I looked after the office and sent out all the correspondence for his wife," says Helen. "By that time, I was living with Mrs. Hudson because she was alone. Their home was right on the river — a beautiful place. I said to her, 'Do you want company? I wasn't going to ask you, but if you want me to come and stay with you at night, I'd be happy to. I can go home during the day to see my mother and father.' She said, 'That would be wonderful!' They were very good to me. And I was very good to them. It was like a mother-daughter relationship."

"There was nobody at the office for about a year," she recalls. "Then, the practice was sold to Dr. Walt Downer. I worked for Dr. Downer for a year. He was there for quite a few years. Then the practice was sold to Dr. Shaw."

After his graduation from the University of Toronto's Faculty of Dentistry in 1959, Dr. John Shaw bought the practice that had originally belonged to Henry Hudson. "Included in the purchase was a dental chair that had belonged to Henry," stated Shaw, explaining his interest in the Hudson/Barilko story. "In 2003, I sold my practice and moved over to the Timmins Square Dental Office. Some of my equipment moved with me, but the chair went into storage — too old to use but too young for a museum," Shaw chuckles.

Dr. Shaw has been an ardent follower of the compelling 50-year saga, specifically chronicling Dr. Henry Hudson's story. "I had learned about Henry from some of my older patients, who told me what a nice guy he was."

In late July 2004, Shaw — who, like Hudson, flies floatplanes — embarked on a fact-finding mission to the site of the crash where Hudson and Barilko lost their lives. "I followed the map to the location 85 miles north from Timmins. I circled over, hoping I could see something — yellow debris or anything — but I just couldn't see anything at all. I had hoped to land at the Island Falls Dam on the Abitibi River, which is about 10 miles away, but there was no road to get closer to the crash site. One day soon, Archie Chenier wants to drive up to Smooth Rock Falls, then branch over to the Island Falls Dam in a four-by-four, but I think it's going to be too difficult even that way."

"Most of my friends were in Toronto, so I decided to make the move," Helen O'Neil says. "I called a dentist named Gordon Johnson whom Henry graduated with in Toronto. He was very well thought of. He used to come to Timmins when they had conventions. I called him and told him I was moving to the city and wanted to work with a good dentist. He said, 'Would you be interested in working for me?' I was surprised because he lectured at the university two mornings each week and he was a very, very good dentist and very well respected. I asked when he wanted me to come and he said, 'As soon as you can get here.' I said, 'I have to find a place to stay.' He said, 'No, you'll stay with my wife and me.'

"I lived with them for about two months, went to work every day with him and then went home every evening with him. Finally, I thought, 'This can't go on,' and I found a place to live. I was broken into the city by that time. I was a small-town girl — I'd never been away before. But it worked out fine. I worked for Dr. Johnson and I loved it."

After the move, Helen maintained a bond with Dr. Hudson's widow. "After I moved to Mississauga [immediately west of Toronto], Phyllis wrote to me and said, 'I really want to move from Timmins to Mississauga and be near you.' My husband and I helped her look for a house." They found the perfect place only about three blocks away. "I either phoned her or she came over every day for the rest of her life." Some time after her husband's remains were discovered, Phyllis remarried, becoming Phyllis Duffy. "She died in May of 1996. She was 90 years old." Helen stops for a moment and summons some wonderful memories of her lifelong friend. "Emil and Anne Klisanich go to Florida every year. They used to see Phyllis Duffy down there. She was part of a group that used to get together when they were in Florida at the home of Vi and Gil Chenier, proprietor of Chenier Motors in Timmins.

"Before my sister and her husband moved to Mexico, they lived with Dr. Lou Hudson for quite a few years. My daughter Maureen was being married in 1975. Dr. Hudson was getting all prepared — we bought him a new suit for the wedding, but he didn't make it." Lou Hudson passed away at the age of 77.

Faye Barilko, though deeply hurt and carrying the tremendous weight not only of losing a child, but, the angst-ridden guilt of not having said goodbye, still held resolutely to her faith that Bill would be found alive.

Anne remembers that someone told her mother of a psychic in Iroquois Falls, about 40 miles northeast of Timmins, who could tell her the whereabouts of her son. "Mother said, 'You take me before snow come, Anne. It worth a try. Maybe she help us find Billy.' I took a couple of girlfriends — Helen Denisavitch and her sister-in-law, Olive — for added company.

"We planned it as a day trip. On our way back, we hit an unbelievable snowstorm. We get our snow early in northern Ontario, but this was way beyond ordinary. The weather was so bad, our windshield wipers couldn't keep up. Mother thought we should stop and wait for the storm to subside, but I said, 'No, we have to carry on.' I had baby Frank at home and I wanted to get home to him."

"We finally made it home," Anne says, with a measure of relief even now. "The psychic didn't tell my mother anything. But it was unusual that every time there was something to do with Bill, the weather was bad. A few months later, my mother said, 'Someone tell me about fortune teller lady in North Bay; she tell us where Billy.' I said, 'Oh, no, Mom! Not again!' North Bay is 250 miles from Timmins. Sure enough, Mom and I drove to North Bay and my mother saw this lady.

"I didn't sit in on their meeting; I'm not sure why. She didn't really tell Mother much. She said, 'They're going to find your son but I can't tell you where he is.'

"Coming home, there was an unexpected rainstorm. My mother and I were driving alone and she said, 'Look, Annie! Every time we do something about Billy, weather bad.'"

Over the course of the next several years, the media would periodically report on the Barilko/Hudson disappearance. "The rumours would start every fall and every spring once the snow left the ground," sighs Anne. "The search would continue and a lot of the pilots thought they would see something out in the bush and they always came back thinking they had some news. There would be a front-page story about Bill Barilko and Dr. Hudson's plane, but there was never anything there.

"Of course, it would get my mother's hopes up again. It got to a point where I contacted many of the major newspapers, TV and radio stations and asked them not to report on stories unless there was some fact behind it. It was very hard on the family; very stressful. The media was very cooperative. They understood."

❧ ❧ ❧

"What happened to Bill Barilko and Dr. Henry Hudson?" asked the Toronto *Telegram* a year after the disappearance. "Almost any guess will do. They crashed and sank in a river or lake — they disappeared in the muskeg trying to land — their plane's wreckage hidden by trees — they crashed in James Bay — they flew out of the North Country altogether and never came back. Take your choice."

In early 1952, with hope having all but evaporated, the *Journal of the Canadian Dental Association* printed a notice: "Albert Henry Hudson, aged 49, was lost in a plane accident in August last and is presumed dead."

In 1953, the Bill Barilko Memorial Trophy was instituted, awarded to the best defenceman each year in the Porcupine Juvenile Hockey League.

* * *

Faye Barilko died February 6, 1982 at Mississauga General Hospital at the age of 82. After a funeral service in Etobicoke, Mrs. Barilko's remains were flown to Timmins for burial beside her husband and beloved son.

"The pain was always in my mother's heart," admits Anne. "She suffered deep, emotional anguish over Billy's death until the day she too died."

"I no miss one day I no cry for Billy," his mother sobbed before her death. "Why my Billy no come home? Why? Why my Billy no come home?"

CHAPTER 19

Never Got to
Say Goodbye

She's still striking today.

Louise (Hastings) Carley is as beautiful today as she would have been more than a half century ago. And there's one other thing — Louise is still in love with Bill Barilko.

The house in northern Toronto that she lives in today is the same one she grew up in. It's also where she first met Bill Barilko. "I met Bill in the kitchen the first day he arrived in Toronto at the beginning of February in '47," smiles Louise. "He came over with Jim Thomson [who had stayed with the Hastings family] and wanted to know if we knew of any place where he could stay." For a short time, Bill lived across the street. Louise remembers a conversation that had taken place with a neighbour. "The couple had a little son and they knew that Jimmy [Thomson] was a hockey player. They wanted to get somebody to teach their little boy how to skate and show him how to handle a stick. So Bill said, 'I'll do it.' That's what Bill did. He looked after that little boy."

"With Bill and I, there was a glimmer the first night we met. There was a spark," admits Louise. "I was married when I met Bill, but the marriage was annulled. I had to go to court and Bill was with me. He walked me through the whole thing." As the months passed, Bill and Louise became boyfriend and girlfriend. "I idolized him. We never argued. We never had a fight."

The Hastings household was a haven for hockey players. "My sister Florrie was going out with a hockey player," Louise explains. "Jimmy Thomson and this player [that Florrie was dating] were going to live together and they had to have their apartment painted. Jimmy asked my mother if he could stay here. Mom said, 'Sure!'" Louise remembers the first time Jim Thomson showed up at their home. "He had on his brother's suit. His brother was a foot shorter than he was and the sleeves came halfway up his arm!" she smiles.

The Hastingses had four daughters. "The eldest is Ruth. I'm next and I'm four years younger than her. Florrie is four years younger than me. We have a younger sister 17 years younger than me. We had three bedrooms upstairs; Jimmy had the back bedroom all to himself. He had it made here — he ran the house," laughs Louise. "Jimmy really wasn't home that much. They were on the road a lot."

Ruth also opened her house to Maple Leafs players looking for a place that offered room and board. "Nick Metz was there for a while. So were Garth Boesch and Cal Gardner. Cy Thomas came to Toronto in the Max Bentley trade and he stayed there too."

The Hastings home quickly became the social centre for the Maple Leafs of the late 1940s. "The boys would be in the living room playing poker or crokinole. Mother used to sit and play the piano by ear. Everybody would be singing. Florrie and I would come home, waiting for our dinner, and Mother would be out getting the boys some beer."

In those days, a hockey game at Maple Leaf Gardens was a social event of such prestige that spectators felt obliged to dress accordingly: jacket and tie for the men and proper dresses for the women. For the players' wives or girlfriends, it was an occasion to dress up and watch their partners at work. "It was a special occasion to go down to the games," June Thomson, the wife of defenceman Jim, recalls. "We got all dressed up. We wore a hat in those days."

"Florrie and I would go to Maple Leaf games together," Louise says. "We always had Jimmy's tickets in the blues. We dressed alike — we had these black coats that had a flap with a button inside. They'd been made by a tailor. We would wear the most exotic thing we could find. We wore these great big black hats with a veil — not over our faces but on top of the hats.

"But Junie McKinnon [later June Thomson] could outdo any of the girls when she started coming to games. She was absolutely beautiful and had lovely clothes."

While the boys were playing, June Thomson recalls that there was one stipulation the management of the Toronto Maple Leafs insisted upon. "Wives were not to sit together," she grins. "They'd have the tickets scattered around the arena, not in a group."

Still, says Louise, "We were all one big group and we were very close. There was no animosity between the girls. When the boys were on the road, the girls would get together. We followed the games very closely on the radio."

After the game, the ladies would often accompany the team to Union Station, where the boys would travel by train to the next city. "If they weren't going away, we'd go to a restaurant for something to eat."

The Leafs had their favourite places, and at the top of the list was the Old Mill, a fine restaurant just off Bloor Street West near the Humber River. The team met there virtually every Monday during the season for dining, dancing and time with their wives or girlfriends. "The boys liked to go to the Old Mill. Bill and I would dance when we went there — he was a pretty good dancer. He liked to cuddle and dance slow. Our special song was 'Because of You,'" — a poignant song that would be a hit for Tony Bennett in 1951. "But you know who was a great dancer?" Louise adds. "Turk Broda was the best dancer I ever met in my life. He was so light on his feet. He has to go down in history as the best dancer ever!"

Louise remembers one particular visit to the Old Mill that got side-tracked. "When we went out to the Old Mill, we usually didn't wear formal clothes. This one time, I don't know why, we were all dressed up — I was wearing a dress that was off the shoulder. Garth Boesch was driving and my mother was in the front seat. Florrie and I were in the back seat with Bill. We were driving to the Old Mill and we were down by where Wayne Gretzky's restaurant is today [near the downtown inter-section of Spadina Avenue and Front Street West]. The boys wanted to stop into this burlesque house on the way. Florrie and I sat in the back and certainly didn't watch. The boys sat down front — with my mother! They got such a big kick out of it."

"We went to the movies a lot," Louise mentions. "Bill usually picked the pictures. He liked action movies. I was more for the lovey-dovey type. We always ate at one particular restaurant on Eglinton.

"I worked for an insurance company [Smith, McKenzie, Hall and Hunter] on Adelaide Street. Bill used to come down and take me for coffee." And Bill could never get his fill of hockey. "I don't think we ever missed a Marlboro game. If there was a game Friday night, we would go. If there was a game Saturday afternoon, we would go. I wasn't a huge hockey fan, but my dad had skates on all four of us girls from the time we could walk. My father always built a skating rink for us out in our backyard. When he was a young man, he played hockey for Little Berlin, which is now Kitchener."

The Leafs players stuck together, both on the ice and off. "We all spent a lot of time at Harry and Lil's place [the Watsons]. A lot of time. They were such nice people. Some of the boys were married and some weren't, but there was a group that always seemed to get into mischief. Jimmy and Bill were the best of pals. Garth Boesch, too. They spent a lot of time together. They were all on the same wavelength."

"Bill loved pranks. He would do anything to get a laugh." Louise's smile broadens into a full-blown grin. "One night, the whole gang of the fellows got together. Bill and I had been out. My sister Florrie had a date with Cy Thomas and came home a little earlier. It was Jimmy and Bill's idea, but they got the boys, about six of them, into the house first. There were French doors, and a few of us hid behind the door — we were hiding all over the place. The lights were out.

"Florrie came in with Cy, and they were sitting on the chesterfield. Cy leaned over to kiss Florrie, and just then the lights were switched on and all the boys jumped out. Cy ran out of the house so fast! Those boys were funny."

"But when Bill was on the ice, he was all business," Louise points out. "'Bashin' Bill.' Bill played hockey to win. He wasn't a dirty player — and he was always a gentleman. I never heard any profanity."

When the boys boarded with the Hastings, they were well taken care of. "Mom cooked steaks for all the boys before every game. The boys who were living with Ruth came over, too. We girls weren't allowed in the house. Mother used to send us out so the boys could eat in peace. We used to go out and shovel snow," Louise laughs. "Bill was different than the other boys. He never ate steak before a game. I don't know if he had a delicate stomach, because he was certainly very healthy, but he always had scrambled eggs and toast."

"Bill was a handsome son of a gun. That blond hair, those beautiful blue eyes..." Louise drifts for a moment, a slight smile tracing her lips. "Bill outshone any of the other boys when it came to dressing. I don't know how many suits that man had — and ties! They made fun of him. He was always very well dressed. He looked good in a tweed suit. He looked good in brown. He wore clothes very well. All the boys were good dressers."

Anne Klisanich agrees with Louise. "Alex and Bill shared a room during the summer. The clothes — oh, my God! There were clothes on the front of the door, the back of the door, the closets were full. They were very well dressed. Bill had quite a collection of suits, that's for sure." The Barilko boys acquired their sartorial flair when they played in the Pacific Coast Hockey League. "Before they played hockey, my mother and Dad wouldn't have had the money to buy nice clothes," observes Anne.

Louise and Bill saw each other in Toronto during the season, but Bill regularly returned to Timmins for the summer. "He'd often phone me, and sometimes he'd come down to Toronto — or sometimes we'd go up there. We'd go up with Jim Thomson or Vic Lynn or Garth Boesch. We were the ones that did the travelling in the summer. Bill had his fishing and his Timmins friends."

Anne recalls Louise coming up to meet the family in Timmins. "I remember Bill asking my mother, 'Mom, can I have some of my friends come up from Toronto?' And Mother said, 'Sure, I do cooking.' My mother was a very kind and generous person who liked to entertain people. Jimmy Thomson, his girlfriend June McKinnon — who later became his wife — Louise and Louise's sister Florrie came up to Timmins that summer."

"The first time I went up to Timmins, I discovered that Bill's mother never sat down at the table," chuckles Louise. "Mrs. Barilko always stood up until everybody had finished." Bill's sister Anne concurs, and admits that that was not unusual. "Mother would say, 'You eat first, I eat after. Me no sit.'"

But there was more to the breakfast menu than Louise was used to. "Before we had our breakfast, Mrs. Barilko would put a shot glass full of whiskey on the table. Bill would down it, Alex would down it. I didn't even know what whiskey tasted like, but I drank it anyways," laughs Louise. Faye Barilko invited all the neighbours over to meet Bill's girl-friend and his friends from Toronto, and with each visitor, out came the whiskey. Anne chuckles and shrugs, "That is a European custom. It was always like that around our house. My mother would serve kielbasa and rye bread with a shot of whiskey." Louise shakes her head and smiles. "I don't know how we kept going. I'll never know!"

There was a place that was very special to Louise and Bill, where they would occasionally rendezvous during the summer. It was a cottage on Lake Simcoe, looking out across the water to Snake Island, that the Hastings family rented each summer. There, they could relax, catch up and visit with friends they'd invited to join them. "Jimmy and Junie Thomson often joined us at the cottage," says Louise.

"I saw Bill twice during that summer [of 1951]," Louise mentions. She comes to a full stop. Unlike the earlier memories that tumbled from Louise's lips so readily, she finds it challenging to recite the chain of events that transpired during the months following August 1951. "Bill was supposed to come to our cottage [on Lake Simcoe] after he went with Dr. Hudson. My mother took the phone call from Bill. He told Mom to tell me that after his fishing trip, he was going back to Timmins to get his car and he was going to drive to our cottage, but he'd be late in arriving.

"We heard the next morning that he didn't come back. We heard it on the news."

Louise never got to say goodbye to the man she loved — in fact, the man she intended to marry. "It's hard to say whether we were engaged or not," says Louise. "I have a ring, and I consider it an engagement ring — Bill picked it out. We talked about getting married. He wanted to be married and he wanted to have a son. He was going to give me the ring at the Old Mill on my birthday, September the fourth." Bill disappeared without a trace 10 days before.

"I certainly wish he had been here on September the fourth," Louise says. "Maybe life would have turned out a lot different for me. From 1951, for five and a half years, I just sort of drifted. I think I was engaged seven times from 1951 until I finally married in 1956. I didn't know how to cope with Bill's death. And some fellows would come along

— they were usually hockey players — and we'd get along well and they'd ask, 'Do you want to get married?' I'd say, 'Sure,' but I always backed out."

The memories are clear as day for Louise, but she still struggles to articulate them properly. "I wanted to find someone like Bill. I never found that person. I looked many times. There was never anybody I met who was like Bill. He had a certain personality. He was always a gentleman.

"When I did get married, I married a man who I thought was very nice, but he wasn't the right man for me. We got divorced and I came home to my father. I returned to the house I grew up in and raised my children all by myself.

"Bill never talked about what he wanted to do when his playing career was over. I don't think he thought it would ever be over," Louise giggles. At 24, everyone feels they're invincible.

Bill's disappearance was devastating to the girl he left behind. "I personally didn't read a lot of the newspaper clippings. It was too difficult. I don't know how Anne and Bill's mother coped, not knowing for all those years."

"I can remember fighting with people when Bill disappeared," continues Louise. "There were so many people around here who thought it was a hoax. They didn't think he and Dr. Hudson had gone fishing at all. They thought they had flown somewhere and picked up gold. I had more fights with people about that. 'Bill would never ever have been involved in anything like that,' I would argue.

"I felt in my heart that if he was alive, he would contact me. Somehow, he'd let me know. I didn't know how far north it was — I didn't know that country. I had never even heard Bill mention Dr. Hudson's name before.

"I lost hope after a while." Louise pauses to catch her breath. "I just thought, 'He's never coming back.' I don't think I went to another hockey game for years and years. I always had Jimmy and Junie [Thomson] around. Jimmy was a very special person. Harry Watson was a dear friend, but I cut myself off from most of the hockey players. I just wasn't interested in keeping in touch.

"Finally, I figured I had to get on with my life. I got married, had children and moved on. But I never fully moved on." The photographs of Bill in her house are evidence of a love that never died.

"I'm a very, very lucky woman," concludes the girl Bill left behind. "I've been blessed with a wonderful family. I've had a lot of fun. I'm quite happy the way my life turned out."

CHAPTER 20

Minus 5
(The Fifties)

In the decade that followed Bill Barilko's disappearance, the Toronto Maple Leafs' fortunes would lead them far from the noble and glorious path they had followed between 1941 and '51. The upheaval affected the club both on the ice and in the front office, causing the once-mighty organization to suffer unprecedented humiliation.

Between the Stanley Cup celebration and the start of the 1951–52 season, the Maple Leafs were rocked by the loss of several members of their extended family besides Barilko.

Early in the summer, while preparing for a fishing trip, the Leafs' chief scout, Squib Walker, died at his home in Fort William, Ontario (now part of Thunder Bay). Walker had known Conn Smythe since 1915, when the Leafs president was captain of the University of Toronto Blues.

Walker is recognized as having had an exceptional eye for hockey talent. Based in Fort William, Squib oversaw an elaborate network of scouts scattered across Canada, and he was personally instrumental in signing Gaye Stewart, Bud Poile, Gus Bodnar, Danny Lewicki, Rudy Migay and Pete Backor, all of whom played for the Leafs during the heady decade between 1942 and 1951 in which the Maple Leafs won six Stanley Cup championships.

Besides his scouting duties, Walker was also a bond and insurance broker. Jack McLean, who joined the Maple Leafs in 1942, shook his head and chuckled when he recalled his signing. "I was offered $100 to sign my first Leaf contract," he grimaces. "On the advice of my Uncle Ed, I asked for $200. Walker wasn't happy but agreed to give me the $200. Then the SOB turns around and says I should buy life insurance and sells me a policy for $100!"

Squib's wit was well known throughout the league. He was regularly seen bantering with fellow scouts Carson Cooper of the Detroit Red

Wings and Baldy Cotton of the Boston Bruins. But during the game, Walker was all business.

When Bill Barilko first arrived in Toronto, Walker welcomed the young prospect and asked him if he'd like to watch the wrestling card at the Gardens that evening. "Here, take my pass or they won't let you in," offered Squib. "Nah, I won't need the pass, thank you," replied Barilko. "I can take care of myself. I'm here to stay, and the gateman might as well get hep to that right now." The scout could only laugh. He realized that Bill Barilko was a confident, although not cocky, young man.

On August 22, 1951, J.P. Bickell died at the age of 66. John Paris Bickell was born in Molesworth, Ontario, a community northwest of Kitchener, not far from the town of Listowel. Bickell moved to Toronto, where he started his own brokerage firm, but left investing to become president and later chairman of McIntyre-Porcupine Mines, an exceptionally lucrative gold producer located in Timmins.

Just before the start of the 1919–20 season, the Toronto Arenas of the NHL were sold to a consortium that included managing director Charlie Querrie, Nathan Nathanson, who was the managing director of Famous Players Canadian Corporation, and J.P. Bickell. The team subsequently changed its name to the Toronto St. Patricks. In 1927, there were murmurs that the team might relocate to Philadelphia; the news prompted Conn Smythe, who had been jettisoned the previous autumn as manager of the New York Rangers, to make a successful bid to buy the team, staked by the severance package he had received from the Rangers. He convinced Bickell to retain his stake in the club, while Peter Campbell and Ed Bickle were also part of the new ownership group. On February 17, 1927, in a contest against the New York Americans, the newly named Toronto Maple Leafs took the ice for the first time.

Smythe and his partners soon realized that it would no longer be viable to continue to play at the undersized Arena Gardens (commonly known as the Mutual Street Arena), and Bickell was instrumental in the construction of Maple Leaf Gardens in 1931. "You could say, without exaggerating, that Bickell was the cornerstone of the whole project," Smythe stated. "He'd call up some person he knew and he'd tell this person what we were doing. Then he'd say we needed $175,000 in a hurry, and he'd tell the party at the other end of the line how much he expected from him. That's how we got the money we had to have when we were threatened with failure."

When the building was completed in five months, an incredible feat at the best of times but even more extraordinary in that it occurred during the Great Depression, Smythe appointed Bickell as the first chairman of the board of Maple Leaf Gardens Limited. Bickell served in that capacity from 1932 until 1943 and remained a director until his death in 1951.

Bickell also initiated the construction of the McIntyre Arena in Schumacher in 1938. The landmark arena was modelled after the Gardens, and it would give many professional hockey players their starts as well as serving as a base for Olympic figure-skating champion Barbara Ann Scott.

After his death, the J.P. Bickell Foundation was established to further his business interests and to perpetuate his benevolent nature. A prime recipient of his generosity was the Hospital for Sick Children in Toronto, although Bickell's philanthropic beneficiaries included medical research projects and scholarships to advance mining education.

Maple Leaf Gardens established the J.P. Bickell Memorial Cup to commemorate his service to the Toronto Maple Leafs franchise. The trophy is awarded "to a player of the Maple Leaf hockey team at such times and for such merit as may be designated and determined by the Board of Directors." Ted Kennedy was the first recipient, in 1953. J.P. Bickell was inducted into the Hockey Hall of Fame as a builder in 1978.

Bickell's death was especially hard on Smythe, who had valued his friendship and financial assistance for a quarter of a century. To lose one of his oldest colleagues was devastating. To discover that the likable Barilko, to whom Smythe had taken a particular shine, had gone missing later that same week was almost more than the Major could stand.

※ ※ ※

The Maple Leafs' training camp opened on September 21. Ordinarily, the first day of camp was like the first day of school — light, good-natured and devoted to catching up on summer activities. But this camp was different. Barilko's disappearance had cast a pall over the proceedings. A Stanley Cup victory celebration had been planned, but no one felt much like celebrating with one of their more popular teammates missing, so it was cancelled.

Nor did anyone seem to be looking forward to the new season with much eagerness. "C'mon boys, we all miss Billy and hope that he's found soon," started Conn Smythe, trying to rally the troops. "But we've got a hockey season ahead, so let's get down to business." In truth, however, the Leafs president was as profoundly burdened by Barilko's absence as anyone in the camp.

Gus Mortson remembers the empty feeling around the Toronto dressing room that September. "When we got to training camp and Bill wasn't there, it really hit that he had gone missing. That was a tremendous search. They sure combed northern Ontario trying to find him. It was a tragedy; it really was."

Bill Barilko's Number 5 sweater hung in his stall in the dressing room, where it symbolized the team's hope that he would be found. But as training camp ended with no sign of the star defenceman, Bill's equipment and sweater were quietly stored away. No one would ever again wear Number 5 for the Toronto Maple Leafs, although the number was not to be officially retired until 1992.

🍁 🍁 🍁

Twenty-seven players reported to St. Catharines for training camp. Only seven boys not considered regulars were invited to skate with the team. Bill Barilko's disappearance left a sizable hole on the blue line, and coach Joe Primeau was paying special attention to Hugh Bolton, Tim Horton and Frank Mathers, hoping that one would step into Barilko's spot.

All three had spent the previous season in Pittsburgh with the Hornets of the American Hockey League. Because the Leafs had been so strong on defence for the previous five seasons, such talented rearguards as Bolton, Horton and Mathers — as well as Frank Sullivan and Leo Boivin — were forced to stay in the minors for longer than they would have liked. Horton had played one regular-season game with Toronto, and another in the playoffs, during 1949–50. Mathers had come to the Leafs system from the New York Rangers organization in 1948 and had played in 21 NHL games between 1948–49 and 1949–50. Bolton had played five games for the Leafs over the previous two seasons.

Tim Horton was a very likely candidate. His game resembled that of Gus Mortson — he took no prisoners in the defensive zone, with more offensive ability than Barilko possessed. In *In Loving Memory: A Tribute to Tim Horton*, co-authors Lori Horton and Tim Griggs state: "Tim was certainly tough enough, but his end-to-end rushing was not a good fit with [the Leafs'] defensive style, and in any case, the Leafs felt Tim's work in his own end could still be improved." In Douglas Hunter's book *Open Ice: The Tim Horton Story*, Ray Hannigan said, "They wanted him to play like Barilko. A lot of the coaches tried to get him to play mean, but he never could. He could hit you, but it was always clean." Toronto's captain, Ted Kennedy, saw Barilko and Horton quite differently. "Barilko was a much bigger man. He could hit and hurt," he said.

Mathers, too, added a spark of offence but was less inclined to drop the gloves than Horton. Bolton, who was the only Toronto native besides Sid Smith in the Leafs camp, was targeted by *The Hockey News* as the likely choice to fill the empty roster spot. "If he can sidestep the injury bugaboo which put him out with a dinky knee and badly-banged-up shoulder last season, he'll probably stick," they reported.

And in the end, it was the six-foot, three-inch Bolton who was chosen to fill Barilko's spot. In 1951–52, the defensive Goliath was paired with

Fern Flaman, who offered a strong physical presence and used his veteran's savvy to cover for Bolton when the rookie was caught up-ice. Bolton proved disappointing to Maple Leafs management and after recording just 16 points and 73 penalty minutes, he was shipped back to Pittsburgh. After a bout with mononucleosis in 1952–53 and a broken jaw in 1953–54, Hugh finally grabbed a full-time spot on Toronto's blue line in 1954–55, but the fragile defenceman suffered a career-ending broken leg six games into the 1956–57 season and was forced to retire.

Ultimately, the task of replacing Barilko would fall to Tim Horton, the muscular native of Cochrane, Ontario, who had originally been found wanting. Leafs' management introduced him into the lineup on a full-time basis in 1952–53, and he would remain a cornerstone of the Toronto blue line for 18 seasons. After he anchored the Leafs defence throughout the dark and desperate '50s, Horton's leadership would help the team evolve into a dynasty during the early 1960s.

There are eerie parallels between Bill Barilko and Tim Horton. Both were born in northern Ontario. Both were entrepreneurs — Barilko with home appliances and Horton in coffee and donuts. Both played on four Stanley Cup champions as a Maple Leaf. Both died tragically and young — Barilko in a plane crash at 24 and Horton in a single-car collision at 44. And Allan Stanley was a pallbearer at the funerals of both.

* * *

By the fall of 1952, Gus Mortson had been traded to Chicago and Bill Juzda had retired, leaving only Jimmy Thomson and Fern Flaman as Leafs defencemen whose jobs were certain. Filling the vacancies, at least in the short term, would be no mean feat. "When you went to the Toronto camp, it was hard work, let me tell you," offers Flaman. "Contracts were never signed until after training camp, so you had to go prove yourself before you could get a contract. At that time, we had some pretty good prospects, like Timmy Horton down in Pittsburgh, and he couldn't crack our lineup at that time. You really had to work because there were some very, very fine players coming up." The Leafs experimented (and struggled) with Jim Morrison, Leo Boivin, Marc Reaume and Al MacNeil through the mid-1950s, before Toronto's junior affiliates yielded a pair of defensive keystones. In 1956–57, Bobby Baun joined Toronto from a Marlboros squad that had just won back-to-back Memorial Cup championships, while Carl Brewer became a mainstay in 1958–59. Through a trade with the Boston Bruins, Allan Stanley was secured, giving Toronto — along with Horton — a foursome that rivalled the quartet of Thomson, Mortson, Boesch and Barilko in the 1940s.

Turk Broda, the Maple Leafs' star goaltender since 1936–37, retired after the 1951 Stanley Cup celebration, although he did play the last half of the final game of the 1951–52 schedule before hanging up his pads for good. Al Rollins, who had played so admirably during the 1951 Stanley Cup run, replaced Turk as the Leafs' number one netminder, but it was clear to Leafs management that Toronto's future wasn't assured with Rollins in the crease, so before the 1952–53 season he was packaged to the Chicago Blackhawks in exchange for Harry Lumley. Lumley played four solid seasons in blue and white before he was sent back to Chicago. The Leafs then struggled in front of Ed Chadwick for a couple of seasons, but it wasn't until Johnny Bower was acquired that Toronto enjoyed the kind of netminding that it would need to win three consecutive Stanley Cup championships between 1962 and 1964, plus a fourth in 1967.

As the decade wore on, Toronto would also overhaul its forward lines substantially; although Sid Smith, Tod Sloan and Ted Kennedy provided a strong presence up front, all would be gone by the time such farm-system products as George Armstrong, Frank Mahovlich, Dick Duff, Bob Pulford and Billy Harris would coalesce into a solid core.

Joe Primeau, who had starred with the Toronto Maple Leafs as a player, centring the renowned Kid Line between Charlie Conacher and Harvey "Busher" Jackson (all three of whom are Honoured Members of the Hockey Hall of Fame), led Toronto to the Stanley Cup in his debut season as an NHL coach. Despite annual rumours that hinted at his retirement from hockey back to the business world, Primeau stayed behind the Maple Leafs' bench for three full seasons before returning to the safety of his concrete-block company. He was replaced by King Clancy, who had played with Primeau on Toronto's Stanley Cup winner in 1932. Clancy remained with Toronto as head coach for three seasons, then was named assistant general manager in April 1956. Howie Meeker took the coaching reins in 1956–57, guiding the Leafs to a fifth-place finish before being named general manager. His tenure was brief. Former Canadiens star Billy Reay was hired to replace Meeker as coach, and Toronto sank to sixth, the first time the team had finished in last place since 1926–27. Twenty games into the 1958–59 season he was fired.

Meanwhile, in October 1954, Conn Smythe had resigned the post of general manager that he had held since he purchased the team in 1927. "What really made up my mind was that my powers as a hockey man were failing," Smythe stated in his memoirs. "I didn't say so but it was true." Although Smythe stayed on as team president, the GM portfolio was handed to Hap Day, who stayed until the conclusion of the 1956–57 season. Meeker succeeded Day briefly before Smythe's son Stafford successfully proposed the idea of forming a "hockey committee" to run the team. Jack Amell, John Bassett, George Gardiner, Bill Hatch, Ian

Johnston, George Mara and Stafford Smythe (as chairman) comprised a group facetiously dubbed the "Silver Seven." Harold Ballard soon replaced Johnston on the committee.

Punch Imlach, who had been part of the Boston Bruins organization, was hired in 1958 as the Leafs' assistant general manager — although, strictly speaking, there wasn't actually a GM for him to assist. Before long, he took over as both GM and coach and, armed with the talent his scouting staff had secured, he would lead the Toronto Maple Leafs to four Stanley Cup victories in the 1960s.

🍁 🍁 🍁

The fifth annual NHL All-Star Game was held October 9, 1951, at Maple Leaf Gardens. This year, the game took on a new format — instead of pitting the Stanley Cup champions against a squad of all-stars, in 1951 the game placed the First All-Star Team, with reinforcements from the U.S.-based teams, against the Second Team, which was embellished with players from Toronto and Montreal.

The game wasn't without controversy. During the summer, after losing seven teeth playing baseball in New Westminster, British Columbia, Leafs goaltender Al Rollins had claimed that without Maurice Richard the Canadiens would be "just a senior team." Montreal coach Dick Irvin was incensed, and as coach of the NHL's Second All-Star Team, refused to name Rollins to the team, despite Rollins' having won the Vezina Trophy the previous spring. Irvin selected his own goalie, Gerry McNeil, instead, saying, "We'll see how McNeil does with a good team in front of him. I know he is much better than Rollins. I don't consider Mr. Rollins a very good goaler."

Irvin, McNeil and the Second All-Star Team did well, skating to a 2–2 tie with the Joe Primeau–coached First All-Star Team. The Leafs were represented by Max Bentley, Ted Kennedy, Gus Mortson, Tod Sloan (who scored one of the two goals), Sid Smith, Jimmy Thomson and Harry Watson. Dick Irvin commented, "There's one other fellow I'd sure like to see out there with us and that's Bill Barilko." The game raised a total of $16,840 for the players' pension fund.

🍁 🍁 🍁

In the fall of 1951, shortly before her ascension to the throne (on February 6, 1952), Her Royal Highness Princess Elizabeth and her husband, Philip Mountbatten, Duke of Edinburgh, made their first royal visit to Canada.

Still reeling from the search for Barilko and Dr. Hudson that was centred at its airport, the town of Kapuskasing officially welcomed the royal couple on October 8. They arrived at the small airport at 3:30 that afternoon, and were taken on a tour of the town. "Residents of Kapuskasing are being asked to keep their homes and lawns as tidy and clean as possible," the local newspaper reported.

While in Toronto on October 13, the princess and duke visited Maple Leaf Gardens and attended their first hockey game — a 15-minute exhibition between the Maple Leafs and Chicago Blackhawks. The same two teams faced off later that evening for the opening game of the 1951–52 season.

Other than at training camp, this was the first time the Maple Leafs had congregated as a team since winning the Stanley Cup the previous spring. That game's hero, Bill Barilko, was conspicuous by his absence. In spite of the pomp and ceremony, there was a definite pall over the Leafs' dressing room.

Ted Kennedy, the team captain, was tutored on the protocol involved in greeting the princess and her consort. He remembers being told, "I don't speak unless they speak to me. I call them each Your Royal Highness. I don't bow, just shake hands and bow my head slightly." In *On the Hockey Beat*, Ed Fitkin reported, "[Princess Elizabeth's] eyes sparkled as she intently followed the play. She recoiled slightly at heavy checks, talked and smiled with Mr. Smythe frequently."

Nearly 51 years later, Queen Elizabeth and Prince Philip were the guests of the Vancouver Canucks for an October 5, 2002, preseason contest against the San Jose Sharks. Before dropping the puck for the ceremonial opening face-off, Her Majesty told both Wayne Gretzky, acting as an ambassador for hockey, and Canucks captain Markus Naslund, that she still had the puck she dropped between Toronto and Chicago on that long-ago day in 1951.

※ ※ ※

On October 27, 1951, *The Hockey News* suggested that "Bill Barilko's Number 5 will be hung up in his locker this season. It might be a nice gesture for the Toronto Maple Leafs to retire the number permanently." It was the first time the idea had been suggested in print. The sweater hung forlornly in Barilko's locker as the season began. "It was back to work and we had our jobs to do, and Conny Smythe, Hap Day and Joe Primeau reminded us we had a job to do," says Hall of Fame member Fern Flaman. "But we all did miss him. He was a real fine young man." By November 1951, the Leafs had removed Barilko's number 5 from the lineup.

In 1951–52, the Leafs finished third. In spite of a decent regular season, Toronto was defeated in four straight games by the Detroit Red Wings in the semifinals. Conn Smythe spoke candidly about the team's disappointing season. "Bill was a great part of our hockey club. With him gone, we just didn't have the punch last year. We were just an ordinary hockey club — a very ordinary hockey club. It's going to be a long time before we find someone to take his place. The old Barilko bounce is really missing." Fern Flaman, meanwhile, says, "Gus Mortson and Jimmy Thomson never really got what they deserved. They were great players and they held that team together, especially back on the blue line that year. Jimmy wasn't that colourful, but believe me, he did his job and he did it well."

In 1952–53, the Toronto Maple Leafs sank to fifth, and missed the playoffs for the first time since 1945–46. They gained enough ground to finish third and make the playoffs in both 1953–54 and 1954–55, but were ousted in the semifinals by Detroit both times. A fourth-place finish in 1955–56 earned one more shot against the Red Wings in the first round, but again they were eliminated. Toronto missed the playoffs in 1956–57 and 1957–58, finishing dead last in the latter season.

Fans watched the dying embers of the Leafs dynasty through the 1950s, and Bill Barilko's body still hadn't been found.

CHAPTER
21

A Glint of Yellow

It was a drizzly morning in northern Ontario on Thursday, May 31, 1962. Gary Fields, a civilian pilot with Dominion Helicopters, was flying Ray Paterick from Cochrane to Newpost Creek, about 60 miles north, to inspect timber in an area slated for a hydroelectric diversion project.

At 8:50, Fields glanced out the side window and saw a glint of yellow. "Ray," he blurted, "do you see a pontoon or something down there?" Fields circled the area as he dropped the helicopter's altitude to the tops of the trees. Both men were able to pick out a pontoon and a strip of metal on the ground below. "It is definitely plane wreckage. I saw part of a tail assembly and a float about 16 to 18 feet long," reported Paterick. There were no nearby landmarks. "If I had known, we would have somehow pinpointed the area." In a 1983 *Toronto Sun* article, Fields added, "When I saw the sun reflecting off something through the trees, my passenger said it was just a well-known wreck, so I didn't mark my map."

They flew over the area but were unable to land because of the denseness of the trees and the thickness of the swamp. "I circled it twice but couldn't land," explained Fields. They completed their mission and capped their flight back to Cochrane by 11:15.

Mindful of Aesop's fable about the boy who cried "wolf," Fields was cautious not to get too excited by his sighting. Both he and Paterick had seen the remains of crashed planes in the wilds of northern Ontario before, and had been rebuked for reporting known crashes. After returning from the flight, Fields casually mentioned to some colleagues that he had spotted some gleaming metal and a pontoon the day before. Although Fields presumed it was wreckage already reported and left in the dense bush, others felt Fields might have stumbled upon the Fairchild 24 that carried Bill Barilko and Dr. Henry Hudson. "Okay, tell me again," Fields asked. "A hockey player crashed 11 years ago and they never found his body?" When Fields learned that the known wreck was 40 miles off the travel line, the idea that the crash site might be that of the long-lost plane — a yellow Fairchild 24 registered as CF-FXT — seemed a distinct possibility.

Officials with the Department of Lands and Forests immediately made plans to renew the search for the wreck. On Saturday, June 2, Gary Fields and District Forester Ted Hall ordered two more planes, a helicopter and a Beaver, to aid in the search. "It is like looking for a needle in as haystack," said Hall, but they did condense their search to a much more targeted area. "It is a tough job because the bush in the area looks so much alike."

Hall intended to keep the story quiet until there were further details, but the possibility that the wreckage of Dr. Hudson's plane had been found was leaked to the Canadian Press, a national news wire service. At 7:15 p.m., an insistent CP reporter tried to get details, but Hall claimed that no wreckage had been reported. Knowing that word was filtering out, however, the Cochrane District Forester intensified efforts to locate the crash site.

It was decided that Ray Paterick and Acting Forest Protection Supervisor Joe Shalla would depart at 8 a.m. on June 2 to search for the plane. Fields and Paterick agreed that the site was "a flat spruce area with no landmarks except an alder creek bed, north of Maher." They believed the plane crash was located in Ireland Township.

Just before midnight, a reporter for the *Globe and Mail* phoned. The word had begun to spread amongst the media. Before the helicopter had even departed on Saturday morning, the telephones were ringing incessantly. First, the *Toronto Star*, then the *Telegram* contacted Ted Hall. The helicopter was airborne earlier than expected, pulling out at 7:20. The skies were overcast, and Paterick was unable to find the site again. In the meantime, the Canadian Press and radio station CFRB in Toronto called. Murray Anglin from the *Toronto Star* also called in search of information. He claimed his father had once coached Barilko and informed the District Forester that the story was on the front page of the *Star* that day. The Timmins *Daily Press* called, too, followed by radio station, CHUM in Toronto, Broadcast News (the CP's radio arm) and the national CBC network.

🍁 🍁 🍁

In contrast to the previous two days, the morning of June 3, 1962, dawned bright and clear. At 8:50 a.m., two helicopters and a small plane carrying search crews embarked on another day of searching for Henry Hudson's Fairchild 24, but they returned home without anything to report.

It was also bright and sunny as morning broke on Monday, June 4. At an early-morning meeting, participants in the Barilko-Hudson search agreed that the press would not be contacted right away, even if something were to be located. The pilots searched all day, and the only conclusion they arrived at was that "the repetition of the scenery is very confusing," according to pilot Woody Pike.

The fair weather held up for a third consecutive day on June 5. Ray Paterick was paired with Ron Boyd in a small plane to search the northern half of the Ireland plot while Gary Fields and Cochrane District Forester Ted Hall scoured the southern portion of the area in a helicopter. The two crews endured a frustrating afternoon, travelling 65 miles north of Cochrane to Maund Township, only to return once again, unsuccessful in locating the crash site. Each day, the same moose carcass had been sighted over and over again, but there was no sign of the lost plane. The idea of using ground crews to track the area was discussed but dismissed.

At 8:35 p.m., CFCL-TV in Timmins announced that the plane had been located. The report proved to be false. Terry Coles of CFCL informed District Forester Hall that the station had picked up the story from the Canadian Press, and Mark Meredith at CP claimed that his syndicate got the story from *Le Droit*, a French-language newspaper in Ottawa.

On June 6, Ted Hall kept a meticulous journal of the day's exploits. At 9:15 a.m., he noted, "Gary continued to fly very accurately without any map. Country wet and uniform when lakes not in view. Very few hardwoods. Creeks outlined by willow or alder. Ticked off landmarks, noting a few times and altitudes. Generally cruising at 300–400 feet, 60 miles per hour at bearing which read from 15 degrees to 330 degrees from passenger side of the cockpit. Turned at Little Abitibi River, then sat down in open muskeg for breather. Took off again, sun in eyes now, feeling a little groggy. Thinking about landing on plot to check footing. Not looking forward to beating up the plot."

Then, at 11 o'clock, Gary Fields shouted, "What do I see?" and tilted the helicopter forward. He was not crying "wolf." Fields had spotted the wreckage of Hudson's Fairchild 24 once again. Hall wrote: "From my side, looks like part of a stump, then the wheels a little and I see the skeleton of a plane float — twisted fuselage — patch of yellow." Gary Fields said: "There are two pontoons, part of the tail assembly and the fuselage. There is also a piece of yellow fabric from the tail. It certainly could be a Fairchild 24." Hall drew a circle around the little lake on the map and showed it to Gary Fields, who added a dot on the creek — the spot they had pinpointed on the map was in McAlpine Township: Lot 24, Concession III. The two men congratulated each other. "Drop to 100 feet and I notice the lake is no longer visible, only swamp," wrote Hall in the log book. "Gary says he'll land at lake and relax — excitement means mistakes."

And excitement did overtake the two men; in fact, the euphoria was briefly too much for Hall to handle — he promptly vomited into his hat. In a calmer moment, he wrote in his log book: "It was like a dream you couldn't quite register. It required a little mental gear shifting to realize that the search was over."

In a *Toronto Sun* interview, Fields explained how the crash site had escaped detection for 11 years. "When I found the spot again, I saw that you had to be directly over the place before you could see anything." Hall insisted that they circle the area so that they wouldn't lose the location again. "We kept right on the spot until the other chopper came along," explained Hall. "I threw out reams of toilet paper to mark the spot. Even then, Gary very carefully marked the spot and I double-checked it before we left. There were no landmarks and no scars on the trees. They must have stalled and gone straight down."

* * *

In 1962, Anne and Emil Klisanich moved from Timmins to London, Ontario. "We decided that hotel life was not for us," explains Anne. "Emil told his mother he didn't want the Pearl Lake Hotel, because you have to work evenings and weekends and there's not much of a family life." After working at Doran's Brewery in Timmins, Emil joined Seagram's and the move south came as a result of his being promoted to a regional manager

"We bought a lovely home near the University of Western Ontario, and my mother came down to visit us in 1962," begins Anne. "A neighbour, Juniece Swift, knew the story about my brother. She called me and said, 'Anne, do you have your radio on?' I said, 'No, I don't. Why?' She said, 'There's some news about your brother and Dr. Hudson's plane and I thought you should know.' I thought, 'Here we go again!' Not only that, but my mother was visiting."

On the afternoon of June 6, Anne's neighbour told her to turn on the radio; radio station CFPL was reporting that a plane believed to be that of Dr. Hudson had been discovered in the northern Ontario wilderness. "I called the station, told them who I was and asked them where they got their information," Anne explains. "They told me the information came from the Department of Lands and Forests in Cochrane, Ontario. The station said, 'We'll contact them and let them know your mother is staying with you and that they can contact you.'"

As promised, the radio station contacted the department, and Anne received a phone call from Lands and Forests Minister Wilf Spooner shortly thereafter. "He told me, 'We think we've found the plane.' I asked, 'What do you base that on?' He explained to me that some of the boys from Cochrane make frequent trips to that area, but they thought they saw something that could be Dr. Hudson's plane. He said, 'We didn't tell the news media until we were certain.'"

The Ontario Provincial Police confirmed the registration of the plane as CF–FXT through letters that were clearly visible on the wreckage. This matched the registration of Dr. Henry Hudson's plane, proving beyond any doubt that the wreckage they had discovered had been the aircraft that had taken Bill Barilko and Dr. Hudson to their deaths. The crash site coordinates were confirmed as North 49 degrees, 45 minutes; West 81 degrees, 12 minutes, 30 seconds. The site is close to shallow Georgina Lake.

The afternoon's events unfolded quickly. Next of kin were to be contacted before the story broke through the media. Attempts were made to reach Anne Klisanich and her brother, Alex Barilko, as well as Dr. Henry Hudson's wife, Phyllis, and brother, Lou. At 12:45 p.m., Anne was telephoned, but she was not at home. Dr. Lou Hudson was called at 1:10, but the office reported he was "hard of hearing and more than a little skeptical" — "I pray that this will finally end the mystery," he stated at the time. Alex Barilko was telephoned at 1:20 p.m., but his phone was busy. Two minutes later, the Ontario Provincial Police tried to call Phyllis Hudson, who had since moved to Port Credit (now part of Mississauga), Ontario, but a neighbour answered and reported that Mrs. Hudson wasn't home. Late that afternoon, Phyllis Hudson returned the call. She insisted on proof of identification, and swore her husband's plane was registered with letters that included DGZ. "We didn't argue," wrote Hall in the search log.

The teletype machines in newsrooms across Canada beat out a staccato bulletin that afternoon. "The wreckage of what is believed to be the plane that carried hockey player Bill Barilko and Dr. Henry Hudson to their deaths 11 years ago was found today about 45 miles north of Cochrane. The wreckage was spotted by a Department of Lands and Forests helicopter crew which has been combing desolate bush lands north of Cochrane since smashed metal was seen glinting in the sun last Thursday." All afternoon, the wire services transmitted a continuous stream of information about the discovery.

At 8:15 that evening, the plane was positively confirmed as having belonged to Dr. Henry Hudson. "We were able to identify it [the plane]

from its official markings," said Joe Shalla, who noted that by methodi-
cally piecing together pieces of the fuselage they discovered at the site,
they were able to read the letters CF-FXT, the registration assigned to
Hudson's Fairchild 24. "The engine was buried in muskeg, but most of
the fuselage was lying on the surface," Shalla continued. The discovery
and positive identification were publicly announced by Lands and
Forests Minister Wilf Spooner, whose department established the date
of the crash as Sunday, August 26, 1951. Records of that time indicate
that winds were strong, at 60 to 70 miles per hour from the southwest,
that day.

Phyllis Hudson was telephoned again with confirmation of her
husband's death. Relieved that Henry's remains had been found after so
many years, she said, "I gave up hope a long, long time ago."

A call was placed to Anne Klisanich at 8:30 on the evening of June
6. She was informed with absolute certainty that the crash site was
where her brother had met his death. For so long, through every potential sighting, the family had held out hope. The ordeal had been
excruciating, especially for Faye Barilko, who steadfastly believed that
her son was still alive. "I told my husband Emil, 'I don't know how to
handle this with my mother,'" remembers Anne. The Klisaniches
phoned a friend, Marion Moore, who had been a nurse for the
Barilkos' family doctor in Timmins, but who, like them, had relocated
to London. "I told her the story and asked her how to handle my
mother," Anne continues. Moore told Anne to get to a drug store and
explain the situation. "They gave me some sedatives for Mother. When
I told her, she went hysterical." It is never an enviable task to break
tragic news, and Anne had to tell her mother that, not only had the
plane not returned, but that, 11 years later, they had finally found Bill's
remains. Faye Barilko wept inconsolably. "Why this no happen long
time ago?" Mrs. Barilko, visiting her daughter Anne, son-in-law Emil
and grandchildren in London, had never stopped believing her Billy
would arrive home.

"Mother, now at least we know," Anne told her. After Faye settled
down, she admitted she felt the same way. "She said, 'Now I have peace.'
Although it was horribly sad, it was a relief," Anne admits.

"It was very difficult for all of us. It was hard on Emil," Anne recalls.
"I now had two boys growing up. Frank was 11 years old then, and Barry
was seven. It was hard on them — they knew the story about their uncle."

The provincial police again tried to call Alex Barilko, who was then
living in Montreal, but as Ted Hall reported in his log book, "Couldn't
understand woman and no one present spoke right language." Hall had
reached Alex's francophone wife, Fern (the former Fernande Dubé).
Anne finally reached her brother, who admitted that the news had
caught him by surprise. "My sister and I are able to take it, but mother

is different. This has been a great shock to her. But she didn't want to die not knowing the truth."

* * *

That evening, viewers of CBC Television watched with rapt attention as anchorman Earl Cameron read the lead story. "The remains of the former Toronto Maple Leaf hockey star Bill Barilko have been found in the northern Ontario wilderness. The provincial minister of Mines and Forests, Mr. Spooner, said tonight that members of his staff had identified the remains of both Mr. Barilko and Dr. Henry Hudson in the wreckage of a seaplane in dense bush 45 miles north of Cochrane. The two men disappeared on a flight on a fishing trip 11 years ago..."

"Northern Ontario's savage bush country has finally surrendered one of its most jealously-guarded secrets — what happened to hockey star Bill Barilko," wrote Peter Worthington of the Toronto *Telegram*. "It is now official: Barilko died in a plane crash with Timmins dentist Henry Hudson. Yesterday afternoon, the moss-covered, weather-worn bones of Barilko and Dr. Hudson were discovered in the twisted wreckage of their yellow Fairchild plane, 60 miles north of Cochrane."

The June 7, 1962, headline in the Timmins *Daily Press* blared, "11-Year Mystery Solved." The bold, red headline offered some measure of relief for Bill's family and friends. "In the past week, one man has twice discovered by accident what dozens of aircraft and hundreds of searchers failed to find 11 years ago." Gary Fields had inadvertently solved the Hudson-Barilko mystery, one that the dense woods of northern Ontario had been reticent to surrender.

Years later, Fields told the *Toronto Sun*, "It looked like the plane had cut a small swath when it went into the bush. It seemed as if [Dr. Hudson] had been flying low, ran out of gas, then tried to stretch his glide but failed."

"The lack of burned material suggested the gasoline tanks were empty at the time of the crash and exploded because of fumes," read Worthington's eye-witness report in the *Telegram*. "Every flier I've spoken to here thinks signs point to the plane running out of gasoline and spiralling into the bush as Dr. Hudson tried desperately to guide it into a clear patch."

"It was as if the pilot was heading for what appeared to be a clear spot," explains Peter Worthington in a 2004 interview. "It looked all brown in midsummer, and quite flat, but it hid all the water in there. It looked like the pilot was heading for that spot to land but fell about 30 or 40 feet short and just buried the plane's nose into the soft, mushy swampland. If he'd gone another 20 or 30 feet — maybe he hit a treetop, who knows — he would have been in the open space and been found a lot quicker.

"The plane had pontoons. It would have landed belly down and bounced. Conceivably, they could have survived. They would have had to wait, as there was nowhere they could have walked to if they had landed. They could have burned gasoline. The search was pretty intense and they would have been found soon enough."

* * *

Cochrane district forester Ted Hall noted that a search team was en route to the crash site. A helicopter was able to land about a half-mile from the site and would then carve out a path to the crash, where the crew planned to clear a landing spot so that a second machine could land a party of police and Department of Transport officials. A four-seater Beaver aircraft equipped with pontoons was then to fly the police to West Trappers Lake, 10 miles south of the crash site, and from there they were to be ferried to the scene by helicopter.

The team from the Ontario Provincial Police agreed that radio and television reporters, as well as newspaper photographers, would be flown into the area, with the local press getting priority. CFCL-TV in Timmins declined the offer, claiming that the station had no one available to send. The Toronto *Telegram* was most eager to expand on their expected story and would be sending a reporter and a photographer.

A helicopter carrying Ron Boyd, a pilot for Dominion Helicopters, engineer Phil Weston and Ray Paterick landed in an open swamp a quarter-mile to the west of the crash site. Battling blackflies and trudging through murky, knee-deep swamp and muskeg, they hacked out a path through the virgin timberland to the crumpled remains of the Fairchild 24. The trek took the men an hour and a half. When they reached the crumpled plane, they discovered two skeletons still strapped in their cockpit seats. "The bones of the pilot [Dr. Hudson] were in the left seat and covered in moss," Boyd reported. "Barilko's bones were sprawled on top. The skull was shattered." The men took photographs of the crash site and then waited for two hours for others to arrive.

A ground party consisting of pilot Gary Fields and Peter Worthington of the *Telegram* landed on a knoll at McAlpine Lake, approximately three miles from the site. "The crash site was too swampy," says Worthington. The men struggled to make their way through the dense bush. "It was very tough going," states Peter. "It took us about half an hour to get to the site. We were both complaining that the pilot could have landed a little closer, but we could see why he landed where he did; you would sink up to your knees in this quick-sandy mud."

The party reached the crash site and stayed for about an hour. "It was this black, swampy mud with swamp grass over it," describes

Worthington. "By that time, the trees had grown around it, and I'm not sure how they even found it then. You could easily see how something would disappear in it. It was no surprise that they didn't find it when it went down. It makes you realize just how rough that country is."

Joe Shalla, the forest protection supervisor, later reached the site and reported that the aircraft had burrowed a hole eight feet wide and three feet deep when it crashed. The wings had been sheared off by the force of striking the dense timber. Shalla was joined by Corporal Albert Duguid of the Ontario Provincial Police detachment in Cochrane.

A working compass was discovered amongst the remnants of the plane. One of the skeletons bore a wristwatch and a ring. A belt buckle belonging to one of the men was found at the site. So, too, were two quarters and a dime. The coins were scorched, indicating that a fire had broken out on impact. In a 1983 interview, Gary Fields told the *Toronto Sun*, "We found the skeletons still strapped in their seats, but the only sign of any clothing was a zipper off one of the garments."

"It looked like one of the gas tanks had exploded," explained Duguid. "There was a bit of charred timber about and some of the bones found at the scene were charred."

"I remember rooting in the cockpit area and finding a tooth. It was a back tooth," reveals Peter Worthington. "I didn't know whose tooth it was, obviously, but for years I assumed it was Bill Barilko's tooth."

According to Worthington's report in the *Telegram*, "Young trees and new foliage are now growing through the plane's twisted and rotting frame. The tail section is bent over the top. The wingtip has been sliced off. A half-buried pontoon stuck above the muskeg; like a tombstone."

The mysterious disappearance of Bill Barilko and Dr. Henry Hudson had prompted all manner of rumours — one of the more outlandish being that Barilko had fled to Russia to teach youngsters there to play hockey. Most were discredited, but one that wouldn't die easily had the two Timmins men smuggling gold out of the north — a practice known as high-grading. Although no proof was ever offered to substantiate the claim, a rationale developed around the allegation. Hudson, being a dentist, used gold to produce crowns and fillings for his patients at that time. Barilko, meanwhile, was a high-profile athlete with access to wealthy entrepreneurs. Being well-known residents of Timmins, both men had a network of contacts who could and would provide gold smuggled out of the mines of northern Ontario. Hudson had his own plane, which he could readily load and fly to the United States to connect with persons working beyond the attention of the law. And finally, there was Henry Hudson's mysterious shooting at the Toronto curling bonspiel — a case in which the assailant had never been caught and no reason had ever been disclosed. Gossip circulating around Timmins at the time hinted at either an affair gone awry or repercussions from high-grading. The weight of the smuggled gold, it was surmised, would surely have weighted down the small plane and could readily have caused the crash.

By the time Peter Worthington arrived at the crash site, he noticed that all the pontoons had been sliced opened with an axe. "I suspect the police thought Hudson and Barilko might have loaded the pontoons with gold because there was a suggestion that people were smuggling gold out of the area. Obviously, this was just to confirm or deny the rumour." The pontoons could not have been damaged by trees, Worthington suggests, because of the presence of what were clearly axe marks.

Worthington's incredibly descriptive reports reflect the surreal feeling he experienced at the site. "Poking around the wreckage seemed somehow like tampering with a grave. I saw several splintered rib bones embedded in seeping bog by the pilot's seat. I stopped looking.

"There was no question that they died immediately. It was not a question of them lingering there being trapped."

Worthington admits to a personal interest in the subject of this 1962 story. "In 1944, I was going to school in St. Catharines and I went to one of the Leafs practices," remembers Peter. "I saw Hap Day and asked for an autograph. He said, 'Sure. Would you like some of the other players'?' I said, 'Sure!' He brought me back a sheet and about 16 players were on it — Ted Kennedy, Wally Stanowski, the whole gang. Can you imagine that today?

"After St. Catharines, I went to university and then to Korea, so I wasn't in Toronto when Barilko played," Peter states. "But Barilko was such a big name back in those days." Reflecting back on that June day in 1962, Worthington describes his feelings as he stood at the spot of Barilko's death. "You know you're in the presence of the place where somebody you admired so much has died. It was almost like visiting his grave. You find the same thing when you visit the war graves in Europe. You see all these tombstones. You look at the ages and they're all young men of 19, 21, 23. You realize that these were such pointless losses. And here you have this hockey player who was revered and who had all this potential, whose whole career was five years, and then all of a sudden, he's no more."

Under the cover of darkness on June 6, Corporal Duguid of the Cochrane OPP and Forest Protection Supervisor Joe Shalla meticulously wrapped the remains of the two men in a towel, then placed them in a haversack to be transported out of the area. What remained of the two Timmins men was flown to Cochrane to be examined by a pathologist and a coroner.

At 8:50 a.m. on June 7, Dr. Lou Hudson and a friend, Gordon Gauthier, arrived in Cochrane expecting to visit the crash site. (Gauthier had the original engine from the Fairchild 24 that Henry replaced back in South Porcupine.) Dr. Lou put up a bit of a fuss when told he would not be able to walk to the crash site. In his logbook, Ted Hall wrote, "Dr. Hudson quite insistent that he go in on ground in low shoes and suit — he's an old man. Couldn't be discouraged. They went to police office to view remains and evidence. Came back later apparently satisfied and not wanting to go in after all."

Later that afternoon, officials decided to proceed to the site with block and tackle in order to hoist the Fairchild's engine out of the crash site. An disagreement ensued, and plans were changed. Now, a Sikorsky helicopter, acknowledged as one of the most reliable helicopters available and capable of hovering low over the site, yet powerful enough to lift out the complete wreck, was to be brought in.

Beginning on June 8, the Department of Transport expressed misgivings that the Ontario Provincial Police, who had visited the crash site early, had disturbed the wreckage of Hudson's Fairchild. This would be an ongoing source of friction between the two departments.

🍁 🍁 🍁

The July 1962 edition of *The Hockey News* reported that the search for Barilko and Hudson had covered 100,000 square miles at a cost of $385,000 — the most extensive and expensive search in Canadian history. Seventeen planes flew more than 1,345 hours in search of the men. At the height of the search, 17 RCAF planes and 135 airmen were involved, scouring the vast northern expanse.

The search had never really ended. Although the RCAF crews and planes returned to their respective bases after several weeks, pilots continued to keep their eyes out for a hint of the plane that had so mysteriously vanished.

Gary Fields, the helicopter pilot with the Department of Lands and Forests who spotted the wreckage, was prodded into inquiring whether he was eligible for the $10,000 reward money offered by Maple Leaf Gardens. "I was lucky enough to spot the wreckage twice. I don't imagine I'll be lucky enough to get $10,000," said Fields. He was correct. Maple Leaf Gardens president Stafford Smythe explained that the reward offer had expired with the flip of the calendar page on January 1, 1952.

🍁 🍁 🍁

Barilko's childhood friend Gaston Garant recalls his return to the site of his friend's death. "About 10 years ago, a group of us went fishing and we flew into the area in a plane that carries about six or seven passengers and their gear. All of a sudden, I was up front with the pilot and he showed me the place where they found the airplane. Of course, we were high up in the air, but it wasn't far from Cochrane. It brought up all the old feelings again."

"That had been quite a time. It was a sad thing," Gaston reflects. "When the air force was looking for Bill and they couldn't find that aircraft, I figured they went down someplace in the dense woods there. My wife cried for days. We were all very close. When Bill would come home in the summer, if we weren't at the Victory Hotel, we were at one of the guys' homes."

Garant knew Dr. Henry Hudson very well, too. "He was my dentist. I always refused to fly with him — don't ask me why. I used to sense something. The other boys flew with Henry. I'm not saying he was a bad pilot — don't get me wrong. I just never liked small planes; that was the reason."

Bill had never before flown with Dr. Hudson in his Fairchild 24, Gaston Garant continues. "Bill just loved fishing, that's the thing. We used to go fishing with our cars or the trucks. Bill, it was his first time with Henry Hudson. Bill had never flown in a small plane before."

"At first, there were hopes that they would be found alive, but as time went on, you just knew they wouldn't," Harry Watson admitted in an August 2001 interview with *The Beaver*, a Canadian historical magazine.

Carlo Cattarello Jr. remembers the day the plane was spotted some 11 years after it had vanished. "I was heading back to Michigan Tech, where I was attending school, when I heard the news. Bill Barilko and Dr. Hudson were almost home — just up in the Abitibi Canyon north of Cochrane. They would have been home in 10 or 15 minutes."

🍁 🍁 🍁

Although the remnants of the crashed plane were positively identified as having belonged to Dr. Henry Hudson, coroner Dr. Philip Bernstein insisted that the remains of the two persons found in the wreckage be legally identified before they were turned over to the respective families for burial. They were sent to the Ontario Attorney General's Toronto laboratory for positive identification, where Dr. Noble Sharp was in charge of the identification effort, but he was unable to positively identify the persons to whom the bones belonged. Scientific examination, strangely, did not prove that the remains discovered at the site were those of either Hudson or Barilko. Ironically, dental evidence was not sufficient to yield a positive identification. Cochrane dentist Dr. A.F.

Dungy tried to identify the teeth from two jawbones he had been given, but could only state that "14 teeth belonged to one group and 14 teeth belonged to another group." He said those facts indicated only that there were two persons. Dungy identified a partial denture he had produced for Dr. Hudson, but no dental records for either Hudson or Barilko were found.

An inquest was held in Cochrane, Ontario, to determine the facts surrounding Dr. Henry Hudson's death. Wilfred Dupont, an assistant Crown attorney in Cochrane District, called five witnesses, but told the five-man jury to concern itself solely with the death of Dr. Hudson and to leave Bill Barilko out of discussions.

Corporal Duguid of the Cochrane detachment of the OPP confirmed that "a number of what appeared to be human bones were found in the wreckage of the cockpit." Dr. Albert Moore of Cochrane, a pathologist, noted that he had received the bones from Corporal Duguid and determined that they comprised approximately 80 percent of each of two human skeletons. When asked if there was any way to determine which skeleton was which, Dr. Moore answered, "With certainty, no." Dr. Moore did determine from examining spinal bones that one skeleton belonged to a person older than the other, but he could only write "tentatively Hudson" and "tentatively Barilko." "The only conclusion I could come to was that the cause of death was multiple fractures of the skull and other fractures. Death would have been pretty well instantaneous."

Corporal Duguid testified that he found a belt buckle with a steer's head on it. Alex Barilko claimed the buckle came from a belt he owned that his brother had borrowed before the fishing trip. Duguid had also found a Swiss-made pocket watch. Phyllis Hudson, Henry's widow, identified the watch as one her husband had purchased in Switzerland in 1950.

A.J. Burleton, an inspector with the Federal Department of Transport, told the jury that the plane's motor was in good mechanical condition and that he was of the opinion that the plane was in operation at the time of the crash. "The plane is believed to have hit the ground at a 50-degree angle," he testified. "The trim tab was in a nose-up position, and that would make the plane difficult, but not impossible, to handle. There was evidence of a fire taking place in the plane."

Reverend Albert Williams, who had been stationed at Rupert's House at the time of the 1951 crash, was called to testify. He stated that he was among the last people to talk to Dr. Hudson while his wife was speaking with Bill Barilko. He explained to the best of his recollection the stop made by the men, spoke of the meeting and conversations, then related his memories of the subsequent taxi and take-off. Although witnesses claimed the plane's pontoons were loaded with fish, Reverend

Williams denied seeing any fish on or about the craft. He did clarify that Barilko "gave three fish to some Indians, but I didn't see where they got them from." When asked by Mr. Dupont if there was any evidence of liquor, the minister replied, "None whatsoever."

The jury took just 13 minutes to reach its anticlimactic verdict. Foreman Peter Hughes announced, "Dr. Henry Hudson was an occupant of the aircraft CF-FXT Fairchild 24, the wreckage of which was found in McAlpine Township on June 6, 1962. We conclude that death was due to multiple fractures caused by impact on the date of the crash."

The coroner's jury made no finding on Bill Barilko.

* * *

On April 21, 1951, Bill Barilko scored the Stanley Cup-winning goal that proved to be the dramatic conclusion to a hockey career so compelling its details are still recited more than fifty years later. Sadly, on August 26 that same year, the lives of Bill Barilko and Dr. Henry Hudson came to tragic ends witnessed by no one, obscured for eleven years by the dense forests that hid the secret to the spectacular finale of Bill Barilko.

After eleven years, Faye Barilko could finally rest. She now knew why her Billy had not come home.

CHAPTER
22

The Prize

"Whenever friends come up here, they always want to see where Bill is buried." Leo Curik chokes on the words as they spill from his lips. It may be more than four decades since his friend's remains were found and subsequently buried, but Curik finds the thought no easier today than he did at the time.

"We had hometown reunions from time to time up in Schumacher, so I would go to the Timmins cemetery and visit the graves of some of the friends I grew up with," mentions Frank Mahovlich. "I stopped in there one day and it happened to be during the Schumacher Homecoming Reunion [in May 1999], and Anne was there visiting Bill's grave."

After the death of family patriarch Steve Barilko in 1946, the family purchased four gravesites at Timmins Memorial Cemetery. Stan Cor, the recently retired manager of the Timmins cemetery, comments, "Every year, we get inquiries for Bill's grave location, which means that people are definitely interested. In the five and a half years I have been involved with the cemetery, interest has been steady. Some people inquire online before coming, while others telephone or come to the office when they are in town."

A gravestone was erected on the Barilko family plot in 1960. Monument maker Eugene Horvath crafted what he affectionately called "my finest piece of work." The headstone is lavishly decorated with hockey images — twin maple leaves, hockey sticks and pucks flank either side of the headstone. Under the proud surname sits a head-and-shoulders photo of Bill wearing his Toronto Maple Leafs sweater. Carved into the stone is "Wm. (Bill) Barilko, 1927–1951." Beneath the dates of his lifeline are the years in which Bill contributed to winning the Stanley Cup: 1947, 1948, 1949 and 1951.

For several years, a solitary hockey puck has lain undisturbed on the monument. No one knows who placed the tribute there.

Bill's monument sat forlornly above an empty grave for nearly two years. His remains were not finally laid to rest until June 15, 1962.

"They shipped Billy's remains to Timmins, and an autopsy had to be performed," reminds Bill's sister, Anne. "About a week later, Mother had a burial for him, just as if he had passed away two or three days earlier that week.

"For 11 years, my mother never gave up hope. It was very sad, but at least now, she knew. We all knew. There was peace of mind for her," says Anne, the tears running down her cheeks.

The Barilkos didn't attend church growing up. "We just said our prayers in our own little way," mentions Anne. Although the family was Greek Orthodox by birth, the funeral was held in Timmins' First United Church on Eighth Avenue at one o'clock on the afternoon of Friday, June 15.

"We are gathered here this afternoon to remind ourselves of our Christian hope and to open our hearts to the comfort which God alone can give," began Reverend William Kitto. "We are here to commend the soul of this person to the eternal care of a heavenly Father, and also to pay tribute to Bill Barilko, who was a great athlete.

"It was not my good pleasure to be personally acquainted with him, but from conversations with the family and from what I have read, certain characteristics stand out clearly. He was friendly. Various pictures suggest it and the witness of his fellow players proves it. We are told he had a smile for everyone except opposing forwards. He was enthusiastic. He was a mere 18 years of age when he was called from the old Pacific Coast league to try out with the Toronto Maple Leafs. But he came with a spirit which said, 'I'm ready to try anything.'

"Lacking in experience, he was quick to learn, and he made up his mind that big-time hockey was for him. He played the game. He used brain and brawn so effectively that he was always a danger to the opposing team. He shared in the four championships Toronto gained from 1947 to 1951, and his winning goal in the overtime period of the final game will go down in the annals of sport. We often say this is the country where we grow hockey players, and we are proud to have contributed such a good one.

"As we think of the career of Bill Barilko, cut short by tragedy, our minds turn very naturally to an illustration by the Apostle Paul to describe the Christian life. As in athletics, Christianity itself is a contest. There is a prize to be gained, but there is also the opposition that would snatch it away. We must, therefore, play a good game.

"Paul expressed it in these words in the third chapter of his letter to the Philippians, verse 14: 'I press towards the goal to win the prize which is God's call to the life above, in Christ Jesus.' Paul notes, first, this pressing forward. The word means to speed or hasten. It was sometimes used in driving a chariot in a race. No athlete himself, Paul must have been impressed with athletics because he also uses the figure of a man stripping off his cloak, lest it should hinder him in the race. The good athlete must put every hindrance aside and press forward; so must the Christian.

"There then is 'the goal.' It literally means 'the object on which one fixes the eye.' During a hockey game, the goal will be under the intense scrutiny of thousands of spectators, to say nothing of the kind of look the hockey players themselves fix upon it, doing their utmost to see the puck gets into the correct one.

"Lastly, there is 'the prize.' The purpose of the hockey player who puts his heart and soul into the game is to come to that happy moment when he gets a hand on the Stanley Cup. There is also a Christian goal. It is 'to win the prize which is God's call to the life above, in Christ Jesus.'

"Today, as we honour the memory of a valiant player who did so much towards winning the greatest prize the hockey world can offer, we find our hearts comforted and reassured in the conviction that by God's grace, he has gained the greatest prize of all, 'the life above, in Christ Jesus.'

"This is our comfort and reassurance, that whether we live in this world or the one above, we are within the tender care of the Eternal. We are still one in the fullness of His love. In that faith we, too, 'press towards the goal to win the prize which is God's call to the life above, in Christ Jesus.'"

🍁　🍁　🍁

Cousin Steve Denisavitch, teammate Harry Watson and childhood friends Leo Curik, Gaston Garant, Mel Richards and Allan Stanley carried the casket of Bill Barilko to its final resting place.

"It was light as a feather," remembers Garant. "Nothing but a few bones."

"On that sad day, my mind drifted back to the overtime goal Barilko scored to clinch the 1951 Stanley Cup," says Harry Watson, who was only four years older than Barilko. Both had joined the Leafs in 1946–47, although Harry already had three NHL seasons under his belt and had spent two years in the military. "It didn't matter where he went. He'd walk into a room and he'd just seem to light up the room. People loved to be with him. It was really something."

Jim Thomson, Bill's closest friend with the Toronto Maple Leafs, also attended the funeral to say goodbye to his friend Bill.

"It was very sad," says Allan Stanley. "But in a way, it was great relief to have closure. People claimed they saw Bill in Russia. There were crazy rumours going around."

"There was no hope of finding Bill," says Stanley as he shakes his head. "You can't even believe the trees up in that country. The tops of the trees are packed so closely together that it looks like a can of asparagus. There was no way to find him unless it was by accident.

"I loved Bill like a brother. We had some arguments just to make it exciting but he was a great friend." After a momentary pause, Allan adds, "It was hard to say goodbye."

❋ ❋ ❋

Former captain Ted Kennedy had intended to pay his respects to the Barilko family on behalf of Bill's teammates, but wires got crossed. "I was at the office one day and Harold Ballard called me. He said, 'You were captain when Bill Barilko played for the Leafs.' He told me that Bill's remains had been found and asked me to drive up to Timmins to represent the Toronto Maple Leafs at Barilko's funeral. I arrived in the town and stopped to ask where the funeral for Bill Barilko was taking place. I was surprised, but no one seemed to know.

"It turns out I was a week early. The remains were going through an autopsy and hadn't been returned for burial. I drove right back home."

❋ ❋ ❋

The National Hockey League agreed to pay the funeral expenses for Bill Barilko. In a letter dated November 30, 1962, league president Clarence Campbell wrote, "Mr. Harold Ballard, Executive Vice President of the Toronto Maple Leafs, has brought to my attention the matter of expenses incurred by you in connection with the funeral of your son, William, a former player of the Toronto Club, with a view to having all or some portion of these expenses reimbursed to you. I took the matter up with the Governors of the National Hockey League at a recent meeting and they have authorized me to reimburse you to the extent of the actual expenses incurred in connection with the funeral itself. Accordingly, I am pleased to hand you herewith our cheque in the sum of $845.

"May I take the opportunity of saying how glad I was to learn of the discovery of the aircraft which removed all possible uncertainty as to the death of your son and to extend to you once more my sincerest condolences in this very tragic loss."

CHAPTER 23

A Curse Lifted

After a horrific decade, starting with the disappearance of Bill Barilko, the Toronto Maple Leafs started to pull out of their tailspin towards the end of the decade. After finishing dead last in 1957–58, Toronto, hired Punch Imlach as assistant general manager in June 1958, at which time he cockily predicted that he would get the Leafs into the playoffs. By the end of November, after Toronto had got off to a lacklustre start, Imlach had assumed the dual roles of coach and general manager, and the team rebounded. However, it was only after winning five straight games to close out the regular season that the Leafs were able to nose out the New York Rangers, 65 points to 64, to claim fourth place and bring Imlach's postseason prophecy to pass. Toronto then shocked second-place Boston in the semifinals and competed against the Montreal Canadiens in the Stanley Cup finals, falling short of the Habs, who won their fourth consecutive Stanley Cup.

But the improvement wasn't solely due to Imlach's investiture. Johnny Bower, a spectacular veteran American Hockey League netminder, would solidify the Maple Leafs goaltending woes. Carl Brewer, a young defenceman who could handle and move the puck, added a dimension not evident on the Toronto blue line in years.

In 1959–60, the Leafs improved by 14 points over the season and jumped to second place in the NHL. Perennial all-star Red Kelly was picked up from the Detroit Red Wings late in the season and, in a savvy move, converted to a centreman from defence. His veteran leadership and skills added much to the Leafs. Toronto dumped Detroit in the semifinals but again encountered Montreal in the finals. The Canadiens swept the Leafs in four games to claim their fifth Stanley Cup championship in a row.

Another second-place finish awaited the Leafs in 1960–61, although their point total increased to 90 from the previous season's 79. Frank Mahovlich exploded, tallying 48 goals, while the exciting Calder Trophy winner David Keon added 20. Eddie Shack was secured from the Rangers, adding a measure of size, skill and spunk to the Toronto front line. But in spite of the promise the team showed through the regular season, the Maple Leafs went down to defeat at the hands of fourth-place Detroit, four games to one, in the semifinals.

The Toronto Maple Leafs, featuring a lineup that combined players developed within their own system (Bobby Baun, Brewer, Dick Duff, Billy Harris, Tim Horton, Keon, Mahovlich, Bob Nevin and Bob Pulford, among others) alongside veterans nurtured elsewhere (Bower, Kelly, Bert Olmstead, Shack and Allan Stanley), demanded to be taken seriously as 1961–62 dawned.

❋ ❋ ❋

The world teetered on the brink of a third world war in 1962. In August, the Soviet Union was set to build missile bases in Cuba, precipitating the Cuban Missile Crisis. United States President John Kennedy ordered a blockade against Cuba, and only lifted the embargo after the USSR hesitatingly backed down in the November stand-off. But the Cold War gradually warmed through the Communist Party's General Secretary Mikhail Gorbachev, who introduced "perestroika" (economic restructuring) and "glasnost" (openness) to the Republic. The thaw took full effect in December 1991 with the dissolution of the Soviet Union under Boris Yeltsin.

Lieutenant Colonel John Glenn Jr. became the first American to orbit the earth, introducing the concept of space travel to North Americans in 1962 by circling the globe three times in four hours and fifty minutes on February 20.

Motion picture icon Marilyn Monroe was discovered dead in her Hollywood home.

While addressing the film world, *West Side Story* collected the Oscar as the best motion picture of 1962. "Moon River" by Henry Mancini was the Grammy-winning song of the year while John Steinbeck won the Nobel Prize for Literature.

New York's Yankees defeated the San Francisco Giants for the baseball World Series and the Boston Celtics took the National Basketball Association championship, beating the Los Angeles Lakers.

❋ ❋ ❋

For the third year in a row, the Toronto Maple Leafs finished the regular season in second place. The Montreal Canadiens were in the midst of a five-season reign at the top of the NHL's regular-season standings. In the semifinals, paired with the fourth-place Rangers, Toronto took the first two games at home, but New York rebounded and won the next two games in their rink. Red Kelly scored the winner in game five, early in the second overtime period. The Leafs emerged as the series victor with a decisive 7–1 win in the sixth game.

In the other series, the reigning Stanley Cup champion Chicago Blackhawks had defeated Montreal, and now faced the hungry Leafs. Again, Toronto won both its home games, while the Hawks did the same. But in game five, with Don Simmons in goal replacing the injured Bower, Toronto doubled Chicago 8–4, raising the possibility that a Stanley Cup celebration might follow game six in Chicago on April 22.

There was no scoring in the first period that evening. None in the second, either. Tensions mounted. Bobby Hull scored from Murray Balfour and Bill Hay at 8:56 of the third, and the ensuing uproar that consumed the venerable old Chicago Stadium took better than 10 minutes to lapse. Bob Nevin replied for the Leafs at 10:29, and the silence was equally deafening. Then, with Eric Nesterenko serving a tripping minor, Tim Horton raced end-to-end and passed to Duff, who was open in front of Glenn Hall. His power-play goal at 14:14 stood, and when the final buzzer went, Toronto had won the Stanley Cup — the eighth in franchise history.

On June 6 that year, a mere 43 days after the victory, the remains of Bill Barilko and pilot Henry Hudson were discovered in the impenetrable forest near Cochrane, Ontario. It was almost as though a curse had been lifted. From April 21, 1951, to April 22, 1962, the Toronto Maple Leafs had gone without winning the Stanley Cup. And once the Leafs' winning touch had at last been recovered, so was Barilko.

"We had just won the Stanley Cup in 1962," reminisces Senator Frank Mahovlich. "We were going to have our parade. I was at Maple Leaf Gardens under the clock there, and Syl Apps was walking towards me to congratulate me. We were going to get into our convertibles for the parade. Just before he was going to speak and say something, a guy came in the front door and said, 'Hey, they found Barilko!'"

❦ ❦ ❦

1962 will be remembered for a great number of reasons, but for hockey fans, the year will be recalled as the year that the Toronto Maple Leafs shed the curse of a fallen hero and captured the Stanley Cup.

CHAPTER
24

Artifacts

Jimmy Main loved attending National Hockey League games at Maple Leaf Gardens. Confined to a wheelchair after being paralyzed in a boyhood diving accident, Jimmy religiously showed up to cheer on his beloved Leafs from an area beside the goal judge at the south end of the historic arena; a spot reserved for him by Conn Smythe. Jimmy usually attended the games with his cousin, George Fletcher. During the pregame skate, the Maple Leafs players would often acknowledge Jimmy with a little nod, or tap their stick on the glass that separated Jimmy from the on-ice play.

On April 21, 1951, Bill Barilko hurled himself through the air to score the Stanley Cup–winning goal at 2:53 of overtime. The puck flew past Montreal Canadiens netminder Gerry McNeil, who was seated on the ice. As Barilko's teammates mobbed him, referee Bill Chadwick skated over, retrieved the puck that had broken the 2–2 tie and flipped it over the glass to Jimmy Main. "Here you go, Jimmy. Take this home to your mother," the official said.

On the way home, Jimmy gave the puck to his cousin. "Give it to Auntie Annie," Main said, referring to Fletcher's mother, who was a diehard Leafs fan. "Jimmy was not one to get excited, not even by a big goal like that," admitted George Fletcher in a *Toronto Star* interview. "I kept it in a dresser drawer, covered just in case someone broke into the house," Fletcher reported.

Jimmy Main died in 1956. George Fletcher decided the puck belonged at the Hockey Hall of Fame, and in January 1985 he donated the legendary artifact. "My grandchildren play hockey, but Bill Barilko means nothing to them," Fletcher admitted. "And my children aren't interested in things like sports mementos, so I thought the Hall of Fame would be the best place for it."

❧ ❧ ❧

When Bill disappeared during that summer of 1951, he left behind a number of personal effects. Most of those related to his hockey past were shared by Bill's siblings, Alex and Anne. "My mother was very fair and gave my brother Alex some of Bill's things and she gave me some of the things Bill had won," reports Anne. "She wanted to make sure they had the right homes."

"Mother gave Bill's Stanley Cup ring to Alex. He also got the tea service that Bill received when the Leafs won one of their Cups. We're not certain what happened to many of the other items Alex received because he died in 1977 and his wife Fern died in 1982," mentions Anne.

"Mom gave me Bill's engraved wristwatch, and I've since passed it along to my son Frank. He has a wonderful display of all the silverware — engraved trays and a rose bowl, for example," Anne says, adding, "When Frank was young, he looked very much like Bill. It was almost as if Frank entered the world when Billy was leaving. Frank was born June 16 and Bill went on the fishing trip two months later."

The pair of skates Bill wore when he scored his final goal were donated to the Hockey Hall of Fame in 1982, while another pair Bill wore that season now reside at the Timmins Museum Centre, having been donated by Anne in 1984.

Most of the hardware earned by Bill Barilko during his career with the Toronto Maple Leafs, from sterling-silver serving trays to his Stanley Cup ring, now reside in Minnesota with Frank Klisanich — son of Emil and Anne and the only nephew Bill ever knew.

There is an interesting postscript associated with Barilko's Cup ring. The Toronto Maple Leafs only began presenting their players with rings in 1947, the year Bill and the Leafs began their dynastic run. The Leafs went on to win three titles in succession and four in five years; rather than award new rings each year, team president Conn Smythe would ask the returning players to turn in their rings, and the size of the diamond would be increased with each additional championship.

In 2002, Ken Dryden, who was then president of the Leafs, agreed to reward the surviving members of the Stanley Cup champions of 1932, '42 and '45 with rings. Although the original moulds, created by Maple Leaf Gardens director Jack Amell, were eventually found, these new rings were replicated from Bill Barilko's 1947 Stanley Cup ring.

One of the appreciative recipients was Jack McLean, a member of the 1945 Toronto Maple Leafs. On the day that he received his ring, McLean announced, "This just might be the greatest day of my life. I've waited 57 years for this ring." He died on October 14, 2003, but left a very happy man indeed.

🍁 🍁 🍁

For the last half of Bill Barilko's life, Leo Curik was his best friend. Once the chattel of the Toronto Maple Leafs, Curik believes his poor eyesight kept him from playing in the NHL. "I remember stepping out of Maple Leaf Gardens one day. It was a bright day and Hap Day asked if he could borrow my sunglasses. I hesitated to let him borrow them because they were prescription glasses and my eyesight was quite poor. I handed the sunglasses to Day and he put them on and said, 'Whoa! You must be blind.' It was a couple of days later that I was sent to Springfield. I wish I had just broken those damned glasses. Just stepped on them. I probably would have played for the Toronto Maple Leafs."

Playing for Eddie Shore's Springfield Indians in 1951, Curik stayed in touch with his best friend. "We had been eliminated from the play-offs, so I went to Toronto and stayed with Bill. After the game, I asked for his sticks. The next day, they had a team meeting and he got the sticks autographed and I brought them home."

After retiring from hockey in 1953, Curik took over the Victory Tavern in Timmins, which his parents had managed for so many years. "We had all kinds of pictures of Bill and other guys from here who made it to the NHL. I had both sticks that Bill used in that game. The sticks hung on the wall in my tavern," he explains. "But when I renovated the place [in 1981], I took them down and put them behind the bar. One day, my brother's two boys came over, took them out and were playing street hockey with them. One of them got broken. I raised hell over that, but he didn't know [any better]."

The other stick was given to Paul Saracuse, a cousin of Leo's. He donated the stick to the Hockey Hall of Fame in January 1985, when he was a 16-year-old high school student playing midget hockey in Waterford, Ontario. "They [the Hockey Hall of Fame] have the puck, the sweater and the skates, so I guess the stick would go better there than here," Saracuse mused from his home. Curik adds, "I'm certain the one Paul has is the one Bill used to score the goal, because it's the one with the autographs of Turk Broda, Harry Watson and the rest of the Leafs."

Hockey sweaters, like most equipment during the Original Six era, were recycled between the parent NHL club and its junior affiliates. At the end of a season in Toronto, for example, the crests would be removed from the Maple Leafs' sweaters, then used the next season by a junior club. "We often used equipment that had been worn by the Leafs," remembers Frank Bonello, who worked his way through the Leafs system from bantam age to senior. "It wasn't unusual for us to see the name of one of the Leafs written into a piece of equipment we'd be wearing."

But as a result, sweaters from that era are hard to come by. That's why it is all but miraculous that the sweater Bill Barilko wore when he scored the Stanley Cup–winning goal in 1951 has not only survived but is on loan to the Hockey Hall of Fame.

The story has more twists and turns than a ride at an amusement park. After the celebrations on April 21, 1951, Max Bentley, who was Barilko's roommate at the time, asked Bill for his sweater. Billy took it off and handed it to him.

Bentley enjoyed the ponies and not only was a regular visitor to the racetrack over the years, but an owner of racehorses as well. One of his jockeys was Randy Mowers, who was also a neighbour. Bentley gave Mowers the sweater in the late 1970s. After going to great lengths to verify its authenticity — a process that involved noting actual holes and stains in the sweater and matching them with photographs and movie footage of Barilko — Mowers brought the historic sweater to the Hockey Hall of Fame in 1990 to exhibit for fans. Since then, the sweater has been sold to Tom Gostlin, who later sold it to Derek Chalmers.

❦ ❦ ❦

Guinness World Records has certified that the largest private collection of sporting photographs belongs to Alex McFadyen, an amiable gentleman from Shaunavon, Saskatchewan. At 174 pounds, it's all Alex can do to move his collection from place to place, but it is the travelling that has made McFadyen a celebrity within hockey circles.

Alex wheels the fruits of his lifelong passion on a dolly. At last count, his hockey scrapbook encompassed 678 pages and 11,811 photographs. Yet Alex doesn't hesitate to travel with his prized collection. "In fact, when I went to the Maple Leafs reunion in Toronto, it cost more for the book to travel than it cost for me," laughs McFadyen, who prefers to be called a "curator" rather than a collector. Alex is a familiar sight to those attending NHL Alumni games, events and card shows, and he can confidently call a number of retired NHL stars his friends.

"I remember Bill's goal from 1951 like it was last week," McFadyen states. "Maybe it was good that we didn't have TV and all the big salaries back then, or we wouldn't have all the great memories that we have now."

In 1988, on the recommendation of Bill's teammate Harry Watson, Anne and Emil Klisanich, along with Watson, spent four hours perusing newspaper clippings, looking at photos and trading stories with Alex McFadyen in a Toronto hotel. "The collection is awesome," Anne enthuses. "Simply awesome."

The Klisaniches were so impressed with Alex and his collection that they gave him a sterling-silver cigarette case Bill had collected for winning the Stanley Cup championship. "I just treasure owning something that belonged to Bill Barilko, but I treasure the friendships I've made with Anne and Emil just as much," Alex says. He calls Anne every year on the anniversary of Barilko's goal.

❦ ❦ ❦

Hersh Borenstein of Frozen Pond, a Toronto-based collectibles' business, states that a Barilko autograph will sell for between $500 to $1000, but to find one is exceptionally rare. He mentions that, through the past several years, he has occasionally seen items for sale from Barilko's career, including a gold medallion given to Barilko that served as a lifetime pass to Maple Leaf Gardens, but it is not a common occurrence. Allan Stitt, a collector of Toronto Maple Leafs' ephemera, secured Barilko's final contract and treasures it as one of his most prized Leaf items. He, too, has seen other items — including earlier contracts — but prices are at a premium, although never short of interested buyers.

Bill Barilko's meteoric rise to NHL prominence has become legend, but it is his tragic disappearance that continues to fascinate hockey fans, making items associated with his abbreviated life among the most collectible in the sports market today.

CHAPTER
25

Fifty Mission Cap

The first chord slashes through the speakers and the song is instantly recognizable as "Fifty Mission Cap" by The Tragically Hip. A staple of rock radio since it was first played on the airwaves during the fall of 1992, the song has an immense and immediate appeal. As one of the most played songs in Canadian rock radio history, it would not be a stretch to identify "Fifty Mission Cap" as one of the greatest songs ever produced in Canada. But as a chronicle of Bill Barilko's story, the song has done more to ensure the survival of the legend than any book, magazine or newspaper story. A generation of fans born decades after Barilko's tragic disappearance and who otherwise would never know of Bill Barilko can now recite the storyline thanks entirely to The Tragically Hip:

> *Bill Barilko disappeared that summer. He was on a fishing trip.*
> *The last goal he ever scored won the Leafs the Cup.*
> *They didn't win another 'til 1962, the year he was discovered.*
> *I stole this from a hockey card, I keep tucked up under*
> *My fifty mission cap.*

*"Fifty Mission Cap"
Written by Robby Baker/Gordon Downie/Johnny Fay/Paul Langlois/Gord Sinclair
Used by permission of Little Smoke Music/peermusic Canada Inc.
From The Tragically Hip album, *Fully Completely*

Formed in Kingston, Ontario, in 1983, The Tragically Hip's name came from a long-form music video called *Elephant Parts*, produced by Michael Nesmith, best known as the toque-wearing member of the Monkees. The band recorded an eponymous debut in 1987, but it was the release of *Up to Here* in 1989 that propelled the band to the upper echelons of Canada's rock hierarchy.

Their third album, *Road Apples*, came out in 1991. The Hip toured throughout that year, culminating with a New Year's Eve show in Ottawa at the Congress Centre. Charismatic front man Gord Downie, as visually arresting as any lead singer, was renowned for breaking into seemingly spontaneous monologues during certain songs, much to the wild enthusiasm of the band's legion of fans. While performing that night, Downie introduced much of the Bill Barilko story over the driving instrumental break in "New Orleans Is Sinking." Many of the band's songs evolved from these monologues, and what began that night as the germ of an idea had been fully developed by the time the group performed at Toronto's Horseshoe Tavern on April 18, 1992, when "Fifty Mission Cap" was performed publicly for the first time.

"Like most kids, everything was hockey and hockey was everywhere," begins Gord Downie, whom the comedian Dan Aykroyd once described as "one of the most dynamic, charismatic performers in the world."

Downie continues: "You could turn anything into hockey, and would — in your rec room or in your garage or on a puddle that's larger than normal. You can make hockey anywhere, and you do, so that's what I did."

In a 1993 *Network* magazine interview, Gord revealed another hockey connection. "My godfather is [Boston Bruins president] Harry Sinden. He and my folks were friends when I was baptized. He was selling real estate at the time, and then when he got back into the game, he promptly won a Stanley Cup with the Bruins." But the singer was already a committed hockey fan. "I didn't need too much of a push for hockey, like a lot of my friends," he explains. "Ultimately, as I got older, it definitely would have tied me to the Bruins at a time when they were interestingly commandeered by him as GM."

"I was goaltender from my second year on," continues The Hip's vocalist. "Hockey is such a strange game that I wanted to check it out from all angles. We had some foam rubber in the garage. I had an older brother who manipulated me into becoming a moving target. That's how most goalies are born. I had a proclivity towards it and I enjoyed it. You either do or you don't. I did. It becomes a love/hate relationship from then on out."

By the age of 16, Gord was finding that, while his passion for the game remained undiminished, the time he had to play it did not. "I was playing major bantam and we had done quite well. The next year, I attempted to go out and play minor midget. But that was probably one of the first few times I was one of the gang to play for the high school dance. A lot of lines are drawn in the sand right there."

Gord Sinclair plays bass in The Tragically Hip, and is a major contributor to the band's writing. Like all the group's members, Sinclair is also a massive fan of hockey. "I played league hockey in Kingston until

I was 12 or 13 years old. I was never all that good at it, but I certainly played it all the time," Sinclair mentions. "Hockey was everything, from playing to collecting the hockey cards. Robby [Baker, one of The Hip's guitarists] lived across the street from us and we traded hockey cards."

Sinclair still vividly recalls driving to Toronto with his father to visit Maple Leaf Gardens. "I got to see my first Leaf game in 1969 — got to see the Oakland Seals play. It was fantastic! I remember my first hockey game much more clearly than I can remember the last few I've been at," shrugs Sinclair. "Hockey is part of the psyche. It's a great backdrop for spending time with your family and your friends. It's a great common ground. I'm finding the same thing with my kids. The four of us will go out and catch a game together, watch *Hockey Night in Canada* together, talk about it.

"It's great. It's a fantastic game."

While Gord Downie followed the Boston Bruins, Sinclair had a different allegiance. "As a kid, I followed the Blackhawks because I was a big Bobby Hull fan. That said, in Kingston, we were always oriented around the Toronto Maple Leafs. Even though we were equidistant between Toronto and Montreal, back in the '60s and early '70s our orientation was always towards the west, be it a cultural thing or what have you. You'd get guys who would end up following the Leafs and some would cheer for the Habs. During playoff time, you were sworn enemies."

Fast off the immense success of 1991's *Road Apples*, a superb album on which Gord Downie fully explored his ability as a lyricist, came the release of *Fully Completely* in 1992. Many of the songs, including "Fifty Mission Cap," would be further developed on stages around the world.

🍁 🍁 🍁

> *Bill Barilko disappeared that summer. He was on a*
> *   fishing trip.*
> *The last goal he ever scored won the Leafs the Cup.*
> *They didn't win another 'til 1962, the year he was*
> *   discovered.*
> *I stole this from a hockey card.*

"The card was sent to me or I picked it up somehow," starts Downie. "We were writing for our record *Fully Completely* at the time. Everything was material. I think I was carrying the card around in my wallet because I found [the story] compelling; I don't know why. I didn't know a lot about him [Barilko] or his story, really. It was like going into a bygone era of hockey. It's a trip that most people don't really make." In an interview with *Maclean's* magazine, Downie admitted, "As a writer, you're always on the search for something new to say, or at least, some new way to shed light on an old word. I'm pretty sure there haven't been many rock songs written about these people, these events, these landscapes, these images."

The hockey card carried by Gord Downie was part of a project that hockey historian James Duplacey was involved with. "I was working on contract for Dan Diamond and Associates, who were NHL publishers. We were at the NHL Awards back in the early '90s and met the president of Pro-Set. He flew up with his family in his private jet from Houston, Texas. This was just as the whole boom in hockey cards was starting. One of the things they wanted was an involvement in hockey. They wanted photos of famous goals. The Barilko goal was always one of the most famous goals ever — I believe it's the finest hockey photograph ever taken. I always loved that photo and had done a lot of research on it, and on Barilko, for my book, *Images of Glory*."

"I found it very interesting that the Leafs never won a Stanley Cup again until 1962, the year Barilko's body was found, so I put that on the back of the card," James explains. "When you're writing [for] cards, the space they give you is very restricted and is done by the number of characters. On the Barilko card, I had 300 characters [at my disposal] so I had to try to find a way to get that one little piece of information in as well as the fact the Leafs won the Stanley Cup and yet still give enough background about the genesis of the photo."

Oddly enough, Duplacey is a music enthusiast. "I have 10,000 vinyl albums and 5,000 CDs and I was in a rock band in high school during the '70s. But I grew out of that so I had never even heard The Tragically Hip. Someone I knew said that they had written a song about the Bill Barilko goal called 'Fifty Mission Cap.' I had never heard it, but had been told that they had actually written in the lyric, 'I stole this from a hockey card.' And I said, 'Oh, okay. That's kind of neat. I wrote that hockey card. I wrote that lyric.'

"What I thought was interesting about the way [Downie] wrote that lyric was that it was blank verse. His lyrics are always surreal anyway. The more you go in depth into the meaning of his lyrics, the more confused you get." Duplacey leans back with a satisfied grin crossing his face. "I do have the *Fully Completely* CD in my collection, yes. It's the only thing I have by The Tragically Hip."

🍁 🍁 🍁

Reading the abbreviated Barilko story on the back of a hockey card further fuelled Gord Downie's passion to explore the story. "I went to the Metro Reference Library in Toronto and got into the microfiche there," Gord continues. "I was compelled by the story, and once you start you can't really stop. I started looking everything up. I basically followed the *Toronto Star* and their coverage of the event — and, obviously, reading pages and pages at the beginning of the disappearance and watching it taper away over the years and then be reignited with the discovery and the reaction to it."

"It was close to closing time and I was right up to the point where they were about to discover his body," Downie adds. "It was dark, and in my mind I was in a bush plane somewhere over Northern Ontario. A librarian tapped me on the shoulder and I jumped right out of my skin."

But "Fifty Mission Cap" is made up of two discrete parts. Through the years, fans have tried to understand the connection between Bill Barilko and a pilot's cap. And although Gord Downie once wrote, "It's better for us if you don't understand" (in the lyrics to "Locked in the Trunk of a Car"), he explains that, although the segments of "Fifty Mission Cap" may appear mutually exclusive, they do in fact have a connection. "They were two disparate parts that were soldered together. Two disparate parts that, to me, connect. The idea of the 'fifty mission cap' occurred to me after a visit to the Smithsonian National Air and Space Museum in Washington, D.C. It was mentioned in an exhibit of wartime artifacts. There was an explanation about its significance but a lot of it evaporated away from me. I was left with the idea of a fifty mission cap being this thing that would denote accomplishment, that would denote experience, that would denote success — all things that a hockey player would aspire to."

Dr. Roger G. Miller, a historian at the Center for Air Force History in Washington, D.C., provides the answer to the most frequently asked question in rock music. "A 'fifty mission cap' was interchangeably known as a 'fifty mission crush' and was the name given a service dress cap worn by World War II fighter pilots. The stiffening ring was removed to allow headphones to be worn over the top of the cap. It altered the cap to look crushed and battered, giving it a distinctive profile. Although the 'fifty mission cap' was steeped in tradition, it was frowned upon by superiors because it was technically out of uniform, but you could wear one if you'd paid your dues and proven yourself worthy by returning from a number of successful missions.

"At one time, 50 was the number of missions one had to fly before being rotated out of the combat theatre, but that number was later reduced. This tradition was started by the Eighth Air Force flying personnel — the Mighty Eighth out of Savannah, Georgia — who became one of the premier air groups to fly during the Second World War. The 'fifty mission cap' separated the fledgling from the battle-hardened survivor who had earned the right to wear it."

Lyrical influences come from everywhere, and both the Barilko legend and the World War II service cap stuck with Gord Downie as he developed the song that became "Fifty Mission Cap." "The hockey card definitely got it going. The lines that were there just connected and we set it to music," he explains. "We were at [drummer] Johnny Fay's folks' place and we had the furniture pushed away in his dining room when we did it for the first time."

Gord Sinclair adds, "They were away on vacation. This was back in the days when we were, like most young bands, a garage band and finding a place to play was always of paramount concern."

"It was an odd song in that it's sort of narrative; there's no rhyming, there's no attempt to rhyme," says Downie. "It was among other songs like it that I was trying at the time. 'Nautical Disaster' — songs like that happened very quickly. It's all there and you set it to music. It has its own certain kind of rhythm."

Gord Sinclair also recalls the writing of "Fifty Mission Cap." "That was a riff that I had had for a while and brought to the guys. As we were jamming, Gord [Downie] sort of grabbed the lyrics almost verbatim from the card right off the bat. The song was formed from there. It's kind of the way we've always worked — any guy in the group can bring in a musical idea, then the five of us will start playing it together. Then, Gord started piecing in words and melody on top of it. This one came together really quickly because Gord had the reference material and it was such a cool story, and the riff was pretty cool and it started falling into place. As we continued to write stuff, it was one of the songs that it became obvious was going to be on the record."

"We monkeyed around with it a little bit," Sinclair reveals. "Arrangement-wise, we wrote a bridge for it a little later. The long and the short of it: it was a quintessential Hip tune in its creation."

The bassist did not know anything about Barilko before his partner presented the lyrics that day. "We always thought it was such an amazing story," states Sinclair. "The way Bill Barilko's life played out was almost like a made-for-TV kind of story. Here was a story that we in the group weren't even familiar with, and it's really quite a heroic kind of thing and a real human tragedy at the same time. It made great fodder for a song."

The band realized they had created something very special. "We knew pretty much right away that it was special because of the ease with which it came together and how quickly we all got behind it as a song," admits Sinclair. "We determine whether something's going to be worth pursuing by how much fun it is to play right off the bat and how quickly it comes together. Certainly the attention it's gotten afterwards and the radio airplay and the fact it seems to occupy such a special place for so many people bears out the fact this was a special song."

The Tragically Hip recorded "Fifty Mission Cap" and the rest of the *Fully Completely* album during July 1992 with producer Chris Tsangarides at Battery Studios, just off Oxford Street in the centre of London, England. The album was released in October 1992.

Joey Scoleri, now the vice president of Rock Promotion at Hollywood Records in California, was the music director and, as "Joey Vendetta," a radio personality at Toronto station Q107 at the time "Fifty Mission Cap" was delivered to his office. "We had close ties to The Hip and I remember hearing that the band had written a song about the Toronto Maple Leafs," Scoleri recalls. "I definitely remember the first time I heard the song. It was such a great rock song and we put it on the air right away."

"Who else but The Tragically Hip could record a song about a dead hockey player? It's only fitting that such an indigenously Canadian band could record such an indigenously Canadian song. I'm a Leaf freak, and I knew Barilko's name, but didn't know the story," mentions Scoleri.

"That was the whole Dougie Gilmour era in Toronto, too," he adds. "The band's from Kingston, Gilmour's from Kingston, I mean, it all came together so unwittingly and for a few years, 'Fifty Mission Cap' became the unofficial theme song of the Toronto Maple Leafs."

🍁 🍁 🍁

Initially, Anne Klisanich was circumspect about the song. "My sons, Frank and Barry, told me that a song had been written about Billy. I thought they were joking. They said it was called 'Fifty Mission Cap.' I said, 'What's that got to do with Billy?' I couldn't figure out what that had to do with hockey. I couldn't believe it when somebody told me there was a song about my brother."

"When I did hear it, I was a bit shocked at first to think that someone would write a song about somebody who died so tragically, but the more I listened to it, there was a lot of thought put into it," Barilko's sister admits. "It was heartwarming to know that people were interested in Bill's life story."

For several years, someone was continually telling Anne Klisanich about "Fifty Mission Cap," the paean to her brother's legacy. Through the song, a whole new generation was introduced to the legend of Bill Barilko, and Anne was pleased that her brother's story endured. "It's amazing how many conversations would start with, 'You know Bill Barilko, don't you?' They'd say 'No,' but then somebody would say, 'You know that song "Fifty Mission Cap" by The Tragically Hip? And they'd be excited about the song and the group who sang it so well in the language they knew," beams Anne.

"My boys said, 'Mother, you should meet the guys in The Tragically Hip.' I said, 'Y'know, I probably should,' but any time they were performing it wasn't easy for me to touch base with them." Most girls who want to meet the band have other ideas on their minds, but 68-year-old Anne resolved to meet the boys to personally thank them for paying tribute to the brother she loved so dearly.

Noting that The Hip would be performing at the Hershey Centre in Mississauga, Ontario, on February 19, 1999, Anne Klisanich made plans to pay a visit. "Because we live in Mississauga, I figured it'd be a good opportunity. I went to the box office at the Hershey Centre and asked if it would be possible for me to meet The Tragically Hip. I said, 'These boys wrote a song about my brother. It's called "Fifty Mission Cap" and my brother's name is Bill Barilko.' She said, 'Yeah, sure. Anybody could tell me that.' I said, 'I'll show you my birth certificate.' She said, 'Nope, I'm sorry. We get too many people telling us stories in order to meet the performers.' So I said, 'Well, if I write them a note, would you take it to their dressing room?' She said, 'Well, I guess so.'"

The woman at the box office gave Anne's note to a manager, who promised to relay it to the band. Anne waited. And waited. Fifteen minutes later, the manager motioned to Anne and said, "They'd like to meet you. Follow me." Anne punctuates the story with, "The girl at the box office couldn't believe it. She just said, 'Wow!'"

"I went to the dressing room and got hugs from the band," says the effervescent Anne. "I noticed that they were wearing hockey jerseys and I saw all these hockey sticks in their dressing room. I asked, 'What are you boys doing with all this hockey stuff?' They said, 'We had a game this afternoon. We like performing in arenas because we can have a game before our show.'"

"I asked them if I could have my picture taken with them, and we did that," Anne giggles. "Then they asked if I'd like to stay for the show, but I said, 'No, I can't. We're leaving for Florida in a couple of days and I have quite a bit of packing to do.' I said, 'This is such a thrill for me to meet you boys!' They autographed a picture for me, too. It was my granddaughter Caroline's 13th birthday and I could hardly wait to get home and tell them about my evening with The Tragically Hip!"

Gord Sinclair remembers that the evening was significant for the band, too. "It was awesome. She's a wonderful person and she really brought the whole thing home for us in terms of our association with Bill Barilko. It made it way more significant and memorable to us as a group when we met Anne in Mississauga."

🍁 🍁 🍁

Although that performance had a magical element for Anne Klisanich, fans still marvel at the show on February 10, 1995, when The Tragically Hip stirred the soul of Bill Barilko in their first appearance at Maple Leaf Gardens. As the unmistakable opening chords to "Fifty Mission Cap" started, the house lights in Maple Leaf Gardens were illuminated and the banner commemorating Bill Barilko's greatest feat shimmied above the crowd, adding an eerie poignancy to the lyrics.

John Sakamoto, then a pop music critic with the *Toronto Sun*, described the uncanny quality of the performance: "At every Tragically Hip concert I've ever been to, there's always been that one instant in which a bunch of seemingly unrelated things rush together into a mind-boggling confluence, and you get to experience The Moment. Last night, The Moment came six songs in during 'Fifty Mission Cap.'

"When Gord Downie got to the line, 'The last goal he ever scored, won the Leafs the Cup,' 14,500 delirious fans looked up, pointed at the 1951 Stanley Cup banner hanging from the ceiling of the very building in which Barilko scored the goal in question and let out a cheer that was probably as loud as the one that greeted Barilko's feat. That was my Moment, but you could've picked a dozen others."

Band member Gord Sinclair realized The Moment from the stage. "As a kid growing up, your whole orientation hockey-wise, rock-band-wise, culture-wise, was towards this legendary mecca, Maple Leaf Gardens. The first time you get a chance to walk into the venerable old barn, sold out, performing in front of your crowd, it really doesn't get much better than that. Mom and Dad are out at the show — it's a big deal. Everyone since the 1930s has gone to that venue to see a significant event, and then all of a sudden, there you are, and *you* are the event in that same building. It was huge! Then you tie it in with what we had written about in the song and how it had clearly gathered the interest and imagination of our fans and maybe helped to give Bill his due, historically, as the hero that he was," says Sinclair. "That was part of what made an incredible night even more incredible."

Maple Leaf Sports and Entertainment commemorated the 50th anniversary of Barilko's Stanley Cup–winning goal before the May 1, 2001, contest between the Leafs and the New Jersey Devils. With everyone in attendance at the Air Canada Centre receiving a Maple Leaf pin emblazoned with Barilko's Number 5, Bill's sister Anne was joined at centre ice by several members of the Stanley Cup–winning Toronto team from 1951: Danny Lewicki, Fleming MacKell, Johnny McCormack, Gus Mortson, Sid Smith and Harry Watson. Gord Downie, Gord Sinclair, Robby Baker and Johnny Fay of The Tragically Hip (Paul Langlois was absent) presented both Anne and former Leafs captain Sid Smith with a magnificent award — a framed handwritten copy of the lyrics to "Fifty Mission Cap" signed by each of the five members of The Tragically Hip.

Radio stations around the world continue to unwittingly honour Bill Barilko by playing "Fifty Mission Cap." In arenas across North America, the song continues to be played during play stoppages. "Fifty Mission Cap" has become synonymous with the passion of hockey and has single-handedly ensured that Bill Barilko's profile remains high more than 50 years after his tragic disappearance.

Gord Downie, who propelled the legacy, declared, "There must be something in Bill Barilko that people relate to. We're all united in tragedy. It's a Canadian story, a tragedy really of someone cut down in his prime. It's as much a story of unfulfilled potential as it is hockey."

> *Bill Barilko disappeared that summer. He was on a*
> * fishing trip.*
> *The last goal he ever scored won the Leafs the Cup.*
> *They didn't win another 'til 1962, the year he was*
> * discovered.*
> *I stole this from a hockey card, I keep tucked up under*
> *My fifty mission cap.*

Bill Barilko died that August day back in 1951. For a new generation, to whom names like Turk and Teeder hold little relevance, The Tragically Hip brought the legacy of "Bashin' Bill" Barilko back to life.

CHAPTER
26

Alex

Born on February 4, 1926, Alexander Barilko was the first of three children born to Faye and Steve Barilko. "Bill had the blue eyes and the blond hair while Alex had dark hair and dark eyes," states their sister Anne. "Both were very handsome. Both were very likable, too. We were taught manners and to respect our elders. That was our upbringing."

Alex was very popular within the neighbourhood, and one of his longest-standing friends was his high-school chum and future NHL star Allan Stanley. "One day, Alex asked, 'Mom, can I invite Allan Stanley over for dinner?' My mother said, 'Yes, but what I make?' Alex said, 'Allan likes spaghetti, and Mom, you make the best spaghetti.' Allan often came for dinner at our house and we always had spaghetti."

"Allan and his family lived on Snob Hill," Anne laughs. "That's what we called the more affluent area of Timmins. Allan's father was the fire chief in Timmins. Alex would want certain things, but being of modest means, my mother would say, 'Alex, we no have money like Stanleys. No forget, Allan's father fire chief.' Our family couldn't keep up with the Joneses back then," shrugs Anne.

Alex was very good in school, unlike his younger brother who was easily distracted and struggled badly. Faye lovingly called her oldest "Smart Alex," but his friends all called him "Bark."

"When we both went to Timmins High and Vocational School, I used to see him in the hallway — this was Grade 12 for him," smiles his sister, Anne. "I was so proud to see my older brother in the hallway, and besides, all the girls were going ga-ga over him. He was a good-looking boy, but he was also very good in so many sports.

"One day, Mother asked me, 'You see Alex in school?' I said, 'Yes, all the time, Mom. Why?' She said, 'I wonder. I no think he go to school.' I said, 'Oh, yeah, he's there,' but that gave me reason to think.

I thought, 'Y'know, I haven't seen Alex for a couple of weeks.' So then I made a point of looking for my brother at school — I never saw him between classes when we were going from one classroom to another. So when Alex came home from school that day, I said, 'Alex, I haven't seen you at school lately. Mother asked me a couple of weeks ago if I ever saw you at school and I lied and told her I did.' He said, 'Anne, I haven't been to school for four weeks.' 'Oh my God, Alex, you're going to get in trouble,' I said. He replied, 'Don't you say anything. I'll handle it in my own way.' I said, 'Okay, but I better not get into trouble because of you!'"

Anne continues: "We were having our lunch at the kitchen table one day. Billy was working driving trucks, so it was just Alex and me. We always listened to 'The Happy Gang' on the radio. They were on CKGB at 10 after 12 every weekday. All of a sudden, there was a knock at the door. There stood Mr. Rose, the principal from the high school. I could just see Alex — he turned white as a ghost. My mother invited Mr. Rose in. The principal said, 'Mrs. Barilko, I'm Mr. Rose. I'm the principal at the Timmins High School. Alex hasn't been to school for a few weeks and we just want to see if there was anything wrong.' She said, 'My Alex go school. I send him to school every day.'

"Mr. Rose stepped into the house and said, 'Oh, hi Alex. Good to see you. I'm glad you're not sick.' That's when Mother found out that Alex had been missing school.

"I got a tongue-lashing," comments Anne. "Then Mother said, 'Alex, what you do? You get up every morning, get dressed, you go school, you come home for lunch, you go back school?' Alex nodded. She said, 'Enough. We work hard and do our best raise you and do right things. You no want education — you be sorry one day! Go get job! What you do every day when you supposed to be at the school?'

"Alex said, 'Mom, I went to the pool room.' He shot pool, and if he made 10 cents or 25 cents, he'd go to the movies. Unfortunately Alex didn't graduate from Grade 12," Anne finishes.

Alex was a gifted athlete from the time he was young. Although neither Steve nor Faye was athletically inclined, all three of their children excelled in sports. Alex was likely the most versatile of the three, and was known around the Porcupine for playing baseball, rugby and track and field as well as for his hockey exploits. "In his late teens, Alex played baseball for the McIntyre Mine," Anne mentions. "If you played baseball for the McIntyre Mine, you were guaranteed a summer job working on the garden crew at McIntyre Park, a beautiful park in Timmins. My husband did the same thing. That's how Emil knew my brother." Alex later played ball in the Northern Ontario Senior League, and was so good that he received an invitation to try out with the Pittsburgh Pirates of baseball's National League in April 1948.

Later, Alex's love of sports earned him a job at the local radio station. "Because our name was Barilko, the management at CKGB thought it sounded too foreign, so they told him, 'On the air, your name is going to be Alex Barton,'" laughs his sister.

Although considered by many locals to be a better prospect than his younger brother, it was Bill who reached the National Hockey League and not Alex. Both Barilko boys were aggressive defencemen, but Alex was acknowledged as being a better skater. In 1941–42, Alex played for the Holman Pluggers. The next year, with Bill tagging along as a stickboy and occasional practice goaltender, Alex and the Pluggers were Ontario's juvenile champions. In 1943–44, "Barks" played with both the Army cadets and with Hollinger Seniors, a strong team sponsored by the local Hollinger Mines.

In 1944–45, Alex signed a C Form and became the property of the Detroit Red Wings, who sent him to what is now part of Cambridge, Ontario, to play with their junior affiliate, the Galt Red Wings. The Red Wings helped Alex line up a job with Ingersoll-Rand, a worldwide supplier of tools. While working in the machine shop, Alex lost the index finger on his right hand. Although his tenure with Galt ended in a clash with coach Al Murray over his injury, the tenacious Barilko caught on with the Brantford Lions, an unaffiliated junior squad of which he was named captain. The *Stratford Beacon-Herald* reported, "His blocking has been strong. He looks like the best defenceman in the league."

Alex returned to Timmins in 1945–46 and finished his junior eligibility playing with the Northern Ontario Hockey Association's Porcupine Combines.

In 1946–47, Alex made the pilgrimage to the west coast, where he joined the Oakland Oaks of the Pacific Coast Hockey League. There was an exodus of hockey talent from northern Ontario to the PCHL that season, including former Holman Pluggers teammates Bill Curik (Tacoma); Bill Adamo, Roy McKay and George Defelice (San Francisco); and Eric Prentice (Hollywood). Alex's kid brother, "Bashin' Bill," also played for Hollywood. Alex collected nine goals and 11 assists in 1946–47 and led the PCHL with 167 minutes in penalties.

For the next campaign, Alex joined the Valleyfield Braves of the Quebec Senior Hockey League. In a league acknowledged as being close in calibre to the NHL, Barilko proved himself again. His single goal and 20 assists gave him a respectable 21 points, while his 107 penalty minutes placed him second to legendary bad boy Jimmy Orlando.

Alex strove desperately to reach the NHL, and younger brother Bill helped by securing him a tryout with the Toronto Marlboros of the Ontario Hockey Association's senior loop. Alex earned a spot on the Senior Dukes' defence, joining a terrific lineup that included Doug Harvey's brother Howie in goal (he was eventually forced to leave hockey due to allergies), Alex Davidson (Leaf scout Bob Davidson's brother), who managed the team and played defence, and a group whose names will be familiar to Maple Leafs fans: George Armstrong, Flash Hollett, Al Buchanan, Johnny McCormack, Ray Hannigan, Chuck Blair, Johnny McLellan and Bill Johnson (a former Leaf and the father of Leaf alumnus Trevor Johansen). Hannigan was from Schumacher, while Blair and McLellan hailed from South Porcupine.

The Senior Marlies were coached by Hall of Famer Joe Primeau, and they won the J. Ross Robertson Cup as Ontario's senior champions in 1948–49, later defeating the North Bay Hawks and Sydney Millionaires in order to meet the Ottawa Senators of the Quebec Senior Hockey League for the Bolton Cup — emblematic of the senior championship of eastern Canada — and the opportunity to challenge for the Allan Cup. The Senators defeated Toronto, and proceeded to win the Allan Cup.

In 1949–50, with a roster virtually identical to that of the year before, the Senior Marlboros won the Allan Cup. But there was one name conspicuous by its absence — that of Alex Barilko.

Alex had failed to stay on with the Marlies for a second season. In 1949–50, while helping run Barilko Brothers Appliances, Alex played in the Toronto Hockey League's major series, often called the Mercantile League. Babe Gresko, Bill's former teammate with the Hollywood Wolves, remembers Alex from that era. "We had a full house at Varsity Arena every Wednesday and Saturday. I played for People's Credit Jewellers one year and West York Motors the next. Alex Barilko played for People's Credit Jewellers a year or two after I quit. I got a concussion when I was hit in the head by one of my own players at a face-off so I figured I should pack it in."

Barilko leapt to the Maritime League to start the 1950–51 season, but by December 1950 had been recruited by the struggling Sherbrooke Saints of the Quebec Senior league. The Saints had been crowned league champions the year before, but had fallen back significantly, and they looked to Alex's experience and leadership to solidify their defence. In fact, the aging team featured a number of former NHLers in addition to Alex — Cliff Goupille and Bob Fillion included — but in spite of Barilko's aggressive stance on the blue line, the Saints finished sixth in the seven-team circuit.

The Senior Marlboros would be as close to the National Hockey League as Alex Barilko was to get as a player. He played in a single preseason exhibition contest with the Toronto Maple Leafs, facing his brother on the opposite side of the ice, but that was as near the big time as he got. Alex chased the brass ring but was never quite able to grasp it. Teammates and foes alike called Alex Barilko a fierce competitor who asked for no quarter and certainly gave none. But for whatever reason or combination of reasons, Alex never played in the NHL. Whether Alex's missing finger played any role, or perhaps his competitive and at times combative nature, it's difficult to surmise. After hanging up his skates, Alex took up residence in Quebec, and was living there when Bill disappeared along with Dr. Henry Hudson.

Alex retired from playing, but not from hockey. He moved into officiating, hoping that path would lead to the NHL. His first assignments were in the Quebec Senior Hockey League, the circuit in which he had most recently played.

Faye Barilko, Alex's mother, had refused to watch another hockey game after the April 21, 1951, contest that proved to be Bill's last, but during December 1954, she acquiesced and attended a game Alex was refereeing.

Although officiating was the path Alex hoped to follow in order to reach the big time, he needed to finance his dream, and in November 1955 he was hired as a sales representative in the Montreal region for Melcher's Distillery. Later, Gaston Garant remembers Alex working with him. "Alex was working for the company I was with, Schenley Distilleries in Montreal, before I was promoted to vice president of sales," Bill's friend recalls.

Alex refereed a series of games at the Montreal Forum between the visiting Moscow Dynamo and the Ottawa-Hull Junior Canadiens on December 1, 1957, followed by the Kingston CKLCs on December 3 in Kingston and the Junior Canadiens again in Ottawa on the fifth. Bob Lebel, president of the Canadian Amateur Hockey Association, stated, "It's a happy coincidence that Barilko, of Ukrainian descent, speaks Russian."

While refereeing a Quebec Hockey League contest on January 18, 1959, between the Trois-Rivières Lions and the Chicoutimi Saugenéens, a rubber overshoe thrown by an overzealous fan struck Alex, knocking him backwards to the ice. Alex suffered a concussion when his head hit the ice. The league president called the game off after Barilko was unable to return for the third period.

Alex was a linesman for two preseason exhibition games at the Montreal Forum in 1957, but that was as much of a taste of the NHL as Alex would enjoy as an official.

While working at the distillery, Alex earned additional money scouting eastern Canada for the New York Rangers between 1965 and 1973. That summer, Barilko was hired as a scout for the St. Louis Blues.

Although hockey had been a lifelong passion and focus for the eldest Barilko sibling, Alex found happiness in another form while playing with the Sherbrooke Saints. He met Fern Dubé. "She was a lovely girl from Rimouski," grins Anne. On March 21, 1953, Alexander Barilko married Fernande Dubé in Sherbrooke. "My mother, my husband Emil and I drove to the wedding," Anne smiles. "When they got married, she spoke very little English, although as the years went by her English improved and Alex's French improved substantially. Fern was a delightful lady and we loved her dearly."

The couple had no children, but Alex had a godchild he adored as well as Anne's two boys, whom he clearly loved. "We visited them in Sherbrooke and they visited us in Ontario," Anne recalls fondly. "They had two adorable poodle dogs that they treated like children," laughs Anne.

During May 1977, Alex Barilko died in Montreal at the age of 51. He had struggled with depression the last several years of his life. His widow, Fern, passed away in April 1982. She was 58 years old.

The fact that his brother was an NHL star had been a source of great pride to Alex. He was fiercely loyal and protective of Bill, and during his brother's five years in Toronto, Alex was regularly included in social outings with the Maple Leafs whenever he was in town. "There was certainly no jealousy towards Bill," states the boys' sister, Anne. "Bill and Alex were very good friends as well as brothers. They had their own set of friends, but they respected and cared for each other. Alex was never envious of Bill; he was so proud of his brother and let him know regularly. They were very close."

CHAPTER
27

Number 5

To followers of hockey in general, and the Toronto Maple Leafs in particular, Bill Barilko and the number five have become synonymous through the years. The irony is that Barilko sported a blue and white sweater with Number 5 on the back for just one season: 1950–51.

Before the National Hockey League was founded in 1917, several hockey leagues had experimented with players wearing numbers to help patrons in the stands identify them. The National Hockey Association, the NHL's immediate forerunner, had used numbers worn on an armband, but this idea proved cumbersome. When the Patrick brothers, Frank and Lester, were organizing their professional hockey league in the west, they were challenged by the complaints of fans over the difficulty in telling players apart. The brothers discussed the matter with their father, Joe, who leafed through a copy of a British magazine, *London Illustrated*, and pointed to a photograph of a British harrier. These long-distance runners were identified by large numbers pinned to the back of their shirts. When the Pacific Coast Hockey Association debuted on January 3, 1912, players wore numbers on the back of their sweaters, a practice that was quickly embraced by virtually every hockey league in North America.

Eventually, the numbering of players' sweaters took on a larger role than merely letting fans identify players on the ice by following the numbers in a program. As leagues grew and built legacies, numbers grew to play significant roles in the hierarchy of teams. Early in the history of the National Hockey League, teams employed anywhere from 11 to 15 players. Generally, a team's sole goaltender wore Number 1; the defencemen wore 2 and 3, and the primary forward line got 4, 5 and 6. Spare players got the higher numbers. Eventually, as the idea of rotating multiple forward lines and defence pairings gained currency,

251

the blueliners tended to wear 2 through 5, while the forwards occupied the higher ranks. And gradually, as the game developed a wider following and stars began to emerge, certain numbers took on added significance. Number 9, for example, came to be known as a sweater number worn by some of the finest players ever to step onto an NHL ice surface: Charlie Conacher and Ted Kennedy in Toronto, Maurice Richard in Montreal, Gordie Howe in Detroit, Andy Bathgate in New York and Bobby Hull in Chicago.

As rosters grew, sweater numbers took on another level of significance, one through which an educated observer might discern a team's pecking order. Through the 1950s, NHL teams travelled exclusively by rail. And although jet travel crept into the picture in the late '50s and early '60s, it didn't become a necessity until the league expanded to 12 teams, including a pair on the Pacific coast, in 1967. In the days of train transport, a team might rush from Maple Leaf Gardens to Toronto's Union Station after a Saturday night game in order to make it to the next town for a Sunday night contest, and sleeping berths were distributed according to a player's uniform number. The highly sought-after lower bunks went to players with lower numbers, leaving the upper berths to those wearing higher double digits. As a result, veterans traditionally wore lower numbers while rookies and younger players were assigned higher sweater numbers.

When Bill Barilko was first summoned to Toronto from Hollywood and played his first game on February 6, 1947, he was handed a Toronto Maple Leafs sweater bearing the Number 21. Earlier that season, Harry Taylor had worn the number, but he played in only nine games for Toronto before being loaned to the Providence Reds of the American Hockey League. Number 5 belonged at that time to veteran Nick Metz.

In 1947–48, Metz again wore 5, while Barilko continued to wear Number 21. Years after Barilko's death, a pair of notable Leafs defencemen would make their names wearing Number 21: Bobby Baun in the 1950s, '60s and early '70s, and Borje Salming throughout the '70s and into the early 1980s.

When Wally Stanowski was traded to the New York Rangers in April 1948, his Number 3 became available and Gus Mortson was given the sweater, leaving his Number 19 vacant. In 1948–49, Bill switched from 21 to 19, while his old sweater was adopted by Bobby Dawes when he joined the team midway through the season. Meantime, Nick Metz retired and his Number 5 was given to Garth Boesch, who had worn 18 to that point in his NHL career.

In 1949–50, Boesch continued wearing 5 while Barilko wore 19 again. After Boesch retired to farm full-time before the 1950–51 season, Bill Barilko was able to secure the Number 5 by which he has become best known. Hugh Bolton, an occasional defensive replacement for the

Leafs, wore Bill's old Number 19. Ironically, there was a point in February 1951 when Barilko was struggling on the ice and strongly considered changing his sweater number from 5 to whatever else was then available.

Barilko was set to wear Number 5 again in 1951–52, and even after his disappearance the sweater remained in his dressing-room stall in hopes he would return to wear it. After it became clear he was gone without a trace, it was decided that no one would again wear Number 5 as a Toronto Maple Leaf.

For more than four decades that convention was respected, but the number was only officially retired by the Leafs on October 17, 1992. That night, the Number 6 worn by Irvine "Ace" Bailey was also officially retired. Bailey had suffered a career-ending head injury in a game against the Boston Bruins on December 12, 1933, an accident that nearly cost Bailey his life. The number remained off-limits until October 13, 1968, when Bailey asked Leafs management to assign Ron Ellis his number. "It was an honour and privilege to be asked to wear the Number 6 by Mr. Bailey, and I treasured the opportunity and made certain I always did both him and his number proud," says Ellis.

After Ron Ellis played his final game on January 14, 1981, the Number 6 was never again given to a Toronto Maple Leaf.

The 1992 ceremony had originally been scheduled for the first of April that year, but a players' strike had shut down the league for 10 days beginning on March 30. Sadly, Ace Bailey was admitted to the hospital on April 1, having suffered a stroke, and he died on April 7 at the age of 88. He never got to see his sweater raised to the rafters in celebration of its retirement.

In the pregame ceremony at Maple Leaf Gardens that night, Ace Bailey's daughter Joyce was joined on the red carpet by Ron Ellis to witness the permanent retirement of Number 6. Also present at centre ice was Bill Barilko's sister, Anne Klisanich, joined by Bill's former teammate and captain Ted Kennedy, as Bill's Number 5 was also officially retired. With the assistance of Maple Leafs captain Wendel Clark, both banners were raised to the rafters of Maple Leaf Gardens. When the team moved to the Air Canada Centre, new banners were commissioned, bearing the two players' numbers and portraits. These hang from the rafters in front of the press box for all to see.

"It was a great honour for me to take part in this wonderful ceremony," says Anne Klisanich. "That was one of the greatest moments of my life." Accompanying Anne and Teeder were Anne's son Frank, his wife, Chris, and their three children, John, Michael and Caroline. Anne's younger son, Barry, was there, too. "My husband Emil, our family and I were treated royally by [Leafs chairman Steve] Stavro and the Toronto Maple Leafs. It was a very special night, although it was melancholy as well. Bill had a magic moment followed by a tragic moment. Retiring his number was very special. It was a very emotional evening."

The Numbers 5 and 6 are the only two to be retired by the Toronto Maple Leafs. In 1993–94, the team began a unique practice of recognizing players who had made significant contributions to the franchise by placing their numbers and images on a banner and raising it to the rafters in an official ceremony, but allowing the number to remain in circulation. During the season in which the player is honoured, the current Leafs player wearing the number wears a special commemorative patch, with the honoured player's name embroidered on it, on the shoulder of his jersey.

On October 3, 1993, Ted Kennedy's Number 9 and the Number 10 worn by Syl Apps were honoured. The Number 1, commemorating the performances of Turk Broda and Johnny Bower, was honoured on March 11, 1995. On November 21, 1995, the Number 7 worn by Leafs defence greats King Clancy and Tim Horton was commemorated in a special ceremony. Numbers 9 and 10 were again raised to the rafters, this time to honour Charlie Conacher and George Armstrong, respectively, on February 28, 1998. Most recently, the Number 27 was honoured twice: for Frank Mahovlich on October 3, 2001, and for Darryl Sittler on February 8, 2003.

Bill Barilko was further honoured on May 1, 2001, in a ceremony to commemorate the 50th anniversary of his 1951 Stanley Cup–winning goal. Anne Klisanich remembers how gratified she was that her brother's achievement was to be remembered. "In my heart, it was one more moment for me to cherish. It was a magical night and I was so proud to be part of it. These lovely tributes have made my life so interesting because of what my brother achieved in such a short period of playing hockey for the Toronto Maple Leafs." Although the historic game was played on April 21, 1951, the anniversary celebration was held prior to a playoff game against the New Jersey Devils on May 1, 2001. On hand were Robby Baker, Gord Downie, Johnny Fay and Gord Sinclair of The Tragically Hip, who had paid tribute to Barilko in their song "Fifty Mission Cap," as well as several teammates from the 1951 Leafs squad: Cal Gardner, Bob Hassard, Danny Lewicki, Fleming MacKell, Johnny McCormack, Gus Mortson, Sid Smith and Harry Watson. Every ticket holder received a commemorative pin with Barilko's Number 5 surrounded by a blue maple leaf. As a special added tribute, Anne received an extraordinary plaque bearing Gord Downie's handwritten lyrics to "Fifty Mission Cap."

"Mother always said, 'Bill is going to be in the limelight again,' and she was right," says Anne in disbelief. "Bill's name keeps coming up; far more than I ever dreamed."

CHAPTER 28

BB 16

Every spring, most hockey teams adopt a slogan to help focus and inspire both themselves and their fans in their drive to win the Stanley Cup. In 1999, the Dallas Stars borrowed the title from the Metallica song, "Nothing Else Matters." In 2001, Raymond Bourque and the Colorado Avalanche unveiled "Mission 16W," referring to the 16 wins — or Ws — the team would need to rack up to win the Cup. That mission was accomplished.

In 2004, the Toronto Maple Leafs faced the Ottawa Senators in the first round of the Stanley Cup playoffs. After game three, Darcy Tucker stood in the Leafs' dressing room at the Corel Centre in Ottawa, his arms folded over his chest. He was addressing a scrum of reporters. With microphones and recorders thrust in front of him, Tucker was every inch the warrior, casually pointing to a sizable welt under his right eye. His left eye sported a good-sized bruise, too.

Tucker was wearing a navy baseball cap embroidered with the legend "BB 16." One of the reporters asked the significance of the navy hat. Tucker explained that he'd had the hats made for his teammates. It was easy to guess that the 16 indicated the number of playoff victories needed to win the Stanley Cup. But what about "BB"? Did it stand for "Bruise Brothers"? Or perhaps Bryan Berard, whose eye was injured during a Toronto-Ottawa series a few years before? Or maybe Bobby Baun's inspiring overtime goal in the 1964 finals, scored on a broken bone?

In fact, it was revealed that "BB 16" was a tribute to the tragic Leafs hero — Bill Barilko.

✳ ✳ ✳

The legend of Bill Barilko has dimmed occasionally through the years, but it has never been forgotten. A Northern Ontario band called the Grievous Angels, led by Charlie Angus, recorded a terrific tribute to Barilko. Later, The Tragically Hip cemented his legacy with the hit, "Fifty Mission Cap." In the spring of 2004, a cap of another sort reminded Leaf fans once again about the tragic story of Bill Barilko; the magic story of Bill Barilko.

※ ※ ※

Mel Woolsey is the president and chief executive officer of Kewl Sports in Barrie, Ontario, the company that produced the caps. "We trade-marked Kewl in 1999," he begins. "[Former Leaf] Shayne Corson and I are great friends; almost like brothers. We started the company and felt that we needed to develop a brand that was specific to the sport we love — hockey. We'd been wearing apparel from Adidas and Nike, but nothing represented hockey.

"We came up with the name over a couple beers. I'm a goaltender, and we're not known for being the sharpest knives in the drawer, so that's where I came up with the spelling," chuckles Woolsey. "Or maybe it was the 12 beers!"

The 2004 playoffs started for the Toronto Maple Leafs on April 8. A chat on April 7 between Woolsey and Tucker, who is Corson's brother-in-law, set the wheels in motion. "I suggested that the Leafs come up with their own little code that means something to the team but doesn't really tell anyone what it stands for. It would create questions and interest — 'What the heck is it?' I suggested 'WAAC–16,' for 'Win At All Costs.'" While the 16 would have been intended to indicate 16 playoff wins, it also happened that Tucker wore Number 16 for the Leafs, "and there are a few guys out there who want to whack *him*, right?"

The two continued to brainstorm. "And I finally said, 'Tuck, take a couple of hours and talk to a few of the guys and give me a call back.' This was at two o'clock Wednesday afternoon. Darcy calls me back half an hour later and says he wants to put 'BB 16' on a hat. I say, 'What's it stand for?' He tells me the story about Bill Barilko — God bless Bill and his family, but I wasn't aware of the story. But I have a co-op student working for me and he says, 'Oh yeah, I know that story.' The kid's 19 and he knows the whole story! I'm embarrassed," admits Woolsey.

In the lounge area of the Toronto Maple Leafs' dressing room hangs a framed copy of the lyrics to The Tragically Hip's "Fifty Mission Cap," handwritten by lyricist and singer Gord Downie. Each day that the Toronto Maple Leafs are at home, the lyrics resonate within each of those players who takes a moment to glance at the souvenir. And it is this chronicle of Barilko's story that inspired Darcy Tucker to choose his 1951 Stanley Cup odyssey as the theme to the Maple Leafs' 2004 quest for the Cup.

"Wednesday night, I got our embroiderer to move stuff off the machines so I could get 30 hats done for Darcy. I had to get them to him by six o'clock. I didn't get there until 6:30, but he waited for them. He took them down to the rink, gave them to the players. A few of them were on TV, and the papers found out what 'BB 16' stood for. We weren't looking at telling anyone," Mel explains.

"The media jumped all over the story. I told production to get the hats going because it was about to go crazy. The phones haven't stopped since the story came out in the papers. We went through 5,000 caps by the end of the first-round series with the Senators."

"The spring is a quiet time for our industry as far as buying goes," explains Woolsey. "We deliver our spring apparel in February. There are some reorders, plus we try to make something for the playoffs, but you never know what's going to happen." In 2003, the selling season for Toronto Maple Leafs merchandise had come to an abrupt end on April 22, when the Philadelphia Flyers knocked the team out of the playoffs with an unceremonious 6–1 spanking in game seven of the first round.

Mel Woolsey smiles as he reflects on the BB 16 phenomenon. "A week ago, I never even knew Barilko. Now, all of a sudden, in game seven against the Senators, I was sitting on my couch going, 'Come on, Bill! Let the Leafs score!'"

The Maple Leafs did eliminate the Ottawa Senators, whom many had favoured to win the Stanley Cup. It was a tough battle, with injured bodies relegated to the sidelines on both sides of the ledger, but in game seven on April 20, 2004, the Leafs pushed the rival Senators aside with a decisive 4–1 victory.

The Leafs met Philadelphia in the second round, but it seemed as though the Ottawa series had taken the spunk out of Toronto. The spirit of Bill Barilko was nowhere to be found. Early on, it became painfully obvious that the Toronto Maple Leafs were not going to get the opportunity to win 16 playoff games in 2004. After losing the first two contests, Toronto battled back to tie the series, but a 7–2 Philadelphia mauling in game five all but finished the Leafs, who limped back gamely and took game six to overtime with a pair of goals in the third period to tie the game at two.

The Toronto Maple Leafs' season, fuelled by the passion of BB 16 and a city dreaming of its first Stanley Cup celebration since 1967, ended abruptly at 7:39 of the first overtime period, as Jeremy Roenick's game and series winner dashed the hopes of a veteran team that believed it had the resources to make it across the finish line.

"I was convinced we were going to find a way to advance," said Leafs coach Pat Quinn through gritted teeth. "When you have those kinds of hopes and dreams, it seems to be devastating right now."

After the Game

In November 2002, the *Toronto Star* polled readers to determine the top sporting moments in Toronto's history. Finishing first in the *Star*'s survey was Joe Carter's dramatic home run on October 23, 1993, that gave the Toronto Blue Jays their second straight World Series championship. The Philadelphia Phillies had led 6–5 going into the ninth inning of game six. Mitch Williams, a relief pitcher known as "Wild Thing," faced Toronto's Joe Carter with two men on base and two down. With the count at two balls and two strikes, Williams kicked and delivered, and Carter connected. His blast flew over the left-field fence to give the Toronto Blue Jays an 8–6 win, and back-to-back championships.

Next on the list was Darryl Sittler's incredible 10-point evening against the Boston Bruins on February 7, 1976. The Maple Leafs' captain assisted on two goals in the first and collected a hat trick and two more assists in the second period. Informed that he was one point away from equalling the record of eight points tallied in a game — a mark set by Maurice Richard in 1944 and matched by Bert Olmstead in 1954 — Sittler decided to insert his upper plate, something he usually played without. It's a good thing — he scored three more goals in the final stanza to set a new NHL mark, a record that also banished Boston Bruins goalie Dave Reece from the NHL for good.

The third-greatest moment in Toronto's sporting history as selected by the readers of the *Toronto Star* was Bill Barilko's electrifying overtime goal against the Montreal Canadiens to secure the Stanley Cup for the Toronto Maple Leafs for the fourth time in five years. The score was knotted at two at the end of regulation time; the fifth game in a row in which a decision would be reached in overtime. At 2:53, Bill Barilko fired a backhand over the shoulder of Gerry McNeil to give his Maple Leafs the Stanley Cup championship. As we subsequently discovered, the breathtaking goal would mark both the end of the Toronto dynasty — and the end of its hero's life.

On December 18, 2003, the *National Post* announced its choice of the greatest Toronto Maple Leafs team of all time. The paper devised a system to level the playing field from era to era by projecting every team's statistics over an 82-game schedule. It was concluded that Bill Barilko's 1950–51 championship team was the greatest Maple Leafs squad of all time, earning 111 projected points (41 wins, 16 losses and

13 ties). The *Post* noted, "Behind Max Bentley and superb goaltending by Turk Broda [and Al Rollins], this squad set the team record for wins in a season; a mark that would stand for 40 years."

※ ※ ※

The saga of Bill Barilko is rife with eerie coincidences that make an extraordinary story that much more compelling.

Following Barilko's Stanley Cup–winning overtime goal, the Toronto Maple Leafs didn't win another championship until 1962 — the year Barilko's remains were finally discovered.

Bill Barilko's spot on the Maple Leafs' blue line was ultimately filled by a hard-hitting, northern Ontario boy named Tim Horton. Like Barilko, Horton died before his NHL career had ended. And Allan Stanley was a pallbearer for both men.

The blond, 24-year-old Barilko disappeared in a plane called a Fairchild 24.

Dr. Henry Hudson, who disappeared in the vicinity of James Bay in 1951, is a namesake of the British explorer Henry Hudson, who in 1611, after having wintered by the coast of James Bay, was cast adrift by his mutinous crew and was never heard from again.

Bill Barilko, the Leafs' playoff hero, was lost in the woods around the Timmins area — as was a different Bill Barilko, who disappeared in 1939. In the latter case, the massive search that ensued ultimately concluded with a much happier ending.

Finally, it is also ironic that the most successful era in the Toronto Maple Leafs' storied history ended with the loss of Bill Barilko.

※ ※ ※

Leafs captain Ted Kennedy reflects on his teammate. "He had a great career ahead of him. No question about it, he was going to be an all-star, but he needed the time — and he was getting it the last couple of years he played for us. It was a terrible, terrible tragedy that something happened to a young man like that."

Howie Meeker says, "He was always happy; always up. He was having the time of his life. He was a born hockey player and he'd be in the Hall of Fame if he'd lived."

Johnny McCormack, another teammate, states, "There were less than a hundred players in the league, so they were tough line-ups to crack. Bill came out of nowhere. He made an instant impact. Bill got in and he never looked back."

Gus Mortson was part of one of the greatest blueline foursomes in Leaf history and reveals, "Bill would be a real friend of mine if he was alive today. He was a very nice person. If something was going wrong, he didn't complain about things.

"He was a great team man. He wasn't looking for individual glory. Hockey was fun for him, and he loved the team and the guys. It was no coincidence that we won four Stanley Cups while he was with the team. He made a big contribution to those clubs."

Max Bentley, quoted in the book *Overtime, Overdue* by John Melady, described his friend, Bill Barilko. "On the ice, he was fearless, aggressive and tough. He wasn't afraid of anyone. Off the ice, he was just the opposite. He never, ever got mad, was very polite and as nice a fellow as you could ever meet."

Leafs president Conn Smythe held Bill in the highest esteem. "There was a great boy, that Barilko — so full of life and vim. He was tremendous and a great team man. And boy, did the girls go for him!"

"He and Smythe got along famously," mentions Louise (Hastings) Carley, Bill's girlfriend at the time of his disappearance. "Bill was Smythe's pet player. Bill could do no wrong in Smythe's eyes."

Allan Stanley was a childhood friend who played opposite Bill in the NHL. "He was a very fine man and I loved him. We ran together quite a bit up there in Timmins. We were always together, doing something like fishing. He was a fun-loving guy. I always felt when he came into the league that he was a diamond in the rough. He was a free spirit, had energy to burn and he had the heart of a lion.

"In the five years that he was with the Leafs, he was smoothing out into a real great hockey player. He was really something."

Another opponent, Maurice Richard, commented on Bill Barilko. "He was very tough and aggressive and his spirit and hard hitting made him a valuable player for the Leafs. He always managed to get a piece of you as you went by."

Frank Mahovlich added, "I asked Maurice Richard, 'If Bill Barilko had lived, would he have compared to all-stars?' He said, 'Oh, sure.'"

Carlo Cattarello Jr. was mascot for the Timmins Holman Pluggers, and later had a fine hockey career himself at Michigan Tech. "Just the other day, my sister brought a friend from Toronto up to Timmins. He is a big Leafs fan and he wanted to go see Bill's tombstone. It's amazing. In Timmins, you hear about Bill Barilko all the time. If any conversation starts about hockey, it's guaranteed that Bill Barilko's name will come up. It's sad; he probably would have had a sensational career."

Broadcaster Harry Neale had the opportunity to watch Bill Barilko play, and later was a defenceman in the Maple Leaf system himself. "We came to Toronto from Sarnia in 1947 or '48. I went to three or four Leaf games a year. I was a defenceman, so I enjoyed watching Jimmy Thomson play and I always liked Gus Mortson. But Bill Barilko was one of those players who stood out. He was a colourful kind of player. He was belligerent; he was noticeable. Jimmy Thomson did a great job staying at home and doing his work and not making many mistakes. Barilko was more rambunctious and was a chance-taker.

"He was a guy with movie star looks who was well known for his spectacular hits. Either he hammered somebody with a check or he led a rush but he did it with some flair."

Nina Weseluck, Bill's cousin, always appreciated him both as a player and as a person. "Even though Bill was in the big league, he always had time for us. He always had a great big smile on his face. He was so warm and loving; it would just come out in his eyes and what he did. He really wasn't 'Bashing Bill,' he was 'Beautiful Bill.' He was so down to earth. He really cared about people. He was a beautiful man."

※ ※ ※

"I'm so proud of what my brother achieved during such a short hockey career," states his sister, Anne. "My mother always said, 'Billy's goal going to be famous again.' I thought, 'Why would that goal be popular again?' But you know something?" she adds, shaking her head in wonder. "She was right."

Faye Barilko uttered a prophetic statement. More than 50 years after her son's tragic disappearance, his star arguably shines even brighter than it did when he manned the blue line for the Toronto Maple Leafs.

But Faye often asked why her grandchildren didn't talk about Bill. "Why Frankie and Barry no talk about Billy? Why? Why they no proud of their Uncle Bill?" What Faye neglected to take into account was that Frank was but two months old when his uncle disappeared, while Barry had yet to arrive. Neither knew their Uncle Bill, but that didn't mean they weren't aware of his accomplishments. And through the years, they proved unconditionally their pride for Bill Barilko.

"Both Frank and Barry did presentations on their Uncle Bill during their public school years," says Anne. But the legacy extends further yet, to another generation entirely: Frank's three children. "John, who was born in 1978, was just 11 years old when he presented Bill's story in the finals of a public-speaking contest at Homelands Senior Public School in Mississauga. Michael, who was born in 1983, was in the finals of a public-speaking contest held in Palgrave, Ontario. He was only 12 and spoke about his great-uncle, Bill Barilko. And Caroline, who was born in 1986, arranged a display of memorabilia about Bill when she was nine. The theme was 'A Collection of Collections' and was held at Sawmill Valley Public School in Mississauga." Anne hesitates for a moment as a tear trickles down her cheek. "Wouldn't Baba be proud of her grandchildren and great-grandchildren?

※ ※ ※

The incredible story of Bill Barilko has taken on a life all its own. The boy from northern Ontario whose skating was so poor that he couldn't play on the local juvenile team overcame his shortcomings and joined the team of his — and almost every young Canadian man's — dreams: the Toronto Maple Leafs. Not only did he make it to the NHL and become an integral part of a playoff powerhouse that won the Stanley Cup four times in five years, but he earned the rare distinction of scoring a Cup-winning goal. His disappearance and death in Canada's vast north, and the astonishing discovery of his remains 11 years later, only add to the Barilko mystique. The story has inspired books, songs, magazine articles and newspaper columns. The legend of Barilko inspires hockey players.

❦ ❦ ❦

We keep the people we love alive by the stories we tell.

ACKNOWLEDGEMENTS

Preparing *Barilko: Without A Trace* was a labour of love; arduous at times but, candidly, the most satisfying accomplishment of my professional career. I have so many to thank for sharing their passion on the subject with me.

First, my love and thanks to Anne Klisanich, who provided memories, contacts, scrapbooks, lunches, photos, tears and laughter through the writing of this book about her beloved brother. I will never be able to express my appreciation strongly enough and hope I have made Anne and her family proud of my compiling of the legacy of Bill Barilko. Right beside her with incredible support and many stories of his own was Anne's husband, Emil. Barry, their youngest son, was also an outstanding resource for this book.

I must also spend a moment finding the words to thank another family — the team in the Resource Centre at the Hockey Hall of Fame. The original notion of writing this book was prompted by Tyler Wolosewich, and I thank him profusely. In addition, Tyler and Resource Centre manager Craig Campbell provided many of the photographs you've seen in *Barilko*. Philip Pritchard was not only a wonderful resource but also an outstanding friend and supervisor who gave me the latitude to write the book. Similarly, the Hockey Hall of Fame's president, Jeff Denomme, offered terrific support. To all the Hall of Fame family who watched me diligently peck out a blue and white tome late each night, I thank you for your support and encouragement.

There is yet another family I have leaned on over the past several years, and that is the incredible team over at Fenn Publishing and H.B. Fenn and Company, the publishers of *Barilko* as well as my three previous books. Their unfailing and unconditional support has been extraordinary. It's time for me to shine a spotlight on specific individuals who have made my efforts so enjoyable. Jordan Fenn, the publisher, has allowed me the opportunity to realize the dream of writing hockey books, nurturing and applauding as I go. Heidi Winter receives eternal appreciation and love for convincing me that I should share my passion for hockey and writing with others. For outstanding publicity efforts on behalf of *Barilko* and my prior books, great thanks to both Heidi and Kari Attwell.

Lloyd Davis did exceptional work in editing, fact checking and smoothing out the wrinkles in *Barilko*. Thank you very, very much. I'll thank Jason Wilson and Paul Patskov for their efforts here, too.

Many of Bill Barilko's Toronto Maple Leafs teammates shared their warm and occasionally sad memories of the Leafs number 5. It was a thrill and honour to speak with Dr. Bobby Copp, Fern Flaman, Ted Kennedy, Johnny McCormack, Howie Meeker, Gus Mortson and Sid Smith who, sadly, died before the publication of this book. In addition, I thank June Thomson, Jimmy's wife, for sharing her stories of that exciting era in Maple Leafs history.

Other hockey stars also shared their stories, and I thank Bep Guidolin, Pentti Lund, Senator Frank Mahovlich, the late Jack McLean and before his untimely passing, Gerry McNeil, as well as his son David McNeil, who added so much to the Barilko story.

Bill's dearest friends — Leo Curik, Gaston Garant and Allan Stanley — added insight into uncovering the person behind the hockey player. Thank you very, very much.

Charlie Angus gave me a better glimpse into Northern Ontario life, while Richard Flohil introduced me to Charlie's band, the Grievous Angels, and "The Bill Barilko Song."

Sincere thanks to Mayor Vic Power of Timmins for memories, great civic pride and hospitality. Stan Cor, the former cemetery manager at Timmins Memorial, found time to assist my research in the midst of his own retirement.

Carlo Cattarello Jr. and Roy McKay provided insight into the Holman Pluggers, while Cec Romain and John Kovich were instrumental in my discovering more about the Timmins Canadians.

Mary Panchuk and Nina Weseluck gave me wonderful stories about the Barilko family. Helen Matus offered a glimpse into Bill's summers in Timmins. Peter Jagla, one of my colleagues at the Hockey Hall of Fame, provided English translations of several Polish documents. And Rolly Poirier donated his files on Father Les Costello.

Thank you to Babe Gresko, Bill's teammate, for sharing stories about the Hollywood Wolves, and to Bob Borgen, who helped me discover more about Bill's year and a half in Southern California. Former child actress Karolyn Grimes was delightful in describing her adventures with Cary Grant in the film, *The Bishop's Wife*. Cathy Kinast assisted in researching Barilko's Pittsburgh connections.

Sandra Neal and Nigel Fernandes provided information about horseracing. Gary Durie and Betti Michael individually gave me assistance in researching the Barilko Brothers Appliance Store. So, too, did lawyer Gary Bruner, whose practice occupies the location where Bill and Alex once owned their store.

Ginny Lowes, the Supervisor of Alumni Records at the University of Toronto, dug deep into her archives to assist my research on both Henry and Lou Hudson. Dr. John Shaw was a godsend, offering incredible information on Henry Hudson. Helen O'Neil, Dr. Henry Hudson's assistant at the time of his disappearance, was a most amiable interview, providing warm recollections of her former employer. Ken Pagan from the North Bay *Nugget* enthusiastically shared terrific stories and contacts, including an introduction to Archie Chenier — one of Henry Hudson's friends. Thank you all for your wonderful stories. And thank you, too, to Dr. Martin Kushner for deciphering dental terms for the book.

So many generously gave me their take on "the goal," and I express sincere appreciation to Frank Bonello, the late Tommy Gaston and Harry Neale who were at Maple Leaf Gardens on April 21, 1951, when Bill Barilko scored his unforgettable goal. But many others assisted incredibly in researching "Bashin' Bill's" final goal. Paul Patskou not only provided extraordinary film footage of the goal, but shared his vast network of contacts with me, too. Rob DelMundo offered research assistance and shared his own passion in Bill Barilko's legacy at his webpage: barilko.penaltybox.com. Rob and his team also host a Toronto Maple Leafs website at tmlfans.ca that proved very helpful. All-star netminder-cum-executive-cum-politician Ken Dryden was gracious to offer his insight into Barilko's goal scored on Gerry McNeil. Michael Burns was one of the photographers that night who captured the enduring moment of Barilko's goal, and gave me a wonderful interview on the subject. Photographer Marko Shark explored photography circa 1951 with me, and took the author shot on the sleeve as well.

James Crawford was one of the last persons ever to see Bill Barilko and Henry Hudson alive, and reflected back on that ominous day. Peter Worthington was the first reporter on the scene of the plane's discovery in 1962, and generously allowed me not only to speak at length about both the day and the era, but also to use his reports of that time from the Toronto *Telegram*. Thank you both from the bottom of my heart.

Louise Carley opened her heart and her home, allowing me to uncover yet another side to "Bashin' Bill" Barilko. At times, I'm certain the memories were painful, but I hope the trip was ultimately enjoyable.

I can't thank Allan J. Stitt enthusiastically enough. Allan allowed me to use much of his collection of Toronto Maple Leafs ephemera for research in *Barilko*. Thanks, too, to Hersh Borenstein of Frozen Pond and Alex McFadyen for their assistance.

The "Fifty Mission Cap" chapter was as thoroughly enjoyable as any I have ever researched or written. First, my sincerest thanks go to Gord Downie and Gord Sinclair of The Tragically Hip for taking time to speak with me during the recording of their album, *In Between Evolution*. In addition, the band, along with Alex DeCartier of Peer Music, allowed me to quote from their lyrics in *Barilko*. David Levinson at Macklam/Feldman Management Inc. assisted greatly in arranging the interviews, as did Shelley Stertz from Management Trust. James

Duplacey, the hockey historian who wrote the hockey card that inspired "Fifty Mission Cap," was a most gracious interview, while Joey Scoleri, now a music industry executive in Los Angeles but one of the first music directors to program The Hip's paean to Bill Barilko, gave valuable background from the radio perspective at that time. Music journalist John Sakamoto wrote a stunning slice of unforgettable music/hockey historical prose in his review of The Tragically Hip's Maple Leaf Gardens show.

C. Chad Martin, the curator of the Canadian Warplane Heritage Museum in Mount Hope, Ontario, Dr. Roger G. Miller, historian at the Center for Air Force History in Washington, D.C., and Michael E. Telzrow, the Director of Research and Interpretation at the Mighty Eighth Air Force Museum in Savannah Georgia, were all incredibly helpful in outlining the story behind the fifty mission cap.

Friends Bill Wellman from the Hockey Hall of Fame and Bobby Hastings of the Toronto Maple Leafs Hockey Club provided me with necessary information behind the BB 16 story, while Mel Woolsey of KEWL filled in the rest of the details.

Michael Oesch shared his passion for both Bill Barilko and the game of hockey. Tim Van Overbeek provided supplementary.

Many thanks also to Ralph Slate and his incomparable statistical hockey database at www.hockeydb.com. Documentary producers Bill Allen of Alleycat Productions and Dave Toms from Ironhorse Productions were extremely generous in allowing me to reference their footage from a Bill Barilko special that aired on Leafs TV.

Innumerable visits to Toronto's Metro Reference Library allowed me to peruse archived editions of the *Toronto Daily Star*, the Toronto *Telegram*, the *Globe and Mail* and the Timmins *Daily Press*, while the Hockey Hall of Fame's incomparable Resource Centre provided *The Hockey News* and both newspaper and photo files on Bill Barilko.

Finally, much love goes to my mother and stepfather, Margaret and Gerry England, brother Dale, Aunt Betty and dearest friends Nancy Niklas, Maureen and Tim Burgess, Andrea Orlick, Cam Gardiner, Steve Waxman, Kim Cooke and Ian Marchant, who inspire me daily with the depth of their love and support, not just on *Barilko*, but in everything I attempt.

Kevin Shea
August 2004

BIBLIOGRAPHY

Mirrors of Stone: Fragments from the Porcupine Frontier, by Charlie Angus and Louie Palu

Timmins: The Porcupine Country by Michael Barnes

Hockey Dynasty, by Jack Batten

The Leafs in Autumn, by Jack Batten

Doug: The Doug Harvey Story, by William Brown

The Best of Hockey Night in Canada, by Stephen Cole

The Last Hurrah, by Stephen Cole

The Trail of the Stanley Cup, 1947-1967, by Charles Coleman

Blades on the Bay, by Bruce Craig and Kenneth Craig

Years of Glory: The Six-Team Era, edited by Dan Diamond

Forever Rivals, by James Duplacey and Charles Wilkins

Images of Glory, by James Duplacey and Joseph Romain

The Rivalry: Canadiens Versus Leafs, by Stan Fischler

Champions: Hockey's Greatest Dynasties, by Douglas Hunter

Open Ice:The Tim Horton Story, by Douglas Hunter

Come on Teeder! The Story of Ted Kennedy, by Ed Fitkin

Max Bentley: Hockey's Dipsy Doodle Dandy, by Ed Fitkin

Turk Broda of the Leafs, by Ed Fitkin

A Fan For All Seasons, by Tom Gaston and Kevin Shea

Golly Gee— It's Me: The Howie Meeker, Story by Charlie Hodge

In Loving Memory: A Tribute to Tim Horton, by Lori Horton and Tim Griggs

Inside Maple Leaf Gardens, by William Houston

Overtime, Overdue, by John Melady

The NHL All-Star Game, by Andrew Podnieks

The Essential Blue and White Book, by Andrew Podnieks

The Goal: Bobby Orr and the Most Famous Goal in NHL Stanley Cup History, by Andrew Podnieks

Portraits of the Game, by Andrew Podnieks

The Blue and White, by T.A. Reed

Behind the Cheering, by Frank Selke with Gordon Green

Life After Hockey, by Michael A. Smith

Conn Smythe: If You Can't Beat 'Em in the Alley, by Conn Smythe and Scott Young

Torontonensis: The Yearbook of the University of Toronto, 1926 and 1928